The
Surreptitious Speech

The
Surreptitious Speech

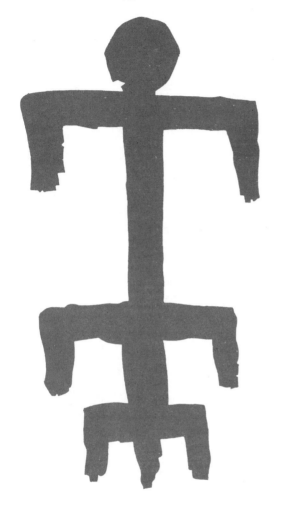

Présence
Africaine
and the
Politics of
Otherness
1947–1987

Edited by
V. Y. Mudimbe

The University of Chicago Press   Chicago and London

V. Y. MUDIMBE is the Ruth F. DeVarney
Professor of Romance Studies and professor
of comparative literature at Duke University.

The University of Chicago Press, Chicago 60637
The University of Chicago Press, Ltd., London
© 1992 by The University of Chicago
All rights reserved. Published 1992
Printed in the United States of America
01 00 99 98 97 96 95 94 93 92   5 4 3 2 1

ISBN (cloth): 0-226-54506-7
ISBN (paper): 0-226-54507-5

Library of Congress Cataloging-in-Publication
Data

The Surreptitious speech : Présence africaine and the politics of
    otherness, 1947–1987 / edited by V. Y. Mudimbe.
        p.   cm.
    Includes bibliographical references and index.
    1. Africa, Sub-Saharan—Civilization.   2. Présence africaine
(Paris, France : 1967)   3. Présence africaine.   4. Blacks.
5. Africa, Sub-Saharan.   I. Mudimbe, V. Y., 1941-
DT352.4.S87   1992
967—dc20   91-23192
                                                         CIP

To the memory of Alioune Diop and Jacques Howlett

Integer vitae scelerisque purus
non eget Mauris iaculis neque arcu
nec venenatis gravida sagittis,
Fusce, pharetra,
sive per Syrtes itere aestuosas
sive facturus per inhospitalem
Caucasum vel quae loca fabulosus
lambit Hydaspes.

> Q. Horatius Flaccus, *Carminum,*
> liber 1.22.1–8

Nous nous sommes, je crois, dépêchés de
juger les nations qui vivent encore sous la
main de la nature, dans la crainte qu'elles
ne nous jugeassent. La Révolution est l'appel bien marqué contre ce jugement in-
nique, et nous nous efforçons de devenir
sauvages pour cesser de l'être . . .

> Lavallée cité par M. Ozouf, p. 216,
> in A. Breuguière, M. Ozouf, and M. N.
> Bourguet, "Naissance d'une ethnographie
> de la France au XVIIIe siècle," 195–228.
> In *Objets et méthodes de l'histoire de la
> culture,* ed. J. Le Goff and B. Kopeczi,
> Paris and Budapest, 1977.

Contents

Contents

Preface Letter

Léopold Sédar Senghor

Dakar, June 17, 1988

To: Professor V. Y. Mudimbe
    Department of Romance Languages
    and Comparative Literature
    Duke University
    Durham, NC 27706 USA

Dear Professor,

Thank you very much for your letter of May 17th, 1988, to which I am pleased to respond. Indeed, the problem posed by *Présence Africaine* is of great importance to those who struggle for the ideas of *Négritude.*

It needs to be recalled that *Présence Africaine,* after *L'étudiant noir,* has been the primary instrument of the Négritude movement. I would like to take this opportunity to point out that Alioune Diop was one of the founders of the movement together with Aimé Césaire, Jacques Rabemananjara, Léon-Gontran Damas, and myself.

This having been said, *Présence Africaine*'s principal role today is, as a publishing house, to be the primary institution for contemporary Black African literature written in French. It should also especially welcome manuscripts of doctoral dissertations.

In order to fully comprehend the importance that *Présence Africaine* has gained, it should be recalled that, since African nations became independent in the 1960's, francophone African literature, including that of the Maghreb, is being taught in the schools, even in France. And it will be taught ever more widely when the French-speaking countries are recognized as a political reality.

As regards to the collective volume to be published on *Présence Africaine* and on the history of *African consciousness,* its timing is excellent. Indeed, as was confirmed by the First International Conference of Human Paleontology held in Nice in October of 1982, "Man emerged from animal 2,500,000 years ago in Africa. And since then and up to the Later Paleolithic Age of 40,000 years ago, Africa has remained at the forefront of human civilization." And I reiterate that this has continued since the fourth millenium B.C., when the Egyptians—who according to Herodotus had "black skin and frizzy hair"—invented the first human writing.

However, that is not all. As I say in my *Ce que je crois, That Which I Believe,* to be published by Editions Grasset in September, Black Africa has once again taken up "the torch of civilization." This began with what I call "the Revolution of 1889," in the realms of literature and the arts, as demonstrated by Surrealist poetry and by the painting and sculpture of the School of Paris.

Very sincerely yours,
Léopold Sédar Senghor

Présence Africaine

foreword

Christiane Yandé Diop

It is difficult for me to speak of *Présence Africaine* since I have been a participant in the adventure. All I can say is that the journal was born from the will of a man who is too close to me for me to be able to speak about him or his work.

The idea of this creation came to him several decades before its realization. He fertilized and nurtured it for a long time, even though in his article "Niam n'goura," which appeared in the first issue of *Présence Africaine* (November–December 1947), he wrote that "the idea goes back to 1942–43." His contagious enthusiasm and his faith in Black Africa, her culture and her peoples, helped him to bring the journal to fruition.

Alioune Diop chose the narrow path. His itinerary at that time—the day right after the Second World War—was not that of an intellectual seeking personal renown. An African through and through, he wanted to rehabilitate the collective memory of the peoples of Africa, and that memory is nothing other than their culture in its various aspects. To bring new life to the Africans from inside their culture was one of the primary goals of the founder of *Présence Africaine*. To disseminate and to make this culture one familiar to and recognized by the entire world was the second goal. Yet another was the place of the Black within humankind as well as his participation in the universal oeuvre.

He preferred listening to talking and was attuned to the ideas of others, especially to the ideas of young people, whom he encouraged to create and to express themselves.

A very open man, Alioune Diop thought that this work of rehabilitation of the Black world was not solely the business of Black Africans but "of all men of good will (white, yellow, or black) given to helping us in defining the African originality and in hastening its insertion into the modern world," as he wrote in that first issue of *Présence Africaine.*

Thus it was that, from the beginning, Alioune Diop was able to form a Committee of Patrons with André Gide, Paul Rivet, Father Maydieu, Emmanuel Mounier, Léopold Sédar Senghor, Paul Hazoumé, Jean-Paul Sartre, Michel Leiris, Albert Camus, Aimé Césaire. On the board of editors of the journal were, among others, Bernard Dadié, Cissé Dia, Georges Balandier, F. D. Cissoko, Mamadou Dia, Roger Mercier, Hughes Panassié, Abdoulaye Sadji, Tidjani Serpos.

Since 1947, many roads have been traveled, filled with joy, but more so with obstacles. This has not prevented *Présence Africaine* from celebrating its thirtieth birthday in 1977 and its fortieth in 1987. *Présence Africaine* could not have lasted this long without the fraternal gathering and the unlimited loyalty of people who were touched by the almost religious commitment of Alioune Diop to the recognition of the dignity of Black people.

Of these people, young and not so young—and it is impossible to name them all—Jacques Rabemananjara was to say in his speech, given in Paris on 13 November 1987, at the fortieth anniversary celebration of this cultural journal of the Black world: "In the course of these forty years of struggle, Alioune Diop's team has not for a moment relaxed its efforts to meet the great, initial challenge. Alioune Diop's zeal, determination, and faith were for him, as for his spiritual heirs, the qualities and the tools that allowed them to overcome the obstacles that had been foreseen by Gide."

It is also thanks to this loyal, ever-present team—which has accepted living in the shadow, sharing the hopes as well as the anxieties of Alioune Diop—that the journal, the African Society of Culture, the publishing house Présence Africaine still continue today with full respect for the identity of each individual, and for its dear, departed founder.

I cannot close without evoking the great moments of *Présence Africaine:* the First Conference of Black Writers and Artists (Paris, 1956), which gave birth to the African Society of Culture; the Second Conference organized by the latter (Rome, 1959); the creation of a World Festival of Black Arts (Dakar, Senegal, 1966; and Lagos, Nigeria, 1977); also, several colloquia and seminars on various subjects as well as the institution of a Day of Black Peoples, that has taken place on the first Sunday of the year ever since 1978. "The Institution of such a day responds to the essential need for the culture of a people to be called upon to speak throughout an entire day, so that the communities may give expression to their authentic values by the means put within their reach."

I would like to give the closing word to Alioune Diop:

> But now we enter the era of the cultural dialogue for the sake of a new economic order. Much is being said about this. And rightfully so. It would, however, be an illusion to believe that the Western world could assign itself a legitimate mission of integrating, absorbing, and assimilating into the vigor of its own vitality, the contributions of other civilizations—and thus appearing in a Harlequin's costume, happy to have killed the soul of other peoples in order to dress in their motley, cast-off clothing. The adventure of Black art (which Western critics have imperiously assimilated into the idea of their own artistic development) is one example of this. In religion they speak of *stepping stones* destined for the construction of a Western Christianity spread across the whole world.
>
> However, I would prefer to speak instead of a *dialogue of cultures*. Cultures do not live in isolation, cut off from their roots, their support system and the source of their own vitality, that is to say cut off from their institutions and plans for civilization. Each living civilization can assume its own history, make use of its own maturity, and give expression to its own modernity, based upon its own experiences, the inspiration of its own environment, the talents specific to its own genius.
>
> From that moment on, no culture could possibly be disengaged from its structures and the sources of civilization in order to have a dialogue with other cultures. Complete and living civilizations must enter into a dialogue. A full-fledged, civilized community must know how to appreciate, through the individual members of its body, the wealth and the meaning of that which it borrows from other civilizations. Undoubtedly, the cultural borrowings are not the least. But there can be borrowing on the social level as well

as on other levels. It is neither correct nor fruitful to cast aside the people of these meetings-dialogues-exchanges in order to reserve those for the Western elite alone.

Particularly in the Black world, the dialogue must first take place within each of the nations, between the people and their Westernized elite—in order to preserve, integrally and organically, the creative vitality of our global civilization.

As for Western civilization, it is definitely murderous—even towards itself. But it is the seat of the most powerful institutions to support democracy, justice, and love. And its voice carried far and wide.

We all need the West. We also need it to master and discipline an all too powerful appetite on its part for domination—so that we may live harmoniously and in peace with the other human civilizations.

Introduction

V. Y. Mudimbe

1947. A French educated Black African, Alioune Diop, founds a journal in Paris. Its name, he decides, should be *Présence Africaine*, which simply means an African presence. Around him and his journal, one finds some of the most prestigious French intellectuals at that time: Albert Camus, André Gide, Michel Leiris, Théodore Monod, Emmanuel Mounier, Jean-Paul Sartre. They encourage the enterprise, serve on a "Comité de Patronage," and seem to believe in its pertinence. What Diop's project represents is a questioning, not of the French culture per se but of the imperial ambition of the Western civilization. Diop still remembers his history classes when he had to recite as many did before and after him that his Gallic ancestors had blond hair.

The *Présence Africaine* of Alioune Diop is, from its inception, a manifesto and a program. It wishes to bring in the very center of the French power and culture what was being negated in colonies, that is, the dignity of otherness. We are in the aftermath of a war. The initiative in itself does not surprise. After all, Emmanuel Mounier's *Esprit* or Jean-Paul Sartre's *Les Temps Modernes* witness to a fundamentally similar project: specifically, the promotion of "the world of the person" and the rights of subjectivity. They, too, want subjective voices to be heard. The only differ-

Dans une même société, il n'y a aucune condition qui ne dévore et qui ne soit dévorée, qu'elles qu'aient été ou que soient les formes de gouvernement ou d'égalité artificielle qu'on ait opposées à l'inégalité primitive ou naturelle.

Denis Diderot, *Histoire des indes*, vol. 8

It is hard to imagine what African and black cultural studies in general would be without Présence Africaine. Once obscure writers who graced its early pages are now major figures in the black cultural world, and indeed in the intellectual world in general. For hundreds of scholars, writers, critics, historians, and readers in the general public, the journal has provided a voice and a supporting "présence" for the African experience in our time.

Donald E. Herdeck, *African Authors*, 1973:576

ence is that Diop's *Présence Africaine* claims to incarnate the voice
of a silenced Africa.

1987. Alioune Diop is no longer there. But the journal and its ap-
pendices (the publishing house and the African Society of Culture)
are alive and well, as Madame Diop and Jacques Rabemanandjara indicate in their contributions to this volume. Celebrations take place,
indeed. The longevity of the enterprise is remarkable.

This collection of essays apropos the fortieth anniversary of *Présence Africaine* would like to concern itself with the meaning of
Alioune Diop's dream and its actualization. Our objective is not a
naive canonization of *Présence Africaine* but a critical reading of its
context, characteristics, and significance. That is the common framework that unites the essays of this volume. Even the most decisively
critical—such as those of Paulin Hountondji and Benoît Verhaegen—
that free themselves from the clearly arranged space of *Présence
Africaine*'s programs in order to face present-day areas of African
nightmares are still concerned with alterations accounted for by an
order whose configurations recount *Présence Africaine*'s passion and
self-imposed missions. The essays establish simultaneously a kind of
biography of *Présence Africaine* as a "figure" and a "mirror" reflecting other depths. They demand a descriptive analysis of its fate as
a sign of displacements that took place in the European imperial
ideology and which directly affected the production of knowledge apropos Africa and discourses about her.

*
**

The first part of this volume, "Text and Context," contains two
types of contributions. Bernard Mouralis and Bennetta Jules-Rosette
perform a physiology of the journal. The second type, represented by
Denis-Constant Martin, interrogates the signifying function of Africanism and its discursive types of knowledge. Bernard Mouralis describes the genesis of *Présence Africaine* focusing on the fact that
the journal is a product of a specific place and context: the postwar
Paris that sees both a gradual reconversion of French colonial policies
and a renewed intellectual vitality witnessed by other new journals
such as *Les Temps Modernes* (1945) or *Critique* (1947). The context
would explain both the collaboration created by *Présence* between
French and African intellectuals and the singularity of *Présence*'s discourse. In effect, *Présence* brings together "a discourse *on* Africa and
discourse *by* Africans" and centers on a universal "right to thought."

This basic feature might indicate the originality of *Présence Africaine*. It also provides explanations for its progressive orientation after the 1960s toward an emphasis on the intellectual and cultural: "its loyalty to the ideals of Pan-Africanism turned it away from the temptation to become the interpreter of the micro-nationalisms" in postindependence Africa. It is this political prudence that a younger generation of Black intellectuals, mainly Africans, sometimes criticizes as well as the so-called idealizing image of the African continent that the journal would have conveyed in an uninterrupted effort. Bennetta Jules-Rosette's reading of the issues published between 1947 and 1987 complemented by extensive interviews with friends of *Présence Africaine* brings about a complex image of the ideology of the journal. According to her, the journal integrates in the same outlook négritude, Pan-Africanism, liberation politics, and Black aesthetics. This effort actualizes itself in a profusion of duplicated metaphors such as "the natural purity of an untouched and idyllic Africa," an "emerging" continent unmasking "colonial repression as the cause of destruction," a "denuded and transformed Africa" which measures herself against antithetical concepts. Jules-Rosette is convinced that *Présence Africaine* was and is still a "movement of [cultural] Revalorization" in the present-day context. It "forged anthropological concepts into literary and ideological tools. This process of cultural semiosis warrants study based upon the texts published by *Présence Africaine* and the actual social events where new ideas were developed and transmitted."

We know that the cultural relativism set free in the 1940s and in which *Présence Africaine* participates—or, more rigorously, a relativism that makes *Présence Africaine* both thinkable and possible—allowed also the constitution of African studies or Africanism. This new field defines itself as a space of knowledge about Africa, which is both an order of relation to the continent and its past and a totalizing discourse of knowledge that can transcend local differences, particularities, dynamics. Such a discourse, thinks Denis Martin, is fundamentally controversial. In the long run, it condemns itself to "intellectual atrophy and desiccation" unless it takes the risk of executing "a double copernican revolution," first by internalizing on the one hand Bachelard's philosophy of openness, that is, a philosophy of a "why not?"; and, on the other, by postulating "that [what] which throws one off [is] an innovation on trial rather than [criticizing] the innovation because it dumbfounds the outside observer;" second, by integrating a comparatist dimension.

Part Two of the volume deals with the biggest challenge that *Présence Africaine* has been facing: the promotion of the concept of an African history. Until the 1950s—and I am not certain at all that things have changed today for the general public in the West— Africa is widely perceived and presented as the continent without memory, without past, without history. More precisely, her history is supposed to commence with her contacts with Europe, specifically with the progressive European invasion of the continent that begins at the end of the fifteenth century.

*
**

Has *Présence Africaine* made a difference in making visible the fact of an African history? Catherine Coquery-Vidrovitch demonstrates that over forty years the journal has published 253 articles and 150 commentaries dealing with history, and particularly "Black" history. Paradoxically, despite the militant support from French intellectuals, only five French historians contributed to the project, probably because "of an instinctive, constitutional mistrust with respect to a non-professional journal, in which an effort had to be made to publish for non-specialists, that is to say, to admit to a bias regarding scientific popularization for an educated but not immediately professional public." One notes also that, in terms of percentages, African history is the most popular theme, followed by the American and Caribbean. Thus the ideological stance of the journal confirms "African historicity, which implied putting a 'Westernized' history of Africa resolutely between brackets." Progressively this choice led to an emphasis on an African history elaborated from "the inside" and in accordance with African identities. One sees here very clearly the delicate problem of the role of subjectivity in the construction of history. Bogumil Jewsiewicki articulates this issue by considering *Présence Africaine* itself as historiography, and he uncovers a curious paradox:

> History . . . is seen to be assigned the double task of producing otherness and identity, which are each other's interface. African otherness is only the lack of Western history that objected to the African societies, and African identity would be a product of scholarly and written history (no less Western) won over by these same societies.

In sum, without questioning the fact that "history in *Présence Africaine* is a science in pursuit of an objective truth," Bogumil

Jewsiewicki insists on the fact that this history is also a "literary activity" imbued with currents that made it functional (Marxism, Sartrean existentialism, psychoanalysis, etc.), and as such its autonomy cannot but be relative to a more general atmosphere. Throughout its density, the *Présence Africaine*'s narrations of history negate and rescue what articulates them from below, their meaning and their condition of possibility: "History, as the collaborators of *Présence Africaine* saw it, did not deliver us in the least from Greek and Roman history as Baudelaire wanted in the middle of the 19th century; it drove us more deeply into it."

Jewsiewicki's provocative argument goes beyond *Présence Africaine* as historiography touching rocky issues apropos the historicity of all societies. How could one delineate the conditions upon which a grid or a language can translate human historicity? In the case of the specificity of Black African cultures and societies, there is a monument: Cheikh Anta Diop, "the" master-thinker historian of *Présence Africaine*. A prolific writer and author of controverted theses such as: the first civilization, that of ancient Egypt, is Negro; Greek civilization, the mother of the West, is the pupil of Egypt, etc. Mamadou Diouf and Mohamad Mbodj take the task of evaluating the "shadow" of Cheikh Anta Diop and its impact. They introduce their essay by noting,

> To question the work of Cheikh Anta Diop, even from a scientific point of view, was for a long time synonymous with African anti-patriotism; to refer to it in passing was an obligation one could readily fulfill, especially in academic work; to repeat its great principles, often without any real knowledge of the work itself, was a certificate of nationalism and pan-Africanism.

They, then, proceed focusing successively on Cheikh Anta Diop problematics and the "epistemological ruptures that it induced in the knowledge of the African societies." As to the significance of Cheikh Anta Diop's "shadow," they believe that "Cheikh Anta Diop has been a victim of the reduction of theses to ideology, which, as a result, excluded them from any serious scientific analysis: 'one believes or one does not.'"

The essays by Catherine Coquery-Vidrovitch, Bogumil Jewsiewicki, Mamadou Diouf, and Mohamad Mbodj situate *Présence Africaine*'s history as well as its practice of history in the more general predicament of what it signifies to write history. Indeed, the questions they raise are about the relationship that historical writings can

have with values. This becomes obvious when one turns to Lilyan
Kesteloot's contribution that closes this part. She demonstrates the
fecundity that oral traditions can, despite their shortcomings, bring
to the construction of the past. As a matter of principle, Lilyan Kesteloot puts myth and epic in dialogue with history. "This oral knowledge," she notes, "and its transmission are . . . not left to chance; at
the least, they guarantee a technique handled by professionals and (in
general) controlled by the notables of the kingdoms . . . or their
descendants."

*
**
Présence Africaine often has been identified with a literary urge
to build new systems of representation with their own rationality
that could phase out a cultural alienation implemented by colonialism. Besides, this urge is, as Léopold Sédar Senghor shows in his Preface Letter, commonly linked to the négritude philosophy with its
double missions: that of articulating theoretically the norms for a
process of disalienation on the one hand, and of illustrating the values
of a cultural difference on the other. The two types of contributions
in Part Three, "Alienation, Voices, and Writing," restate and analyze
this double dimension of *Présence Africaine*'s literary engagement.
They complement each other. Richard Bjornson and Abiola Irele focus on alienation and its mechanisms; the first, by referring to conceptual and emotional bonds existing between *Présence Africaine*,
négritude, and the literary products of writers such as Paul Hazoumé
and Ferdinand Oyono; the second, by reinterpreting the dialectic of
alienation and expanding it to the whole of the African experience.
The second group of essays in the chapter detail concrete illustrations
of a cult of alterity. Mildred A. Hill-Lubin establishes the affinity existing between Blacks that *Présence Africaine* thematized; Elisabeth
Mudimbe-Boyi makes visible similarities of motifs existing between
the Harlem Renaissance movement and négritude; finally, Bernadette
Cailler examines texts by Paul Niger, Langston Hughes, and Keita
Fodeba, thus bringing in the same textual space three types of creativ-
ities: an African (Fodeba), an African-American (Hughes), and a Caribbean (Niger).

These essays echo each other. They structure an emotional field of
thought, its derivation, and its character. Richard Bjornson writes:

> The négritude movement was . . . both a product of the as-
> similationist doctrine and a reaction against it. The am-
> bivalence of this situation deeply marked the works of

négritude writers like Senghor, but the process of alienation that it implies actually led them to a heightened state of awareness that has remained at the center of Francophone African intellectual debates since the late 1940s.

To refer to Sartre's *Black Orpheus*, négritude is a negative and an antithetical statement, as, in an identical fashion, Harlem Renaissance was in the name of otherness. Their sociopolitical contexts might have been different. They were, nevertheless, in agreement in the position they assumed about the Black's role in a White dominant culture. On the other hand, as moments of refusals, as negativities, they were in a relation of adjacency with the alienating paradigms they were opposing. In the "voices of ancestors," to use a felicitous expression of Mildred Hill-Lubin, as well as in the thematic binding of consciousnesses unveiled by Elisabeth Mudimbe-Boyi, the words of alterity decipher the whole of a negative, disordered experience and, simultaneously, as described by Bernadette Cailler, render audible mute invocations, references, or silent extensions to the myth of Africa.

In sum, in order to transcend the négritude literature one has to extend the elucidation of its dreams, illusions, political investments to the very fact that makes this literature significant: African colonization and alienation. But, as Abiola Irele puts it in his essay, the "one who causes you injury also teaches you wisdom." Alienation, as a concept or as a reality, is always jumbled in a historical rhythm. Its signs as well as the expressions that oppose it side with particular motivations. It would be naïveté from what the concept or the reality of alienation meant or still means to posit a sole and static signification about them. "We cannot do without a thorough-going revolution of the mind," insists Abiola Irele. Indeed, alienation is not an African disease if we bear in mind that all consciousnesses are, strictly speaking, slaves. If the particular African experience of colonialism determined forceful procedures of conversion, say, to external intellectual and sociopolitical models, it also taught us at least two things: first, that we can call into question the history of the cartesian subjectivity or the mathematization of nature; second, as pointedly illustrated by Irele's essay, alienation is always a weak moment in a dynamic dialectic, that is, in a historical work of searching for truth, liberty, and a more egalitarian world.

The alternative emerging from *Présence Africaine* is a political philosophy. Sartre, as already noted, tried to account for its authority and internal limitations. But *Présence Africaine*'s ambition needed concrete models, organized local systems of thought that could, in their own right, respond to and justify its theoretical theses about the tension between the other and the self. Alioune Diop found an argument in Placide Tempels's *Bantu Philosophy* that Présence Africaine published in 1949. At that moment, the book already had a history. A slightly different French translation had been made by Antoine Rubbens in 1945 in Elisabethville (Belgian Congo) from the Deutch original which itself was made available in six issues of the Belgian journal *Band* in 1945–1946, and subsequently published, in 1946, as a volume by De Sikkel publishing house in Antwerp (Belgium). It is only in 1959 that an English version was published by Présence Africaine itself. In any case, the title of the book and its project could not but please Présence's desire to unveil indigenous African systems of thought. Yet, the ambiguity of Tempels's *Bantu Philosophy* vis-à-vis the colonial system, its uncertain and vague philosophical terminology and propositions aroused almost immediately uncomfortable questions. Among these questions, we may note, at least, two major ones: Should one, in the name of a good cause, confuse a worldview with philosophy? What does it mean to postulate, as Tempels did, the possibility of an implicit philosophy?

The essays in Part Four explicitly ignore the debate imprudently initiated by Tempels. These texts succeed each other dialectically. Anthony Appiah in his "Inventing an African Practice in Philosophy" and Paulin Hountondji in "Recapturing" propose a transcending of illusions and mystifications. The first, theoretically, indicates a possible locus for the emergence of a philosophical practice; the second, practically, outlines the fact of an extraversion that imbues through and through African discourses and practices. The second set of essays constituted by Emmanuel Terray's and Peter Rigby's articles point toward more concrete issues. Did the French Marxist anthropology as an intellectual paradigm and a political praxis fail in its ambition of rejuvenating anthropology and contributing to African liberation? asks Emmanuel Terray. Yes, indeed, he notes that one could question the ways Marxist anthropology tried to resolve "the difficult problem of the relationship between 'professional' practice and political." Yet, the challenge represented by the current has radically transformed the field of anthropology and the discourse about the primitive. On the other hand, Terray thinks that "in France today, Marxism resembles a palace that has been abandoned by its inhabitants: it is deserted but intact, and one can foresee that it will not remain unoccupied indefinitely." As a complement to this, Peter

Rigby formulates a Marxist practice as he conceives it among Ilparakuyo Masai, bringing together *Présence Africaine*'s representations,
Marxist logic, and the demands of an autocritical anthropology. For
Marx, and historical materialism, he writes, "an epistemology cannot
be found theoretically; epistemology for Marx is the relation between
theory and practice in all human activity which, by definition, is conscious." The third and last set of philosophical essays goes further.
Kwasi Wiredu focuses on questions of translating and formulating
modern thought in African languages, insisting that "a concept, problem, or thesis expressed in a given language [which] is not expressible
in another language will never be a sufficient reason for dismissing it
as in some way defective." Benoît Verhaegen, from the governing policies of Zaire, interrogates politics of failure in a description of a social
decomposition and its consequences for an African university, which
should be a strategic basis for the germination of students' political
consciousness and the organizing locus of knowledge and its transmission. Extending Verhaegen's critique, Paulin Hountondji, in a critique of the African daily life, concentrates on what seems to him a
generalized type of perversion destructuring all domains of life and
whose effects may seem intrinsic to a negative mutation.

These essays on philosophy and the practice of everyday life disar-
ticulate Tempels's dream and at the same time go beyond the romantic essentialism of some of his disciples celebrating the virtues of
négritude. They not only face taboo issues but magnify their effects
and problems in analytic descriptions that directly invite a renewed
reflection and original political actions. In short, one could think that
by disconnecting themselves from the field in which *Présence Africaine* has been defining and, somehow, confining philosophy, they
deduce what was and, perhaps, is still compromising for *Présence
Africaine*. In fact, the essays by Anthony Appiah, Emmanuel Terray,
and Kwasi Wiredu belong strictly to the domain of methodology and
are principally concerned with the usage of a discipline and its pertinence. On the other hand, Paulin Hountondji, Peter Rigby, and Benoît
Verhaegen refer back to the founding of a maligned authority from
which they enunciate sites of possible sociopolitical transformations.
We clearly are dealing here with complementary positions, yet they
are, and very visibly, caught up in different webs.

It was only normal that, apropos *Présence Africaine*, I should bring
in also another dimension, a more emotional one, in order to offer a
picture that could render exactly its complexity. I interviewed historic witnesses in France (Simone Howlett and Jacques Rabemanan-

jara) and in the United States (the late Albert Berrian, Maurice Lubin, and Emile Snyder). They spoke frankly from their minds and their hearts. I then interviewed analysts from different horizons expecting some kind of surprise. They include Lilyan Kesteloot from Dakar (Sénégal), who in the 1960s with her book on Francophone literature canonized négritude; two academicians, Fernando Lambert from Canada and Henri Moniot from France; a journalist, Marc Rombaut, from Belgium; and a young African intellectual from Guinea (West Africa), Manthia Diawara, presently a permanent resident in the United States. Despite differences of accents in their evaluations, their unanimity on the historic role of *Présence Africaine* is striking. Part Five presents these conversations, and is followed by a conclusion in which the very project of this book and its content is discussed by specialists of African cultures: Roberta A. Dunbar, Eileen Julien, and Christopher Miller.

*
**
I would like to thank the many people who helped me to shape and realize this project. First are the authors of the essays and the interviewees. I am grateful also to Marjolijn de Jaeger who translated from the French into English the contributions of Catherine Coquery-Vidrovitch, Christiane Yandé Diop, Mamadou Diouf and Mohamad Mbodj, Paulin Hountondji, Simone Howlett, Bogumil Jewsiewicki, Lilyan Kesteloot, Denis-Constant Martin, Henri Moniot, Bernard Mouralis, Elisabeth Mudimbe-Boyi, Fernando Lambert, Maurice Lubin, Jacques Rabemananjara, Marc Rombaut, Léopold Sédar Senghor, Emile Snyder, Emmanuel Terray, and Benoît Verhaegen. Catherine Porter translated Bernadette Cailler's text.

The translations were made possible by a grant from the Florence Gould Foundation.

I am also sincerely grateful to Gaurav Desai, Mary Michelle Moessinger, and Lila Weinberg who administratively handled this project with competence and efficiency; to Stanley Blair who edited the manuscript and whose careful work went well beyond that normally expected of a copy editor; and to the staff of the Duke University Romance Studies Department, particularly to Rita Henshaw. Finally, my thanks to my editor, David Brent, who believed in this project.

part one
Text and Context

Présence Africaine: Geography of an "Ideology"

Bernard Mouralis

The first issue of *Présence Africaine* appeared at the end of the year 1947. It was an impressive volume of 196 pages which was, in itself, quite a feat in that postwar period when paper was a rare commodity. The journal was introduced as a monthly publication, and the second issue appeared, as planned, in January 1948.

It is doubtful that anyone could have predicted then what would become of this publication and what role it was to play. Forty years later, the journal continues to be published quarterly, and we are able to measure to what extent it is justifiably called by the title that its founders gave it. It remains one of the major voices of Africa.

But of which Africa? That is what I would like to try to identify here by recalling a certain number of historical givens and by analyzing a few basic aspects of the discourse that *Présence Africaine* has held for forty years on African culture and literature.

The journal was born in a specific place and context on which it would be good to dwell for a moment. Paris, 1947: the political changes that followed the Resistance and the Liberation brought into question, at least in terms of principles, the traditional relationship that the metropolis entertained with the co-

lonial territories. The French constitution of 1946, in its section dealing with the "French Union," officially sanctioned this evolution and
set up a new political entity from which colonialism was supposed to
have disappeared. This was translated specifically by the recognition
of the right to citizenship for all those under the jurisdiction of the
union and their parliamentary representation in the assemblies anticipated by the new constitution, the suppression of the indigenous
penal code and conscription (forced labor), the suppression of the colonial educational system and the introduction of the French system.

Of course, in practice the application of these measures came up
against obstacles, but the participation of the territories in the political life of the new entity that was the French Union was a fact. Thus,
for the first time, the colonizer truly involved himself in a politics of
assimilation that, in the shorter or longer term, was bound to entail
the abolition of the colonial system.

From then on, the choice of Paris as the place in which the journal
would be produced assumed, perhaps, a specific importance. The Paris
of 1947 was no longer that place of exile that it was for the négritude
writers during the 1930s but a place where the African writers belonged, because the city was, from then on, one of the theaters in
which the political and cultural future of Africa was being prepared.
More specifically, as far as the cultural question is concerned, it should
be noticed that the new journal, by establishing itself in Paris, escaped
the risk of marginalization inherent in any attempt to have a peripheral voice be heard. In this regard, one can appreciate the discrepancy
that separated *Présence Africaine* from *La Voix du Congolais* (which
appeared from 1945 to 1959 in Léopoldville), or from the *Bulletin de
l'Enseignement en AOF* (which in 1935 became *L'Education Africaine*), each of which was an important vehicle for African writing.

In a parallel manner, the journal found itself endowed with the
status of those journals that bore witness to the renewal of ideas in
the intellectual climate that followed the Liberation: *Les Temps
Modernes* (founded in 1945 by J. P. Sartre), or *Critique* (founded in
1947 by G. Bataille). Thus, *Présence Africaine* found itself placed side
by side with journals that were going to become prestigious, prolong-
ing a movement initiated between the two wars with *Europe* (founded
by R. Rolland) or *Esprit* (founded by E. Mounier). This status is very
clearly apparent in the circulation that was established, throughout a
number of years, between the collaborators of those journals and
Présence Africaine, to which Sartre, Gide, and Mounier contributed

writings. This status is equally apparent in the advertisements one can read for those magazines in the issues of *Présence Africaine:* nothing to do with those venerable institutions such as *La Revue des Deux Mondes, Le Mercure de France,* and even less with *La Nouvelle Revue Française* (disqualified by Drieu La Rochelle who sided with the Nazis and was its editor under the Occupation), and many others.

This context explains the makeup of the Committee of Patrons and of the editorial board of the journal, as can be seen in the first issue. It also helps us to understand the plan developed by Alioune Diop in his founding text, entitled "Niam n'goura ou les raisons d'être de *Présence Africaine"*:

> This journal is not subservient to any philosophical or po-
> litical ideology. It wishes to be open to the collaboration of
> all men of good will (white, yellow, or black) capable of
> helping us to define the African originality and to hasten
> its insertion into the modern world. *Présence Africaine* in-
> cludes three essential sections. The second one, the most
> important one in our eyes, will contain texts by Africans
> (novels, short stories, poems, plays, etc.). The first section
> will publish studies by Africanists on African culture and
> civilization. We will also examine the ways and means by
> which to integrate the Black man into the Western civili-
> zation. The last section, finally, will review works of art or
> thought concerning the Black world.[1]

Thus, from the very start, Diop's plan involved both receiving and assembling, and the journal chose to introduce at the same time a discourse *on* Africa and a discourse *by* Africans.

Furthermore, the Africa in question was not an Africa fixed in an immutable totality, the appearance of which would be sufficient. It was an Africa in alteration, at a specific moment in its history. And, evoking the origin of the project, Alioune Diop writes:

> The idea goes back to 1942–43. We, a certain number of
> students from overseas, were in Paris in the very middle of
> the suffering of a Europe that was questioning itself on its
> essence and the authenticity of its values; we gathered to-
> gether to study the situation and the characteristics that
> defined us, too. Neither White, Yellow, nor Black, unable
> to return completely to our original traditions nor to as-

---

1. Alioune Diop, "Niam n'goura ou les raisons d'être de *Présence Africaine," Pré-sence Africaine,* no. 1 (November–December 1947): 7.

similate to Europe, we had the feeling that we were a new
race, mentally cross-bred, but one that had not been taught
to know its originality and that had barely become aware
of it.[2]

That was the point of departure. But the author immediately thereafter extends the invitation to pass beyond the stage of gaining awareness of a particular situation forced upon a given group. What
mattered, in fact, was the refusal to "renounce thought" and to act in
such a way that Africans would fully share "the responsibility for
thinking and improving the lot of the human species."[3]

This confirmation of the right to thought, which supposed an "un-
shakable faith in man," could be interpreted as a concession to Western humanism and to its universalizing ambitions, which many saw
as a dangerous trap. It also translates the will not to be completely
enclosed in the heritage of Pan-Africanism, that nevertheless would
be one of the major concerns of the journal, as what follows will show.

But the position of Alioune Diop can only be understood when put
in the perspective of the anticolonialism that is manifest in the journal from the first issue on. The rather disconcerting contribution of
Mounier, "Lettre à un ami africain," aroused some reservations, and
A. Diop was opposed to its publication. On the other hand, the
articles "Présence noire" by Sartre, "Le noir est un homme" by
Balandier, "Présence africaine" by Naville, as well as the preliminary
text of Gide's, "Avant-propos," are enough to indicate the militant
direction the journal intended to take.

On the whole, it is a question of demonstrating the *présence* of
Africa by continuously recalling the conflictual context[4] in which
this presence finds itself placed because of its historical relationship
to Europe, a dialectic defined by J. Howlett when he writes:

The self-affirmation of Africans entails the criticism of
the West and its different forms of subjugation, of suffocation of the Black consciousness; this polemic has itself
been bypassed by a plan for reconciliation that would be
accomplished by a universalist humanism, enriched and
authenticated by the values of the excluded peoples, differ-

2. Ibid., 8.
3. Ibid., 9.
4. On the relationship of *Présence Africaine* with Pan-Africanism, one may refer to
the analysis I offer in Bernard Mouralis, *Littérature et développement: Essai sur le
statut, la fonction et la représentation de la littérature négro-africaine d'expression
française* (Paris: Silex Editions, 1984), 387–461.

ent in fact from the abstract universalism as thought by the West.[5]

This orientation was characteristic of the first two years of the journal, years that made known a certain number of African writers and that opened debates such as, for example, those that took place on the "mythe du nègre" (nos. 2 and 5) or in connection with the book by Tempels, *La philosophie Bantoue* (no. 7), which was the first work published by the journal.

Equally remarkable is that this book appeared in the period during which *Présence Africaine,* renouncing a periodical publication, published, between 1950 and 1954, a series of special issues: *Le Monde Noir* (nos. 8–9), *L'Art Nègre* (nos. 10–11), *Haiti, Poètes Noirs* (no. 12), *Le Travail en Afrique Noire* (no. 13), *Les Etudiants Noirs Parlent* (no. 14), *Hommage à Jacques-Richard Molard* (no. 15), and *Trois Ecrivains Noirs* (no. 16).

Eventually returning to regular periodical publication, the journal continued in the same direction, but the concern to stick to the social and political reality of the day was perhaps more clearly stated. In defining the new formula, the editorial board specified: "All articles will be published on the condition . . . that they concern Africa, do not betray our anti-racist, anti-colonial cause, nor the solidarity of the colonized peoples."[6]

The tone taken is explained by a Franco-African context marked by the beginning of the Algerian War and by the perspective of *independence* as the political solution to the problems posed in the African territories. This same text referred to it explicitly:

> Our common national aspirations are the very foundation of our union in the face of a dangerous colonialism. It is also the road to positive construction in the matter of culture. There is no production, no cultural initiative, without the confidence and the lucidity, without that memory of our personality that only free political institutions can guarantee us.[7]

Thereby, *Présence Africaine* began a new phase in its existence: from now on, Africa, as a producer of culture, would be thought of as

5. Jacques Howlett, "Esquisse d'une histoire de la politique culturelle de *Présence Africaine,*" in *Mélanges (Réflexions d'hommes de culture)* (Paris: Présence Africaine, 1969), 42.

6. Editorial Board, "Notre nouvelle formule," *Présence Africaine,* nos. 1–2 (April–July 1955): 4.

7. Ibid., 4.

having a political future that will, by necessity, pass through the form of independence.

This preoccupation became apparent from the First International Congress of Black Writers and Artists in Paris (19–22 September 1956) and also from the Second International Congress in Rome (26 March–1 April 1959), both organized under the aegis of the journal.

These two conferences (to which should be added the "Debate on National Poetry" that was developed in the wake of the Paris conference) provided a particular opportunity to define the place and the role of the artist and the writer in the independent Africa of tomorrow. The first conference was, however, more of an appraisal of the cultural creativity in the Black world. The second conference dealt with the cultural politics of the new African States, notably in the resolutions drawn up by its different committees. Indeed, in 1959 we were on the eve of the Independences; as far as the French context is concerned, both the 1956 Loi-Cadre and the Communauté installed following the 28 September 1958 referendum together opened the way to political autonomy and subsequent independence. (Let us not forget the role played by Guinea, which after its "no" vote on the referendum then became independent.)

Paradoxically, it was at the moment that *Présence Africaine* expressed itself in the most narrow fashion on history that it most forcefully stated the interdependence of the cultural and the political, and escaped from the real as it concretely formulated itself in the early part of the 1960s. Without a doubt, therein lies its specificity as it can be perceived throughout the issues published since that period.

In fact, during the 1950s, Alioune Diop and the others who were the life and soul of the journal were praying for an independence and recommending a nationalism that was undoubtedly very different in their mind from the reality that we see today. The independence they envisioned was supposed to confirm and reinforce the solidarity of the African peoples as well as their unity, based on their common culture and history.

If it was utopian to think that the United States of Africa could be realized (the old dream of Pan-Africanism which Nkrumah had tried to make true), then one could at least envision independence on the basis of political entities of a certain geographical dimension (for example, on the scale of the former federations of the AOF or the AEF, and not in the form of the balkanization of States, to which the Loi-Cadre and the Communauté led, and which correspond very clearly to the interests of the colonizer). It is known how much the African political leaders as well as their parties were divided in the face of a form of independence that sanctioned the division and the weakening of Africa.

Confronted with this situation, *Présence Africaine* proved its pragmatism. It could have become the ultimate refuge of the supporters of a nationalism inherited from Pan-Africanism, on the scale of the entire continent, awaiting the day and the hour of Africa's salvation in a messianic atmosphere. But it preferred to act as *institution,* side by side with the publishing house and the Société Africaine de Culture, and to animate the intellectual and cultural debate that Africa needed and still needs.

In choosing this option, *Présence Africaine* avoided two pitfalls. Its loyalty to the ideals of Pan-Africanism turned it away from the temptation to become the interpreter of the micronationalisms and the ideologies that emerged in a certain number of states and whose function was to legitimize the new powers (Marxism-Leninism, authenticity, consciencism, etc.) that had come forth out of the Independences. It reported on them, answering the obligation of giving information, but it never gave up its independence. In this respect, the editorial politics of the journal as well as those of the publishing house undeniably reveal a will to lead a debate on all the problems broached. Besides, it is surely not a coincidence that the "round table" is a concept especially favored by *Présence Africaine.*

On the other hand, the fact that *Présence* has maintained contact with the fabric of the African institutions, notably the political, cultural, and academic ones, has preserved it from the second pitfall, a drift toward nostalgia, toward the ideology and spirit of the "groupuscules." From that point of view, the Africa that it has been facing is not a mythical Africa but the very real Africa, with its strong points, its burdens, its women, its men, its youth, its languages, its political regimes, which must be taken into account.

After this rapid description of the interior of this land named *Présence Africaine,* one might begin to measure its originality. As has been seen above, although *Présence Africaine* was born in Paris, it avoided the trap of exile right away. On the other hand, it played a basic role in the debate and the movement of protestation against colonialism that ended in independence. But, once independence had been attained, it detached or protected itself from what it had helped to create. This reserve, however, does not signify a flight into other-worldliness, an aversion with regard to the process through which, fatally, mystique lowers itself (as Peguy said) to politics.

It is precisely by keeping the necessary distance from reality that one is allowed to think the real, in compliance with the demand that Alioune Diop formulated in the first issue of the journal in "Niam n'goura." In that sense, one could say that the place in which *Présence Africaine* is situated is a utopian place—but one must not forget that Utopia often consists of a framework that allows thought topreserve its independence and critical effectiveness.

APPENDIX 1:   Committee of Patrons and Editorial Board after the Foundation of Présence Africaine

OCTOBRE-NOVEMBRE 47

N° **1**

——————— COMITE DE PATRONAGE ———————

MM. André GIDE

P. RIVET	P. MAYDIEU
TH. MONOD	E. MOUNIER

C. S. SENGHOR

P. HAZOUME

RICHARD WRIGHT

J.-P. SARTRE	Direction " REVUE
M. LEIRIS	INTERNATIONALE "
A. CAMUS	AIME CESAIRE

COMITE DE REDACTION

B. Dadié, Cissé Dia, Ayouné, Balandier, F.-D. Cisso-kho, Mamadou Dia, Mercier, Meyé, H. Panassié, A. Sadji, T. Serpos, M. Sillaret.

ADMINISTRATION ET REDACTION

16, Rue Henri-Barbusse, 16

Téléphone : DANton 78-57

Directeur : Alioune Diop

A partir de janvier 1948 la revue sera mensuelle.

Les abonnements 'ne commenceront qu'avec le numéro de janvier 1948.

APPENDIX 2: Synopsis of the First Issue

APPENDIX 3:   Fourth Page of the Cover of the First Issue

Prochainement ────

PRÉSENCE AFRICAINE

publiera

DES NUMÉROS SPÉCIAUX

CONSACRÉS

1. A une enquête sur « Le Mythe du Nègre » et « Le Mythe du Blanc ».

   Des articles de :

   J.-P. SARTRE : Du paternalisme.

   A. PATRI : A. Césaire et L.-S. Senghor.
   Etude sur « La Philosophie bantoue » du P. Tempels.

   D.-H. KAHNWEILER : « L'Art nègre et le cubisme ».

   Alioune DIOP : « Attitudes devant 'e monde exotique » :
   1) Psichari, P. Valéry, A. Camus.

   M. WATTEAU : « Situations raciales et condition de
   l'homme dans l'œuvre de J.-P. Sartre. »

   Michel LEIRIS.

   Albert CAMUS.

   L.-S. SENGHOR : « Marxisme et humanisme. »

   XXX... : « L'Homme selon le Christ. »

   A. BAYET : « La Colonisation romaine en Gaule. »

   Un roman d'Ousman SOCE.

   Une nouvelle de R. WRIGHT.

2. Aux valeurs africaines.

3. A la vie et aux aspirations des étudiants noirs dans
   le monde.

4. Au Nègre à travers 'a littérature européenne.

5. A la vie quotidienne du Nègre dans l'Afrique actuelle.

   Etc..., etc...

Octobre-novembre 1947.   Prix : 9.50

APPENDIX 4:   Synopsis of the Second Issue
(January 1948)

PRÉSENCE AFRICAINE

2

─── SOMMAIRE ───

Premières réponses à l'enquête sur le " Mythe du Nègre"
GEORGES MOUNIN, EMILE DERMENGHEM,
MAGDÉLEINE PAZ

AIMÉ PATRI .... Y a-t-il une philosophie bantoue ?

MAURICE WATTEAU .. Situations raciales et condition
de l'homme dans l'œuvre de
J.-P. Sartre (1ʳᵉ partie).

JACQUES ROUMAIN .... Bois d'ébène.

DAVID DIOP .... Trois poèmes.

Ballade khassonkaise de DIOUDI.

J. RABEMANANDJARA.. Chant.

MARTHE ARNAUD ...... Mythologie et folklore du Haut-
Zambèze.

L'histoire du singe fidèle, conte kabyle recueilli et présenté
par EMILE DERMENGHEM.

MOUASSO PRISO ...... Le cultivateur et la belle-mère.

ABDOULAYE SADJI ...'. Nini (roman).

RICHARD WRIGHT ...... Claire étoile du matin (fin).

CHRONIQUES

MICHEL DÉCAUDIN .... Guillaume Apollinaire devant
l'art nègre.

XXX .... L'U.N.E.S.C.O. fera-t-elle ap-
porter l'éducation dans les
contrées arriérées ?

PAULHA .... Les coloniaux doivent-ils con-
naitre les langues africaines?

NOTES DE LECTURE

La Poésie, par LEOPOLD SEDAR SENGHOR.
Les Essais, par M. M. DAVY.
Les Romans, par RENE MARAN et P. MINNE.
Le Jazz, par H.-J. DUPUY et MADELEINE GAUTIER.
L'Art, par J. CAILLENS.
Les Revues, par J. HOWLETT.

Conjugating Cultural Realities: Présence Africaine

two

Bennetta Jules-Rosette

Introduction

The original founders of the Présence Africaine publishing house exploited the cultural imaginary of "Africa." In turn, they were supported by French culture brokers, including Balandier, Camus, Leiris, Rivet, and Sartre, who discovered a revalorized sense of self and of their political objectives, fueled by a radical representation of "the other." Moreover, these brokers were part of a larger, self-validating French intellectual audience that stood in contrast to the emerging foreign (African, Caribbean, and U.S.) audiences for Présence Africaine. The preference for written literary expression (as opposed to representations in the visual and plastic arts) is a further indication of the tension between conventional artistic strategies and innovative cultural content in the Présence Africaine movement. This tension reflects the abrupt social and aesthetic changes characteristic of what V. Y. Mudimbe has termed the conjugation of the cultural and political aspects of expression. Présence Africaine as a publication network and an intellectual movement was both a source of cultural innovation and a vehicle of social and political mobility for members of the group. Seen from an anthropolog-

14

ical perspective, Présence Africaine is equally a new creation and a stimulation; it is simultaneously a reinvigorated source of intercultural communication and a reiteration of the sociocultural status quo.

During the course of this study, my understanding of Présence Africaine has changed many times. I began this research with myths and prejudices about the elitism of the négritude movement and its relationship to Présence Africaine. I responded to stereotypes of political outcomes. Now I have emerged with a fresh perspective on African writers in Paris and on the African continent. In this paper, I shall make no pretensions of a grand synthesis, because I believe that my interviews with African writers in Paris mark the beginning of a long journey and the opening of many new doors. This journey takes us back to the France of the 1940s and 1950s, to the interconnections of art and anthropology. The journey then moves forward into the present and calls for a reinterpretation of the realities of social science and art today—for African writers, for Africanists, and for anthropologists. Of only one fact am I certain: that the Présence Africaine publishing venture was a catalyst in a major intellectual movement that forces researchers to reenvision Africa in text and deed.

Rebelling against the referential illusion of an idealized Africa emerging from what Paul Niger termed "the theories of the ethnologists, sociologists, and other scholars who study humans in a glass case," the founders of the Présence Africaine journal and publications network formed an ideological movement (see Niger 1958:30). The international intellectual activities surrounding the Présence Africaine publishing house are challenging and still vital. Motivated by a vision of social, political, and economic autonomy, this movement reinvigorated the culture of its participants. At the same time, Présence Africaine and the négritude movement more generally may be analyzed as simulacra of existing artistic and intellectual networks in mid-twentieth century Europe (see Touraine 1984:32–34).

The concept of conjugating cultural realities is drawn from V. Y. Mudimbe's exhortation that it is necessary to delineate the relationship between cultural and political forms of expression about contemporary Africa.[1] I am concerned with the ways in which the writers

1. See Nantet (1972:239–240). Nantet quotes V. Y. Mudimbe's recommendation for a new and subtle strategy of political and cultural engagement among black writers. Commenting upon this recommendation, Nantet suggests that this engagement contrasts with a European approach to literary production by situating the problems described in an African cultural and philosophical context.

and artists who participated in the Présence Africaine movement have interpreted images of Africa as a means of making their voices heard on the international scene. This process involves creating a cultural reality as a point from which to speak to a diverse audience. Africa as a cultural imaginary becomes the source and symbol for a unique, although not unified, discourse. In a study of tourist art in Africa, I argued that the artists were engaged in projecting exotic and idyllic images of Africa for consumption by a foreign audience.[2] Writers have engaged in a similar but more complex process of devising counterimagery to identify and reaffirm themselves while simultaneously regenerating idyllic images. Bernard Mouralis (1984:419) describes the hybrid discourse that ultimately emerged in the publications of Présence Africaine as "multiform, polemic, and prospective." Whether the result is either (as Mudimbe claims) a "neatly ambiguous ideology" of artistic and political expression or a comprehensive literary and artistic framework is a question that can be answered only by listening to the voices of the writers themselves.[3]

In 1941, Alioune Diop spearheaded a new group of young black writers and intellectuals. Although previous publication efforts had been made among black students in Paris, these publications were sporadic and short-lived. *Légitime Défense*, a review published by a group of students from the Antilles, first appeared on 1 June 1932.[4]

Etienne Léro and other authors connected with *Légitime Défense*

2. Jules-Rosette (1984:19–20). Here I suggest that African artistic communication with a foreign audience involves a system of symbolic and economic exchange. See also Baudrillard (1972:118–119).

3. V. Y. Mudimbe (1988:177–178). Mudimbe argues that the conjugation of cultural and political forms of expression achieved by *Présence Africaine* was based upon a combination of the works of Marcel Griaule, Placide Tempels, and other "apostles of African otherness" with a political program emphasizing the analogy of universal human suffering. This process is evident in my discussion of the five images of Africa found in the writings of *Présence Africaine* authors.

4. A. C. Brench (1967:3–4). Brench contends that many African students and writers viewed the efforts of *Légitime Défense* as "inapplicable to Africa." They claimed that African writers already possessed the traditional values that the Antillian students were just beginning to explore. In contrast, Kesteloot (1974:83–84), considers *Légitime Défense* and *L'Etudiant Noir* to be cultural antecedents to the Présence Africaine movement. The writers themselves appear to share Brench's interpretation. M. Ngal (1975:53–54) discusses *La Revue du Monde Noire* established in 1931 under the direction of Paulette Nardal as a predecessor of both *Légitime Défense* and *L'Etudiant Noir*. The *Revue du Monde Noire* is significant because of the major roles played by women in its intellectual and publication activities.

criticized uninspired imitations of French literature and culture found in West Indian poetry of the 1920s and 1930s. Their publication called for a return to authentic African and West Indian cultural traditions in literature and the arts. The review folded after a single issue because of threats to the editors and financial difficulties.[5] Although some African students and writers were associated with *Légitime Défense,* many African students felt that the West Indian call for authenticity did not apply to them, for *Légitime Défense* advocated political activism as well as cultural change. Shortly after this group disbanded, another circle—including Aimé Césaire, Léopold Senghor, and Léon Damas—began to distribute a newspaper that first appeared in 1934 under the title *L'Etudiant Noir.*

Although Senghor and other African students were involved, the *Etudiant Noir* project acquired the reputation of being a West Indian effort rather than a collaboration of all black students. Its life span, too, was short. Alioune Diop, however, declared that his efforts were entirely different from those of any previous groups. In commenting on these early publication efforts, Christiane Diop, now head of the Présence Africaine publishing house, reiterated her late husband's concerns in an interview with me: "They always confuse us with *L'Etudiant Noir.* They were not our generation. We did not know them."

Established as a journal, *Présence Africaine* grew into a larger publication enterprise, an intellectual group, and a cultural movement. Initially published in the wake of the war, the journal reflected and capitalized on the turbulent changes in France. It was the time of the awakening of political protest in Algeria and Indochina and of disillusionment in France over economic stagnation and the slow recovery from the war. These social changes triggered ideological challenges to colonialism and French cultural hegemony. The first copy of the *Présence Africaine* journal was 196 pages long and was distributed simultaneously in Paris and Dakar in December of 1947.

Summarizing the history of Présence Africaine, Diop warns against confusing the publication with related cultural and political activities, including Pan-Africanism. He asserts that Présence Africaine was born

5. Kesteloot emphasizes that the publications of *Légitime Défense* and *L'Etudiant Noir* were short-lived for political reasons. Kesteloot (1974:85) further states: "Thus most of the contributors to *L'Etudiant Noir* recognized socialism as a valuable 'method of research' and as a 'revolutionary political technique,' but would not permit it to interfere in philosophical and religious domains."

out of protest against the colonization and assimilation produced by "Latin" culture.[6] Diop frames the goals of Présence Africaine as a liberating search for African identity and values in art and culture.

Présence Africaine's objective is to renew pride in African culture. This raises several questions. How do we define Africa apart from specific societies and cultures? What is "Africa" as a concept and a practice? Why do the authors need to reconceptualize and reevaluate Africa? The Africa to which Diop refers is a cultural imaginary, an aesthetic inspiration, and a rallying point for social and political action. The founders of Présence Africaine and the approximately twenty members of the editorial and patronage committees ideologically invested in Africa as a cultural construct in order to achieve self-expression, to reaffirm dignity, and to assert their political views in a hostile environment. Achieving these goals required recognition and the opportunity to publish African works in a new voice. As a cultural enterprise, Présence Africaine has served as a broker and facilitator in this process.

In an interview, Madagascan poet and founding member of Présence Africaine Jacques Rabemananjara outlined for me his conception of the goals of the organization and the journal. He summarized these themes as a revitalization (*réhabilitation*), illustration, and creation (*suscitation*) of new values.[7]

> In sum, there are three themes of *Présence Africaine:* first revitalization, second illustration, and third creation of new values in the black world. The goal is to revalorize the black world, the black man, so, from one perspective, to revitalize the specific values of the black man in today's world. What I mean is that these values have been despised. They have been ridiculed. Now the role of *Présence Africaine* is to affirm this revitalization. But, *Présence Africaine* is not content to stop at revitalization. We must go beyond that to illustrate these values, to place them in their proper context. And finally, *Présence Africaine* wants to create new values for the African of today, the black man of today, values that belong to the *black* world [*monde noir*]. So, if you say to me that there has been a change in our

6. In his "Itinéraire" (1987:43–52), Alioune Diop outlines the goals and history of *Présence Africaine.*

7. I recorded this interview with Madagascan poet Jacques Rabemananjara at the offices of Présence Africaine in Paris on 12 July 1988. In the interview, Rabemananjara outlines the history, evolution, and objectives of Présence Africaine as a publishing house and a cultural movement.

goals since the early days, it is as a result of the milieu in which we live. Times change. There has been an evolution. Consequently, values become married to their era, which is what *Présence Africaine* has done in identifying itself with the conditions of the world in which it exists today.

These three themes reflect the global ideology of *Présence Africaine*. They rationalize the motivations of its founders and demonstrate the historical flexibility of the movement. The goals of *Présence Africaine* are so general that they do not belie any individual point of view. Within their sphere, diverse political ideologies and styles of expression operate freely. All points of view may be claimed if they support the universalistic values of a revitalized black world. Philosophies of négritude, Pan-Africanism, liberation politics, and black aesthetics are embraced under the same cloak as long as their effect is one of revitalization and new creation.

The three terms that Rabemananjara uses to describe *Présence Africaine* imply action. They are the predicates of a sentence in which "l'homme noir" is the apparent subject. Yet, there is another unstated subject in the phrase "the adversaries of a revalorized Africa." In his introduction to Senghor's *Anthologie de la nouvelle poésie nègre et malgache de langue française,* Jean-Paul Sartre refers to this unstated subject as colonial domination by the European world.[8] Sartre's interpretation of the négritude movement in "Orphée noir" is widely quoted as a description of the philosophical ingredients of négritude. Sartre (1948:xli) saw colonialism—the unstated subject—as the thesis, black reaffirmation as the antithesis, and "human realization of a society without races" as the synthesis of the dialectic of domination. Regardless of whether one accepts this interpretation from a semantic perspective, Sartre highlights the limitations of this discourse as a political strategy. The Présence Africaine project makes sense in terms of the intentional absence of Africa as a source of value in European thought. Africa is reclaimed by the founders of Présence Africaine because it has been dominated and misinterpreted as a forgotten cultural sign.

The Referential Illusion of an Idealized Africa

Ideal images of Africa portrayed by some of the writers and artists associated with the Présence Africaine movement are by-prod-

8. See Jean-Paul Sartre (1948:ix-xliv, esp. xli). Sartre's philosophical recasting of négritude has been the source of much debate among African writers and scholars of the négritude movement.

ucts of what Roland Barthes (1975:271) has termed "the adventure of language." These images create a reality effect of shared meaning by anchoring a cultural vision in time and space. Africa provides a historical source for the significance of the writers' present challenges. Nevertheless, what is intended by the term "Africa" is neither uniform nor obvious. According to anthropologist Manga Bekombo, the referential illusion of Africa is employed to evoke a sense of unity ("quelque chose d'unitaire") for the "black world." This unity is inspired by alluding to a shared history and a common creative spirit. The image of unity depends on a narrative structure derived from the combination of three temporal sequences into a single expression: traditional past, colonial history, and emergent present.[9] A pristine and natural Africa is envisioned as the source of tradition and pride; colonized Africa is depicted as a state of affairs to be rejected and psychologically transcended; modern Africa embodies the hope of recaptured cultural authenticity and new political solidarity.

In documenting the trajectory of the Présence Africaine journal and the publishing house, Mouralis (1984:423–424) isolates three distinct periods: 1947–1949, 1950–1954, and 1955 to the present. During the first period, from 1947 until 1949, the journal published articles reaffirming a unified African identity and debunking misleading cultural stereotypes. This period coincided with a rise of interest in Africa among French ethnologists and the rethinking of anthropological conceptions of universality. Paul Rivet and Michel Leiris (of the Anthropology Laboratory of the Museum of Natural History at Trocadéro, now the Musée de l'Homme) were members of the supportive committees of the Présence Africaine journal. At the end of this period, the first book published by Présence Africaine in 1949 was Placide Tempels's La philosophie bantoue, which provided an essentialist view of the African aesthetic and creative spirit. In his effort to rediscover universalities of so-called Bantu thought and culture, Tempels confounded form, content, and action through inspiring generalities. This period was characterized by cultural reaffirmation.

An important strategy of reaffirmation was enlisting the aid of French scholars and intellectuals, including not only Leiris and Rivet

9. This combination of narrative sequences may occur within a single image or across several images and narrative utterances. In the image of emerging Africa, for example, traditional past, colonial history, and present conditions are united in an unfolding juxtaposition. See A. J. Greimas and J. Courtés (1979:247–250), and Gerald Prince (1987:63–64).

but also Jean-Paul Sartre, Georges Balandier, and Emmanuel Mounier. Balandier's "Le noir est un homme" appeared in the first issue of the journal (see Balandier 1947:31–36). In it, he denounces colonial stereotypes of Africans and counters them with the measured sociological analysis of African village life. Sartre's "Orphée noir" places a similar argument within a Hegelian framework, in which colonialism is the thesis and reclaimed African identity is the antithesis. Alioune Diop (1949:3–8) comments on these views in an editorial (appearing in the sixth issue of the journal) in which he criticizes Sartre's article, as well as essentialist stereotypes of traditional Africa, while advocating black cultural solidarity.

During the second period, the journal's cycle of publication became irregular, apparently due to financial problems. A series of special editions was published on poetry, art, and literature. Although cultural expression was the primary focus of these special editions, socioeconomic and political problems were handled in three of the nine issues published by *Présence Africaine* during this period. States Mouralis (1984:424):

> In this regard, the volumes *Le Travail en Afrique, Hommage à J. Richard Molard* and *Les Etudiants Noirs Parlent* were particularly indicative of the new orientation emerging in the journal in which the editors intended henceforth to place an emphasis squarely on the social, economic, and political dimensions of African problems.

Dating the third period from the middle of 1955 (when the first issue of *Présence Africaine* was published that year), Mouralis gives us no real end point. He appears to believe that the foci of the *Présence Africaine* journal and cultural activities have been constant since that time. Indeed, his view is supported by Rabemananjara, who states that the three basic themes of *Présence Africaine* have remained unchanged over the years. Although continuing its focus on cultural issues during the third period, the journal moved further toward the conjugation of political realities by advocating the anticolonialist solidarity of all oppressed people. In this instance, Africa became the symbol of resistance. The journal turned away from nostalgic cultural representations of Africa in favor of political exhortation. These changes surfaced in the numerous seminars, conferences, and festivals sponsored by Présence Africaine.

Although this diachronic overview is incomplete and subject to debate, it shows an evolution from nostalgic images of Africa framed in an essentialist mode to a more active combination of cultural revital-

ization and political action in the context of modern Africa. Although
a diversity in the interpretations of the African imaginary emerges
through historical description, this approach does not uncover the
fundamental differences and semiotic oppositions implied by the contrasting visions of Africa characteristic of the Présence Africaine project. By turning from chronology to imagery, it is possible to isolate
five contrasting themes that support but also fragment the discourse
of cultural reaffirmation.

1. Afrique-nature

In this image, the natural purity of an untouched and idyllic
Africa is envisioned as a source of strength and unity. Africa is viewed
nostalgically as an ancestral source and a splendid memory that
unites past glory and present dignity. This view is part of the praise
song animating the early stages of the négritude movement. Senghor's
poem "Congo" (published as part of the 1956 collection entitled
Ethiopiques) epitomizes this praise of natural Africa. The opening
lines of the poem, "Oho! Congo oho! Pour rythmer ton nom grand sur
les eaux sur les fleuves sur toute mémoire," set the tone for a nostalgic journey through idyllic Africa, complete with burning sun, palm
trees, canoes, dancing, and drumming.[10] The image evoked here resembles tourist art paintings of a lost and unblemished Africa.

This lyrical imagery reappears in critical and philosophical works.
In alluding to what he terms the "charm" and "magic" of African
poetry in "Orphée noir," Sartre (1948:xvi) describes this lyrical Africa
as "the last circle, the navel of the world, the source of black poetry,
dazzling Africa, on fire, slippery like the skin of a serpent." No longer
the dark continent, Africa is the source of a new, positive, and hyper-
bolic imagery. As with the paintings of the tourist artist, the poems
inspired by "Afrique-nature" and the nostalgic longing for a pristine
past create a powerful and innocent image, an incantation that con-
jures up the presence and memory of a lost land.

2. Afrique en combat

Idyllic Africa is challenged by social and political upheavals.
The image of emerging Africa resembles the burning landscape or village in tourist art (see Jules-Rosette 1984:154–155). Paintings of the

---

10. The poem "Congo" appears in *Anthologie du la nouvelle poésie nègre et malgache de langue française* (1948:168–170); and in Léopold Sédar Senghor, *Ethiopiques*.
The poem praises the nostalgic return to an ideal Africa.

burning village depict an idyllic landscape in flames, the source of which is ambiguous. The village may be burned as part of a political plan or simply as a result of natural causes. The image of emerging Africa, however, unmasks colonial repression as the cause of destruction. Two versions of this image may be designated: an optimistic vision in which the ancestral strengths of Africa result in victory, and a more pessimistic resolution that emphasizes the negative consequences of change. These two versions of the image of emerging Africa are aptly exhibited in the works of Aimé Césaire and Paul Niger. As West Indian poets, they looked toward Africa as a distant source and a cradle of ancestral hopes but were disillusioned by what they found in the living, modern Africa, uprooted from this poetic ideal.

"Afrique" ("Africa"), published in Césaire's *Ferrements* (1960), illustrates a combative yet optimistic approach to change. Although it is a song of praise, the poem contains metaphors of destruction describing the "blemishes" and "scars" suffered by a continent in transition. Echoing the spirit of revolt and liberation that appeared in his early *Cahier d'un retour au pays natal* (1939), Césaire depicts Africa, first as a locus of struggle and conflict, then as a natural and glorious ancestor. Describing "Afrique" and the other poems in *Ferrements*, Eshelman and Smith (1983:23) state: "The 'African' poems, in particular, celebrate decolonization in a tone that carries praise almost into political speechmaking." James Arnold (1981:267) considers "Afrique" to be typical of Césaire's "combative voice" and adds: "The poem expresses confidence in the eventual, indeed the imminent, success of decolonization and in sum exhorts the continent as a whole to persevere to that end." More than an elegy and an exhortation to act, "Afrique" unites nostalgic and combative imagery to mark the passage from the old Africa to the new.

Césaire opens this poem by describing an oppressed Africa.[11]

Africa
Your solar tiara knocked down to your neck by rifle butts
they have turned it into an iron-collar; your clairvoyance
they've put out its eyes; prostituted your chaste face;
screaming that it was guttural, they muzzled your voice,
which was speaking in the silence of shadows.

11. This translation of "Afrique" appears in *Aimé Césaire: The Collected Poetry* (1983:347), ed. Clayton Eshelman and Annette Smith. The poem cleverly combines nostalgic and combative images of Africa. The poem was originally published in Aimé Césaire's 1960 collection of poetry entitled *Ferrements*.

An image of change is evoked in the next stanza: "Africa, do not tremble, this is a new fight." The poem closes by harking back to the ancestral Africa, now scarred but still surviving.[12]

hidden things will again climb the slope of dormant musics,
today's wound is an oriental cavern,
a shuddering issuing from black forgotten fires, it is,
sprung from blemishes from the ash of bitter words
from scars, all smooth and new, a face
of long ago, bird concealed spewed, bird brother of the sun.

The metonymy "bird," like Senghor's Congo river, links Africa and nature. The figure of the bird suggests that Césaire has not completely abandoned an idyllic view of Africa. In fact, the natural Africa is the wellspring of hope for the emerging Africa in revolt. In a 1967 interview and lecture given in Paris, Césaire elaborated on the vision of Africa that he and the poets of négritude wished to convey in their early work.

We thought that it was an immense injustice to say that Africa had done nothing, that Africa did not count in the evolution of the world, that Africa hadn't invented anything of value. And at the same time it was an enormous mistake to think that nothing of value could come out of Africa. But let me add that our loyalty to Africa did not lead to a sort of philosophy of the ghetto.

A more pessimistic view of emerging Africa is presented in Paul Niger's poem "Je n'aime pas l'Afrique," first published in 1944. Lilyan Kesteloot (1974:279) describes the trip to Africa made by Paul Niger (whose real name is André Albert Béville) and his colleague Guy Tirolien as a failed pilgrimage. Niger returned to Paris bitter and disillusioned. He rejected both the idyllic images of Africa and social scientists' descriptions of Africa as a laboratory for studying human evolution. In "Je n'aime pas l'Afrique," Niger speaks of an oppressed Africa, riddled by disease, threatened by famine, and exploited by neocolonial middlemen and politicians. Yet Niger, too, hopes for a return to ancestral and natural strength. In the poem, he laments: "I wanted an earth where the land is nurturing, where the seed is a seed. Where the harvest is made with the scythe of the soul, a land of Redemption and not Penitence." Niger's poem begins with a litany of faults found in the Africa that he does not like.[13]

12. The last stanza of "Afrique" unites the suffering of the past with hopes for future strength. See Eshelman and Smith (1983:23–24).

13. Paul Niger's "Je n'aime pas l'Afrique" was published in Senghor's 1948 *Anthol-*

I Do Not Like Africa

Me, I do not like *that* Africa!
The Africa of the *"nayas"* (here)
The Africa of the *"makou"* (silence)
The Africa of the *"a bana"* (ended)
The Africa of the yesmen and blessed yes-yes
The Africa of men lying down awaiting like a grace to be
    awakened by a kick.
The Africa of *boubous* floating like flags of surrender, of
    dysentery, of the plague, of yellow fever, and of chiggers . . .
The Africa of "the man from Niger," the Africa of desolate
    plains.
Farmed by [a] murderous sun, the Africa of obscene loincloths,
    of muscles knotted by the effort of forced labor.

Oppressed, corrupt, and disease-ridden, Africa is the continent
emerging from idyllic dreams into the nightmares of modernity. Although this image of Africa achieves a reality effect by incorporating
modern political changes, it too is a stereotype. Implicit in Niger's
image of Africa is a longing for the continent to live up to its natural
and historical ideal. Dejected and frustrated because the new African
reality was not what he had expected, Niger presents an ambivalent
portrait of the Africa that he does not like superimposed upon an
implicit ideal. A hypotactic relationship exists between the two Africas. The ruined and corrupted Africa appears as such only in opposition to the ideal. Moreover, Niger hopes for a return to the seed, the
rich and nurturing ancestral Africa.

3. Afrique dénaturée

A third image of a denuded and transformed Africa emerges in
the writings and ideologies of the *Présence Africaine* authors. Although transformed, Africa remains a source of unity and inspiration.
Its strength derives from the experience of oppression and colonization. The Africa that Niger does like is now ready for "insertion into
the modern world" (see Diop 1947:7). African originality is the abil-

---

ogie (93–100) and reprinted with an English translation in *Voices of Négritude: The
Expression of Black Experience in the Poetry of Senghor, Césaire, and Damas*, ed.
Edward A. Jones, (1971:82–93). In Ellen Conroy Kennedy's 1974 English translation of
Kesteloot's *Black Writers in French: A Literary History of Négritude*, the line "the
Africa of *boubous* floating like flags" is mistranslated as "the Africa of tom-toms wav-
ing like flags" (279). Nevertheless, the impact of Niger's criticism of emerging, modern
Africa remains unchanged.

ity to transcend fragmentation and oppression through cultural and political unity. In his editorial introducing the first issue of *Présence Africaine*, Diop emphasizes the importance of developing an African consciousness and sensibility in the context of the modern world. The April 1955 issue of *Présence Africaine* introduces a new formula ("Notre nouvelle formule") stating that all articles published concerning Africa should reflect "anticolonialist" and "antiracist" perspectives in order to promote solidarity among oppressed people.

Some of the clearest statements about a transformed Africa appear in prose rather than in poetry. In a 1974 summary of the history of Présence Africaine, Diop states:

> The linguistic unity of our people has been destroyed since time immemorial. Their historical consciousness is fragmented into multiple universes of which the horizons are as limited as their linguistic arenas. Our cultures, in Africa, are *oral;* our monuments in *wood* do not resist the onslaught of time. Our political powers are limited in space. The equilibrium of our spiritual personality is easy to destroy. Neither the intellectuals nor the people (deprived of writing) have scientifically and realistically mastered our cultural heritage. No common vision of the future of the world sustains our coexistence on earth. Deprived of ways of thinking correctly about the modern world, based on sufficient information and exchanges, we let strangers construct our future and impose on us ideas that we have not created from personal experience of history and action in the world.[14]

Diop's image of Africa is not that of a nurturing phantom and a natural source. He sees Africa in motion as it progresses from its past to an unstable present. As with Niger, Diop (1987:46) proposes a solution to the problems of fragmentation, isolation, and oppression. He argues: "A real cultural solidarity of our people is, thus, indispensable to our salvation and our faith in ourselves. But this solidarity among black people must begin with an organic solidarity between the Westernized elites and their own people."

The Africa described by Diop is not just a geographical location in

14. This quote is taken from A. Diop (1987:43–52). This translation is my own, and it differs in several minor points of emphasis from that provided by Présence Africaine in its 1987 catalogue (48–52). Here Diop emphasizes the importance of providing new and transformed images of Africa.

time. It is an ideological construct and a cultural sign. Africa's existence and unity depend upon conscious political and social acts.

4. Afrique antithétique

In "Orphée noir," Sartre presents the vision of antithetical Africa. This Africa is the antithesis of European colonial domination. Sartre (1948:xvii) states: "It is necessary to break down the walls of a culture-prison, to return one day to Africa: thus in the cauldrons of négritude the themes of return to the native land and a redescent into hell are inextricably combined." Antithetical Africa, as Sartre envisions it, is a logical step in the progression toward liberation of the human spirit. Sartre considers this liberation to be a fundamental necessity for both European and black writers. As with Diop, Sartre conceives of the African situation as synonymous with the condition of all oppressed people. Sartre (1948:xxxix) asserts: "[R]ace is transmuted into historicity, the black Present explodes and is temporalized; Négritude introduces its Past and its Future into Universal History . . . "

Sartre (1948:xli) sets up a dialectic in which "the theoretical and practical assertion of white supremacy is the thesis; the position of négritude as an antithetical value is the moment of negativity." For Sartre, the synthesis is "the realization of the human element in a society without races." For him, Africa is thus a reminder of a negative moment in logic and history. It is the source of revolt, rejection, and negativity. Although Sartre acknowledges that ancestral Africa is an inspiration for black writers—the Eurydice toward which the writers turn—he rejects Africa as a final philosophical solution. Africa is important as a stunning reminder to European intellectuals that the "other" exists and that their expressions of liberalism can be undermined by Africa's stark experience of oppression. In the progression toward human liberation, Africa represents the combative element. Sartre is not concerned exclusively with the details of the African experience or their translation into the poetry of Black writers in Paris. Instead, he sees Africa as an analytic proposition and a source of universal political engagement. Sartre's complete statement of the dialectic of négritude in "Orphée noir" (1948:xli) is:

> Négritude appears to be the upbeat of a dialectical progression; the theoretical and practical assertion of white supremacy is the thesis; the position of négritude as an antithetic value, is the moment of negativity. But this negative moment is not sufficient in itself, and the blacks

who make use of it are aware of this. They know its aim is
to prepare a synthesis or realization of the human in a society without races. Thus négritude exists in order to be
destroyed. It is a transition, not a result, a means and not a
final ending.[15]

Sartre wished to establish a parallel between the condition of an
oppressed proletariat in Europe and the situation of blacks on a worldwide scale. Although he acknowledged that the social problems resulting from differences in class and race were not equivalent, Sartre
reduced them to logical comparability as a phase in the dialectical
movement toward human liberation. Both Alioune Diop and Frantz
Fanon considered Sartre's view to be relativistic and distorting. Fanon
(1952:135) stated of Sartre's assertion: "When I read that page, I felt
that I had been robbed of my last chance." In different ways, Fanon
and Diop saw African reaffirmation as an end point rather than an
antithesis in a dialectical movement. For them, the image of a transformed Africa was both a motivation and the end point in a long
struggle for self-realization.

Yet, in spite of his rational philosophical synthesis, Sartre, too, re-
verts to the image of natural Africa in exhorting his readers to consider the consequences of political action. He states that the African
situation may be depicted realistically and without anger: "It will be
enough for us to feel the scorching breath of Africa in our faces, the
sour smell of poverty and oppression."[16] This "scorching breath"
emanates from an idealized Africa that evokes both natural grandeur
and a sense of guilt for the nations that have colonized and exploited
the continent. Sartre vacillates between an acceptance of the poetic
images of a natural and emerging Africa and a final resolution that
Africa should be considered as a correlate in the logic of human
liberation.

5. Afrique scientifique

At the same time that the *Présence Africaine* authors were constructing idealistic and affirming images of Africa, French anthro-

15. This translation of Sartre (1948:xli) is quoted from the English version of Kesteloot's *Black Writers in French: A Literary History of Négritude* (1974:111). The passage summarizes Sartre's philosophical interpretation of the négritude movement as a
literary development and strategy of political action.
16. See Kesteloot (1974:286). This statement combines Sartre's commitment to political liberation with the ideal of idyllic and untouched Africa. The original statement
in French appears in Jean-Paul Sartre (1947:28–29).

pologists were beginning to conduct a new type of scientific research on the continent. The Dakar-Djibouti Mission extending from 1931 to 1933 was organized by anthropologist Marcel Griaule and included two participants in the *Présence Africaine* movement, Paul Rivet and Michel Leiris. The mission resulted in one of the most comprehensive efforts of field research conducted in sub-Saharan Africa. The researchers returned with ethnographic accounts, photographs, primary documents, and 3,500 objects designated for study in the Museum of Natural History at Trocadéro (see Clifford 1983:121–122). Griaule advocated using every available method for the study of Africa— geography, archaeology, aerial photography, ethnography, and oral history. He was among the first French scholars to penetrate "African thought" with his detailed recordings of conversations with the Dogon sage Ogotemmêli (Griaule 1948).

Not all of Griaule's methods were revolutionary and innovative. The term "mission" had long been used to describe colonial forays into Africa during which conquest and acquisition, rather than ethnographic study, were the goals. In his "Introduction Anthropologique" to Jules Rochard's *Encyclopédie d'hygiène et de médecine publique* (1889), ethnologist A. De Quatrefages defined anthropology as "a branch of zoology and mammalogy" in which "man should be studied as an insect or a mammal."[17]

The objects of study were to be scrutinized, described, and displayed. Although Griaule's spirit of comprehensive cultural inquiry departed from this conception of anthropology, he clung to the mythos of scientific objectivity and used Africa as a laboratory. While daily social life and ceremonies were analyzed holistically by the Dakar-Djibouti Mission, many aspects of material culture were taken out of context and studied as curiosities. The new anthropological movement overlapped in time, space, and personnel with the emerging black intellectual movements in Paris, but its objectives were different. James Clifford (1986:9) refers to the founders of *Présence Africaine* as "ethnographically aware" and argues that the journal "offered an unusual forum for collaboration between these writers and social scientists." Although a common ground existed between the anthropology of Africa and the renewal of pride in Africa through

17. See P. Rivet, P. Lester, and G.-H. Rivière (1935:507–531, esp. 508–509). The authors use A. De Quatrefages's zoological conception of anthropology as a point of departure for redefining the new mission of the Museum of Natural History. They criticize De Quatrefages for failing to distinguish between the ideas of race and civilization.

poetry and novels, anthropologists continued to view Africans as objects of study and to consider Africa as a laboratory for the investigation of human evolution and variation. Even when the African subjects spoke (as did Griaule's Dogon informant Ogotemmêli), the perceptions of the subject were not used to revise anthropological theory or to modify the methods of scientific analysis.

The tension between African intellectuals and anthropologists has not abated. In his introduction to the mission's report, Griaule (1933:1–2) outlined extensive and intensive methods for the study of African societies. Extensive methods involve the comparative study of several societies, while intensive methods focus on in-depth research on a single society. Although these conventional methods are sound, their success and effectiveness depends upon the questions asked and the access that the anthropologist obtains to the society under study. In many cases, the mission's researchers gained enough access to observe and photograph events while collecting objects of interest to the museum. However, the interpretation of these findings posed problems when the artifacts, detached from their cultural context, ultimately reached France. Griaule (1933:2–3) summarized his mission's approach:

> It is a question of proceeding with observations that become day by day more urgent, with a certain and rapid method. This certainty, like this rapidity, derives from the division of labor within a team of experienced observers working in constant collaboration. The quantity of results—to which one can add the quality—that one can hope to obtain is thus proportional to the number of researchers.

In a 1965 debate with anthropologist and ethnographic filmmaker Jean Rouch, one of Griaule's students, Senegalese filmmaker and *Présence Africaine* author, Ousmane Sembène, reproaches anthropological researchers for "considering Africans as insects" (see Cervoni 1982:78). Rouch ironically retorts that there is a virtue in this anthropological approach because even ants have a culture of their own. Although the new anthropology introduced African societies and culture to France with an unprecedented degree of methodological care and detail, the voices of the African subjects remained strangely silent. The collaboration between the black writers and French anthropologists was uneasy at best.

Commenting on the role that Présence Africaine has played in introducing a new anthropological perspective, Manga Bekombo re-

marks upon a similar problem of definition and ambiguity in the use
of technical terms:

> In my opinion, I think that a special problem faces those
> who claim to do what they call African anthropology.
> There is a problem of terms or of conception that means
> that they cannot fully accept the attitudes of the previous
> [African] writers, those who spoke of Africa as a human
> reality, a social reality and an object of study. I am not in
> total agreement with them.

The five images of Africa reflect these conflicts of definition. They
demonstrate that *Présence Africaine* from the early days forward encompassed the contradictory images of Africa as an ancestral source,
a continent in turmoil, a beacon of hope for the future, and an object
of scientific research. Some of these problems may be delineated by
examining the process of audience reception with regard to the Présence Africaine movement (see Holub 1984:159–161). As indicated
by its simultaneous distribution in Paris and West Africa, as well as
its choice of French as a language of publication, the audience for
Présence Africaine's early publications included African and European intellectuals in France, African scholars and writers at home,
and potentially a larger public of interested individuals ranging from
Parisian café society to the African and West Indian bourgeoisie. Each
shift in audience focus required a change in communicative register
and thought. Moreover, each image of Africa had a multiple appeal
across these audiences. Christiane Diop explained to me her view of
the diverse responses to Présence Africaine:

> It's like Don Quixote: that's where we are. We have this
> vision of the black world of Africa, and each time that
> we think that we have arrived there it's always receding,
> always disappearing because there is no respondent for
> us in the cultural domain. Culture is not profitable, you
> could say.

The absence of a cultural audience, described by Christiane Diop,
may result from the presence of too many respondents. Africa is defined as a source of inspiration for black writers. At the same time,
the authors reshape and revalidate Africa for European and African
readers. Despite the differences in definition, a common theme per-
vades the five images of Africa presented to these audiences. This
theme is the core definition of an ancestral and idyllic Africa that
becomes transformed by the writer's pen and the colonial experience.

Even the image of scientific Africa that was sacred to French anthropologists and certain *Présence Africaine* authors embodies overtones
of the natural and untouched ideal. It is an evolutionary point of departure that, for better or worse, stands in contrast to modern European society. These problems of interpretation may be explored in
more detail by applying the semiotic concept of homologation (see
Greimas and Courtés 1979:174).

Sartre places Europe in a relationship of contrariety to Africa. The
opposition of Africa and Europe leaves two other logical possibilities:
non-Africa and non-Europe. Herein lies a logical problem. Alioune
Diop defines non-Europe as all oppressed people. On the other hand,
Sartre revises this typology by a process of homologation in which
the African situation and the condition of the proletariat in European
capitalist societies are considered to be equivalent. Hence, the following homology emerges—Africa: Europe::non-Europe: non-Africa. In
this formula natural Africa is oppressed and colonized by Europe. Do
we consider the term "non-Europe" to include the African masses
who stand in a relationship of contradiction to non-Africa, or the European masses? Sartre (1948:xli–xliii) responds to this question by
conceding that although the concepts of race and class are different,
both the "proletariat" and the "black man" seek an egalitarian and
humanistic society without distinctions among groups. In this case,
non-Europe (that is, oppressed people of the Third World) and non-
Africa (that is, the oppressed classes of Europe) should share the same
social and political goals. The logic of homologation establishes this
equivalence, but in doing so it removes the uniqueness of Africa and
the "black man." The Présence Africaine movement, however, emphasizes African uniqueness as part of the process of renewing cultural pride.

Renewing Pride

Présence Africaine organized the First International Congress of
Black Writers and Artists that took place at the Sorbonne 19–22 September 1956. Numerous accounts of the proceedings of this conference are available in the *Présence Africaine* journal and other sources
(see Frutkin 1973:32–36; Kesteloot 1974:103; and Mouralis 1984:
425,432).[18] A perusal of these accounts suggests that the ambiguities

18. Two special editions of the *Présence Africaine* journal were devoted to the First
International Congress of Black Writers and Artists. *Présence Africaine* 8–10 (June–
November 1956) contains a summary of the congress and includes the papers and de-
bates actually presented at that time. *Présence Africaine* 14–15 (June–September

inherent in the five images of Africa surfaced in public debates. The problems with defining Africa as a cultural sign moved from the printed page to the domains of speech and social action. The congress took eighteen months to prepare. Sixty-eight writers, artists, and scholars were involved. Participants came from several African countries—Congo, Ivory Coast, Sénégal, Cameroon, Niger, Togo, Angola, and Mozambique. Others arrived from Martinique, Guadaloupe, Haiti, Jamaica, Barbados, India, and the United States. Diop framed the objectives of the congress as the affirmation of African culture and Western humanism (see Mouralis, 1984:425). In a 1959 interview about the congress, Senghor summarized its significance to him:

> To enable our négritude to be, instead of a museum piece, the efficient instrument of liberation, it was necessary to cleanse it of its dross and include it in the united movement of the contemporary world. This was, after all, the conclusion of the First Congress of Black Artists and Writers, which gathered symbolically at the Sorbonne in September 1956. (Kesteloot 1974:193)

Three themes were examined at the congress: the richness of black cultures; the crisis in these cultures, and the prospects for the future. The second theme appears to have received the lion's share of press coverage and is often represented as the theme of the entire congress (see Frutkin 1973:32). Three types of presentations were made at the congress: synthetic cultural statements about natural Africa and emerging Africa, scholarly papers based on social science research and observations of particular topics (such as religion in Africa and the tonal structure of Yoruba poetry), and programmatic political statements.

Senghor's "L'esprit de la civilisation ou les lois de la culture Négro-Africaine" represented the first approach in its call for a synthetic vision of universal black culture with its roots in Africa. The second set of expositions combined scientific and critical views of emerging Africa in the scholarly papers of Paul Hazoumé and A. Hampaté Ba. The third set of papers appears to have opened a series of logical and

---

1957) summarizes the papers that were not presented and several additional commentaries. See also Bernard Mouralis (1984:426). Interesting discrepancies emerge between the oral histories of the congress and the written summaries of its proceedings. These discrepancies suggest that a detailed case study of the congress as an event would yield beneficial results for historians and other analysts of the *Présence Africaine* movement.

programmatic debates concerning transformed and antithetical Africa. Both Aimé Césaire and Richard Wright objected to Senghor's holistic formulation of black culture on the basis of the historical and cultural differences affecting diverse populations, particularly in the Americas. In "Culture et colonisation," Césaire argued for the integrity of diverse black cultures in Africa and the African diaspora but stated that all were united by a common condition of colonial oppression. Wright and other American delegates, including Mercer Cook and John A. Davis, objected to imposing the concept of colonialism on black Americans and argued that their situation of racial oppression was different. Characterizing the congress and this debate in a personal interview, Rabemananjara recalled:

> You know, the most fantastic thing was the success of the
> First Congress of Black Writers and Artists held here at
> the Sorbonne. The Americans sent a strong delegation, and
> we ask ourselves even to this day how so many people
> accepted to come. There were Americans, delegates from
> the Caribbean, people from the Pacific, the Indian Ocean,
> continental Africa, and even India. How do you explain
> this type of meeting in Paris under the direction of Alioune
> Diop, who, once again, was not assisted financially? You
> must remember that no one gave money to finance us at
> that time. It was Alioune Diop with his small and loyal
> team who united these people from all corners of the
> world . . . Writers like Richard Wright were there with
> the North American delegation. These were the intellec-
> tuals from your country. But that does not mean that they
> shared the same vision of the world. We were all evidently
> dominated by the cultures that shaped our ideas. Yes, but
> a common cultural base was there. We wanted to express
> our commonalities across the diverse cultures that sepa-
> rated us. And there were conflicts—even very bitter con-
> flicts— because what dominated our thinking at that time
> was our colonization. And the Americans did not under-
> stand that because they said that they were *not* colonized.
> They could not understand. And some of them feared that
> they would not be able to return to America after the
> congress.

Here Rabemananjara is referring to the political fear that some of the Americans apparently had of associations with a Marxist perspective during the era of McCarthyism. James Ivy presented a paper entitled "The NAACP as an Instrument of Social Change," and

Wright addressed the problems of what he labeled the "tragic African elite" in "Tradition and Industrialization." Césaire and Fanon, however, preferred to dwell on the shared problems of colonialism and racism as issues affecting blacks throughout the world. Fanon warned against placing too much faith in purely literary and artistic endeavors, which he termed "the culture of culture." According to Mouralis (1984:429), Fanon's presentation was so controversial that no one referred to it throughout the remainder of that day's discussion.

Other participants had more positive memories of the congress. Recalling his experiences, a founder and participant in the Présence Africaine movement, Paulin Joachim of Benin, enthusiastically reported to me:

> The First Congress of Black Writers and Artists took place here in Paris in 1956 at the Sorbonne. And we were all there. There were Americans who came. I particularly remember Langston Hughes, who was my friend. We traveled to Uganda together later. And there was Richard Wright. We stayed in the Latin Quarter until five o'clock in the morning discussing ideas. In those days, this was our place. It's nothing now. And there was Frantz Fanon at this First Congress. The theme was "Modern Western Culture and Our Destiny." This congress gave a great boost to Présence Africaine. Alioune Diop and Aimé Césaire worked hard to organize it. Black Americans participated and so did French poets. The congress resonated throughout the negro-African cultural movement. They started to take us into consideration and to respect us in France. They began to discover our writings.

For Joachim, cultural crisis and conflict were not the fruits of the congress. Instead, he saw the principal results as respect and public recognition. The congress provided publicity and a new forum within which the opinions of African writers could be heard. Problems of definition and debates over terminology faded into the background as Présence Africaine savored its new success.

Although buried in memory, the terminological disputes were not erased. They may be interpreted with reference to the five images of Africa and the logical problems that these images pose. Senghor and the scholars focusing on cultural, literary, and scientific topics looked to the timeless and idyllic Africa as their ideal. Césaire and Fanon invoked the colonial experience of Africa as a description of the present situation and a clarion call for action. Rejecting idyllic and emerging Africa as models, the black Americans described their struggles and experience of marginality, but they were uncertain about their identification with Africa as a cultural ideal or a model of political activism. Probably figuring in these controversies were political debates and personality conflicts not recorded in the congress proceedings. Nevertheless, the conflicting images of Africa implicit in the broad agenda of Présence Africaine surfaced repeatedly in the conference presentations. The congress was a point of departure for publicizing the efforts of Présence Africaine on an international scale, a reflection in microcosm of its ideological dilemmas, and a forecast of future challenges.

Voices of Writers and Artists in Contemporary Context

Writers and artists discussing Présence Africaine today do so with a nostalgic regard for the pioneering role of Alioune Diop and his circle of followers. Through a series of interviews, I have explored the sources and directions of change as perceived by individuals who participated in or were inspired by the activities of Présence Africaine. Three major themes surfaced in my interviews: recognition of the past successes of Présence Africaine in redefining cultural identify and authenticity, attempts to continue these efforts and to adapt them to the contemporary context, and observations that the conditions for expression and action require a new synthesis and the use of alternative methods.[19]

Reviewing the continuity of Présence Africaine's efforts, Rabemananjara reflected:

> The writers composed and created. Présence Africaine has always been there to support them and help them to flourish, to bring out their insights and values. So, at present, this does not have the same meaning, but the objective is still the same: to revalorize the black man in every domain. Voilà! That's what I can say overall about our evolution—Présence Africaine has always functioned as a midwife that has given birth to others. Voilà! A midwife! It has supported the creativity of writers from the black world for the simple reason that European publishers were reluctant to publish the works of black writers. Présence

19. In July of 1988, I conducted a preliminary series of interviews with black writers and artists in Paris. The presentation of the voices of the writers is based on these interview materials. I conducted follow-up studies with additional interviews in 1989, 1990, and 1991.

Africaine took up this task as its vocation, nurtured the talents of black writers, and literally gave birth to great authors.

Although Rabemananjara remarked that many of these writers initially could not publish elsewhere, he emphasized the creative and supportive role still played by Présence Africaine in the translation and publication of African works. Publication is, of course, part of the larger goal of reshaping a sense of cultural identity by challenging world views that have excluded an African creative presence.

Following the pattern of many intellectual movements based in Europe, Présence Africaine centered around a core of writers and students. It used the university system as a model and a source of intellectual support. In France, where the literary intellectual has often become a public hero by combining art and political activism, Présence Africaine was an apt vehicle for exploiting as well as challenging existing patterns of cultural expression (see Clark 1987:165). The founders enlisted the support of successful literary heroes such as Sartre, Camus, and Leiris. They also cast themselves in the mold of literary heroes and intellectuals speaking on behalf of the "black world." Although this strategy offered an effective means for publicizing new ideas, it also marked an acceptance of the system that had excluded the writers in the first place. In other words, Présence Africaine opted for both symbolic protest and cultural assimilation during its early years.

Anthropologist Manga Bekombo described how the early Présence Africaine movement functioned.

So how was the movement organized? Essentially by work commissions. The African Cultural Society [or SAC] of Présence Africaine saw itself as a veritable university. There were commissions that resembled university departments. They worked on history, geography, philosophy and so on. These were specialized departments. That was the ideal. And on the concrete level it translated into departments that were veritable little societies in themselves. And these commissions operated for a long time, perhaps until the 1960s, and they produced I don't know how many issues of the journal. There was the journal itself to publish reflections. And there were books and edited volumes. The objective of all of this collaborative work was to bring Africa into the public view as a human reality, as a great people. Voilà!

Bekombo's description reveals the organizational coordination and scholarship behind the Présence Africaine publishing efforts. This work was influenced by the fervor of Parisian intellectual life during the 1950s. Paulin Joachim describes the excitement and sense of anticipation surrounding the meetings of the early Présence Africaine group.

> There were several of us grouped around Alioune Diop, who was a great pioneer in his work for African culture. He brought together French intellectuals such as Mounier, Sartre, and Leiris, the great surrealist. All of them knew Africa. And there was a small group of students: David Diop, a great poet who is now deceased; René Depestre, a Haitian poet; and Jacques Stéphen Alexis, now deceased, from Haiti. He wrote marvelous books. We were all in the small group around Alioune Diop, and we had a mission. Essentially it was to implant African culture in European civilization, to affirm our presence. And in Paris in those years we wanted to launch an African cultural renewal aimed at the white world in which we had been immersed. We wanted to assert our culture and our presence in this world.

Joachim continues to explain the relevance of the early publications on négritude as an inspiration for the young students.

> And these efforts were related to négritude, which was for us in the beginning a political position that grew into a cultural movement. Aimé Césaire, who coined the word "négritude," had been there at the birth of Présence Africaine. There were about ten students around Alioune Diop. We were loyal followers. First we met at Rue Chaligny in the twelfth arrondissement and later we moved to Rue des Ecoles in the Latin Quarter where all the students could meet easily. Césaire's *Cahier d'un retour au pays natal* was our bible. We found a certain purity in the writings of Césaire and many of us tried to imitate him. Césaire, our elder, had achieved a synthesis. In Africa, it became a bible of black cultural renewal.

Césaire recalled his student days when the term "négritude" was coined.[20]

20. On 4 December 1967, Aimé Césaire presented a lecture and presided over an open question-answer session on his work at the Maison Helvétique in Paris. I have quoted from this lecture and interview session courtesy of Serge Tornay, a participant in these discussions.

Thirty years ago when Senghor, Damas and I were students in the Latin Quarter the term "négritude" was coined during our discussions and debates. It appears that at that moment we used the term among us as a little bit of jargon. But it happens that, in fact, I have the dubious honor of having used the word in a literary sense for the first time. Since then, it has become part of a literary repertoire and has been consecrated. Books and articles have been devoted to the term, and I become singularly embarrassed when I personally am called upon to define what we meant by négritude in those days. We were students at Sorbonne then and we confronted a cultural void in the black world. It was a period when the notion of African civilization was very controversial. And for the first time Leo Frobenius's book on African civilization was translated into French. It was extremely revolutionary, extremely shocking. Well, you need to have these facts in mind in order to grasp what we meant when we used the word "négritude" for the first time.

Past successes of *Présence Africaine* still inspire young writers and artists in Paris. Benjamin Jules-Rosette, Martiniquan founder of the Théâtre Noir of Paris, claims that the efforts of Présence Africaine have been important for his work:

I think that Présence Africaine is still necessary, first of all as a source of cultural reassertion, and second as a means of showing us that black culture is extremely rich and dense, despite alienation and efforts to stamp out and ravage that culture. Présence Africaine reclaims black culture without beating its fists on the table. Présence Africaine simply says that we must take a stand and display this cultural richness. It says to Europe that we have our own culture and that we can play your game. When Césaire, Damas, and Senghor spoke of négritude, they advanced this cultural battle. But now everything has become a bit stagnant. Perhaps it's necessary. I am trying to analyze that. And young black students today do not understand this cultural assertion and this reaffirmation of dignity. They think that these ideas are outmoded.

Christiane Diop expressed a similar skepticism about the relationship of Présence Africaine to the new generation of black students.

Young people are so impatient. They must always speak of the present. But the present is built upon history. So they

say that we at Présence Africaine are old-fashioned and focused on the past. Can you believe that?

This remark returns us to the present. Although the content of
Présence Africaine's message of cultural affirmation remains the
same, its audience has changed. Perusing the shelves of the Présence
Africaine publications outlet, one finds an eclectic mixture of literature of past and present characterized by a persistent theme of cultural protest.

Prospects for Future Research

A study of Présence Africaine raises several interrelated anthropological, historical, and interpretive problems. Analyzing the
evolution of ideologies, Karl Mannheim (1936:83) states that "the
variation in the meaning of words and multiple connotations of every
concept" provide "an index of social and cultural change." Accounts
of the early days of Présence Africaine demonstrate how a new universe of discourse was shaped and popularized. The reenvisioning of
Africa, the evolution of négritude as a term and a philosophy of action, and the literary forum opened by Présence Africaine are indi-
cators of its impact as a social and cultural movement. Présence
Africaine forged anthropological concepts into literary and ideological tools. This process of cultural semiosis warrants study based upon
the texts published by Présence Africaine and the actual social events
where new ideas were developed and transmitted. Before it is too late,
a documentation of the oral history of the movement is essential as a
supplement to the voluminous writings of its authors. This task emphasizes the crucial methodological distinctions between oral discourse, in what Walter Ong (1982:104) refers to as its "chaotic
existential context," and the apparent precision of the written text
that imbues utterances with a sense of finality. Voices of the writers
and artists introduce an alternative interpretive perspective that
modifies analysts' and literary critics' views of the meaning of texts
and events.

Significant foci for further research include the following six
points.

1. More extensive study of what Mouralis has termed the third period of *Présence Africaine* (from 1955 forward) should be conducted in order to establish the contemporary impact of the
   movement. This analysis should also examine various generations of the intellectual movement placed in social context.
2. Additional oral historical and interpretive sociological data gath-

ered in France, Africa, the Antilles, and the United States would be useful for studying the diffusion of Présence Africaine and related movements focusing on African culture. This process of diffusion also warrants analysis in its own right.

3. The ambiguities that scholars find in the messages of the Présence Africaine movement are produced by specific textual and communicative strategies that should be analyzed semiotically and culturally. Audience reception should also be examined. Considerations here include the gendered and culturally specific language of *Présence Africaine*, the concept of négritude, and the meaning of "*l'homme noir.*"

4. These concerns should lead to a further consideration of the role of women in black intellectual movements in Europe and an analysis of the contemporary situation of black women writers, domains of study that appear to have been neglected in previous analyses of Présence Africaine.

5. French anthropologists of the 1940s and 1950s began to transform scientific conceptions of African "civilization" and to remodel views of Africa as a laboratory for studying the universal elements of human culture. Investigation of the relationship between anthropological thought and the literary and artistic efforts of Présence Africaine is a productive area of research for the history of both anthropology and of the Présence Africaine movement.

6. In order to gain a fuller understanding of Présence Africaine in its own right and as a point of departure for the analysis of the diffusion of intellectual movements, its audience neeeds to be studied in more depth. This audience includes the press, African and European intellectuals, the scientific world, and the general public.

Conclusion

Inspired by the rediscovery of Africa in European social science, a young group of black writers and scholars expressed their experiences of cultural marginalization and protest. In so doing, they modified the concepts and tone of social science and assured themselves a place in literary history. Présence Africaine offers a fertile terrain for the study of the dynamics and diffusion of an intellectual movement. Many anthologies contain texts of the authors who participated in or were directly influenced by the movement, but few studies examine the social context of this cultural production. By analyzing five images of Africa in conjunction with the early Présence Africaine movement, I have attempted to demonstrate that categorical distinctions in the texts have reflected the social experiences of the writers and have simultaneously engendered further social conflicts. Contradictory but thematically linked images of Africa resurfaced in the debates at the First International Congress of Black Writers and Artists and reappear in the writers' oral description of their experiences.

Yet the social experiences and the texts are not the same. Interview data reveal the emergent quality of literary terms and ideological constructs that originated in speculation, debate, and conversation. This process of cultural semiosis is not a singular event, as Sartre's concept of the white supremacy thesis and the négritude antithesis implies. Teleological movement toward a unique synthesis is not the outcome of these texts and discussions. Instead, the Présence Africaine movement graphically demonstrates a process of constant reinterpretation, or infinite semiosis, in which the meaning of Africa recedes from view and reemerges to haunt and challenge us once again.

BIBLIOGRAPHY

Arnold, A. James. 1981. *Modernism and Negritude: The Poetry and Poetics of Aimé Césaire.* Cambridge, Mass.: Harvard University Press.

Balandier, Georges. 1947. "Le noir est un homme." *Présence Africaine* 1 (November–December):31–36.

Barthes, Roland. 1975. "An Introduction to the Structural Analysis of Narrative." *New Literary History* 6, no. 2:237–272.

Baudrillard, Jean. 1972. *Pour une critique de l'économie politique du signe.* Paris: Editions Gallimard.

Brench, A. C. 1967. *The Novelists' Inheritance in French Africa: Writers from Senegal to Cameroon.* London: Oxford University Press.

Cervoni, Albert. 1982. "Une confrontation historique en 1965 entre Jean Rouch et Sembène Ousmane." *CinémAction* 17:77–78. This interview was first published in *France Nouvelle* 1033 (4–10 August 1965).

Césaire, Aimé. 1947. *Cahier d'un retour au pays natal.* Paris: Bordas. This collection was first published in the Parisian review *Volontés* 201 (1939) and was reprinted by *Présence Africaine* in 1956.

———. 1960. *Ferrements.* Paris: Editions du Seuil.

———. 1967. "Entretien et Débat." Paris: La Maison Helvétique. (Audiotaped lecture and interview courtesy of Serge Tornay.)

Clark, Priscilla Parkhurst. 1987. *Literary France: The Making of a Culture.* Berkeley: University of California Press.

Clifford, James. 1983. "Power and Dialogue in Ethnography: Marcel Griaule's Initiation." In *Observers Observed: Essays on Ethnographic Field-*

work, ed. George W. Stocking, Jr., 121–156. Madison: University of Wisconsin Press.

———. 1986. "Introduction." In *Writing Culture: The Poetics and Politics of Ethnography*, ed. James Clifford and George E. Marcus, 1–26. Berkeley: University of California Press.

Diop, Alioune. 1947. "Niam n'goura ou les raisons d'etre." *Présence Africaine* 1 (November–December):7–14.

———. 1949. "Malentendus." *Présence Africaine* 6, no. 1:3–8.

———. 1987. "Itinéraire." *Catalogue 1987: Présence Africaine*, 43–52. Paris: Présence Africaine. This article is reprinted from *Présence Africaine* 92, no. 4 (1974).

Eshelman, Clayton, and Annette Smith, eds. 1983. *Aimé Césaire: The Collected Poetry*. Berkeley: University of California Press.

Fanon, Frantz. 1952. *Peau noire, masques blancs*. Paris: Editions du Seuil.

Frutkin, Susan. 1973. *Aimé Césaire: Black between Two Worlds*. Miami: Center for Advanced International Studies, University of Miami.

Greimas, A. J., and J. Courtés. 1979. *Sémiotique: Dictionnaire raisonné de la théorie du langage*. Paris: Hachette.

Griaule, Marcel. 1933. "Introduction méthodologique." In special issue of *Minotaure* titled *Mission Dakar-Djibouti, 1931–1933*. *Minotaure* 2:7–12.

———. 1948. *Dieu d'eau: Entretiens avec Ogotemmêli*. Paris: Chêne.

Holub, Robert C. 1984. *Reception Theory: A Critical Introduction*. New York: Methuen.

Jones, Edward A., ed. 1971. *Voices of Négritude: The Expression of Black Experience in the Poetry of Senghor, Césaire, and Damas*. Valley Forge, Pa.: Judson Press.

Jules-Rosette, Bennetta. 1984. *The Messages of Tourist Art: An African Semiotic System in Comparative Perspective*. New York: Plenum.

Kesteloot, Lilyan. 1974. *Black Writers in French: A Literary History of Négritude*. Trans. Ellen Conroy Kennedy. Philadelphia: Temple University Press. This book was first published in French as *Les ecrivains noirs de langue française: Naissance d'une littérature*. Brussels: Editions de l'Université Libre de Bruxelles, 1963.

Mannheim, Karl. 1936. *Ideology and Utopia: An Introduction to the Sociology of Knowledge*. Trans. Louis Wirth and Edward Shils. New York: Harcourt, Brace, and World.

Mouralis, Bernard. 1984. *Littérature et développement*. Paris: Editions Silex.

Mudimbe, V. Y. 1988. *The Invention of Africa: Gnosis, Philosophy and the Order of Knowledge*. Bloomington: Indiana University Press.

Nantet, Jacques. 1972. *Panorama de la littérature noire d'expression française*. Paris: Librairie Arthème Fayard.

Ngal, M. 1975. *Aimé Césaire: un homme à la recherche d'une patrie*. Dakar, Sénégal: Nouvelles Editions Africaines.

Niger, Paul. 1948. "Je n'aime pas l'Afrique." In *Anthologie de la nouvelle poésie nègre et malgache de langue française,* ed. Léopold Sédar Senghor, 93–100. Paris: Presses Universitaires de France. This poem is also reprinted with an English translation in *Voices of Négritude: The Expression of Black Experience in the Poetry of Senghor, Césaire and Damas,* ed. Edward A. Jones. Valley Forge, Pa.: Judson Press, 1971.

———. 1958. *Les puissants.* Paris: Editions du Scorpion.

Ong, Walter. 1982. *Orality and Literacy: The Technologizing of the Word.* New York: Methuen.

Présence Africaine. 1956. "Le premier congrés des ecrivains et artistes noirs et la presse internationale (Paris—Sorbonne 19–22 Septembre 1956)." *Présence Africaine,* nos. 8–10 (June–November).

———. 1957. "Contributions au 1er congrés des ecrivains et artistes noirs." *Présence Africaine* 14–15 (June–September).

Prince, Gerald. 1987. *A Dictionary of Narratology.* Lincoln: University of Nebraska Press.

Rivet, P. P. Lester, and G. H. Rivière. 1935. "Le laboratoire d'anthropologie du muséum." *Archives du Muséum d'Histoire Naturelle*: Volume Tricentenaire 6, no. 12: 507–531.

Sartre, Jean-Paul. 1947. "Présence noire." *Présence Africaine* 1 (November–December): 28–29.

———. 1948. "Orphée noir." In *Anthologie de la nouvelle poésie nègre et malgache de langue française,* ed. Léopold Sédar Senghor. Paris: Presses Universitaires de France.

Senghor, Léopold Sédar. 1948. "Congo." In *Anthologie de la nouvelle poésie nègre et malgache de langue française,* ed. Léopold Sédar Senghor, 168–170. Paris: Presses Universitaires de France. This poem also appears in Léopold Sédar Senghor. 1956. *Ethiopiques.* Paris: Editions du Seuil.

Tempels, Placide. 1949. *La philosophie bantoue.* Paris: Présence Africaine.

Touraine, Alain. 1984. *Le retour de l'acteur: Essai de sociologie.* Paris: Librairie Arthème Fayard.

Out of Africa! Should We Be Done with Africanism?[1]

Denis-Constant Martin

three

Put differently and badly, if epistemology is reduced to a logic of the functioning of methods that matches a concrete sociology of groups in conflict, then science is nothing more than common rubbish. Within it, everything comes from power and is changed into power, comes from glory and is transformed into glory, comes from gold and is transmuted into gold. Contemporary science, which has pierced the secrets, the old secrets of transmutation known long ago, will be covered with historical shame for having discovered the philosopher's stone the wrong way up. In the end, everything is transmuted into gold, but the worker remains unchanged.

Michel Serres[2]

As manifested in Africanism, the African presence in the world is scoffed at. Such an assertion may appear unfair and outrageous. However, if Africanism is understood to mean the wish, academic or journalistic, to report the continent in a double unity—it is one, it is unique—that is, to isolate it within specificities that are attributed (but not verified as such through comparative analysis) in order to create a unity that is artificially reinforced by the generalizing temptation to infer general facts from the imperfect knowledge of local phenomena, then this presence appears as an imprisonment, an isolation. It is the result of enclosure.

Like all other parts of the planet, Africa has lived in open communication to the outside, in a relationship of interaction—be that peaceful, conflict

1. These remarks, deliberately polemic and occasionally almost caricatural, come out of twenty years of "Africanist" research from within a French institution that is officially dedicated to political science. Thus, they are very largely self-critical and have been heavily marked by the French history of political science as applied to the African societies after the independences. They constitute, as the reader will have understood, what is called a *papier d'humeur*.

2. Michel Serres, *Détachement, apologue* (Paris: Flammarion, 1983), 140–141.

laden, dramatic, or hateful—which implied both its transformation through foreign contributions and interventions as well as its influence on the societies with which it had contact. It is today no longer necessary to dwell upon the fact that, like the rest of humanity, contemporary Africa is the result of history; her organizations have known all kinds of forms, have produced all kinds of goods at different periods in their existence neither more nor less than have the others.

Thus, this history is a plural one in every sense: a plurality of contacts, a plurality of societies, bonds between societies within the continent, exchanges with societies abroad. From this plurality, the dynamics of African history have derived their energy. All of this, too, is well-known since Georges Balandier so admirably summarized these processes in the "dialectics of the dynamics of the inside and the dynamics of the outside."[3] Nevertheless, to accept Africa as history, plurality, meeting place, and source of influence (as numerous works by historians and anthropologists[4] invite us to do) implies the consideration that the events and the phenomena that unfold and have unfolded there could have been, are being, and will continue to be found outside of Africa, even if the forms that they take, the expressions that make them known, differ from one place to another. This is precisely what Africanism tends to deny; it stresses alleged characteristics or evades the confrontation of its results with those gathered in other places. It makes of Africa a closed universe, an incomparable world that in its most pessimistic versions is doomed.[5]

Is Africanism Possible?

Africanism is an ideological notion; such a term cannot claim some sort of scientific discipline as basis. Africanism, as a wish to globalize and to attract attention to the events and the phenomena that occurred in one part of the world, is a mask, an alibi that, de-

3. Georges Balandier, *Sens et puissance, les dynamiques sociales* (Paris: Presses Universitaires de France, 1971).

4. We are not concerned here with contesting the quality of the works—at least of many of the works—produced under the title of "Africanism" but with questioning certain ideological implications of this term.

5. Note, for example, in the daily newspaper *Le Monde* the revival of the components—"tribalism," "magic," "corruption"—of the Africanist vulgate in order to present a rough sketch of a catastrophic Africa: for example, on tribalism: *Le Monde*, 3 January 1986; on sorcery: *Le Monde*, 11 December 1987. See also on this topic: Denis Martin, "Les méfaits du tribalisme (dans *Le Monde*)," *Politique Africaine* 21 (March 1986):102–108.

pending on the era, has been able to serve as a justification for oppression (which, in turn, was used to eradicate what was presented as atavistically idiosyncratic, therefore inhuman or, in other words, barbaric), or as a formulation for the more or less sorrowful condemnation of an incapacity to manage the present (which serves, this time, as a pretext for other interventions such as those organized by the IMF or the World Bank).

Once again, the paradox is that the scientific literature devoted to Africa demonstrates exactly the opposite. Everything shows that the very relevance of the word "Africa" is of a geographic nature. In that realm there is no problem. The continental boundaries are clear, indisputable, and operative. But as soon as this realm is left behind, it is all over: the diversity of social realities sheltered in the continent is such that Africanism as encountered in books, texts, and courses has never succeeded in defining a common Africa for itself. There are maximalists who claim to envisage the totality of the continent's societies in one fell swoop. They have a hard time in dealing with the differences, unless they choose to give descriptions region by region or country by country, but at least they espouse a certain logic. Larger in number are those who, from the start, carve it up in small pieces; and then the difficulties abound. What Africas does one encounter: Sub-Saharan Africa as opposed to North-Africa (Maghreb-Machrek), Black Africa as opposed to White Africa, the inheritance of a hierarchy of barbarisms where the Moslem Arab endowed with the ability to write is worth more than the pagan and illiterate Negro? The Africans who have become Moslems and who have mastered (at least, the scholars among them) the Arabic script are problematic, while on the other hand one can amuse oneself by figuring out when and for whom Mauritania, the Sudan, and even Ethiopia and Madagascar are or are not part of Africa.

Colonialism has created other lines which Africanism has sometimes repeated. Africa is also former French colonies facing former British colonies, a border that frequently reinforces the caesura between East and West as well as the linguistic differences. Thus, one had to wait a long time for French Africanism to leave its "own turf" so to speak, and to take an interest in something other than the societies of the African West, in which Zaire was included by dint of linguistics, as were Rwanda, Burundi, and, on occasion, out of political-economic necessity, Nigeria as well.

Hence, many works presented as "Africanist,"—that is, claiming to deal with the continent or at the very least embellished with a title in which Africa is mentioned—are in reality only works that evoke a region or that are based on the systematization of knowledge acquired in a single area or a single country. What is normally called African-ism has been also constructed at the risk of error and misuse.

These practices testify not simply to a lack of rigor (which would be tolerated with difficulty in studies devoted to other parts of the world) but also without a doubt to an impossibility. If one takes the diversity and the plurality of the African realities into account, then an honest and authentic continental Africanism is probably unattain-able. Of course, there are admirable syntheses based on the compila-tion of studies of cases more or less covering the whole of Africa. Such works are necessary and useful when they are truly balanced and know how to indicate the convergences and the divergences as well as the overtures and the coming together of Africa and other parts of the world.[6] But, today as yesterday, the claim to know is a vain one, even more an absurd one, when to know means to possess a sufficient degree of empathy in order to break through the facade of appearances and to grasp the logic and the reasons of the political mechanisms and the behavior from the inside. In confronting one single country after only twenty or twenty-five years of sovereignty, the foreigner already has difficulty enough in keeping his bearing to produce one monograph after a certain amount of time spent work-ing. How then could he come to terms with the whole of the conti-nent? All the more so because it is not yet sure that we possess an acceptable case study per African country, even while cumulating writings in French and English.

From this point of view, the methodological discretion of Africanist political scientists is remarkably paradoxical once again: on the one hand, they insist on the specific characteristics, on what distin-guishes one African society from another; while on the other hand, either they do not explain how they work there or they content themselves with applying prescriptions used and revised elsewhere, sometimes with baffling results. A generation of legal writers has thus devoted itself to paraphrasing African constitutions, only to be astonished later that these hardly seem to shed light on the real prac-

6. In this field, the primary example of the genre remains without a doubt and de-spite the years Yves Bénot, *Idéologies des indépendances africaines* (Paris: F. Maspéro, 1972). Also excellent resources are Catherine Coquery-Vidrovitch and Henri Moniot, *L'Afrique noire de 1800 à nos jours* (Paris: Presses Universitaires de France, 1974) as well as Elikia Mbokolo, *L'Afrique au 20ème siècle, le continent convoité* (Paris: Edi-tions du Seuil, 1985).

tices, to the point where today, through inverse excess, the very study of African laws as such seems disqualified and not (as might more reasonably be expected) the approach that prevailed a short time ago. Teams of investigators crashed down upon the African societies, armed with finely honed questionnaires, without having given the least preliminary thought to the place of the spoken word, its hierarchies, its functions, its techniques, to that which is provoked by the creation of a querying situation. They returned from their quest with only a meager harvest.[7]

Then, too, while political studies are more and more interested in popular behavior and movements (in the "grassroots" ways of making and speaking politics among ordinary citizens), while the moral, aesthetic, and symbolic dimensions of social and political practices are the object of more systematic studies, we are present at a stimulating flowering of theoretical developments which, undoubtedly, would be more convincing if it were explained on what investigations these developments were based and how those investigations were conducted. It would also be good if it were clarified in which language the materials used had been formulated. For one of the essential givens, regularly forgotten by political scientists, is the fact that the majority of citizens of the African States live and think politics in a language that is neither French nor English, Portuguese nor Spanish. And it is obvious that political expression, conceived and stated in an indigenous language, carries impulses, visions of the world, symbols, and ethical valorizations not reducible to what one can find in more or less skillful translations, or in the official discourses dressed in the idiom of the former colonizer, whether those discourses were obtained in the course of interviews with rulers or university graduates or after the reading of and listening to other means of information. As

7. An attempt at reflection on the problems posed by the polls has begun to be made in Tatiana Yannopoulos and Denis Martin "Les questions d'Endama, de quelques problèmes méthodologiques posés par les enquêtes en milieu africain et en particulier chez les étudiants camerounais" (Doctoral diss., 3d cycle, Université René Descartes, 1973); Tatiana Yannopoulos and Denis Martin, "De la question au dialogue . . . à propos des enquêtes en Afrique noire," *Cahiers d'Etudes Africaines* 18, no. 71 (1978):421–442. Other methodological questions are raised in Denis-Constant Martin, "A la quête des OPNI (Objets politiques non identifiés), comment traiter l'invention du politique?" *Revue Française de Science Politique* 39, no. 6 (1989):793–815. Finally, two classic works stress the way in which the gathering of data mold the gathered data: Gérard Althabe, *Oppresion et libération dans l'imaginaire, les communautés villageoises de la côte orientale de Madagascar* (Paris: F. Maspéro, 1969); and Benoît Verhaegen, *Rebellions au Congo* (Léopoldville: IRES, 1966; Brussels: CRISP, 1969).

a matter of fact, while there are few works that have taken the importance of the facts of language into account, they open up some very exciting perspectives.[8] Impossible in fact, Africanism remains passably superficial in what it produces. Its methodological deficiency and its linguistic failings make it a mediocre partner in the conception of a comparative politics built on a truly worldwide scale.

Is Africanism Useful?

Nevertheless, such a case against Africanism cannot lose sight of the fact that the search for what is African, the will to put the continental realities together, the desire to find therein the foundations for a common enterprise, the energies of a shared sensitivity have all responded to an intellectual demand by Africans confronted with the dehumanizing work of colonialism. In the fact of the global denial of cultures, of values, of African practices, it was absolutely necessary to forge and brandish a unified defense of Africa's peoples and societies. It was a matter of turning back against the invader, holding him with the weapons he himself had brought and whose force he therefore knew in the realm of both politics and religion. Knowledge cast into certain molds indubitably furnished one of these weapons, and if some colonial administrators were able to claim that they were Africanists as well, why should not some Africans also have tried to produce their knowledge of their societies, but to their own ends?[9] Thus, Africanism and Pan-Africanism thereby found themselves intimately linked.

That time is gone. The majority of African territories reached the status of independent statehood twenty or more years ago. The image of Africa in the world has changed considerably, and its unity and its standardization that Pan-Africanism rendered somewhat mythical not so long ago feeds attitudes today that are all too often attitudes of incomprehension. They can be attitudes of rejection, of condemnation, or they can be attitudes of attraction, without having thereby become better grounded.

For many among the Western public, Africa is again in fashion, as it was during the heyday of colonial exoticism about sixty years ago. Through music classified as African, but reworked in European or

8. See Comi M. Toulabor, *Le Togo sous Eyadema* (Paris: Editions Karthala, 1986).
9. Cheikh Anta Diop admirably represents this effort of protest and heuristic reconstruction: *Les fondements culturels, techniques et industriels d'un futur Etat fédéral d'Afrique noire* (Paris: Présence Africaine, 1960); and *Nations nègres et culture* (Paris: Présence Africaine, 1965).

American studios, the West offers material (as yet not much used) for the dreams of uncertain youths who, furthermore, find an opportunity to pour out their generosity in spectacular events of rock music meant to highlight the African "misery," even though they know nothing more about these misfortunes.[10]

In a more general sense, the work of academics (who for some time now have been eager to prove the arbitrariness as well as the weakness of the African States, their abuses of power as well as their mismanagement) is going in the same direction. They make Africa conspicuous in a negative sense, and support it intellectually by ghettoizing it.

On the one hand, the academics spot phenomena whose existence and prevalence in African societies cannot be denied: violence, the preponderance of solidarity based on origin ("tribalism" as it is called today, although no satisfactory definition of the "tribe" has ever successfully been given), corruption, fascination with what lies abroad, and escapism. But, on the other hand, only rarely are historical and relational analyses proposed to show the complexity of causes the intermingling of internal and external factors that maintain these phenomena. Furthermore, the academics limit themselves to describing their consequences in Africa without making the effort to identify comparable phenomena, either in the present or in the history of the other parts of the world. Nor do they ever take the trouble to indicate what puts these phenomena apart and what brings them closer. With what right can the French, the Europeans, or the Americans denounce the "endemic effects" of an Africa that "is off to a bad start," "sick," "strangled," "tormented by the demons of tribalism," "ravaged by the misdeeds of corruption" and "lost its compass"? I mean, with what right can they generally denounce, globally condemn Africa, and not, of course, legitimately rise up without complacency in the name of the universal rights of man against a specific event, against a particular practice in Africa, as one would do for anything similar happening elsewhere? But it is not frequently so: on the contrary, from the heights of a clear conscience, they judge Africa on the basis of what has occurred during the span of one generation, thereby "forgetting" the past, even recent, of their own societies, offsetting what may be happening still in their own countries. France giving amnesty to the "Carrefour du développement" embezzlements, America of the Rea-

10. Héléne Lee in *Rockers d'Afrique* (Paris: Albin Michel, 1988) provides an example of this mythification of the new African music, based on an investigation that is geographically limited to a small number of West-African nations.

gan scandals, and Great Britain eroded by the Irish canker: how dare they denounce African corruption, negligence, and tribalism! Another paradox: the "historicity of the African societies" is no longer questioned. All too often, however, Africanists do not assess what two or three decades represent in the whole history of humanity. Let us take a thirty-year period in Europe—1914-1944, for example—and let us draw some definitive conclusions on the civilization and the peacefulness of the Europeans, only to see—another great lack in the field of African political science is the reasonable perception of time.

When generalizing, the Africanist rarely knows of what he speaks, since there is neither the material nor the intellectual means by which to grasp the continent integrally. He barely admits from where he speaks, what interest motivates him, how he proceeds in order to come to the conclusions that he draws. He gladly makes pronouncements without any regard for history, without seeking to put things in perspective or to compare. This is perhaps—but who shall define the psychopathology of the Africanist?—caused by a lover's spite, disappointed hopes put into the new experience of the independencies, investments too emotionally made in the different societies, whose difference proves in the long run to be frustrating and wearing. Many of the enthusiasts of the 1960s have changed into the prosecutors of the 1980s without truly asking themselves whether their hopes had been formulated in response to deficiencies, to aspirations that were theirs alone, or from a respect for the Africans, who would choose by *themselves*, including the ways of *their* domination, including *their* decision regarding motives and the forms of *their* conflicts. To affirm this in no way covers up the dramas that the African societies know today. On the contrary, it prompts a search for better understanding before making judgments (if that is still possible), in order that foreign observers can participate in solving the African predicaments from the place that must be theirs as observers only, not from a position as scorners and directors.

In short, Africanism continues to be a paradox in that it insists upon differences in order to deny the right to differences, instead of showing the similarities in order to demand respect of being other. But Africanism, notably that of the former colonial powers or that of the most recent world powers, cannot accept its futility. It cannot do so out of self-respect, of course, but also because, small as it may be, it constitutes a world of influence, of powers, of honors, if not always of material privileges. Africanism has its rostrums, its scholarly societies, its journals; it has its reputations and its coteries. It is also riddled with conflicts that are rivalries of ambition and power. It must protect itself, however, for—and that is the other side of the coin—by dint of wanting to make Africa conspicuous, by dint of wanting to isolate the continent, Africanism has ensconced itself as an academic discipline, and it seems even more difficult to extricate oneself from it than to enter into it. Its slight taste for comparatism and the stress laid on what might appear to be aberrant have partly discouraged the rest of the political scientists' community from becoming interested in the Africanists' work and from delving into it. In sociology, in political science, it seems that one can attain an acceptable reputation as a "generalist," on and after practical experience of the Orient, of the Arab countries, of Latin America, even if the great road still passes through the "developed" countries and, in France, especially through the study of French political life. However, one can hardly cite names which are "in" emerging from Africanism, but not because there is an absence of qualified people in the profession.[11]

For African Studies in a Comparative Perspective

So, then, is Africanism impossible? Have the efforts that it instigated not improved our knowledge of the societies of the African continent? Or, have these efforts participated in a vast enterprise of misrepresenting the realities that are prevalent there and have only furnished another demonstration of "Western arrogance?"[12] Without coming back on what has been written in necessarily general terms in the preceding sections, I do not mean that, or, more precisely, not that only. Written in the short term out of an exterior and necessarily partial experience of "Africa," under the influence of visions of the world, of non-African conceptions of its management (especially of its material administration) taken up again and simplified in journalistic commentaries—texts that generalize and globalize certainly have perverse effects and illustrate a temptation of Africanism to preach, merging the good civilizing conscience of colonialism and the bad social conscience awakened by the contemporary dramas and dis-

11. For example, in skimming the index of authors cited in the four volumes of *Traité de science politique,* Madeleine Grawitz and Jean Leca (Paris: Presses Universitaires de France, 1985), it seems that barely more than 1 percent of the names mentioned are those of Africanists or of "generalists" who have written about Africa (if my count is correct: sixty-eight out of a total of 6,163 entries).

12. On this "Western arrogance" see particularly Annar Cassam, "La Tanzanie, la France: Nous n'avons qu'un seul monde," in *La Tanzanie, vingt ans après Arusha,* ed. François Constantin and Denis Martin (Pau: Université de Pau et des Pays de l'Adour, Centre de Recherche et d'Étude sur les Pays d'Afrique Orientale, 1988).

asters. Next to these, and in fact legion, are those writings devoted to exact phenomena within clearly circumscribed terrain, on a given time period, asking theoretical (sometimes even methodological) questions of interest to the whole of the human science in whatever area they may apply their resources. But the specialization of such studies and their not very striking style will make them less easily accessible, limiting the dissemination of the knowledge they harbor.[13] The publisher who owns a house (and keeps an eye on the breakeven point) will find them too "limited," the journalist too difficult, and the public at large will have few opportunities to know that they exist. But, starting with these works, syntheses are possible; the enormity of the continent and the vastness of the accumulated materials make the task more and more difficult, but we have seen that it is not impossible. And such syntheses, be they achievement of African authors or of collective efforts, can contribute to making that which happens in Africa better known and better understood.

Nevertheless, we cannot be satisfied with that. For Africanism must execute a double Copernican revolution in order to avoid the intellectual atrophy and dessication in which it tends to take a delight. First, it must be equipped with an equivalent of Bachelard's philosophy of openness, of pluralism, of a "why not"?;[14] in other words, it must make itself available to the facts of Africa—as perturbing as they may seem, as dreadful as they are for those who live them—in order to study the indigenous structures from those facts: to postulate that which dumbfounds as a potential innovation (rather than to criticize the innovation because it dumbfounds the outside observer), and to draw the theoretical teachings from it after this very specific form of experience.[15] Only thereby will Africanism, or better African stud-

13. The popular press is thrilled with a work of sensationalist popularization, the one by Guy Sorman, *La nouvelle richesse des nations* (Paris: Fayard, 1987), and does not make note of the factual mistakes nor of the bias in a chapter devoted to Tanzania, but it passes over the admirable book by Bernard Joinet, *Tanzanie, manger d'abord* (Paris: Editions Karthala, 1981), practically in silence. See on this subject François Constantin, "Les images de la Tanzanie en France, mythes et parti-pris," in Constantin and Martin.

14. Gaston Bachelard, *La philosophie du non, essai d'une philosophie du nouvel esprit scientifique* (Paris: Presses Universitaires de France, 1962).

15. See Denis Martin, "Par delà le boubou et la cravate: pour une sociologie de l'innovation politique en Afrique noire," *Revue Canadienne des Etudes Africaines* 20, no. 51 (1986):4–35. Recent works devoted to property rights and to informal economies show the direction to be taken: Claude de Miras, "De la formation de capital privé à l'économie populaire spontanée, itinéraire d'une recherche en milieu urbain africain,"

ies, show itself capable of restoring Africa to the world—that is, restoring to Africa its score in the concert of knowledge. For (and this constitutes the second revolution to be fomented) these African facts will truly make sense, even in the double light of their partially unveiled internal economy and in this confrontation with the facts and knowledge gleaned in other places. Africanism has no future except in comparatism: first, an internal comparatism that will allow the true establishment of Africa as a geographic place of similar and different experiences; and second, an external comparatism that draws parallels, no longer with an artificially generalized Africa but with African realities and other non-African realities.

What will result is a freeing of the scholarship on Africa. Proceeding from an already considerable and constantly increasing store of knowledge, it would stimulate new research, redirected by the discovery of the universality of certain phenomena and the specificity of others as well as the conditions of production of such specificity, of their expression. To take just one particularly flagrant example, if Africa can contribute to a general theory of social classes, it must also help in understanding that these classes exist in every culture in conceptions and expressions belonging to their culture. In the same way, placed in the domain of comparatism, the facts of Africa will allow new approaches to non-African societies and will direct observers of Africa to focus where they have not turned willingly.[16]

This African presence in the social sciences must recover another form of dialogue, more precisely, it must pursue, amplify, and systematize the collaboration of foreign and African researchers, combining the impulses of different experiences, backgrounds, and relationships to the studied reality when these are opposed to each

Politique Africaine 14 (1984):92–109; Alain Morice, "A propos de l'économie populaire spontanée,' pour une vision socio-politique de la reproduction urbaine," *Politique Africaine* 18 (1985):114–124; Emile Le Bris, Etienne Le Roy, and F. Leimdorfer, eds., *Enjeux foncier en Afrique noire* (Paris: Editions Karthala, 1982), 391–399. And, of course, the innumerable works devoted to the religious innovations and their significance should be mentioned, beginning with those of Georges Balandier and Marc Augé.

16. Among others, two recent works of research in progress show what anthropology and political anthropology of the "developed" societies, the French in particular, can draw from the teachings of the anthropology of the African societies. See Georges Balandier, *Le détour, pouvoir et modernité* (Paris: Fayard, 1985); Claude Rivière, *Les liturgies politiques* (Paris: Presses Universitaires de France, 1988); see also Marc Abélès, "L'anthropologie et le politique," in *Anthropologie, état des lieux* (Paris: Navarin/Le Livre de Poche, 1986), 207–233; and "Le temps des labours," *Le Monde,* 8 June 1988.

other. Such a collaboration would not in and of itself resolve the problem of linguistic understanding of the political and social facts, but it would help if, over and above all that, methodological thinking were to be brought to the subject at the same time.

Thus, Africanism will perhaps risk its disintegration in a comparative anthropology of contemporary human societies that will finally permit no further barriers to be erected in order to devote itself better to the study of what makes humanity one, of what connects its fragments, of what constitutes its cultures without thereby altering its universality. But, at that price, the funeral will be a happy one.

part two

The Question of an African History

Présence Africaine: History and Historians of Africa

four

Catherine Coquery-Vidrovitch

An eminent literary journal, *Présence Africaine*, has not been any less attentive to history in a time of major political upheaval of the African continent through the genesis of the Independences, and more generally of the Black world of the diaspora: it was assuredly no coincidence if, among others, the process of desegregation began in the United States in the same period. It is, therefore, important to question the journal's role and influence in this domain, to determine to what extent it was a militant action (that is, both active and innovative) that could have influenced the conception and the ulterior evolution of the *discipline* of history in some privileged fields: Black Africa and the diaspora, as much in France as in other places, especially the Caribbean, South America, and the United States.

Our first goal is of a quantitative nature: to register the body of work whose outstanding feature is *history* and to determine what its major characteristics were that will permit us to judge better the breadth of the contents in a second part of the analysis.

The first step in our research, therefore, consisted of noting the articles in

question. The list will be found in the Appendix. The analyst's subjectivity naturally reveals itself from this stage on: we have given the
term *history* the widest possible content, retaining not only those
texts that refer to a chronicle-history but all that (closely or from
farther away) refer to the field of history—including not only the
methodology or problematics of the discipline but also any cultural
fact that refers more or less explicitly to the past.[1] In the same category, we have grouped in-depth articles and more or less specialized
notes whose content is generally (but not always) shorter, in order not
to lose an area that would be treated only in this form. The only items
we have considered in a separate category are the reports (properly
speaking),[2] and we have noted the distribution of the special issues.

The overall result is as follows: over a period of forty years (from
1947 to summer of 1988) and 161 issues,[3] we found 253 articles and
150 commentaries on written works (of which 132 were in the form
of the reports and the rest gathered together in half-a-dozen columns).
This represents an average of 6 articles and a little more than 4 reports
annually (clearly more than 1 article but less than 1 report per issue).
As for depth, this is not negligible; it echoes very little the works
published in the field during the same time. In other words, while on
the one hand the authors published in *Présence Africaine* had something to say (or, if one prefers, a message to deliver) to the field of
history, on the other hand the journal was not very interested in
outside contributions, perhaps quite simply because it never really
organized a specialized critical column—which in itself can be seen
as indicative.

The distribution over time corrects the lukewarm appraisal (see
fig.): after a beginning that was rather little concerned with a history
then barely in existence and not the first objective of the editorial
team, the journal became enormously interested in the historical
roots of decolonization; most of the early articles on history cover the
years of the creation of Independence, 1958–1962. Then, a fresh interest in history in the middle of the 1970s corresponds, at least in
part, to the emergence of a second generation of African academicians

1. Our choice does not necessarily overlap that of the alphabetic Index of the Appendix and the material over thirty years old published in 1977.

2. For lack of time and because their distribution seemed too random to us to be
conclusive, we did not submit the reviews to the file reserved for the articles.

3. Apart from the 15 special issues of the first series, the journal had reached no. 146
of the second series (begun in 1955) with the second quarter of 1988, the last issue
consulted for this article.

Evolution of number of articles on history

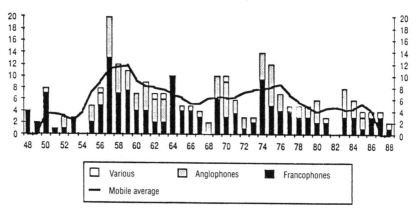

(as, for example, Boussoukou-Boumba, Kabongo, Maryse Condé, Madina Ly, Makosso-Makosso, Salifou, Simiyu) who begin to write side by side with their elders; this fresh interest also corresponds (and this is surely no coincidence) to a second nationalist wave that at the same time rose up against the "neocolonialism" of the years that immediately follow upon Independence (for example, by demanding the revision of the agreements of cooperation with France, in the political arena). In the academic arena, this tendency was accompanied by a thesis of a xenophobic nature that once again showed its mistrust of Western science: at least, that was a palpable current among the students at the time. Since then—and one should question the reasons for this turning point—the journal seems to have devoted itself once again primarily to its original literary inspiration. Since the beginning of the 1980s, the interest in history is more rare. Would that simply be because the discipline, having reached maturity, has lost part of its militant dynamism to enter instead into the classical field of the professionals of history whose interest in a journal that is relatively marginal to their preoccupations has decreased?

The articles are distributed among 178 authors. Few of them have been regular contributors: 18 among them have written twice (of whom 3 on the same subject divided over 2 issues), and 4 among them—Louis Béhanzin, Raymond Mauny, Jacques Rabemananjara, and Jean Suret-Canale—have written 3 times. Another 4 appear 4 times: Basil Davidson, Joseph Ki-Zerbo, Oruno Lara, and Léonard Sainville. But it is rare that these few contributions took place with a time lapse of more than three or four years (with the exception of Jacques Rabemananjara and Léonard Sainville, that is, of members of the journal's staff.)[4] This indicates a reciprocal interest between journal and author that is real but occasional, either on the occasion of a thesis that must be defended or simply because of relatively fleeting affinities.

Two authors produced five articles: Richard Pankhurst (1960–1985) and Mody Cissoko (1964–1983). Finally, the name John H. Clarke returns 7 times (1960–1988), that of Ibrahima Baba Kaké 9 times (1953–1979), and the most prolific author is Théophile Obenga with 10 articles (1969–1988). These 5 authors are, therefore, regular collaborators, whose permanence signifies the journal's loyalty to a certain conception of the practice of history. To that group, it can be noted, no Frenchman belongs. In a general way, the majority of these authors (whose international distribution is clear) are well-known among Africanists.

Présence Africaine and the French University

But the ties between history at *Présence Africaine* and French universities appear astonishingly loose: only 13 authors—that is, 6.6 percent of the total—are French academics or researchers. Among these, only 3 or 4 have contributed as intellectual patrons of French Africanism: Georges Balandier, in an introductory article at the time of the first issue; Théodore Monod, director of the IFAN, who organized the special issue on "Le Monde Noir" (1950); the historian Raymond Mauny, professor at the Sorbonne since the beginning of the 1960s; and the sociologist Paul Mercier (then a relative newcomer), in a note of a few pages in 1952. If one were to refer to the academic discipline of *history* (in the strict sense of the term), the number decreases even more. There are only 5 Frenchmen who have contributed somewhere along the line to *Présence Africaine:* Henri Lhote (prehistorian), Raymond Mauny (medievalist archeologist), Henri Moniot (historical anthropologist), Jean-Louis Triaud (Black Islam), and Jean Suret-Canale (contemporary historian-geographer). The number is low, even more so when compared to that of the English-speaking

---

4. For example: the 2 articles by Cheikh Anta Diop are from 1959 and 1964, those by Reverend Mveng from 1963 and 1965, the 3 by Mauny from 1961 and 1964, the 4 by Davidson from 1955, 1956, and 1957, the 4 by Lara from 1974, 1975, 1976, and 1979. One hardly notices greater time lapses, except for E. O. Egbo, who writes in 1970 and 1978, Léonard Sainville (1969–1978), and, above all, Jacques Rabemananjara, who shows himself only in 1957, 1959, and 1987.

academics who have contributed to the journal: even though my knowledge of their university affiliation is less exact, there have been at least 15 of them, more in number than their French counterparts. As for the African writers, practically all of them come from the university elite or from the world of arts and letters. This is, at least, a striking fact and certainly significant. It reveals a double blockage, on the part of the academics and on that of the journal.

From the "academic" end, it could truthfully and quite simply be partly a question of an instinctive, constitutional mistrust with respect to a nonprofessional journal, published for nonspecialists; that is, academics were biased regarding scientific popularization for an educated but not immediately professional public. That is hardly a natural attitude in French academics. It is not necessarily always shared; thus, one finds in the journal certain articles of history that the specialists consider fundamental, such as the reference text by Thomas Hodgkin on "Mahdisme, messianisme et marxisme" (1970), or the one by Mody Cissoko on "L'intelligentsia de Tombouctou aux 15è et 16è siècles" (1969). One has to recognize that nothing like this appears signed by the French historians, who rather have tended to offer the journal—when they did offer anything, which seems rather exceptional in itself—some light pieces (des bonnes-feuilles), or a resumé of research published elsewhere (Lhote 1958; Suret-Canale 1958, 1960, 1964), or bibliographical items (Moniot 1966; Triaud 1977). Without judging what my attitude would have been had I been invited or had the opportunity presented itself, it is probable that I would have acted in the same way. The only French historian of international rank who offered original articles, on 3 occasions, seems to be Raymond Mauny (1961 and 1964). And this is all to his credit.

There is another, more basic, academic mistrust: that of withdrawing, with a certain coldness, into the rigor of the discipline in order to avoid any risk of surrendering to what might not obey strict "scientific" rules. These were barely in existence in African history, whose very recent genesis has followed a chronology that runs parallel to that of the Independences. Hence the militantism of a "new" history that answered the expectation of that history's objects, who had finally become subjects or claimed to be so: the Africans. The claim has been felt, consciously or unconsciously, as an assault by a number of European academics, and it is probable that the distance kept from the young nationalist scholars often has no other cause. The traditional historians at the time were only suspicious of what was then the innovation of the oral sources. Moreover, one knows the

kind of academic hue and cry provoked internationally by Cheikh
Anta Diop's revolutionary theses on the relationship between Egypt
and Black Africa and the ostracism that followed. Today, the merits
of his intuitions are known, even if one might discuss the manner in
which he sometimes conducted his demonstrations, which barely escape the shortcut—common to a number of researchers—to want to
explain too much starting from the newly introduced theory (which
is no less valuable); since then we have become conscious of the
philosophical significance of a new way of conceiving the world, thus
also of conceiving history.[5] Diop's deed certainly exercised its influence, since *Présence Africaine* resolutely took sides from the beginning, not so much by publishing Diop himself (who appeared only
twice, in 1959 and 1964) but by making his disciple, Théophile
Obenga, its beacon: for twenty years, Obenga has continuously been
the most faithful historian of the journal, with 10 articles, at least 2
of which (1970 and 1978) were devoted to Cheikh Anta Diop.

The mistrust, however, did not come from one side only. Having
adopted a combative attitude, the journal considered with caution the
possible contribution of the historical traditions that came out of the
metropolis: the accusation of ideological bias is explicitly formulated
in at least 5 articles that question Western objectivity.[6] In fact, with
the exceptions of Georges Balandier (whose preliminary declaration
in the first issue 1947 was obviously a militant action), Alfred Mé-
traux (1957), and Daniel Guérin and Henri Lhote (1958), no French
specialist in the social sciences offered his cooperation before Independence. The first contribution by Jean Suret-Canale (whose affec-
tion to the cause of the Independence was obvious) goes back to 1960.
If participation has hardly been any more active since then, it is
surely also because the possible contributors were hardly ever invited
for a variety of reasons, one of which was undoubtedly rightly or
wrongly the resentment linked to the implicit conviction that they
were misunderstood, indeed, despised by a scientific community that
can easily seem imbued with its superiority of people of science.
Hence another characteristic of the journal: its manifest lack of inter-

5. See the contribution of Bogumil Jewsiewicki (Chap. 5, this vol.), and of Mamadou
Diouf and Mohamad Mbodj (Chap. 6, this vol.).

6. St. Clair Drake (1959) and, again, Ibrahima Baba Kaké (1975) against the Hamitic
myth in 1959; Georges Ngango on "cultural colonialism" in 1963; Honorat Aguessy
on négritude in 1971, and Nazi Okoro Ojiaku on the attitude of the Western scientists
when facing "traditional" African thought in 1974.

est in the official scientific accomplishment of its contributors, many of whom obtained university degrees in the Parisian universities in subjects that related very directly to the interests of the journal. All in all, we locate only 1 report on a dissertation defense for this kind of work.[7] Nor does the journal echo the international academic events of non-African origin, such as the various colloquia held in Parisian universities or the annual meetings of the *African Studies Association* (A.S.A.) in the United States. However, the initiatives of African origin or with predominantly African participation commonly gave rise to announcements and exact reports: for example, the International Conference of African History (announced in Abidjan, in 1974), the conference of the Association of African Historians, the conference of Brazzaville for the centennial of the International Conference of Berlin,[8] the plenary meeting of the Committee for General History of Africa of UNESCO. It should also be stressed that the journal in no way missed out on Western scientific production in terms of reports: two-thirds of them (65 percent) deal with works written by Europeans or American Whites, as opposed to 27 percent written by Africans and about 8.5 percent by African-Americans. It is probable that these percentages correspond more or less to the respective divisions in scientific production.[9]

Thus it can be seen that in a world in which Africanist historiography was just beginning to emerge with the publication of the first works by Basil Davidson in Great Britain (1956) and by Jean Suret-Canale in France (1958), *Présence Africaine* had already been publishing articles on African history in the most varied fields for ten years: from 1948 on, themes and periods covered a vast spectrum, including precolonial history (with an article by Alioune Sar on the Siné-Saloum), colonial history (with a study by Georges Balandier on the gold of French Guinée), slavery (and on its abolition by the French Revolution, P. Naville), the history of ideas (the White genesis of an

7. Report on the thesis of the third cycle on slavery in the Caribbean by Oruno Lara, contributor to the journal from 1974 to 1976, by Nelly Schmidt; this has been her only contribution to the journal (1971).

8. This one, as several other numbers of these manifestations, were promoted or supported by the Société Africaine de Culture.

9. Percentages are calculated on a partial total of 139 reports: with 91 titles having come out of the West, the production in African history over forty years is far from having been covered. But the same thing can be said, to some extent, with only 38 titles by African authors (all languages mixed) and the dozen titles by African-Americans.

idea of the Black, J. Howlett), or cultural history (the African roots of American music, E. Bornemans). Until the Loi-Cadre (1956), 21 articles dealt with the most diverse historical themes, going from the history of Madagascar to that of the Yoruba women, and touching on the Belgian Congo, Angola, or the relationships of colonialism to education or Christianity. This point had not yet been reached by research at French universities, which to this day have hardly been touched by the journal's motivating role in the realm of history.

Involved is a double dynamism that tunes a double current of influences (sometimes complementary ones) with respect to African history: not only the history having come *from* Africa, or course, but also the history having come in the English and French languages. This original aspect is not the least of the journal's contributions.

Présence Africaine, International and Multicultural Journal

After a few openly Francophone years in which some articles in English were systematically translated, the journal soon wished to present itself as bilingual, equally bringing together those nationals who earlier were subjected to French or British imperialism. The results were numbers 31–59 (from March 1960 to December 1966), double editions in French and in English (only the order in which the articles appeared would occasionally vary in one version from the other). The experiment did not last long, probably for financial reasons of distribution on the Anglophone side; but the bilingual bias, confirmed on the cover, was not abandoned, since from then on the articles written in English have been published in their original language. The experiment is not unique: the *Cahiers d'Etudes Africaine,* for example, has the same policy, which assures them the loyalty of a market that is above all American. What is more striking, of course, is the participation of a high number of contributors of African or African-American origin.

Bearing in mind the variations of the politics of translation, we have not taken into account the language of publication but the language in which the authors originally wrote, which seemed more significant to us. Of a total of 253 articles, 147 (58 percent) are in French, 101 (39.5 percent) in English, and the remainder in other languages translated into French (2 articles in German, 1 in Russian, 1 in Spanish, and 1 in Portuguese). The respective length of the articles is very similar: the articles of English origin covered 38 percent of the journal, the French articles 61 percent. And if there were some years without any Anglophone articles, especially in the beginning (1948–1949,

1951, 1953, and 1964), there was at least one without a single French article cn history (in 1968). As for the reports, the percentage confirms a balance of the same order, even if the French works hold a slight advantage (64 percent) against the English works (33.5 percent) and the German works (2 percent).[10] In other words, the wager of a very real participation of Africanist culture in the English language has been fully kept throughout the existence of the journal, especially from the appearance of the second series (1955) onward. The fact is sufficiently exceptional to be emphasized, especially as the cultural gulf between writing in English and French (especially academic writings) has been maintained too long. It is only very recently that the French-speaking intellectuals and students have begun to feel the pressing necessity not only to read the few great translated texts but also to keep up-to-date with the Africanist production in the English language. The curiosity of the English-speaking intellectuals is perhaps even more limited, in view of the relative and steadily growing abundance of writings in their own language. It can be proclaimed, loudly and clearly, that *Présence Africaine* has made Africanist production in the English language into one of its warhorses from the very start. A major incitement was probably the wish to break with the tenacious legacy of the linguistic division, bequeathed by the language of colonization.

On the Anglophone side, it is not always obvious who among the writers is British and who is American, since both nationalities circulate in the institutions of both countries. One might also try to identify the importance of the writers of Caribbean or African-American origin. But this leads to another question: that of the distribution of the contributors to the journal in terms of their continent of origin. There again, the journal seems exemplary.

The African supremacy is obvious, with 87 authors, against 42 of European origin, about 30 from the Americas (15 for the United States, 13 from the Caribbean, and 3 from Latin-America).[11] Once again, the balance is notable even if the French-speaking dimension remains dominant, as is normal for a journal situated in Paris.

On the level of African participation, on the other hand, a regional imbalance becomes quite clear. The journal represents West Africa to a very large extent. One can even state that, despite a few attempts, the rest of Africa appears only as a reminder. On the Francophone

10. On a total of 146 titles.
11. The difference of the total and the total number of authors comes from a few cases that remain inexact.

side, there are 31 West-African authors (75 percent), as opposed to 6 from an African Equatorial State, 4 from Zaire, and 3 from Madagascar. On the Anglophone side, regionalization is even more marked: 25 authors (86 percent) hail from West-Africa (16 Nigerians, 6 Ghanaians, 2 from Sierra Leone, and 1 from Liberia); the remaining 4 are scattered between Kenya (2), Lesotho, and Zambia. Finally, one should add 1 author from Somalia, 1 from Ethiopia, and only 2 from the Maghreb. In other words, despite a common colonial past, the separation between North Africa and Black Africa seems, at least in the realm of history, to be stronger still than the one between West Africa and the rest of the continent.

The division is evidently explicable through the very personality of the founders-organizers of the journal, whose Senegalese connection has strongly (although not exclusively) marked the whole, as we shall soon see. Certainly the journal has struggled to overcome this split, but the result has hardly been decisive, at least with respect to authors (for we have not yet broached the issue of themes): the interest shown in ancient history or the theme of Egypt, for example, tended to reestablish the regional balance. Nevertheless, the journal cannot be considered representative of the totality of the continent. Even if a recent issue touched upon the problems in South Africa today, all told one can find only (for example) 3 articles on the history of that country[12] (of which not a single one on the history of colonialism and *apartheid*), 2 on that of East Africa, and 3 on that of the islands in the Indian Ocean (only 2 on Madagascar, and 1 on the Grand Comoro Islands). The first objective of the West African authors was obviously to give a theoretical and factual account of the past and the becoming of the land to which they belonged. Who could blame them for this?

The Historic Thematics of the Journal

Africa is the subject to a very major extent (if not exclusively so) with 209 articles (or 83 percent of the total), against 30 dealing with American subjects (12 percent)—especially with respect to the Caribbean (16, or 7 percent), secondarily with the Blacks of the United States (6)—and almost nothing on South America, apart from 2 articles on Brazil.[13] As for Europe, it appears incidentally (and especially after the 1980s only when the opportunity presents itself) in 4 arti-

12. Of these, 1 is a biography of Shaka (Balandier 1947), 1 of Bambata (Clarke 1963), and 1 essay on precolonial culture (Jaspan 1958).

13. One by Thomas Blair on the emancipation of Afro-Brazilians (1965), and another by Spencer Leitman on slavery in the south of Brazil (1974).

cles, all of them dealing with issues relating to Blacks:[14] it was clearly a matter of confirming African historicity, which implied putting a "Westernized" history of Africa resolutely between brackets.

One-third of the articles dealing with Africa (76) are written with a will to generalize that forbids a regionalizing of its scope. For the rest (as we have already stated), West Africa very largely remains the focus, but far from being exclusively privileged. Apart from a little more than 20 articles dealing either with West Africa in general, or more particularly with Francophone West Africa (a dozen), or Anglophone West Africa (2), certain countries such as Senegal, Mali, Nigeria (11 articles for each one) are covered extensively. This fact corresponds quite well with the relatively high number of contributors that come from these three countries. Ghana follows with 7 articles—notably on the occasion of the special issue devoted to its Independence[15]—and Guinée with 5. On the other hand, the rest of West Africa is dealt with very little: Burkina Faso merited 2 articles, as did Benin. As for the Ivory Coast, it is surprising to find it directly discussed only once,[16] and the same is true for Liberia. This reveals, at the very least, if not a lack of interest, then a lack of contact between the editorial staff and the growing school of Ivoirian historians, which has become quite numerous.[17] Finally, Guinée-Bissau is mentioned only twice, once in the only article devoted to the lusophone zone in its entirety.[18]

West Africa aside, the two areas covered in an entirely satisfactory manner are Zaire and Ethiopia, each with 8 articles.[19] Ancient Egypt merits 3 articles, all written by Théophile Obenga. But another surprise: the appearance of the States inherited from the former A.E.F. is slow and remains limited, with 5 articles on the Congo (the first not

14. Howlett on the White genesis of the idea of the Black (1948); Fikes on the Black erudites in Renaissance Europe and the Age of Enlightenment (1980); Françoise Thésée on the Société des Amis des Noirs in 1789 (1983); and Keith Cameron on René Maran (1987).

15. No. 12 (1957), 3–85.

16. In a short article by A. Roux on "Harrisme," nos. 8–9, first series (1950): 133–140.

17. Nevertheless, 2 Ivoirians are present: Bernard Dadié in 1957 and Christophe Wondji in 1986, both of them involving West-African themes of a general scope.

18. Buanga Fele on the crisis of education in the Portuguese colonies (1956), and C. Mahala on Portugal in Angola and in Guinée (1960).

19. Richard Pankhurst, it is true, has written 5 times on Ethiopia. Still, 3 other articles by different authors remain. As for Zaire, the authorship there is very diverse, except for 2 articles by Kabongo.

until 1969), which, with respect to quantity, thus arouses the same interest as that devoted to Angola; there are two articles on Gabon (1969 and 1984), one on Chad (1974), nothing on the Central-African Republic. As we have said earlier, the rest seems almost negligible.[20]

Bearing in mind the importance of articles of a general scope, one must not draw conclusions from this enumeration that are exaggeratedly regionalistic. Nevertheless, what the analysis of the geographic fields confirms (and it is not surprising) is the same point that was foreseen based on the dominating nationalities of the authors: namely, a vision of Africa through the prism of West Africa—that is, very different from what might emanate from an apprehension having come from Southern Africa. There would be great interest in confronting one with the other in order to elicit reflections of truly continental interest.

The dimensions of history, on the other hand, seem to have been grasped in a remarkably balanced fashion: aside from about 30 general articles on a considerable time span (11 percent), 18 (6.5 percent) articles deal with ancient history (of which 6 with prehistory), 87 are concerned with precolonial history, 86 with the colonial period, or almost a third each of the total; and 40 with the contemporary period (14.5 percent) of which about 10 deal with the phase of decolonialization and about half a dozen with independence.[21] As for the articles concerning the Caribbean or the American continent, a dozen of these (or 3.5 percent) broach the problems of the Black diaspora, in the form of Pan-Africanism (2 percent) or, more generally, of African-American cultural roots. In other words, the journal proved itself to be open to all the domains of African history from the start. Of course, it offered a wide span to the new discoveries of historical techniques used specifically in the study of the societies without writing, techniques popularized by the anthropologists in the face of traditional Western historians who remained backwardly hostile to the oral tradition. But it must be noted as well why primarily African and Caribbean historians explored the colonial period early and widely, without the blockage or false shame that characterized European and American academics; for the Europeans implicitly refused to ques-

20. Apart from the infrequent articles on South Africa and the Indian Ocean previously cited, there are 2 articles on Somalia and on Kenya and 1 on each of the following countries: Rwanda, the Sudan, Zambia, Zimbabwe.

21. One must not seek an exact correlation with the number of articles to the extent that there might be a cross-checking of key words (principal and secondary), notably in the case of an overlapping of periods.

tion their nationals, while the Americans favored the research of pre-colonial "innocence" that was supposed to be more "African." Only about 20 of these articles (out of 89) were written by Europeans: it is altogether remarkable to note that the dominant current of cultural "négritude" in no way finessed the colonial past—on the contrary. It is even more interesting to note that almost all of the articles concerned with the Independences are written by Africans or African-Americans;[22] in fact, at that time, the classical historians (European or American Whites) did not take the risk, in the name of the objectivity of a necessary distance that masked, above all, the refusal to broach "dangerous" themes: the "scientific" argument is still much heard in the French university, according to which it would still be too early (keeping the national sensitivities in mind) to broach the history of the war of independence in Algeria. It is, of course, true that the passions on this subject have not been extinguished and that the historian, like anyone else, is a victim of subjectivity. But the very acceleration of history opposes such handy feelings of reticence that avoid questioning a recent, national, historical heritage. The African historians had no choice: in a new country everything had to be tried, including an "immediate" history rethought even if the dangers of a certain awkwardness or of a sometimes advertised militantism were not always avoidable.[23] And that is why, in this area, *Présence Africaine* gave the impression of being a pioneer.

In the realm of themes, the journal appears clearly targeted. In this realm, the analysis through key words shows itself to be delicate, and we have instituted a rather large number of cross-checks. We have, finally, grouped the retained themes into four categories: those very clearly dominant, those fairly frequent, those treated in moderation, and finally those that are only very rarely treated.

It is through the first group of dominant themes that the journal clearly states what it is: preoccupied first by facts of civilization. The most dominant theme is that of the new mission and new tasks incumbent upon the African historian. In one form or another, it re-

22. With the exception of Pierre Clément (1962) on Lumumba, Basil Davidson (1955) on the Belgian Congo, Marc Gazel (1973) on the forest exploitation of West-Africa, Claude Meillassoux (1964) on Bamako, Immanuel Wallerstein (1961) on the national identity, and Peter Waterman (1970) on African trade unionism, that is, authors who are considered to be "committed" to the anti-imperialist struggle.

23. On the interest and difficulties of immediate history, see C. Coquery-Vidrovitch, Alain Forest, and Herber Weiss, eds., *Rébellions/révoluntion au Zaire, 1963–1965* (Paris: L'Harmatten, 1988), particularly the "Epilogue," vol. 2.

turns 47 times: the necessity to formulate a theory of history (21), to do so in full consciousness (10), with objectivity (3), by adding to it the meaning and the knowledge of historiography (16), by being wary of the prejudice of the Whites (5), and of the colonial ideology (2).

Facts of *culture* follow very closely (39 times), hiding a very specific interest, not only for the history of civilizations but also for the history of the arts.[24] Evident as well is the attention paid to *political* history (32 times). This basically deals with questions linked to the formation of the State (especially precolonial—7—but infinitely less so with respect to chieftaincy—only 1) or, more generally, linked to the workings of colonial or postcolonial power. But the Loi-Cadre and the evolution of the French Union is of little interest (2), direct references to nationalism are relatively rare (5), and the concept of democracy is hardly broached (3).

The second group refers to recurrent themes that intervene a little bit on every level of history and that bear on the genesis of the African identities: basically it is equally concerned with *slavery* and *religion* (16 articles on each). Then again, the religious aspects are quite equally distributed between Christianity, animism (5 articles each), and the syncretic cults (6 articles, including 2 on Voodoo), although Islam is of very little interest (3 articles only, of which 2 are biographies of Marabouts).

The major themes of history appear in the third group, of which the journal is clearly aware without being impassioned: thus economic problems (11, of which only 2 brand colonial exploitation with infamy, though that gave rise to so many academic works) and social problems are relatively neglected if one breaks them down in facts of society on the one hand (5), and questions linked to the history of labor on the other (7, including a special issue that made a mark in its time).[25] On the other hand, as might be expected from a cultural journal, the interest in *education* is tangible (8 articles, of which 3 are on traditional education). The genre of *biography* is readily discussed (10), above all for political or religious personalities of the precolonial period. But it is astonishing to see, in the same way as for the nationalist currents, a relatively limited interest in the pair *conquest*

24. Four articles on the history of the plastic arts, 3 on the genesis of the theater, 6 on literary history, and 1 on music history. Here again, beware of the totals—which, in any event, have only an indicative value—because the key words are sometimes double but rarely triple.

25. *Le travail en Afrique noire*, no. 13, first series (1952).

and especially *resistance* (6 each). On a somewhat related order, *military* facts, properly speaking, are of no interest (2). Finally, although in principle the journal attaches great importance to these themes, the history of the *diaspora,* properly speaking, is dealt with only moderately (7 articles), and the same is true in the methodological field for the question of *oral sources,* even though that is the warhorse of the academicians (only 8). In the same group of themes, it should be noted that the infatuation with the myth of *"tradition"* is rather weak (8 articles). But the journal may be proud of having dealt with, early on and regularly, the theme of the history of *women* (5 articles); these have, in fact, given rise to two special issues, in 1972 and 1987.[26]

A few peak areas remain in which the interest of the journal has been only episodic, indeed accidental. Surprise: it is even less interested in rural history (2 articles)[27] than in urban history (4 articles, innovative, especially at the time that the first 2 appear, in 1958); neither the theme of ecology nor that of the droughts have any acceptance (only 1 article), nor the history of health (1). The history of international relations is mostly absent (1), unless it deals with the thorny question of the frontiers (also 1, but on the precolonial frontiers). Even if the theme of nonalignment gave rise to only 1 article, *Pan-Africanism* is of greater interest (5 articles); but African *unity* gives rise to only 3 articles, of which 2 find their origin in the precolonial background (Cheikh Anta Diop 1959, and Ibrahima Baba Kaké 1964), the other in the colonial past (Rabemananjara 1959). Neither *racism* (2 articles) nor *segregation* (also 2) appear as major themes. The birth of student thinking offered hardly any food for thought (except for a small note by David Diop), no more than Marxist thought (2) or the interrogation of Nazism (1). As for the multidisciplinarity of the social sciences, it barely emerges on the occasion of Nigeria;[28] outside of a critique of colonial ethnology, brief mention is made of the contributions by linguistics (1 article), by archeology and paleontology (1), and by historical anthropology (2).

In the meantime, the journal has echoed almost the entirety of the

26. *La civilisation de la femme dans la tradition africaine,* and *La femme noire dans la vie moderne: Images et réalités.*
27. One on the peasantry of the Sudan (Jir Messaoud 1987), the other, theoretical, of Rosa Luxembourg (1952).
28. E. J. Alagoa, "The interdisciplinary approach to African history in Nigeria," no. 94 (1975).

fields of history, but with an undeniable penchant for cultural history, political history, and the history of ideas. It is with this last aspect that we will conclude.

The Historian's Profession

History, as defined by the contributors of *Jeune Afrique*,[29] appears "above all suspicion."

It is therein that the originality of the African historians (with respect to the Western school) is most clearly distinguishable. In fact, what strikes us (aside from a few exaggerations or expressions of xenophobia that need not be stressed) is the extreme awareness of having to find a new language that is both rigorous and efficient. The theme of the responsibility of the African historian recurs frequently.[30] S. Biobaku emphasizes the need for intellectual honesty, since the African historian must both overcome the prejudices carried by the Western historical tradition and elaborate new techniques of manipulation, starting from sources of an original type (oral sources); but at the same time he owes it to himself never to lend himself to the politics of the moment, nor to deform the image of the past through the mirror of a nationalism that has not been thought through. That presupposes an analysis of the nature and the modalities of expression of the European outlook on Africa, in order "to study *our* history and to straighten out the one that has been made without us and against us."[31] This was done in a few insightful articles that were badly needed, since a similar work had not yet been undertaken by the Westerners responsible for this history: several texts thus make an effort to understand the ethical and ideological foundations of the White outlook on Africa,[32] which immediately implies the need for a different outlook.

29. See Leonard Sainville, "L'enseignement et la recherche en histoire: Expériences, méthodes, perspectives," no. 94 (1975).

30. M. Achefuri, "Responsabilité des noirs d'Afrique en fait de culture scientifique," and J. Ki-Zerbo, "Histoire et conscience nègre," no. 16 (1957); Saburi Biobaku, "Les responsabilités de l'historien africain en ce qui concerne l'Afrique," nos. 27–28 (1958); Ibrahima Kaké, "Histoire et unité," no. 49 (1964).

31. J. Ki-Zerbo, no. 16 (1957).

32. See R. Codjo, "Colonisation et conscience chrétienne," no. 6 (1956); J. K. Sundiata, "The Mores of Expansion, 1837–1914," no. 70 (1969); Nazi Okoro Ojiaku, "Traditional African Social Thought and Western Scholarship," no. 90 (1974); N. Tidjani-Serpos, "L'ethnologie coloniale et la naissance de la littérature africaine," no. 136 (1985).

As Louis S. Béhanzin explains on the occasion of a colloquium reproduced in *Présence Africaine,* all this runs counter to the stereotypes to be cast aside, such as the one of Africa, continent of emotiveness that would be the contrary of Europe, continent of objectivity: "[T]he Greek spirit, the Egyptian genius, the Black soul, these expressions have no explanatory meaning . . . What is true is that the Black has been cast aside from the rational construction of the world." It is true that the summary of the debate that followed this article shows to what point (in 1957) the idea of a "scientific and technical" Europe face-to-face with an "artistic and spiritual" Africa was openly defended by the European participants of the time: it is Cheikh Anta Diop who then defends the theme of the universal unity of intelligence.

While making their history, the African historians were perfectly aware of the affective mode from which they could not escape because of both the recent wounds inflicted by Europe and the urgency to construct a new political and cultural identity. African history claimed itself to be objective, but not neutral: "The memory of past greatness as of past suffering must make real the necessary union so that the Negroes are no longer the materials of history, the mould on which many European states have built and still build their fortune" (Ki-Zerbo 1957). Strengthened by his experience of the past, the historian thus feels himself invested by the mission of "guide and . . . political advisor of his people" (Achefuri 1959), not in a partisan fashion but because his object is to answer the questions: "What happened? Why did that happen? What will happen?"

The elaboration of a history "from the inside," guarantee of the collective identity, appears inseparable from the problem of acculturation: Africans have been steeped in the judgment that for centuries the Westerners have brought upon "any culture that does not derive from the Greco-Latin patrimony."[33] Like the Malagasy evoked by E. Andriantsilaniarivo,[34] the African "is a man who got lost and who, in his anguished search for himself, first thought he had to identify himself with another, then found himself again, but how much changed": history must help him to reconstruct this itinerary, to understand it, to accept it, and to elaborate a common vision of a common cultural heritage. The consciousness of history existed among

33. Mohamed Aziz Lahbabi, "Propos sur la civilisation et les cultures," no. 16 (1957).
34. E. Andriantsilaniarivo, "Le malgache du 20è siècle," nos. 8–10 (1956).

the precolonial people.[35] It was, and has therefore to become again, a
dimension of African unity,[36] by permitting the individuals to rediscover their identity with the help of their past. History, historical
awareness, and national consciousness become inseparable:[37]

> History is, finally, the work of the people who live it and
> who make it . . . The history of Africa will remain unfin-
> ished as long as it is not lived and expressed by the Africans
> themselves [for] to develop oneself is first of all to become
> aware of oneself, that is to say, to situate oneself in today's
> world and to situate oneself with respect to one's past."[38]

The new history is, then, a key element in the quest for a national
identity in the new States. In this regard, Cheikh Anta Diop was
explicit:

> It is only a real knowledge of the past that can bring the
> feeling of an historic continuity to the consciousness, a
> continuity that is indispensable for the consolidation of a
> multi-national State.[39]

In this "devouring need for paternity"[40] one finds again a characteristic of the history of young States wherever they may be in the
world: irresistibly, one thinks of the role played by the newly born
modern historiography in the genesis of republican good citizenship
of the French Third Republic—particularly on the level of primary
education (the famous school text "petit Lavisse" of the elementary
classes). Thus it is not surprising that the African intellectuals wor-
riedly study the weaknesses of their education,[41] which must be decolonized as soon as possible as a priority on which a round table
especially organized by the journal gets to work.[42]

35. Raph Uwechue, "The awareness of history among indigenous African communities," no. 73 (1970).

36. I. Kaké (1964).

37. Marian Naïdeyam, "Histoire et conscience historique," no. 92 (1974); Alioune
Diop, "Colonialisme et nationalisme culturel," no. 4 (1955).

38. Christophe Wondji, "Histoire et conscience nationale en Afrique," nos.
137–138 (1986).

39. *L'Unité culturelle du monde noir,* cited by I. Wallerstein, "Recherche d'une
identité nationale en Afrique occidentale," nos. 34–35 (1960–1961).

40. Georges Balandier, *L'Afrique ambiguë* (Paris: Plon, 1957), 279.

41. Bernard Dadié, "Misère de l'enseignement en A.O.F.," no. 11 (1957); Sar and
Fofane, "Esprit et situation de l'enseignement en Afrique noire;" Buanga Fele, "Crise
de l'enseignement dans les colonies portugaises," no. 7 (1956).

42. "Table ronde sur l'enseignement de l'histoire en Afrique noire," 20–21 October
1969, no. 81 (1972), 49–132.

Quest for identity, national history, so be it. Militant history but scientific history: at the moment that an African history of rehabilitation began to develop—a tendency that can be seen both in the African historians and in the European academicians (in the latter through a "bad conscience of the Whites")—it is interesting to note that the editors of *Présence Africaine* are aware both of the necessity of the enterprise and of its dangers. One will notice with interest, for example, Tshijuke Kabongo's reprimand of Ibrahima Baba Kaké for having unduly exaggerated the dimensions of the historic kingdom of the Kongo and thereby having embellished African history in contempt of the demand of erudition and rigor.[43] Let us note in passing the distance taken in the journal by the African historians with respect to the négritude movement, carefully situated in its time: one stresses the influence of colonial ethnology, admitted by

> literary negritude [that thus introduced] in its own foundation a mystified and mystifying element, as gospel, as a neutral place, while that is one of the intellectual ways of adapting the colonial fact to the demands of the hour."[44] Another presents "the phase of negritude"[45] for what it objectively was in African cultural history: the literary expression of the revolt of the African intellectuals of France against assimilation, in response to the assault of the culture in which they had been academically educated.

We do not, then, claim here that the African historians, any more than the others, have been free from the subjectivity that came out of their time, their ideology, their will to act. But what is obvious is that *Présence Africaine* did not cease to alert the conscience of African historians to the risks and the duties of the profession. This constantly repeated concern clearly shows the sharp awareness of the "nationalist" dangers that lie in wait for the militant historian. One understands the basic reasons for a relatively weak participation in the enterprise on the part of the Western historians: whatever their good will may have been, they were hardly up to contribute in this dimension. All historians know it well: they seek—we seek—to encourage the greatest rigor possible by controlling the sources and accepting their verdict, especially when their analysis invalidates the hypotheses of the starting point. But historical science does not re-

43. "Histoire zairoise et critique historique" (no. 90, 1974).
44. Tidjani-Serpos, "L'ethnologie coloniale et la naissance de la littérature africaine."
45. Title of the article in honor of Aguessy, (no. 60, 1971).

main any less a human science because it is necessarily subjective through the point of view and the horizons of its operator. That the Western academicians remained present in the journal was the necessary counterpoint of the historical projections that came forth from the Black continent. But bearing in mind the very objectives of the journal, it was normal, indeed necessary, that this remain a minor current.

APPENDIX: Articles Published in *Présence Africaine*

Author	Year Published	No. Pages	Title
	1951	45	L'art ancien (références historiques: W. Fagg, J. P. Lebeuf, etc.)
	1959	3	Résolution soumise par le sous-comité d'histoire de la commission des sciences humaines, 2° Congrès des Ecrivains et Artistes Noirs
	1971	3	1° réunion plénière du Comité Scientifique pour la Rédaction d'une Histoire Générale de l'Afrique
	1974	6	Congrès International d'Histoire Africaine
	1977	1	Deuxième Congrès Ordinaire de l'Association des Historiens Africains
	1985	13	Centenaire de la Conférence de Berlin, 1884–1885 (Colloque sur). Rapport final
Abou-Siril	1950	8	Civilisations africaines au pluriel
Abraham, Arthur	1978	14	Cannibalism and African Historiography
Achebe, Christie C.	1981	14	Continuities, Changes and Challenges: Women's Role in Nigerian Society
Achefuri, M.	1959	15	Devoirs et responsabilités des historiens africains

Author	Year Published	No. Pages	Title
Adeloja, Kola	1969	21	Sources in African Political Thought. I. Blyden and the Impact of Religion on the Emergence of African Political Thought
Adeloja, Kola	1976	12	Traditional Power Control among the Mossi and the Yoruba: A Comparative Study
Aguessy, C.	1956	10	Esclavage, colonisation et tradition au Dahomey (sud)
Aguessy, Honorat	1971	16	La phase de la négritude
Ajayi, J. P. Ade	1983	5	The State in Colonial Africa
Akalaguelo, Aganga	1984	30	Esquisse d'histoire ethnique du Gabon
Alagoa, E. J.	1975	13	The Interdisciplinary Approach to African History in Nigeria
Ambouroué-Avaro	1969	7	La notion d'Ayamole (dieu) dans les civilisations claniques du Gabon avant les blancs
Andriantsilaniarino, E.	1956	10	Le malgache du 20è siècle
Andriantsilaniarino, E.	1959	16	Le colonialisme
Asiwaju, A. I.	1983	10	The Concept of Frontier in the Setting of States in Precolonial Africa
Assane, Sylla	1955	29	Une république africaine au 19è siècle, 1795–1857 (République Léboue de la Presqu'ile du Cap-Vert)
Autra, Ray	1956	19	Historique de l'enseignement en AOF
Ba, A. Hampaté	1966	30	Manzon et le roi de Koré (poème épique, Ségou)
Bal, Willy	1963	16	Le royaume du Congo aux 15è et 16è siècles
Balandier, Georges	1948	11	L'or de la Guinée française
Balandier, Georges	1950	10	Un chef: Shaka

Author	Year Published	No. Pages	Title
Barnet, Miguel	1967	5	Un vieil esclave se souvient . . . propos recueillis par . . .
Béhanzin, Louis S.	1957	6	Signification historique d'une indépendance (Ghana)
Béhanzin, Louis S.	1957	10	Responsabilité des noirs d'Afrique en fait de culture scientifique
Béhanzin, Louis S.	1958	6	Fondements historiques de la loi-cadre
Beier, H. U.	1955	7	The Position of Yoruba Women
Beier, H. U.	1962	8	Les anciennes religions africaines et le monde moderne
Bernus, E., and G. Savonnet	1973	26	Les problèmes de la sécheresse dans l'Afrique de l'ouest
Béséat, Kiflé Sélassié	1983	23	Autopsie de l'empire Ethiopien
Biobaku, S. O.	1959	4	Les responsabilités de l'historien africain en ce qui concerne l'histoire de l'Afrique
Biobaku, S. O.	1963	5	Aspects historiques de l'acculturation
Blair, Thomas L. V.	1965	7	Afro-Brazilian Freedom Movements from Slavery to Modern Times
Boahen, A. Adu	1983	12	State Formation in Lower Guinea and the Chad-Niger Basin
Bornemans, E.	1948	14	Les racines de la musique américaine noire
Boussoukou-Boumba	1978	24	L'organisation de la chefferie indigène à Ntime et à Divenié (Congo)

Author	Year Published	No. Pages	Title
Brandl, Ludwig	1975	29	Early Christianity in Africa: North Africa, the Sahara, Central and East Africa (a Contribution to Ethno-History)
Buffon, Jacques	1964	27	Sur "l'avènement de l'Afrique noire"
Cameron, Keith	1987	6	Il y a cent ans—René Maran
Carion, Jabaru S.	1975	16	Black Civilization and the Problem of Indigenous Education in Africa: The Liberian Experience
Carter, Robert L.	1959	19	La cour suprême des Etats-Unis et le problème de la discrimination raciale depuis 1940
Césaire, Aimé	1956	16	Culture et colonisation
Cissoko, S. M.	1964	8	L'humanisme sur les rives du Niger au 16è siècle
Cissoko, S. M.	1964	12	Le siècle de Kankan Moussa
Cissoko, S. M.	1967	17	Civilisations Wolofo-Sérère au 15è siècle d'après les sources portugaises
Cissoko, S. M.	1969	25	L'intelligentsia de Tombouctou aux 15è et 16è siècles
Cissoko, S. M.	1983	22	Formations sociales et Etat en Afrique précoloniale: Approche historique
Clarke, John H.	1960	7	Le Nigéria ancien et le Soudan occidental
Clarke, John H.	1963	7	Portrait de Bambata
Clarke, John H.	1971	14	The impact of the African on the New World: A Reappraisal
Clarke, John H.	1972	14	Slave Revolts in the Caribbean Islands

Author	Year Published	No. Pages	Title
Clarke, John H.	1979	20	African-American Historians and the Reclaiming of African History
Clarke, John H.	1984	11	Ancient Civilization of Africa: The Missing Pages in World History: (C.R. du vol. 2 de l'histoire générale de l'Afrique)
Clarke, John H.	1988	31	Pan-Africanism: A Brief History of an Idea in the African World
Clément, Pierre	1962	12	Patrice Lumumba (Stanleyville, 1952–1953)
Codjo, R.	1956	11	Colonisation et conscience chrétienne
Colvin, Lucie G.	1975	16	International relations in precolonial Senegal
Condé, Maryse	1975	11	Civilisation noire de la diaspora
Cook, Mercer	1957	10	Les relations raciales aux Etats-Unis vues par les voyageurs français depuis la 2è guerre mondiale
Crowley, D. J.	1959	18	L'héritage Africain dans les Bahamas
Dadié, Bernard	1957	11	Le rôle de la culture populaire des noirs d'Afrique
Dadié, Bernard	1957	14	Misère de l'enseignement en AOF
Davidson, Basil	1955	15	Angola: Economie du colonialisme
Davidson, Basil	1955	15	Le Congo Belge au carrefour de son destin
Davidson, Basil	1956	7	African Education in British Central and Southern Africa
Davidson, Basil	1957	6	A Note on "Pre-European" Africa

Author	Year Pub- lished	No. Pages	Title
Davis, John	1957	20	The Participation of the Negro in the Democratic Process in the United States
Dia, Amadou Cissé	1986	5	Le Damel Teigne Lat Dior (Ngoné Latir Diop)
Diagne, Pathé	1965	31	Les royaumes Sérères
Diop, Abdoulaye Sokhna	1974	8	Aperçu sur les cultures pré- historiques en Afrique
Diop, Alioune	1955	12	Colonialisme et nationa- lisme culturel
Diop, Cheikh A.	1959	6	L'unité culturelle africaine
Diop, Cheikh A.	1964	11	Evolution du monde noir
Diop, David	1953	4	L'Etudiant africain devant le fait colonial
Drake, St. Clair	1959	13	Détruire le mythe chami- tique, devoir des hommes cultivés
Dreshiar, Horst	1962	12	L'Allemagne et l'Angola du Sud (1898–1903)
Du Bois, W. E. B.	1956	18	Africa and the American Negro Intelligentsia
Du Bois, W. E. B.	1957	10	La foi des ancêtres
Duffy, James	1962	16	La présence portugaise en Angola
Echeruo, Michael J. C.	1972	17	The Lagos Scene in the 19th Century
Egboh, E. O.	1970	15	The Nigerian Trade-Union Movement and Its Rela- tions with World Trade- Union Internationals
Egboh, E. O.	1978	14	The Nigerian Gum Arabic Industry: A Study in Rural Economic Development under the Colonial Regime
Ekondy, Akala	1965	43	Colonisation, décolonisa- tion et préjugés raciaux en Afrique noire, 1 et 2

Author	Year Pub-lished	No. Pages	Title
Ekwueme, L. E. N.	1975	19	Nigerian Performing Arts: Past, Present and Future, with Particular Reference to the Igbo Practice
Eluwa, G. I. C.	1971	19	The National Congress of British West Africa: A Study in African Nationalism
Esedebe, P. O.	1970	19	Origins and Meaning of Pan-Africanism
Fall, Mar	1984	11	Le mouvement syndical sénégalais à la veille de l'Indépendance: Un lieu de formation des élites politiques
Fele, Buanga	1956	6	Crise de l'enseigne-ment dans les colonies portugaises
Fikes, Robert, Jr.	1980	12	Confirming Intellectual Capacity: Black Scholars in Europe during the Renaissance and the Enlightenment
Gatera, Augustin	1971	18	Les sources de l'histoire africaine: Exemple du Rwanda
Gazel, Marc	1973	30	Le développement de l'ex-ploitation forestière en Afrique de l'ouest
Gerbeau, Hubert	1967	19	Un mort-vivant: L'esclavage
Graft-Johnson, J. C. de	1957	8	African Empires and the Past
Greenberg, Joseph	1963	11	Langues et Histoire en Afrique
Guérin, Daniel	1958	7	Controverse autour de l'héritage africain aux U.S.A.
Hagan, George P.	1980	16	The Rule of Law in Asante, a Traditional Akan State

Author	Year Published	No. Pages	Title
Hamidullah, M.	1958	11	L'Afrique découvre l'Amérique avant Christophe Colomb
Harris, Joseph E.	1966	12	Les précurseurs de la domination coloniale au Fouta Djallon
Hazoumé, Paul	1957	17	L'humanisme occidental et l'humanisme africain
Herskovits, Melville	1950	10	Le noir dans le nouveau monde
Herskovits, Melville J.	1961	8	Traditions et bouleversements de la culture en Afrique
Hill, Adélaide	1958	20	Revolution in Haiti, 1791 to 1920
Hodgkin, Thomas	1970	26	Mahdisme, messianisme et marxisme dans le contexte africain
Howard, Laurence C.	1961	18	Des différences entre l'impérialisme et le colonialisme
Howlett, J.	1948	3	Genèse Blanche d'une idée du Noir
Huxley, H.	1952	6	Visite à l'est africain en 1946
Ijera, Martin O.	1974	19	Marcus Garvey as Pan-Africanist: A Study in Contrast
Imoagene, Oshomba	1975	32	The Impact of Industrialisation and Urbanisation on the People of Nigeria
Irele, Abiola	1980	11	The correspondence of Edward W. Blyden (1832–1912)
Janvier, J.	1958	15	Autour des missions Voulet-Chanoine en Afrique occidentale
Jaspan, M. A.	1958	23	La culture noire en Afrique du Sud avant la conquête européenne

Author	Year Published	No. Pages	Title
Kabeya Muase, Charles	1964	12	Bref aperçu sur le mouvement syndical en Afrique noire
Kabongo, Tshijuke	1974	4	Histoire zairoise et critique historique: Le cas de l'étendue de l'ancien royaume du Kongo
Kabongo, Tshijuke	1977	14	Les cultes africains comme manifestation de la résistance au colonialisme belge (1920–1948)
Kaké, I. Baba	1953	7	Evocations historiques
Kaké, I. Baba	1964	13	Dinah Salifou: Roi des Nalous
Kaké, I. Baba	1964	18	L'histoire comme facteur d'unité
Kaké, I. Baba	1966	10	Un grand érudit soudanais du 17è siècle
Kaké, I. Baba	1969	6	Aventure des Bukhava (prétoriens noirs) au Maroc, au 18è siècle.
Kaké, I. Baba	1975	9	De l'interprétation abusive des textes sacrés à propos du thème de la malédiction de Cham
Kaké, I. Baba	1976	26	La civilisation de la boucle du Niger du 11è au 16è siècle
Kaké, I. Baba	1979	18	L'influence des Afro-Américains sur des nationalistes noirs francophones d'Afrique (1919–1945)
Kaké, I. Baba	1981	6	Dimensions géographique et historique du monde noir
Kamian, B.	1958	5	L'Afrique occidentale précoloniale et le fait urbain
Keita, L.	1987	10	Africa's Triple Heritage: Unique or Universal?

Author	Year Pub-lished	No. Pages	Title
Ki-Zerbo, J.	1957	3	L'histoire recommence
Ki-Zerbo, J.	1957	17	Histoire et conscience nègre
Ki-Zerbo, J.	1957	23	L'économie de traite en Afrique noire ou le pillage organisé (15è au 17è siècles)
Ki-Zerbo, J.	1961	4	L'histoire: Levier fondamental
Kwamena-Poh, Michael A.	1975	15	The Traditional Informal Sector of Education in Pre-colonial Ghana
Lahbali, Mohamed Aziz	1957	30	Propos sur la civilisation et les cultures, 1 et 2
Lara, Oruno D.	1974	9	Les racines de l'historiographie afro-américaine
Lara, Oruno D.	1975	31	Traite négrière et résistance africaine
Lara, Oruno D.	1976	54	Esclavage et révoltes négro-africaines dans l'empire musulman du haut Moyen-Age
Lara, Oruno D.	1979	16	Témoignages afro-américains sur l'esclavage
Leitman, Spencer	1974	7	Slavery and Racial Democracy in Southern Brazil: A Look Back to the 19th Century
Lem, F. H.	1951	12	Variété et unité des traditions plastiques de l'Afrique noire
Lhote, Henri	1958	10	L'extraordinaire aventure des Peuls
Luxembourg, Rosa	1952	15	L'expropriation des terres et la pénétration capitaliste en Afrique
Ly, Abdoulaye	1957	39	Economie sucrière et marché d'esclaves au 17è siècle, 1 et 2

Author	Year Published	No. Pages	Title
Ly, Madina	1979	11	La femme dans la société traditionnelle mandingue (d'après une enquête sur le terrain)
Mahala, C.	1960	15	Le Portugal et les colonies d'Angola et de Guinée
Makosso-Makosso, Sylvain	1975	7	"Le mouvement religieux congolais" de 1921 à nos jours: Contribution à l'étude des formes de résistance et de nationalisme
Maran, René	1948	16	Gide et l'Afrique noire
Margarido, Alfredo	1965	17	La domination Lunda: Un empire construit sur la guerre et la force
Markakis, John	1968	43	An Interpretation of Political Tradition in Ethiopia
Markovitz, Irving L.	1969	18	The Political Thought of Blaise Diagne and Lamine Gueye
Martin, Ch.	1973	32	Nkrumah's Strategy of Decolonization: Originality and Classicism
Mauny, Raymond	1961	4	Ancienneté de la variolisation en Afrique
Mauny, Raymond	1961	12	Noms de pays d'Afrique occidentale
Mauny, Raymond	1964	5	L'Afrique tropicale de la période pharaonique à l'arrivée des Arabes
Meillassoux, Claude	1964	35	La Kotaba de Bamako
Mennesson-Rigaud, O.	1958	26	Rôle du Vaudou dans l'Indépendance d'Haiti (1804)
Mensah-Browne, A. K.	1967	27	An African Chiefdom in Modern Ghana
Mercier, Paul	1952	8	Travail et service public dans l'ancien Dahomey
Messaoud, Jir	1987	19	La paysannerie soudanaise et les problèmes qui entravent sa mutation

Author	Year Pub-lished	No. Pages	Title
Métraux, Alfred	1957	16	Histoire du vaudou depuis la guerre d'indépendance jusqu'à nos jours
Mohamed, Marioan Y.	1961	3	La femme dans la société
Mohome, Paulus M.	1976	12	The First Decade of Africa's Independence: A Balance-Sheet
Moniot, Henri	1966	23	Notes d'histoire
Moniot, Henri	1966	11	Notes d'histoire: 2
Monod, Théodore	1950	10	Un homme de Dieu: Tierno Bokar
Monod, Théodore	1950	11	Un empereur: Moussa 1°
de Moraes, Nize Isabel	1974	19	Relations de Lazaristes français concernant la petite côte (Sénégambie)
Moyangar, Naïdeyam	1974	17	Histoire et conscience historique
Mveng, E.	1963	17	L'art africain d'hier et l'Afrique d'aujourd'hui
Mveng, E.	1965	6	Les sources de l'histoire négro-africaine
Naville, P.	1949	1	L'abolition de l'esclavage et la Révolution française
Ndiaye, Alphonse Raphael	1980	15	Les traditions orales et la quête de l'identité culturelle
Ndonko, Wilfred A.	1976	15	From Economic Domination to Association: Africa in the E.E.C.
Ngango, Georges	1963	7	Colonialisme culturel en Afrique
Ngoma, Albert	1950	14	L'Islam noir
Niane, D. T.	1974	16	Histoire et tradition historique du Manding
Niane, Djibril Tamsir	1974	17	Dynamisme des foyers de culture africaine
Nicol, Davidson	1980	10	The African and the Jewish Diaspora: A Comparative Study

Author	Year Pub- lished	No. Pages	Title
Nicol, Davidson	1984	16	Brazil, Canada (Nova Sco- tia) and the Guinea Coast: A Literary and Historical Overview of the African Diaspora
Nkrumah, Kwame	1957	16	La naissance de mon parti et son programme d'action positive
Nkrumah, Kwame	1962	8	De l'histoire culturelle du Ghana
Ntloedibe, Elias L.	1970	11	Nazism in Africa
Obenga, Mwene Ndzale	1969	12	L'Afrique dans l'Antiquité
Obenga, Mwene Ndzale	1969	18	Le royaume de Makoko
Obenga, Théophile	1970	26	Méthode et conception his- torique de Cheikh Anta Diop
Obenga, Théophile	1971	22	L'Afrique et l'évolution hu- maine (éléments biblio- graphiques)
Obenga, Théophile	1972	24	Esquisse d'une morpholo- gie de l'histoire africaine
Obenga, Théophile	1975	21	Contribution de l'Egyptolo- gie au développement de l'histoire africaine
Obenga, Théophile	1978	16	Cheikh Anta Diop et les autres
Obenga, Théophile	1983	21	De l'état dans l'Afrique précoloniale: Le cas du royaume de Kouch dans la Nubie ancienne
Obenga, Théophile	1986	22	La philosophie pharao- nique
Obenga, Théophile	1988	23	Esquisse d'une histoire cul- turelle par la lexicologie
Ochieng, William R.	1985	19	Moralism and Expropria- tion in a British Colony: The Search for a White Do- minion in Kenya, 1895– 1923

Author	Year Pub-lished	No. Pages	Title
Ogunsheye, A.	1958	10	Société traditionnelle et démocratie
Ogunsheye, F. Adetowun	1960	18	Les femmes du Nigéria
Ojiaku, Nazi Okoro	1974	11	Traditional African Thought and Western Scholarship
Okonga, Salem	1961	18	La Somalie, hier et aujourd'hui
Ola, Opeyemi	1979	30	Pan-Africanism: An Ideology of Development
Oloruntimehin, B. Olatunji	1983	9	The Nature of Local Power (or Government) under Colonial Rule
Opoku Agyeman	1977	27	Non-Alignment and Pan-african Trade-Unionism
Ousmane, Diallo	1960	8	Connaissance historique de la Guinée
Padmore, George	1957	5	Ghana: L'autobiographie de Kwame Nkrumah
Pageard, Robert	1961	20	Soundiata Keita et la tradition orale
Pankhurst, R.	1960	26	L'indépendance de l'Ethiopie et son importation d'armes au 19è siècle
Pankhurst, R.	1962	13	Portrait de Ménélik II, empereur d'Ethiopie
Pankhurst, R.	1963	22	Théodore II, empereur d'Ethiopie
Pankhurst, R.	1969	11	Ethiopia and the Loot of the Italian Invasion
Pankhurst, R.	1985	8	The Napier Expedition and the Loot from Maqdala (1867–1868)
Potekhine, I.	1970	4	Lénine et l'Afrique
Price-Mars, J.	1959	11	La paléontologie, la préhistoire et l'archéologie au point de vue des origines de la race humaine et du rôle joué par l'Afrique dans la genèse de l'humanité.

Author	Year Published	No. Pages	Title
Rabemananjara, Jacques	1957	5	Madagascar 1947–1957
Rabemananjara, Jacques	1959	16	Les fondements de notre unité tirés de l'époque coloniale
Rabemananjara, Jacques	1987	14	Quarantième anniversaire de la revue P.A.
Ropivia, Marc	1981	13	Les fang dans les grands lacs et la vallée du Nil: Esquisse d'une géographie historique à partir du Mvett
Roux, A.	1950	8	Un prophète: Harris
Sadji, A.	1949	4	Littérature et colonisation
Saint-André Utudjian	1980	30	Le thème de la folie dans la littérature africaine contemporaine (1960–1975)
Sainville, Léonard	1969	24	Document inédit: A propos de la mise en valeur des établissements français du Sénégal à partir de 1816
Sainville, Léonard, ed.	1970	12	La captivité et la mort de Toussaint-Louverture
Sainville, Léonard	1977	29	Les fondements négro-africains et la culture dans les Caraibes et la lutte pour leur sauvegarde
Sainville, Léonard	1978	20	L'enseignement et la recherche en histoire: Expériences, méthodes, perspectives
Salah, Ali	1970	5	El-Marouf, grand maabout de la grande Comore (19è–début 20è siècle)
Salifou, André	1974	12	L'éducation africaine traditonnelle
Sar, Alioune	1948	6	Histoire du Sine-Saloum
Sar, Alioune, and I. Fofane	1957	13	Esprit et situation de l'enseignement en Afrique noire

Author	Year Pub-lished	No. Pages	Title
Shelton, Austin J.	1968	8	The Problem of Griot Interpretation and the Actual Causes of War in Sondjata
Simiyu, Vincent	1974	46	Ukambani from the End of the 19th Century up to 1933
Singh, Raja J.	1984	9	Trade-Union Development in Zambia
Soromenho, Castro	1962	7	Portrait de la reine Jinga
Sundiata, I. K.	1969	21	The Mores of Expansion: 1837–1914
Suret-Canale, Jean	1958	3	El Hadj Omar
Suret-Canale, Jean	1960	36	La Guinée dans le système colonial
Suret-Canale, Jean	1964	23	Le contexte social et les conséquences de la traite des esclaves
Thésée, Françoise	1983	79	Autour de la Société des Amis des Noirs: Clarkson, Mirabeau et l'abolition de la traite (août 1789–mars 1790)
Thomas, L. V.	1959	17	Animisme et christiannisme. Réflexions sur quelques problèmes d'évangélisation en Afrique occidentale
Tidjani-Serpos	1985	18	L'ethnologie coloniale et la naissance de la littérature africaine
Tolémée, P.	1950	16	Hier et avant-hier
Traoré, Bakary	1976	5	La colonisation et le problème de la démocratie
Triaud, Jean-Louis	1977	13	A propos d'un manuel d'histoire destiné aux élèves d'Afrique
Tura, Rogalio Martinez	1974	13	Les Lyesos
Uwechue, Raph	1970	5	The Awareness of History among Indigenous African Communities

Author	Year Pub-lished	No. Pages	Title
Verdier, Raymond	1960	10	Civilisations agraires et droits fonciers négro-africains
Verkijika, G. Fanso	1986	18	Traditional and Colonial Boundaries: Concepts and Functions in Inter-Group Relations
Wade, Abdoulaye	1953	27	Afrique noire et Union française
Wallerstein, Immanuel	1961	13	La recherche d'une identité nationale en Afrique occidentale
Warner, Garry	1976	24	Education coloniale et genèse du théatre néo-africain d'expression française
Waterman, Peter	1970	17	Towards an Understanding of African Trade-Unionism
Wondji, Ch.	1986	15	Histoire et conscience nationale en Afrique
Yagi, M. A.	1956	5	Les origines de Khartoum
Zousmanovitch, A. Z.	1964	12	La révolte des Batetela au 19è siècle

Présence Africaine as Historiography: Historicity of Societies and Specificity of Black African Culture

Bogumil Jewsiewicki

History is one of the most prevalent disciplines between nations and races. Common people want to know it. Kings, leaders seek it emulously . . . It offers ground for meditation, for an effort to find an access to truth, for a subtle explanation of the causes and the origins of the facts . . . Thus, history finds its roots in philosophy.[1]

Ibn Khaldun 1967–1968: vol. 1, p. 5

We are not any less innocent regarding history.[2]

Alioune Diop 1959:48

The concept of history that seems to dominate the writings published in *Présence Africaine*[3] contradicts the radical attitude, the desire to be done with Western domination, and the promise of a profound transformation in the history of humanity.[4] It is immersed in the

1. Momigliano (1966a:217) emphasizes the alliance between history and philosophy of which Voltaire had been the one to say: "Racy and generalizing, historiography offers its services to the propaganda of the enlightened."

2. Melone (1963:143) says: "At this stage in his adventure, the Negro-African is a man without memory. He does not have the pleasure of planning. No voice heard in the olden days has been prolonged in his memory."

3. The texts that appeared in *Présence Africaine* do not claim to prove my theses on the conception of history and historicity of the peoples of Black Africa as my reading of this journal perceives them. I offer these extracts above all to give the tone, the spirit, and the formation of theses. These extracts also allow us to see the nuances and the change, which the space available to me does not permit me to present in this account.

4. Morin (1959:372): "The affirmation of an African culture . . . opens the era that will give birth to the universal culture; whereas for Fanon (1956:124): For the Third World, it is a question of beginning the history of man again; Sartre said

paradigm of "progress history" and its pressing optimism. The thesis of progress obstructed by Western intrusion—whether that intrusion takes the form of slave trade or colonialization—does not contradict the value of the idea of progress. The following might be said of it: "It is not a question . . . of clarifying our relationship to the past but of suppressing the distance that separates us, of acting as if its representation restores it, in effect, to the present" (Vidal-Naquet 1985:52).

Progress will once again become the providential motive of an upward trend, once political independence has been recovered. Organized around a linear axis, certainly shattered in one part of its covered distance, history is capable both of bringing the creative forces of the past[5] into the present and of propelling society onto the axis of progress from which it had been arbitrarily and fraudulently deprived.[6] This optimism contrasts sharply with the present attitude: "Critical thinking cannot stem from such defensive positions [academic knowledge and capitalist economy], nor from the strangeness that affirms that 'historicity' is agent and cause and that past is intrinsically present" (Cohen 1986:326).

For the contributors to *Présence Africaine*, history is a moral force from which societies drink deep in order to reconstruct their consciousness and their identity, a moral reincarnation that precedes their regaining control of their future.[7]

To deprive a society of its history, to forbid it the production and

---

that the West cannot write the history of the world by itself. Marcus (1968:52) wrote: "Revolutionary power . . . can be expected only from the encounter of the Third World and the movements that are working towards an upheaval in the very bastions of capitalism"; and Maspero (1962:133–134), in speaking of Fanon's work, said, "To pray for a human brotherhood that makes a clean slate, that is not a slave of an eternally alienating past."

5. C. A. Diop (1959) insists upon "an historic continuity essential for the consolidation of a multi-national State."

6. Suret-Canale (1959:347) says that there is not a completed nation in Africa because trade and imperialism "have for centuries halted historical evolution." In turn, Potekhin (1958:66) asserts in his lesson on the study of the formation of nations: "Colonialization interrupted the *natural* [my emphasis] course of the history of the peoples of Africa." Cheikh Anta Diop (1957:19) states, "Egypt civilized the world."

7. Ki-Zerbo (1957:53): "The fact of once again becoming conscious of one's history is a sign of rebirth for a people." See also the Société Africaine de Culture (1947a:208). One of the four themes proposed to the International Congress of African History is "History and African Rebirth."

knowledge of its history, is to assassinate its genius,[8] to render it foreign unto itself. The falsification of history is a crime against its people,[9] the search for historical truth (for the recent debate see Gadoffre 1987; and Novick 1988) is a mission entrusted to the "organic" intellectuals:[10] we find therein the double echo of the verse, unresolved in the Western tradition. History is a manifestation of objective laws, whether these be divine or natural; historiography is their decoding through the study of the past. History is also the collective conscience that produces otherness, since the temporal distance is that of nonreturn.[11]

In the production of Africanist knowledge by the conquering West,[12] summarized in *The Invention of Africa* (Mudimbe 1988), the cultural distance produced by anthropology[13] is burdened by otherness as long as the primitive and the villager constitute the same category. The African rupture with this equation, to which *Présence Africaine* bears vigorous witness, brings anthropology back to ethnology—indeed, to sociology—in order to establish the respective identities of a people and of an elite.[14] History, then, is seen to be

8. Nkrumah, 1962:12, by quoting his own 1958 declaration, stresses that: "At present, an effort is being made to regenerate Africa . . . within the framework of a social system adapted to traditions, to history. . . . Despite the breaches opened by the Western influence, this remains in large measure unchanged."

9. Rabmananjara (1959): "After having been the pitiless architect of the dispersion of the Negroes through the slave trade . . . The West has revealed itself as a complex of Negrophore values" (67) which is all the more weighty of consequence because of "culturally French ontologically Malagasy, my personality" (75).

10. " . . . stripped of his history, he is a stranger to himself" (Ki-Zerbo 1957:53).

11. Biobaku Sabusi (1959:98) insists on "the urgency to write the true history of Africa." He adds later that "it is incumbent upon the African historian to ensure that the image that comes forth not be deformed through the mirror of a rash nationalism." As early as 1953, Dike asserted: "The question is not that the Africans have no history but that this history has been seriously ignored" (225).

12. A. Diop (1962:12): "Is history not science and passion at the same time." The two articles published in *Présence Africaine*, nos. 27–28, 1959 (Biobaku 1959; and Achufasi 1959) on responsibilities of the African historian translate this dichotomization well. While Biobaku (1959) speaks on the "great challenge of objectivity" (96), Achufusi stresses mission and political commitment.

13. Ki-Zerbo (1957:63) says this: "Local culture has been diverted to become no more than a folkloric appetizer" (63).

14. Wallerstein (1961:80): "The ideological justification for cultural superiority has been one of the principle arguments for maintaining colonial domination." Possoz (1962:93): "There is today . . . an ethnology that thinks of itself as classical, unique, fundamental, true, because it is supported today by recent observations, by mores of

assigned the double task of producing otherness and identity, which are each other's interface. African otherness is only the lack of Western history that negated African societies. African identity would be a product of scholarly and written history (no less Western):

> What transformation represents is precisely a synthesis of difference and resemblance; it connects two facts without their being able to identify themselves. Rather than a double-faced unity, it is a two-fold operation: at one and the same time it confirms resemblance and difference; in one single movement it throttles time and suspends it; it allows discourse to acquire a meaning without the latter becoming pure information; in a word, it makes the narrative possible and delivers its very definition to us.

The continuity of history[15] allows a closing of the rupture caused by Western intrusion without, however, forgetting it,[16] since it is the

---

people of color illiterate . . . very 'other' than we, who are White, who publish books . . . As a scientific method there is none crazier. Indeed, naming something that one does not know well is one of the least 'scientific' things to do." It is somewhat surprising to read such radical criticism of anthropology from the pen of a colonial magistrate who inspired Tempels, even if he subsequently disagreed with *La philosophie bantoue*.

15. The question of a possible specificity of genius, of consciousness, of Black culture was widely, even if practically always indirectly, debated. Here are a few examples of two attitudes. While for Obenga a Negro specificity is a Western invention that contradicts the Negro origins of civilization (Obenga 1964): "The Africanists must rid themselves, once and for all, of the idea that the African Blacks would constitute a humanity apart" (160); and "Thus, the essential point today, after an affirmation of this sort (pharaonic Egypt is Black African—UNESCO 1974), is to lay the foundation for a true African history" (119), which for him means a central element of the history of humanity since its origins merge with African history. Gurvitch (1959:375) asserts that all vitalist conceptions originate from Black African culture." He thus confirms the specificity of the African genius, in agreement with Senghor on the one hand, for whom sensuality is black, but above all with Tempels. It is "a theogenic and cosmogonic mythology that intervenes directly in the working of the social structure (and conversely) that defines the cultural specificity of Africa as a "global society" (Gurvitch 1957:213). Bastide (1962): "As for me, I object to misrepresenting that which I believe to be the truth. I no more accept the recent definition of Africa of Anta Diop through matriarchy, than I do the old definition of Africa through fetishism" (33); "Western and monistic thought . . . African thought is pluralist" (42); "Western thought is abstract . . . African thought, on the contrary, discovers a logic of images which allows us to think the *concrete* [emphasis by R. B.]—instead of destroying it" (42). For Bastide, analogic epistemology defines African thought.

16. Morin (1959:372) glimpsed a possibility that could, in fact, have transformed anthropology, but it was a wish that forgot that knowledge cannot be completely dis-

fact on which the diaspora (hence négritude as much as Africanism) is founded. This continuity also imposes the way in which history is practiced. Narration and its written form distinguish it from the "re-cited" and oral history, and make literate intellectuals out of the modern griots of the new nations (who pride themselves just as much on their being guardians of tradition), thereby leaving to the traditional griots only the archival role, only the technicality of positive history vouching for objective truth.[17] They can only do this by confusing two meanings of history: "1) the total of all that has ever happened, 2) a kind of understanding reached in the course of historical inquiry" (Oakeshott 1982:1–2).

Thus, the rebirth of the African personality, of Black conscious-ness, and of the national identities that legitimize the independent States manifests the reincarnation of the Black genius in its specific (national) expressions.[18] In the meantime, this manifestation is not automative; it needs an "organic brain power that will change the fracture into a bracketed part of history" (Piault 1987) by attach-ing the two ends of the broken rope, by translating the oral into the written, by producing a true narrative that will give the value of an identity, as in a monument to the dead, to the traumatism (Lagarde 1979; Prost 1983). The historian endeavors to approach this great traumatism as a historical fact, whereas he should do so on another level, different from that of interpretation and of historical explana-tion, as Deutscher (1968) has said.

The concept of cultural cannibalism (which seems to have been constructed around 1920 by Oswald de Andrade) characterizes well this procedure, one that produces not only a type of knowledge but

---

sociated from power and that African scholarly knowledge, then in development, was only working a transfer not a revolution: "You can become *the ethnologues of Europe* [emphasis by E. M.], return the ethnologic look back to the West . . . which reopens the problem of man."

17. Agblemagnon (1959) says that Westerman, Frobenius, Delafosse, and Griaule offered nothing but a "kind of vast phenomenology" that rejects the continuity of his-toriography which Obenga partially claims.

18. Rabemananjara (1959:71): "Blessed, then, are our masters in rule for having revealed us to ourselves!" and the Commission des Sciences Humaines (1959:399) rec-ommends: "To found great research activity concerning Africa's past . . . with the goal of teaching our people about their equality with respect to other human beings." Later, the Société Africaine de Culture (1974:92) recommends: "The historian—as erudite as he needs to be—should teach the meaning of history to the people."

also its shape—the narration.[19] René Girard would have said that it is a perfect example of the founding of a new identity on a ritual murder. I personally prefer Mudimbe's *L'odeur du père* (1982). The narration's form is not neutral. Quite the contrary, its demands command and select that which is worthy of a place in the historiography, to become official recognition and memory of a nation. The narrator—the historian—becomes its trustee, the guardian of truth and the priest of the national genius which is none other than the Black genius. The ideology of the State, which is the translation in real terms of the nationalist dream, can only be narrative history. It makes a historical necessity out of the nation-state, since it identifies its premises in the past and organizes them into national consciousness (on this subject see Brown 1987).[20] It should not be surprising, then, that one grasps tradition in a way Freud described: "Tradition frequently contains more truth, less distortion than fixed history. It is a psychic document that allows the construction of historical truth with certainty" (Freud 1967 : 7). And one could add: "That which you have inherited from your fathers must be acquired in order to be owned" (Freud 1965 : 11; for critical views see Meltzer 1988).

History in *Présence Africaine* is a science in pursuit of an objective truth, but also a literary activity that recounts the past as it did indeed take place (we shall come back to this). Thus it sheds full light upon the laws of evolution. The circle of *Présence Africaine* is immersed in Marxism, in Sartrean existentialism, and in psychoanalysis, which allow for a combination of the theory of history and of philosophy as a condition of consciousness. The future is seen from the historical necessities onward. This historicization of the future has caused the African independences to be perceived, for a very long time, as an autonomous process (the expression of a historical law seen from a Leninist angle) in relation to the immediate stakes of the economic and political European evolution—that is, the formation of the European Community and the Common Market (Marseille 1984). This vision conformed to the political and intellectual history of the

19. Bastide (1959:371), in his message to the Second Congress of Black Writers and Artists, calls the black peoples to "make of your future a continuation and not a betrayal."

20. Commission des Sciences Humaines (1959:399) recommends that the governments of already independent States "encourage historians to write history books of African history."

intellectuals who were nourished by an altogether idealistic vision of the past, even if they were inspired by Marxism as much as by Christianity and Existentialism. The concretization by Lenin and Stalin of the Marxist theory of history (Suret-Canale 1959:344, cites Stalin's definition of 1912 in *Le matérialisme et la question nationale*) legitimizes the voluntarism that allows the progress of history. It is advisable, therefore, to state the priority of the nation over the State and of nationalism over the creation of the middle-class culture.[21]

The writing of history becomes the vanguard of the political struggle for independence,[22] by virtue of the law of narrative causality (Jameson 1981), which permits the grasping of an awareness in such a way that it makes of the present not the simple outcome of the past but a realization of the promises of the past.[23] The narrativization of a sequence of historical events annuls the present as location of its production; it betrays the operation in order to substitute for it a "future past" or a "past future." Awareness grasps hold of the past in order to define the future as a realization of a plan that the past would have already held.

It is thus that Black humanity takes its right to produce meaning, its freedom to choose a past from among the options that the (Western) culture offers it.[24] The only misunderstanding (but one with serious consequences) resulted from the fact that narration is not a

21. Deuxième Congrès (1959b:385) states that "every effort towards the personification and enrichment of national cultures . . . constitutes *progress* [my emphasis] towards the universalization of values and . . . a contribution to human civilization." In 1955, the editorial staff of *Présence Africaine* asserts: "Not much imagination is needed to understand that our common national aspirations are the very foundation of our union."

22. Rabemananjara (1959:70) speaks of the European language used by the colonized in the following words: "We seized it, we appropriated it, to the point of claiming it for ourselves . . . in truth, our Congress is the Congress of the values of languages," and he adds: "The foreign culture could only be embodied in us by feeding upon the material of our torment: a veritable restoring of itself by swallowing our intellectual molecules. But at the same time a strange reversal of functioning is at work: in order to assume it fully, we must, in turn, feed upon it, use it as an indispensable nutriment."

23. Fanon (1959:2): " . . . it is national liberation that causes the nation to be present on the scene of history. It is in the heart of the national consciousness that the international consciousness is raised and invigorated."

24. Obenga (1969:84): "The historic consciousness of each of the precolonial nations is still so alive that at the least crisis . . . it is always ready to invade the modern national consciousness."

culturally neutral[25] form and cannot be stripped without simultaneously adapting oneself to the content that this form implies (White 1987).[26]

Perceived in this light, history-narration can be nothing other than the reversal of the Western discourse on the nonhistoricity of African societies. History ceases to be a "long nightmare" (as Benjamin has said) in order to become both a positive science of Africanism in rebirth and a dream of a return to the world of justice.[27]

Concerned with the meaning produced by the choice and the articulation of the events, the process cannot avoid the dichotomization of science and ideology typical of Western epistemology of the nineteenth century. The disappearance of one of the terms—*ideology* in this case—is envisioned as the only solution to the story. Under the influence of Mannheim and Heidegger, the circle of *Présence Africaine* then borrows the dominant current of thought of "devaluation of ideology and reevaluation of autonomy of culture through sociology and knowledge" (Momigliano 1966b:234).

History-narration that (in the tradition going back to Herodotus) tells "true stories that have been lived," whose truth lies in the correspondence between the narration and the past praxis, permits us to grasp the framework of the human drama. In this way, history as knowledge promises an in-depth understanding of the phenomena of which we presently see only the surface. By seizing onto the laws of change, it becomes possible to construct the future in the midst of the present thanks to the wisdom of the past, since "man has thought, for a long time, that the world knew as much about it as he did"

25. Wallerstein (1961:84): "The nationalist movements have realized, while in development, the political values inherent in a revalorization of the African heroes and empires."

26. A. Diop (1959): "Négritude born in us from the feelings of having been frustrated in the course of history, from the joy of *creating* and of being considered at our rightful worth" (43); and "Négritude, then, has the mission to restore its true dimensions to history" (43). Sartre (1948:xxvii) said, "Négritude defines itself against Europe and colonization."

27. Bastide (1962:43): "University studies have carried along with them at least one modification of intelligence and of the new forms of intelligence which cause them to want to save Africa . . . but they rethink it in Western terms, and not in African terms any longer: they reconstruct, they do not continue it." Maspero (1962:133) said of those whom one would call 'fellow travelers' today: "The French liberals will continue to be this Cartesian center of the world, that gives the latter its meaning and definitive form. Beyond their thinking and their norms, there is no history at all that can be written."

(Gribinski Nysenbaum 1985). It is only normal when the Marxist historians, on the one hand, and H. I. Marrou, on the other hand, exert a great influence on this work of reconstitution of the true "future past." In the 1960s efforts were made not only to create changes but, especially in the dominant culture which is that of the West, to shape a future that gives, if not a central place, at least one of importance in humanity, back to Africa. It is then impossible to escape from the realism of the nineteenth century (Barthes 1974) that substitutes for the real an already textual image that claims to represent reality iconographically. The African historians are thus torn between professionalism and the moral responsibility that is identified with political commitment; they seek the security of the former in order to call for objective history as a positive science that authorizes the practice of the latter as a historic mission that is incumbent upon them.[28] Prisoners of the vision incarnated so well by the British historians (who saw in history a manifestation of progress [Arx von Jeffrey 1985] culminating in the elite of their own society), they share with Lord Acton (Butterfield 1959) the conviction that the conscientious approach to history, guaranteed by professionalism, will insure objective history. This attitude implies the perception of the historian as an agent able to raise himself above his society.[29] B. Verhaegen, who was associated with *Présence Africaine* as were almost all radical Africanists, characterizes the task of the historian as follows: "I let the present consciousness, that the actors and the plans they form for the future have of it, be traversed by the movement of the praxis, whose meaning—never completely uncovered—unties with or adds to the completed action" (1974:190).

Contrary to the Ecole des Annales or to British social history that recognize only the analytical philosophy of history (Bann 1981) and refuse to debate truth and objectivity, the circle of *Présence Africaine*

28. Rabemananjara (1959) writes: "To rob our master of their cherished identity, the motive of their thought, the golden key to their soul, the magic Sesame that opens wide the door of their mysteries to us, of the forbidden cave where they have piled up the spoils stolen from our fathers and for which we have to ask them to account" (70). The great poet rejoins popular thought, especially syncretic thought. But as Tchicaya U Tam'si says (1980): "Because, in truth, every civilization is a syncretic encounter of at least two worlds, barbaric one to the other, and both barbaric. And obviously, that produces a new barbarism, so controversial in itself that it is by necessity a tragic being, and fatal because inhabited by two deaths, those of the two worlds that bore it" (8).

29. Moyangar (1974): "But the long history of this land [Chad] has not yet had its national expression" (103).

prefers the speculative philosophy of history. This comment by Momigliano (1966b:234) with reference to the first who "underline problems rather than solutions" explains the slowness of the awakening of the history of Africa to a current that is nevertheless dominant (Clarence-Smith 1977; Vansina 1978).

The dichotomization—of science and ideology, of the historic method and the moral responsibility—contributes to the fact that the evaluation of the work of Cheikh Anta Diop, J. Ki-Zerbo, I. Kaké, or of the speculative philosophy of history would have been and still risks being perceived as a violation. Paradoxically, in this century dominated by the great ideologies of the nineteenth century, philosophy was discredited to the advantage of a scientific illusion. Only the adversaries would practice ideology; the followers of the good cause only practice science. Utopia then becomes planning, prophetic determinism becomes the law of history, and so on. One pretends to forget that, instead of being an imitative operation to represent the developmental process of real events, historical narration constructs a meaning by starting from certain epistemological and ontological choices that have ideological and political implications.[30] These choices precede the construction of a concrete historical narration, since the structure of the narrative itself imposes a coherence and produces meanings that inspire and do not flow from the historical events analyzed, which are more constructions than givens. Narration is a discursive system of the production of meaning that imposes upon the individuals an unreal but highly significant relationship to the social formations amidst which they realize their social role. The "content of form" (White 1987) carries a burden that is far from neutral, and this fact explains the violence (at least verbal) of certain debates on the form of history as scholarly narration, as was the case for négritude in pharaonic Egypt.[31] If it is still possible, as in 1959, to qualify Europe as an "advanced peninsula of Asia" (Deuxième Congrès 1959:9), the power of its form has not been lessened.

Thus it happened—not only for psychological reasons but essen-

---

30. Hountondji (1970), quoting Cheikh Anta Diop, says that "history in Africa has a practical function, a revolutionary function that aims to give the consciousness of their continuity in time to our people"; he adds that "this task can be assumed only by the revolutionary intellectuals, the revolutionary historians" (89).

31. Ki-Zerbo (1962): "The Negro uniqueness was being professed by the Black intellectuals of the period, in the form of literature . . . Thus, they expanded the revendication of the African personality by carrying it to a political plane . . . Historical analysis was a weapon of choice for them" (138); see also n. 11.

tially for reasons both strategic and structural—that the group of *Présence Africaine* turned this marvelous tool of narration, which once served to subjugate the Africans, into the true narrative of cultural and political affirmation,[32] not only in the face of but especially in the midst of Western culture.

The Independences have achieved the process of the transfer of knowledge, creative and man-eating on the popular level but normative and conservative on the institutional and political level. Inevitably, historical narration could only be an Afro-centered variation on the Judeo-Christian background of historicizing history (Bourdé and Martin 1978). The production of history calling for the monopoly of objective and positive knowledge is accompanied by the political formation of the citizen as the subject of a nation-state inserted into the worldwide capitalist system (Wallerstein 1983; and Jewsiewicki 1987). This official recognition of a political order by history organizes the production of a future past.[33]

The demonstration of the antecedence of the African civilization, of the historicity of the societies of Black Africa, and of their humanity could only be made through a masterful plunge into the epistemology of the long nineteenth century, which explains a relative chill between African history as historic domain and the approaches whose ambition it was to produce a new methodology on the wreckage of the historicizing or Whig history (Butterfield 1959). *Présence Africaine* appealed to those in charge in the African societies and to the cultured Western public.[34] If it promised a more just, more moral, and more accomplished humanity because it would be decentered from the West,[35] *Présence Africaine* never promised there would

32. Rabemananjara (1959): Conscious of the weight of the West, which he would like to appropriate instead of rejecting it, he is worried by it nevertheless: "Will the invasion of our cultural field by the categories of thought and the intellectual modelling of the occupier not provoke the parching suffocation of our seeds and our hereditary concepts? In any case, it presents the risk of contaminating us" (71).

33. It must be recognized that certain authorities of the time have accepted the basic argument of Cheikh Anta Diop. Gurvitch (1959), who supports an African specificity, has stated: "The civilization of ancient Egypt would not be possible without the great example of the Negro-African culture, and most probably it was only its sublimation" (375).

34. Ki-Zerbo (1957): "Our desire is to study our history and to rectify the one that was made without us and against us" (67).

35. A. Diop (1962): "[E]verything conspires to assign a political function to our cultural works. The nature of these works is to appeal more to the West . . . they appeal to the cultural authority of the West, first of all to challenge it . . . to persuade its legitimacy of that political sovereignty" (119).

be an epistemological revolution,[36] a plan that is sometimes attributed to it. Hence my conviction that despite our disappointment—for which *Présence Africaine* cannot be held responsible—the intellectuals of its circle have kept their initial promise. They constructed and widely legitimated, as much in the West as by the Africans in charge, a philosophy of history—or, rather, a chronosophy (Pomian 1984)—of Hegelian inspiration, articulated around a broken line whose break loses its definitive character thanks to the idea that anthropological knowledge comes from the African concept of the present characterized by the permanent position of the past.[37]

The thesis on the colonial digression (Ajayi 1968, 1969)[38] that makes the precolonial history into a future present is already implicitly present in the chronosophy of Cheikh Anta Diop. Anchored in their past, the African societies firmly hold on to the Ariadne's thread of their civilization, of their unity, of their consciousness, and will in time establish at one bound the bridge, over barbarism and rupture, between the glorious past and a radiant future. This chronosophy abolishes duration, since time is nothing but a container for the bene-

36. Obenga (1972), who is inspired by Heidegger 1964 (see Lacou-Labarthe 1987) as to the determination of the being by historicity, thinks that Africa must develop its conception of man, "a role that Africa must assume, for all that it is profoundly historian in holding the solution to the problems of origin of manufacturing man" (27). He adds that "the *contemporaneity* (emphasis by T. O.) of African history . . . comes down to focusing clearly on the fact that the Africans will truly be liberated not by oblivion . . . but, indeed, by history, their history that emerges from and is blended in with universal history." It is useful to compare this text by Obenga with the one by Bastide (1962): "The Africans know history just as much as we do, individual history and collective history, but they do not have the same reaction when face to face with 'events.' The event is what shatters the web of Eternity inserted into Time . . . There is a socially cultivated mistrust of individual history: see 'the confession of sins' to cast away the event—and as far as collective history goes: see the effort towards packaging wars or revolutions . . . inside the categories of mythical thought, and the Messianism that appears with colonization that deeply cracks the equilibrium," equilibrium is thrown into the future since time takes on a "meaning," becomes history (39–40).

37. *Présence Africaine* (1955): "Our task is to encourage national cultures and the awakening of the consciousness" (6). Hountondji (1970) is among the rare contributors who see the role of the African intellectuals in a more radical way: "Theory, at this point in time in Africa, only makes sense if it is above all demystifying" (89).

38. Ki-Zerbo (1957): "The place . . . of the notion of time . . . is one of the constants in the traditional mentality of the Negro" (54). Agblemagnon (1959) in contrast, interprets it as a hypertrophy of the present, since the cult of the ancestors would aim to render the past present. Ki-Zerbo, whom I have just quoted, sees there rather an attitude that places the present in the past. For each one of them, it is a question of "ontological" time, as Agblemagnon says (222–232).

fit of a conceptual time. On a linear axis it situates three sections—
the origins, the present, and the future—that the principle of evolution not only ranks by devaluating the present but also by determining it. The present here seems to be a moment of articulation of the
origins of the future.[39] Thus it gives the value of the past to the distance that separates the origins of the future. To tell the truth, the
knowledge of the past has only a secondary usefulness, since the past
is largely the time of the others. It is only by establishing the direct
link between the time of the origins and the future that the present
can effectively contribute to the advent of a becoming (see, for example, Price-Mars 1959). The essential role of history is to establish
the true African and national origins, to render them useful to the
political construction of African and national unity.[40]

One must be very careful not to see in this an African cultural
specificity, unless one admits to an African antecedence from that
Western almost-obsession with origins (*Autrement* 1987; Lowenthal
1986). Which nation-state of the old continent did not fabricate ancestors for itself, customs and costumes (Trevor-Roper 1983) possibly
dating back to antiquity? It is not without reason that Ki-Zerbo
(1957:67), who probably recited "our ancestors the Gauls" from his
elementary school desk, compares the republication of Vercingetorix
to the suicidal but heroic end of Fafitini of Kenedougou.

This chronosophy abolishes duration in the immense effort of constructing a vast narrative museum of the African antiquities. The
truly "archeological"—or "antiquarian," as Momigliano says (1966)—
passion for a current that is so much present in the Western historian's practice represents that other window of historic interest of
Présence Africaine, in which the African antiquities adjoin those one
could call Pan-Negro.

If the academic Western history of Africa rejects the Egyptian thesis
on behalf of its own scientific paradigms upon which its mission depends, it devotes itself body and soul to the archeology of the antiquities. The historic narration that more or less explicitly links the

39. Ki-Zerbo (1972): "Having broken the colonial interruption, these countries
somewhat resemble the freed slave who begins to try and find his parents and the origin
of his ancestors again" (10); and Kabongo (1974): "Africa has a history in which the
contact with Europe is nothing but an accident" (222).

40. A call of the Second Congress of Writers and Artists (1959): "Paleontological,
prehistorical, and historical studies could release the first foundations of a unity of our
African universe from our past" (11). Biobaku (1955) emphasizes this fascinating research of the origins (5).

legitimacy of the sovereign practice of political authority in precolonial Africa to the grandeur of a given empire or kingdom participates with a chronosophy similar to that of Cheikh Anta Diop. Both put the Western discourse of political legitimacy on its feet (to take the expression that Marx used with regard to Feuerbach) by turning the hierarchy upside down; from the last conqueror to the first occupant, only the last term is preserved while the first is marginalized. So it is that the nineteenth century in Africa, so important for understanding the present, was more or less forgotten by the historians. Very effective in the 1960s, the operation of legitimizing African politics rapidly made scholarly history unable to offer a basis for the construction of a nationalist historiography. The hierarchy of the reasons for legitimacy of a power ruptured, opening in the midst of each society a Pandora's box of research in the authentic first occupant, far less evident than the last conqueror, whose attributes are often possessed by the present State, which cannot claim them without touching the other dogma of the 1960s, that of the communal character—indeed prematurely socialist—of the original African society. The class struggle, and thus the social conflict, having been banished from the domestic scene and pushed onto planetary level,[41] there cannot be conquering indigenous middle classes in Africa.

Thus, curiously—but only for the superficial observer—the metropolitan version of the past seems more and more in the place of honor for internal use, such as for teaching. For lack of being able to present Mobutu Sese Seko as the conqueror of the "territory" of the popular masses, it is still possible to do so through the intermediary person of Leopold II (Tshimanga 1976). In this way the wave of interest of almost celebrations is explained by the historians of the centenary of the Conference of Berlin. Vidal-Naquet in his analysis of *Zakhor* (1984) offers another hypothesis, a most correct one, it seems to me, for the Jewish memory, but where our ignorance of this memory (and not of the "tradition") does not yet allow us to apply it to the societies of Black Africa; he says that the weight of memory makes it impossible for history to exercise its rights.

41. The statements below and those of Maquet compel one to question the dialectics of African universalism vis-à-vis Western relativism. As Berque says (1962): "One might fear that the rehabilitation of pluralism in a politically liberated world holds technicist reasoning in store for some, the enjoyment of their Me for others. An illusory qualitative emulation would follow upon the former imperialism, born from the excesses of quantity" (118–119). Dampierre et al (1959) 355, say, for example, "[S]uch a movement would only have an enriching effect if, beyond this unity, it aims for the following goal: the unfolding of all the diversities of the cultures" (355).

The era of origins, of Black or African unity and consciousness seems to me to have come full circle.[42] This vision of history being ill-suited to serve a nationalist historiography, the former chronosophy of *Présence Africaine* can no longer dress Clio (Bann 1981), which is what every African state needs. Contrary to the unity that the experience of the colonial era, the metropolitan education, and the political and cultural struggle for independence offered to or imposed upon the group of *Présence Africaine*, the new chronosophy risks being splintered. History—as the collaborators of *Présence Africaine* saw it—did not deliver us in the least from Greek and Roman history (as Baudelaire wanted in the middle of the nineteenth century) but drove us more deeply into it. Without any hesitation one can refer to Loraux:

> [T]he construction that sought to reconstitute what is played out in the narrative—that is to say, before the narrative, or at least before writing, had begun. For, it was faithful to its practice—not to say to its ethic of closing all access roads to the workplace of the historian. Thucydides does not begin to write . . . until every too visible trace of the scaffold of intelligibility has been erased. (1985:21)

The French Revolution could claim the Athenian heritage, Germany that of Sparta, and the Socialist States the revolt of Spartacus; in that context, nothing can contradict the legitimacy of the appeal to Egypt in order to build a unified African State, nor the more targeted appeals to the closer heritages such as that of Ghana. If we accept Dan Sperber's definition of rhetoric (1975) as a function both of a text and of a shared knowledge, the discourse on the origins, especially the Egyptian ones, lacks the potential for building a national historic consciousness.[43] The shared knowledge is inseparable from the Western culture nourished by the Greek and Roman cultures, which makes of the debate on their origin a quarrel that is purely internal to the intellectuals.

42. Wallerstein (1962): "Class struggle does not exist in Africa, partly because it exists on the international level" (46). Touré (1959b:394) affirms: "We formally reject the principle of class struggle, less out of philosophical conviction than by reason of a desire to preserve African solidarity at any price."

43. Hodgkin (1959) spoke as follows: "The work that *Présence Africaine* accomplishes by interpreting and clarifying history, the institutions, the literature, and the arts from Africa, has been extraordinary for the Africans and the Europeans. No other organism or group has undertaken a similar task on such a scale, nor shown the same combination of energy and unity of spirit, of perspicacity and universalism" (353).

I close with a remark about the place of historic narration in *Pré-sence Africaine*, which reserves a large place for works of fiction.[44]
Louis Mink (1978:149) lets us understand this cohabitation not as an
accident but as a necessity. He insists upon the obligation to contrast
fiction and history in order to assert the scientificity of the latter: "If
the distinction were to disappear, fiction and history would both collapse back into myth and be indistinguishable from it as from each
other."

Just as Western professional history emerged from the nineteenth-
century romantic movement (Haddock 1980:90–105)—whence was
derived the inspiration of Dilthey, whom the circle of *Présence Africaine* reads for his "national genius"—so, too, does African professional history emerge in the 1960s and 1970s from the négritude
movement, in its widest sense. To this phenomenon one can extend
White's judgment on the historic imagination of the nineteenth century.[45] The unity of rhetorical structures between historiography and
the philosophy of history refers us to the archetypes of Northrop Frye.
History is a narrative guided by the narrative reason, since we know
it only through historiography. This look at *Présence Africaine* as
historiography poses an agonizing question for the present on the link
between historiography and politics in contemporary Africa and,
hence, on the place of narrative reason in political culture and
practice.

The historiography of *Présence Africaine* has not succeeded in constructing a durable myth, torn as it was between its own contradictions and those of Western culture, whose reincarnation with the
Black values did not take place.[46] The man-eating enterprise of the
intellectuals seems to me to have turned sharply and in the opposite
direction of the hopes of the 1960s, presented by J. Rabemananjara

44. The double link between cultural activity, especially writing, and politics on
the one hand, and between history and politics on the other, should be noted as much
as the place of literary language in the Soviet theory of the formation of nations, of
great influence on the African intellectuals. It is useful to stress that the Soviet theory
of the formation of nations insists upon literature (a common *literary* language; my
emphasis) as an element in the formation of a nation (Potekhin 1958:68). It was very
influential in the 1960s.

45. Andrade (1962): "The nationalist and literary activities are blending" (98); and
A. Diop (1962): "The concern with culture is, on the contrary, the seed from which all
profound political initiative is born in the Third World . . . in Black Africa today. Politics has a cultural origin and inspiration" (98).

46. Hountondji (1974): "All things considered, the real problem is that of liberating
the theoretic creativity of our peoples" (13).

(1959). Once again, it is the Western culture that feeds upon the African cultures through the Western contributions. The ideologies are our myths, and the African societies appropriate them through the philosophical and religious syncretism with which the intermediaries succeed where intellectuals have failed. The myths

> are the world's dreams. They are archetypal dreams and deal with great human problems. I know when I come to one of these thresholds now. The myth tells me about it, how to respond to urban crises of disappointment or delight or failure or success. The myths tell me where I am. (Campbell with Meyers 1988:15).

The explanation of the failure is perhaps elsewhere, not in the incapacity of the African intellectuals but in our collective incapacity: "The only mythology that is valid today is the mythology of the planet—and we don't have such a mythology" (Campbell with Meyers 1988:22).

To take as necessary an equation that is true only on the formal basis is the great temptation: Vernant (1981:129) says, "The thought is daughter of the city." In our past there is a link between historic narration, citizenship, and the State—the advent of historiography is associated with the civic conscience of the intellectuals blended with the life of the city (Gusdorf 1967, and Chaunu 1964). To make a universal rule of this leads us to appropriate history as thought in the nineteenth-century Western culture. Leaving the debate on the Western character of narration aside for the moment (Ricoeur 1984, and Carr 1986), we should question ourselves rather on the exceptional character (hence limited and not at all universal) of this link that the Judeo-Christian culture establishes between authority, writing, narration, and historicity as the condition for historic consciousness. Our historiographical practice exaggerates in claiming to be the direct heir to the Greek practice: "modern historiography, in leaning on Herodotus, and Thucydides, and their Greek and Roman pupils, has appropriated a method highly suitable for orally based historiography, but much less so for research drawing upon archives." This wealth of our culture, which allows us to "think against oneself" (Nordon 1987:192), has become law (Momigliano 1966a:218). It is time to recognize that we practice a *form* of history and not history.

It is important to add that in my opinion there is no *Présence Africaine* doctrine, which does not contradict the existence of a remarkable convergence of the points of view expressed. What should be noted, however, is that *Présence,* despite its political role (which is a partly desired and partly imposed one—let us recall the bomb attack of 1962), remains remarkably open to those points of view that the editorial staff and the majority of the collaborators do not share.

This critical reading is meant to be a sincere homage to *Présence Africaine,* whose work deserves better than fulsome flattery.

BIBLIOGRAPHY
Achufasi, Mondolim. 1959. "Devoirs et responsabilités des historiens afri-cains." *PA* 27–28:81–95.

Agblemagnon, F. 1959. "La responsabilité de sociologue africain." *PA* 24–25:195–209.

———. "Du 'temps' dans la culture 'Ewe.'" *PA* 14–15:222–232.

Ajayi Ade. 1968. "The Continuity of African Institutions under Colonial-ism." In *Emerging Themes of African History,* ed. T. O. Ranger, 189–200. Nairobi: East African Publishing House.

———. 1969. "Colonialism an Episode in African History." In *Colonialism in Africa, Vol. 1,* ed. P. Duignan and L. H. Gann, 497–509. Cambridge: Cambridge University Press.

Andrade, Mario de. 1962. "Littérature et nationalisme en Angola"; *PA* 41:91–99.

Andrade, Oswald de. 1929. "Manifeste anthropophage." In issue titled *Le Mal Brésilien. Europa,* March 1970:43.

Arx von Jeffrey, P. 1985. *Progress and Pessimism.* Cambridge, Mass.: Harvard University Press.

Autrement. 1987. Special issue of *Autrement* titled *Passion du Passé les 'Fabricants' d'Histoire, Leurs Rêves et Leurs Bataille,* no. 88.

Bann, S. 1981. "Toward a critical historiography: recent works in philosophy of History." *Philosophy* 56:365–385.

Barthes, R. 1968. *Elements of Semiology.* New York: Harper and Row.

———. 1974. *S/Z.* New York: Columbia University Press.

Bastide, R. 1959. "Message." *PA* 27–28:371.

———. 1962. "L'Africain à travers sa religion traditionnelle." *PA* 35:30–43.

Baudelaire, Ch. 1964. *The Painter of Modern Life and other Essays.* London.

Berque, J. 1962. "Hommage à Frantz Fanon" *PA* 40:118–119.

Biobaku Saburi. 1955. *Origins of the Yorubas.* Lagos: Federal Information Service.

———. 1959. "Les responsabilités de l'historien africain en ce qui concerne l'histoire et l'Afrique." *PA* 27–28:96–99.

Bipoun-Woum, J.-P. 1976. "Vers un blocage culturel de la démocratie dans l'Afrique des Etats?" *PA* 97:3–10.

Bourdé, G., and H. Martin. 1978. *Les écoles historiques.* Paris: Seuil.

Brown, D. E. 1987. *Hierarchy, History and Human Nature. The Social Origins of Historical Consciousness;* Tucson: University of Arizona Press.

Butterfield, H. 1959. *The Whig Interpretation of History.* London: Bell.

Campbell, J., with B. Meyers. 1988. *The Power of Myth.* New York: Doubleday.

Carr, D. 1986. *Time, Narration and History.* Bloomington: Indiana University Press.

Chaunu, P. 1964. *Histoire science sociale.* Paris: Presses Universitaires de France.

Clarence-Smith, G. 1977. "For Braudel: A Note on the 'Ecole des Annales' and the Historiography of Africa." *History in Africa* 4:275–282.

Cohen, S. 1986. *Historical Culture: On the Recording of an Alphabetic Discipline.* Berkeley: University of California Press.

Commission des Sciences Humaines. 1959. "Résolution soumise par le sous-comité d'histoire de la Commission des Sciences humaines." *PA* 24–25:399–401.

Dampierre, E. de, et al. 1959. "Message." *PA* 24–25:355.

Dawidowicz, L. S. 1981. *The Holocaust and the Historians.* Cambridge, Mass.: Harvard University Press.

Desmond, W., ed. 1988. *Hegel and His Critics: Philosophy in the Aftermath of Hegel.* New York: State University of New York.

Deutscher, I. 1968. "The Jewish Tragedy and the Historian." In *The Non Jewish Jew.* Oxford: Oxford University Press.

Deuxième Congrès des écrivains et artistes noirs. 1959a. "Appel." *PA* 24–25:9–22.

———. 1959b. "Résolutions et motions. Notre politique culturelle." *PA* 24–25:385–421.

Dike, K. O. 1953. "History and Autonomy." *West Africa* 14 (March): 225.

Diop, Alioune. 1959. "Le sens de ce congrès: Discours d'ouverture." *PA* 24–25:40–48.

———. 1962. "Solidarité du culturel et de politique." *PA* 41:117–122.

Diop, Cheikh Anta. 1957. *Nations nègres et cultures.* Paris: Présence Africaine.

———. 1959. Unité culturelle de l'Afrique noire. Paris: Présence Africaine.

"Documents de la mémoire." 1985. *L'Ecrit du Temps* 10.

Fanon, F. 1952. *Peau noire, masques blancs.* Paris: Editions du Seuil.

———. 1956. "Racisme et culture." *PA* 8–10:122–131.

———. 1959. "Fondement réciproque de la culture nationale et des luttes de libération" *PA* 24–25:82–89.

Freud, S. 1965. *Totem et tabou.* Paris: Payot.

———. 1967. *Moïse et le monothéisme.* Paris: Editions Gallimard.

Gadoffre, G., ed. 1987. *Certitudes et incertitudes de l'histoire.* Paris: Presses Universitaires de France.

Gribinski Nysenbaum, S. 1985. "Longtemps l'homme a cru que le monde en savait autant que lui." *L'Ecrit du Temps* 8–9:25–37.

Gurvitch, G. 1957. *La vocation actuelle de la sociologie*. Paris: Presses Universitaires de France.

———. 1959. "Message." *PA* 24–25:373.

Gusdorf, G. 1967. *Les sciences humaines et la pensée occidentale*. Paris: Payot.

Haddock, B. A. 1980. *An Introduction to Historical Thought*. London: Arnold.

Heidegger, M. 1964. *L'être et le temps*. Paris: Editions Gallimard.

Herskovits, M. 1965. "De l'humanisme en anthropologie." *PA* 46:14–34.

Hodgkin, T. 1959. "Message." *PA* 24–25:353.

Hountondji, P. 1970. "Intervention dans le débat: Elites et peuples dans l'Afrique d'aujourd'hui." *PA* 73:39–108.

———. 1974. "Histoire d'un mythe." *PA* 91:3–13.

Jameson, F. 1981. *The Political Unconscious: Narrative as a Socially Symbolic Act*. Ithaca: Cornell University Press.

Jewsiewicki, B. 1987. "The African Prism of Immanuel Wallerstein" *Radical History Review* 39:50–68.

Kabongo, Tshijuke. 1974. "Histoire zaïroise et critique historique." *PA* 90:276–279.

Kaké, Ibrahima. 1969. "Signification historique de la passion de Dona Béatrice, la Jeanne d'Arc congolaise, 1704–1706." *PA* 51:195–209.

———, 1975. "De l'interprétation abusive des textes sacrés à propos du thème de la malédiction de Cham." *PA* 95:241–249.

Keita, L. 1974. "Two philosophies of African history: Hegel and Diop." *PA* 91:41–49.

Khaldun, Ibn. 1967–1968. *Al-Muqaddima: Discours sur l'histoire universelle*. 2 vols. Trans. V. Monteil. Beiruth: Sindbad.

Ki-Zerbo, J. 1957. "Histoire et conscience nègre." *PA* 16:53–69.

———. 1962. "La personalité négro-Africaine." *PA* 41:137–143.

———. 1972. *Histoire de l'Afrique noire*. Paris: Hatier.

Lacou-Labarthe, P. 1987. *La fiction du politique*. Paris: Christian Bourgois.

Lagarde, P. de. 1979. *La mémoire des pierres*. Paris: Editions du Seuil.

Loraux, N. 1985. "Enquête sur la construction d'un meurtre en histoire." *L'Ecrit du Temps* 10:3–21.

Lowenthal, D. 1986. *The Past is a Foreign Country*. New York: Cambridge University Press.

Marcus, H. 1968. *La fin de l'utopie*. Paris: Editions du Seuil.

Marseille, J. 1984. *L'empire colonial et capitalisme français: Histoire d'un divorce*. Paris: A. Michel

Maspero, F. 1962. "Hommage à Frantz Fanon." *PA* 40:129–134.

Melone, T. 1963. "Les thèmes de la négritude et ses problèmes littéraires." *PA* 49:137–150.

Meltzer, F., ed. 1988. *The Trial(s) of Psychoanalysis.* Chicago: University of Chicago Press.

Mia-Musunda, M. B. 1976. "Le viol de l'identité négro-africaine." *PA* 98: 8–37.

Mink, L. 1978. "Narrative form as cognitive instrument." In *The Writing of History: Literary Form and Historical Understanding,* ed. R. Conary and H. Kozicki. Madison: University of Wisconsin Press.

Momigliano, A. 1966a. "Historiography on written tradition and histori-ography on oral tradition." In *Studies in Historiography,* 211–220. London: Weidenfeld ans Nicolson.

———. 1966b. "Historicism in contemporary thought." In ibid., 228–238.

Morin, E. 1959. "Message." *PA* 24–25:372.

Mudimbe, V. Y. 1988. *The Invention of Africa.* Bloomington: University of Indiana Press.

———. 1982. *Odeur du père.* Paris: Présence Africaine

Mveng, E. 1963. "L'art africain d'hier et l'Afrique d'aujourd'hui." *PA* 46: 35–51.

Neto, A. 1962. "Aspirations."; *PA* 41:100–101.

Nkrumah, Kwame. 1962. "De l'histoire culturelle du Ghana." *PA* 41:5–11.

Nordon, D. 1987. "La peur de l'errance." *Le Débat* 46:187–192.

Novick, P. 1988. *The Noble Dream.* In *The "Objectivity Question" and the American Historical Profession.* Cambridge: Cambridge University Press.

Oakeshott, M. 1982. *On History and Other Essays;* Oxford: Blackwell.

Obenga, T. 1969. "L'Afrique dans l'antiquité." *PA* 71:73—84.

———. 1972. "Esquisse d'une morphologie de l'histoire africaine." *PA* 83: 9–32.

———. 1974. "Science et langage en Afrique." *PA* 91:149–160.

———. 1975. "Contribution de l'égyptologie au développement de l'histoire africaine." *PA* 94:119–139.

Pavel, T. H. 1988. *Univers de la fiction.* Paris: Editions du Seuil.

Piault, M., ed. 1987. *La colonisation: Rupture ou parenthèse.* Paris: L'Harmattan.

Pomian, K. 1984. *L'ordre du temps.* Paris: Editions Gallimard.

Possoz, E. 1962. "La magie des primitifs." *PA* 40:58–117.

Potekhin, I. 1958. "De quelques problèmes méthodologiques pour l'étude de la formation des nations en Afrique au sud du Sahara." *PA* 17: 60–73.

Présence Africaine. 1955. "Liminaire." *PA* 11:5–8.

———. 1959. "Notre politique de culture." Editorial. *PA* 24–25:5–7.

———. 1963. "Cultures économiques et Tiers-Monde." Editorial. *PA* 46: 3–6.

———. 1969. "Mélanges: Réflexions d'hommes de culture." *PA* 63 (special edition).

———. 1976. "Pour une renaissance de la civilisation noire." Editorial. *PA* 99–100:i-iii.

Price-Mars, J. 1959. "La paléontologie, la préhistoire et l'archéologie au point de vue des origines de la race humaine et du rôle joué par l'Afrique dans la genèse de l'humanité." *PA* 24–25:49–59.

Prost, A. 1983. "Les monuments aux morts." In P. Nora (ed.), *Les lieux de la mémoire: I la Republique,* ed. P. Nora: 193–227. Paris: Editions Gallimard.

Rabemananjara, J. 1959. "Les fondements de notre unité tirés de l'époque coloniale." *PA* 24–25:66–81.

Ricoeur, P. 1984. *Temps et récit 2: La configurtion dans les récits de fiction.* Paris: Editions du Seuil.

Ruch, E. A. 1973. "Philosophy in African History." *Africana Studies* 32, no. 2:114–120.

Sartre, J.-P. 1948. "Orphée noir." In *Anthologie de la nouvelle poésie noire et malgache de langue française,* ed. Léopold Sédar Senghor. Paris: Presses Universitaires de France.

———. 1963. "Le pensée politique de Patrice Lumumba." *PA* 47:18–58.

Senghor, Léopold Sédar. 1963. "Négritude et civilisation de l'universel." *PA* 46:8–13.

———. 1983. "Préface." In *La pensée africaine: Recherches sur les fonde-ments de la pensée négro-africaine,* by Alassane Ndaw. Dakar: NEA.

Société Africaine de Culture. 1973. "Congrès international d'histoire afri-caine." *PA* 89:207–208.

———. 1974. "Africaniser les disciplines de la culture." *PA* 91:91–92.

———. 1976. "Identité culturelle négro-africaine: Texte d'orientation." *PA* 98:3–5.

Sperber, D. 1975. "Rudiments de rhétorique cognitive." *Poétique* 23:410–423.

Suret-Canale, J. 1959. "Message." *PA* 25–45:344–348.

Tchicaya U Tam'si. 1980. *La main sèche.* Paris: Lafont.

Todorov, T. 1978. *Poétique de la prose.* Paris: Editions du Seuil.

Touré, Sékou. 1959a. *L'action du Parti Démocratique de Guinée et lutte pour l'émancipation africaine.* Paris: Présence africaine.

———. 1959b. *L'expérience guinéenne et l'unité africaine.* Paris: Présence africaine.

Traore, Bacary. 1963. "Les damnés de la terre." *PA* 45:197–204.

Trevor-Roper, H. 1983. "The invention of tradition: The highland tradition of Scotland." In *The Invention of Tradition,* ed. E. Hobsbawm and T. Ranger, Cambridge: Cambridge University Press.

Tshimanga wa Tshibangu. 1976. *Histoire du Zaïre.* Bukavu: CERUKI.

UNESCO. 1974. *Le peuplement de l'Egypte ancienne et le déchiffrement de la langue méroitique Rapport final.* Paris: UNESCO.

Valesio, P. 1980. *Novantiqua: Rhetorics as a Contemporary Theory.* Bloo-mington: University of Indiana Press.

Vansina, J. 1978. "For oral tradition (but not against Braudel)." *History in Africa* 5:351–356.

Verhagen, B. 1974. *Introduction à l'histoire immédiate;* Gembloux: Duculot.

Vernant, J.-P. 1981. *Origine de la pensée grecque.* Paris: Presses Universitaires de France.

Vidal-Naquet, P. 1984. "Zakhor, souviens-toi." *Libération* (29 October).

———. 1985. "Le héros, l'histoire et le choix." *L'Ecrit du Temps* 10:47–55.

Wallerstein, I. 1961. "La recherche d'une identité nationale en Afrique occidentale." *PA* 34–35:79–91.

———. 1962. "L'idéologie du P.D.G." *PA* 40:44–56.

———. 1983. *Historical Capitalism;* London: Verso.

White, H. 1987. *The Content of the Form.* Baltimore: Johns Hopkins University Press.

The Shadow of Cheikh Anta Diop

Mamadou Diouf and Mohamad Mbodj

This study is concerned with discovering whether the work of Cheikh Anta Diop can be examined only with reference to the origin of Black Egypt, the Continental Federation, or Pan-Africanism, and whether this work is readable only in reference to *négritude* and colonization. This is certainly an important evaluation, given an oeuvre that has set up a theoretical horizon for the intelligentsia of both Africa and the diaspora, a horizon that could not be exceeded.

The sudden referential appearance of the unanimous praise that began at the moment of Diop's disappearance did, indeed, take on the form of deification. "The last pharaoh has died!" to quote the daily Senegalese newspaper, *Le Soleil:* he will no longer light our Black-Egyptian lantern. As regards deification, is it not simply (from a political point of view) a recuperation, a shadow that could create the unanimity of the Senegalese consciousness and that would drain both the vitality of the discourse and its challenge? There is the problem: to question the work of Cheikh Anta Diop, even from a scientific point of view, was for a long time synonymous with African antipatriotism; to refer to it in passing was an obligation one could readily fulfill, especially in academic work; to repeat its great principles, often without any real knowledge of the work itself, was a certificate of nationalism and Pan-Africanism. In any case, a dynamic oeuvre—paradoxically—paralyzed the African intellects or caused them to look elsewhere. And yet, it was his ambition to provide historical coordinates in which specific stories and monographs that contain only a partial and fragmentary history must be fitted (*Civilisation ou barbarie*, p. 274).

The entire work takes exception to regional history, the history that the micro-States inherited from the independences, the history that for them sketched an ideology as well as a national culture, especially in the African part of the colonial French empire. From its problematics, from the Negro origins of Egypt to the Africa of today, there is a historic continuum inscribed in the cultural and historic unity (archeological plan according to Mbengue);[1] the Federal African State becomes a categorical imperative (teleological plan according to Mbengue). The work of Cheikh Anta Diop has produced, strictly speaking, a new theoretic continent and a geographic continent—a theoretic continent whose matrix is an intimate knowledge of Egyptian history for the reestablishment of the African social sciences (*Civilisation ou barbarie*, p. 12), and a geographic continent: the Federal African State.

Our approach will focus first on the uncovering of the problematics brought into play and how it induced epistemological ruptures in the knowledge of the African societies. Then we will trace the imprints that Cheikh Anta Diop left in historiography and the social sciences, at least in the case of Senegal.[2] His shadow has shifted, in fact, following the changing manifestations of what is political and scientific in the area of Senegal. Seized by the "progressive left"—at little cost and with a bare, noncritical knowledge (the Marxists closed their eyes to it)—the oeuvre tends to become an ideology of compensation substituted for négritude in the context of Senghor's departure and Cheikh Anta Diop's death. In addition, Diop's disappearance seems to remove, from now on, all political hindrance that every criticism (scientific and disciplinary?) used to imply. An oeuvre public from now on, it undergoes the assaults of a generation confronted with the bankruptcy of the ideological models of nationalist inspiration.

1. Mbengue, C.S.A., *Histoire et projet politique dans l'oeuvre de Cheikh Anta Diop* (Master's thesis, Department of Philosophy, Université de Dakar, 1986–1987).

2. We shall use primarily the "major" works, that is, the books, as the articles and lectures seem fairly limited to us.

Therein, the shadow of the "last pharaoh" loses its efficacy and is summoned to speak its truth or its truths. At the same time, sanctified, erected into a statue, and becoming encrusted in mausoleums and other monuments, the work slips away more and more from a leftist territory in search of its own personality.

Problematics and Epistemological Rupture in Cheikh Anta Diop

Generally, the following few points in the work of Cheikh Anta Diop are maintained:

—Humanity made its appearance in tropical Africa; the first man is Black, and his whole evolution took place in Africa.

—The first civilization, that of ancient Egypt, is Negro.

—Greek civilization, the mother of the West, is the pupil of Egypt, matrix of civilization.

—One must refuse the civilizing characteristics of the colonial enterprise, which is an ideological mystification founded on the concept of the superiority of the White race and of Western civilization.

—One must rehabilitate the traditional African societies that all issue forth from the same origin and that are fundamentally different from the others, from the Indo-European one in particular.

—The cultural unity of Black Africa should coincide with a Federal African State, the only road to development and true independence.

—Black Africa must, in the concert of nations, occupy a place equal to that of others, especially that of Europe.

—African social sciences can only play their role by finding their resources in the Egyptian humanities.

One immediately notices the continuity of the thinking of Cheikh Anta Diop, even though beginning from a historic, academic plan one ends up with a political and teleological plan. In fact, history is nothing but a means to serve the realization of a political plan. Hence, one can hardly hope to find pertinence in the work of Cheikh Anta Diop through the mere dialectic of observation-hypothesis-demonstration that is the basis of history. Furthermore, the pertinence of a philosophy of history should be acknowledged. A philosophy is original in that it opposes a particularistic, therefore triumphant, ethnology; but still, although a globalizing plan, its vision is not enslaved to economic mechanisms, thereby distancing itself from the Annales school. By connecting Black Africa's place and role in humanity to the demonstration of the Negro personality of ancient Egypt (indeed, of the négritude of homo sapiens), Cheikh Anta Diop offers the elements of the problematics of a universal history. Thus presented, the problematics of Cheikh Anta Diop become disproportionate in relation to the usual academic practice of the Africans. By refusing the logic of the usual monographs and specializations, Cheikh Anta Diop reduces the breadth of this activity, or else offends it by considering it a dead end. For, far from being case studies, Cheikh Anta Diop's work postulates a theology and does so from the start.

The first echoes of Cheikh Anta Diop's scientific preoccupations are heard in a lecture given at Saint-Louis du Sénégal during the school vacation of 1950, on the theme "Les fondements d'une civilisation moderne," a title that revealed ambitious preoccupations. Already he asserted there that the civilizations of the Nile Delta were Negro-African ones.[3] Two years later, in an article published in the first issue of the journal of the Association des Etudiants du Rassemblement Démocratique Africain, he advanced the thesis that Egypt was the mother of civilizations.[4] Nations nègres et culture, published in 1954, is the first major publication in which he takes up all these ideas in an attempt to rehabilitate Black civilizations: pharaonic Egypt, the first civilization, is Black African; the Valley of the Nile is the cradle of all Black African populations, both ancient and modern; and, finally, Africa has civilized the rest of humanity.[5] In 1960, Cheikh Anta Diop publishes the two sections of his doctoral dissertation—L'unité culturelle de l'Afrique noire—and reasserts the existence of a single matrix for the Black African civilizations, based on matriarchy, in contrast to the Indo-European civilizations which are patriarchal. In L'Afrique noire précoloniale (1960) he studies the political Indo-European and African institutions in a comparatist perspective and shows that they are irreducible, thereby destroying the dream of assimilation once and for all. Nevertheless, independence was already the order of the day with its foreseeable consequences, balkanization in particular. It is then that Cheikh Anta Diop suggests an alternative solution with Les fondements économiques et culturels d'un Etat Féderal d'Afrique Noire (1960), which is his "least scientific"—or, rather, his "most political"—work, surely the one he himself considered the most important, going so far as to revise it in

3. Account in Paris-Dakar, no. 4451, 7 September 1950.
4. "Vers une idéologie politique africaine," La Voix de l'Afrique Noire (February 1952).
5. Nations nègres et culture (Paris: Présence Africaine, 1954).

1974. From 1960 on, the books that follow will frequently only be
systematizations, clarifications, or syntheses of theses already stated.
Thus, *Antériorité des civilisations nègres: Mythe ou vérité historique?* (1967) reorganizes the already known arguments in an attempt
to respond to his detractors, who accuse him of placing himself
outside of the academic principles. *Parenté génétique de l'egyptien
pharaonique et des langues négro-africaines* (1977) is more original:
it emphasizes the historical continuity between ancient Egypt and
present-day Black Africa through linguistics, which then appears a bit
like the "exact science of the social sciences."[6] The last work published during his lifetime is *Civilisation ou barbarie: Anthropologie
sans complaisance* (1981). There, although he once again takes up the
essentials of his earlier ideas, Cheikh Anta Diop tries his hand at
producing a philosophy of history. What seems especially important
to him—for the survival of Black Africa as a nation subject to a process of change that it must master—is the identification of an acti-
vating, historical consciousness. This book is the sum of Cheikh
Anta Diop's scientific production, and many researchers consider it
his masterpiece. In any event, the range of his thinking firmly lays
the foundation for a new humanism.

Having thus posed the problematics of Cheikh Anta Diop and announced the epistemological rupture (which claims to be globalizing),
we now ask whether or not he is correct. To answer this question, one
must first raise an ambiguity that has settled in from the beginning
of the readings of his oeuvre. The Negro origin of ancient Egypt and
its affiliation with the African civilizations has been the focal point
of the work. The controversies and the questionings begin when the
author is disqualified as historian and Egyptologist. And yet, it is clear
from the first publications on that the archeology undertaken by
Cheikh Anta Diop claims to be complete, encompassing the totality
of the scientific disciplines mobilized in the service of a rationalist
cause. Later, in 1967, he explained this approach explicitly, observing
forcefully: *"It is not a question of a theory of Negritude. It is our
intention to clarify a precise point in human history, to establish a
unique fact in that history,* to detach it from the pile of false statements under which it is buried" (*Antériorité*, p. 9; our emphasis). The
pharaonic design is thus inscribed on the canvas of human history,

6. Martin Bernal, *Black Athena: The Afro-Asiatic Roots of Classical Civilization*
(New Brunswick, N.J.: Rutgers University Press, 1987), 393–415.

which becomes readable only by the addition of Black Egypt and its daughters. From then on, the metaphor "Mother Africa" finds all its meanings in the work of Cheikh Anta Diop, a singular work that was the singularity of the object that it reconstructs: a pharaonic memorial for Africa, a memorial that is built by the mechanisms of a historic quest that articulates scattered pieces of an Africa of tribes that was constructed by the triumphant ethnology of the nineteenth century ("the pile of false statements"). And it is precisely therein that Cheikh Anta Diop is modern, for he does not work the distinction between "historic consciousness" and "consciousness of the past." An entire fringe of African historians and Africanists has been engaged in the process of showing how the perceptions of history are at the service of both a political cause and a social cause, the construction of the memory of a generation on the eve of the transfer of power. First Cheikh Anta Diop removes that which is fictitious both historically and in terms of colonial politics. He opposes the evolutionist and civilizing historicity structured by the dominating powers with the dynamics of "Nations Nègres" and their "cultures." He mobilizes the disqualified (from Herodotus to Volney) historiographic discourses preceding the birth of modern Egyptology and, thereby, gives meaning to collective reminiscences and to the social memory inscribed in the political institutions, in the social and cultural organizations, and in technology, through the pharaonic light shed and through the comparisons with the Indo-European civilizations. In the author's conception, the historiographic scientific discourse that he produces alone is capable of giving birth to a social memory.[7] Thus Cheikh Anta Diop inscribes himself in the historic approach, described as a climb upward "from the cellar to the attic," a little in the manner of Le Roy Ladurie as regards the passage from economic and social history to the history of mentalities. Only there, exhumation explanation in no way takes precedence over revitalization. In that sense, contrary to the author himself, his work is at the same time myth and history; it is a knowledge of the emotions and an individual sensitivity, a social and political situation in the course of the postcolonial phase, translated by a polemic writing, under constant tension. Having in no way postulated any break between colonization and independence, he maintained the corrosive characteristics of his writing that became the target of the most virulent criticism. Writing

7. The teleological ambition of Cheikh Anta Diop is clearly apparent here.

that is constitutive of the oeuvre and that best translates its political dimension (for the constitution of a new society—that of an independent Africa) will go into effect through the construction of a history.

The totality of these observations is the basis of characterizing the work as an epistemological rupture, not a rupture in its confirmation of the négritude of ancient Egypt (witness to this are the facts that Cheikh Anta Diop said he was initiating a "rereading" and that there exists an entire body of Negro-American literature, whose peaks are Blyden, Du Bois, Garvey, Césaire, and John Hope Franklin) but a rupture in its approach and the methodological instruments it used. In the context of a triumphant negritude—expressed in the poetry and the philosophy and the African theologies, consecrated by the preface of J. P. Sartre,[8] recognized in the possibility of putting forward both an academic historiographic discourse on Africa (together with J. Ki-Zerbo and A. Ly) and monographs of the territories and ethnic groups that are preparing independence—Cheikh Anta Diop stands by himself, even in relation to the most radical discourse, that of the African Marxists who remain Euro-centered.[9] However, in the entire work there is no frontal attack on all these other tendencies, even if in *Civilisation ou barbarie* his deconstruction of the modes of production and his discussion of the revolutionary processes reduce the Marxist approach to the African realities to nothing. With regard to the academic system—its modalities, procedures, and historical contents—Cheikh Anta Diop remains a rebel. Jean Devisse, in an article devoted to Cheikh Anta Diop after his death, situates that rupture very well when he writes,

> Europe, France most specifically, has long hesitated to take this man and the ideas that he advanced into consideration. Concerned with showing that, in the very long term, Africa was at the origin of a good number of human civilizations, Cheikh Anta Diop, in full mastery of Western historical positivism, made use of history that would not have been repudiated in Europe, neither by Fichte, nor Marx, nor Sorel.[10]

8. J. P. Sartre, "Orphée noir," preface to *Anthologie de la nouvelle poésie nègre et malgache,* ed. Léopold Sédar Senghor (Paris: Presses Universitaires de France, 1948).
9. M. Diop, *Contribution à l'étude des problèmes politiques en Afrique noire* (Paris: Présence Africaine, 1959); and *Histoire des classes sociales dans l'Afrique de l'Ouest: 2. Le Sénégal* (Paris: Maspéro, 1972).
10. J. Devisse, "Cheikh Anta Diop," in *Encyclopedia universalis,* Universalia (1987), 546–547.

If we follow Devisse's reasoning, the work of Cheikh Anta Diop is inscribed in a logic marginal in Western historical discourse. In this regard, allusion has often been made to the reversal of Hegelian logic and to the reconstruction/subversion of the two poles Europe/Africa (Hegel), Africa/Europe (Cheikh Anta Diop), to the unfolding/revealing of reason in history. And yet, even if the invested temporal sequences can be opposed—the outcome in Hegel is the emergence of the Modern European State, while in Cheikh Anta Diop this reason (historic consciousness) must be exhumed in order to reactivate the Federal African State that has been waiting since the pharaonic era—the two approaches have a plan and are inscribed in the perspective of a unity of reason, of a logic of history. If Hegel's thought can be interpreted as the philosophic expression of the constitution of a social class, the bourgeoisie, then Cheikh Anta Diop's thought is surely an ideological weapon—of the radical wing?—of an ascendant social movement, that of the elite to whom the power must be transferred. The paradigm of modernization that Cheikh Anta Diop sets in motion is inscribed in a historic continuum, slowed down by the slave trade and colonialism, and thereby rejects mimicry and its corollary ("second hand modernity") of which Alf Schwartz[11] speaks. It is a categorical refusal of the confiscation of the memory and the historicity of Black nations. More than a refutation or an inversion, Cheikh Anta Diop goes around Hegel in order to establish his own teleology.

Where Cheikh Anta Diop does work, an inversion is on the premises of the European civilizing mission from the "Greek civilization" to the "industrial revolution," the sequence during which Africa loses its historical initiative. And yet, with regard to a reading of the work of Cheikh Anta Diop, this inversion poses a problem that would take the works of Finley, Vernant, Vidal-Naquet, Detienne, and especially Havelock and Hartog[12] as its support. Is such a reading legitimate, all the more so because these works seem to have left no traces in Cheikh Anta Diop's work? The need to question imposes such a de-

11. A. Schwartz, *Le tiers-monde et sa modernité de seconde main* (Natal: Foundation Jose Augusto, 1982).

12. F. Hartog, *Le miroir d'Hérodote: Essai sur la représentation de l'autre* (Paris: Editions Gallimard); *Hérodote: Histoires* (Paris: La Découverte, 1980); and "Les Grecs egyptologues," in *Annales Economies-Sociétés-Civilisation,* 1986; E. Havelock, *Preface to Plato* (Cambridge, Mass., and London: Belknap Press of Harvard University, 1983).

tour, which enables one to follow the order of the discourse that proceeds from a writing that either imprisons the one who thinks it in a noncritical acceptance—for political reasons—or gives him refuge in an embarrassed silence.

Two sites of analysis are privileged—philological archeology and the semantic quest of Havelock—in order to situate a rupture that Diop detects in the configuration of Greek thought from Homer (the pole of a preponderant orality), whose poetry, sanctioned by the audience, constitutes "a tribal encyclopedia" to *The Republic* of Plato, who attempts to dissociate "logos" and "mythos," wherein the written carries him away from the spoken word in order to give birth to philosophy and to constitute a fixed memory, that of the Platonic ideas. This process occurs to the detriment of the tribal encyclopedia, which through the demand of a sanction repeats itself only because it is transformed.[13] If Herodotus is inscribed between these two poles, and even if he writes "in the Greek world of the 5th century, orality remains preponderant,"[14] Herodotus is one of Cheikh Anta Diop's primary sources; it is from him that he takes the basics of the thesis of "Greek plagiarism" from Black Egypt. It is this thesis that unleashed the polemics around the existence of an "African philosophy" and its relationship to the written word and orality, but more basically still, of its relationship to the birth of philosophy in Greece, and of the relationship between philosophy and myth.[15] This reading opens up a much wider field for the philosophical debate and allows the Egyptology of the Greeks both to be replaced in the Greek contexts and to work on a critique of the sources of Cheikh Anta Diop and their pertinence, especially since he dispensed himself of it.

In fact, the works of Hartog provide another entryway into the dialogue that may necessarily be initiated between the results of contemporary Hellenist historiography and the work of Cheikh Anta Diop. Indeed for Hartog, from the Mycenaean epoch to the Ptolemaic conquest, the Greeks were never indifferent to Egypt. In his article "Les Grecs egyptologues," he specifies from the start that the investigative dimension—the degree of reality or veracity of the reported facts—is considerably reduced since Egypt inscribes itself in the de-

13. M. Détienne, *L'invention de la mythologie* (Paris: Editions Gallimard, 1981).

14. Hartog, "Les Grecs egyptologues," 956.

15. P. F. Diagne, *Ethnophilosophie et europhilosophie: Pour une herméneutique néo-pharaonique* (Dakar: Sankore, 1984); A. A. Dieng, *Les problèmes de la philosophie en Afrique* (Paris: Nubia, 1985).

sign of the Greek culture: it is not autonomous but a paradigm. According to Hartog, the procedures that sanction the narrative of Herodotus are those of "inversion, first of all, a well-known form that moves the real of the other in simple inversion to itself or to ours; then the constant concern to survey, to measure, to enumerate, and to quantify" (Hartog, p. 954). This observation permits us to understand that Herodotus is not only a gold mine of information for Cheikh Anta Diop but that he steps into his traces and constructs his historical paradigm in an identical fashion: the symmetry and inversion North/South for Herodotus becomes in Cheikh Anta Diop those of Indo-European civilizations/African civilizations, the domain of the patriarchy/the domain of the matriarchy, nomadism/fixedness. The analogy of the methods of Cheikh Anta Diop and of Herodotus must arouse reflection in African historiography's global framework. Diffusionist like Herodotus, "he marks the itineraries and registers the relay points" (Hartog, p. 955). In this sense, he is rather more the heir of ancient historiography than of the modern one which goes from historic positivism to the Annales school which seems to have no echo in his work at all. Its explanation is simple. From the ancients to the birth of modern civilizations (eighteenth century), the established idea was that Egypt belonged to Black Africa.[16] The advent of Europe and its design for domination has falsified the history of humanity.

But if Egypt is a "borrowed land," is it a geographic and historic reality and/or a theoretic concept in the Greek ideological matrix? From the symmetry/inversion of Herodotus, we usher in with Plato— still guided by Hartog—another Greek form in Egypt: "as the Atlantis is a fiction of Platonic discourse, one might think that Egypt, also intervenes as a largely fictional land, unoccupied and plausible, to be inhabited by the Platonic discourse" (Hartog, p. 957).

If these thoughts impose another reading of the Greek sources on Egypt, the issue at hand is not that of challenging the Black characteristics of Egypt; they impose a shifting of the quest for the sources, or at least a radical critique, an imposition that they escape in the works of Cheikh Anta Diop. They place on a different ground not only the questions of plagiarism but also the debate on philosophy and the reestablishment of the African social sciences from Egypt onward. If the "going" poses no problems, the question of the "re-

16. Bernal, *Black Athena*.

turn," to use an expression of a Senegalese philosopher,[17] is obviously a limitation for "ressourcement."

A unique and grandiose work, draped in a style of writing that imposes, if not a skirting, then acceptance or silence on the part of the Africans, it must today be questioned, not on the historical facts exhibited but on the logic that underlies their organization, in order to offer that sumptuous philosophy of history that has paralyzed the critical mind of generations of Africans. More than a history, it is the product of a perception of history in the service of a political plan.

And this political dimension has been an obstacle to the archeology of the knowledge of Cheikh Anta Diop. Today, we dream of being able to scrutinize his library attentively in order to find the intellectual history of the man, to follow the trace of the genesis and the blossoming of the work. Today, silence is no longer in fashion. To criticize Cheikh Anta Diop implicitly amounted to siding with the neocolonial camp of négritude/servitude.[18] The strategy of skirting the work, referring to it only in passing, became common to an entire generation. And so the work was raised into a "pyramid," and its author into a "pharaoh" escaped from the realm of fertile epistemological polemics that perhaps could have allowed the author to consider African literature on Africa, notably the history, historical sociology, and anthropology. And it is this resignation of the scholars that today opens the way to the recuperation of that work, distant and disdainful work, scrutinizing the seized independences and the delays that stand out in the face of technical progress. Even today, it is still reduced to a shadow that is cast, a thicket in which everyone comes to poach for causes that are never innocent. The victory of politics over thought has permitted this betrayal.

The Shadow Cast By Cheikh Anta Diop

The imprint of Cheikh Anta Diop on the Senegalese social sciences, particularly in historiography, is very ambiguous. For, on the one hand he is rarely contested or simply discussed, but on the other he is just as rarely credited for his contributions. This is not so much the product of ignorance as it is the effect of a tutelary shadow that is present but, paradoxically, cannot be found. Of course, the peripatetics of his academic career and his political action explain to a great

17. Abdoulay Kane, symposium around the work of Cheikh Anta Diop, Dakar, April 1982.
18. M. Towa, "Conditions d'affirmation d'une pensée philosophique africaine moderne," *Présence Africaine,* nos. 117–118 (1981).

extent the absence of true disciples, but do not at all explain the absence of the critical apparatus.[19] In fact, Cheikh Anta Diop has been victimized by the reduction of his theses to ideology, which consequently excluded them from any serious scientific analysis: "one believes or one does not!" For those "who believed," Cheikh Anta Diop became the object of an adulation that was more symbolic than instrumental. Put on this pedestal, a series of rather trivial formulas was all that was noticed from his work: *"The Blacks were the first people to be civilized," "The political unity of Africa is the key to its emancipation," "There is only one nation in Black Africa," "Precolonial Black Africa knew a political, social, and economic harmony that the West came to destroy,"* and so on. Sheltered by these shock formulas, the work was not evaluated, and thus the critical mind could not correctly exercise itself. As a result, the works of Cheikh Anta Diop could not easily be deepened or surpassed in the sense of making progress. In fact, it became impossible to escape from unanimity: there was no room for a classical academic discussion in which the points of agreement could coexist with the points of disagreement. This attitude was justified—quite wrongly, for it responded to other imperatives—by Cheikh Anta Diop's attitude; his legitimate intransigence was based on the fact that he "knew very well that as soon as he would yield an inch on the terrain of global demonstration, the latter would lose all political effectiveness to be dissolved in debates on erudition."[20] This unanimous tendency produced a predictable effect. For the most part incapable of answering the prerequisites of Cheikh Anta Diop (for example, the apprenticeship of the Egyptian or also the admiration for the precolonial societies), many did not know how to use his works;[21] then again, through his obvious reservation vis-à-vis the monograph, Cheikh Anta Diop was not aware of the major part of African scientific production, whose authors did not feel themselves to be coauthors with him. One might even say that in the absence of co-option, Cheikh Anta Diop was not able to establish a school in Senegal. We find here less the failure of a plan than the dead end of a diffusionist logic: for example, the small group of Senegalese Egyptologists was formed by others in Paris in the 1980s. Another difficulty, more important than appearances show, resides in the fact that Cheikh Anta Diop is a

19. The noteworthy exceptions are the works of Dieng and Diagne, cited above.
20. Devisse, "Cheikh Anta Diop," 547.
21. Dieng, A. A., "R d'un bilan critique de l'oeuvre de Cheikh Anta Diop" (unpublished article).

physicist who branched off, but whose principal activity would be more that of a historian. In a unique judgment, A. A. Dieng says that Cheikh Anta Diop "never read anything on pharaonic civilization as a functional system. He did not criticize the concepts by which Egyptology is moved forward and he did not create any new ones. When all is said and done, he did not create a true school of Egyptology."[22] And this does not appear a small obstacle when one is familiar with the rigidity of the academic system of French inspiration that only recently has put the multidisciplinary approach in a place of honor. In fact, it is a sociologist, Pathé Diagne, who appears as the disciple, rather late and in the field of philosophy.[23] Diagne systemizes, for example, the principal thesis of *L'unité culturelle de l'Afrique noire* (1960), the one on an irreducible difference between Black Africa and the West in order to reject Marxism, which was then only a product of Euro-philosophy.[24]

The work of Cheikh Anta Diop is frequently in touch with the political and scientific predicament of the 1950s, which may have made it somewhat out-of-date in the eyes of a number of academicians, for example, around the quasi-general challenge of the racial framework's validity. But could an African nationalist of that period escape from it? The accusation of racism (backlash/or reversed) should be admissible only if the prejudices suffered in the name of "race" were equitably shared, which quite obviously is not the case. Furthermore, this "Black racism" could possibly have value only by creating a guilt complex in the Europeans, which is not Cheikh Anta Diop's plan. Nor does he seek to comfort popular feelings; he writes for an elite that is already armed with the conviction of the equality of the human species. Nevertheless, there will exist still a refusal—a nearly obsessed refusal—to discuss Cheikh Anta Diop either in the name of the "defense of the Black race," or, less legitimately, in the name of the denial of the concept of race.

This unfavorable situation also functions on the level of the anticolonialist battle. Not only is Cheikh Anta Diop's anticolonialism expressed within a political framework that has always been in the minority in his own country (from the RDA to the Rassemblement National Démocratique, the RND), but after the Independences it seems to have lost its pertinence: it is the African leaders who incarnate this new evil, while the physical erasure of the former colonizers

22. Ibid., 10.
23. Diagne, *Ethnophilosophie et europhilosophie*.
24. Ibid.

puts the different partners in the anticolonial struggle face-to-face. For the intellectuals this situation sanctions the triumph of anti-imperialist and anticapitalist ideologies, while anticolonialism is discredited and relegated to a discourse that justifies the irremovable position of the elite in power. Thus, even if the breadth of the anticolonialist discourse of Cheikh Anta Diop did not undergo the test of power, it still remains that the generations born between 1940 and 1950 are no longer satisfied with the fine earlier unanimity against the metropolis.

As Cheikh Anta Diop chose to be a philosopher of history, he owed it to himself to use all scientific production available, a little in the manner of the traditional philological erudition that dominated French historiography until the triumph of the Annales school in the 1950s. Still, the 1960s announce the victory of the specialist, sharp in profile, which by contrast makes the works of Cheikh Anta Diop at least somewhat outdated on the methodological level, and in any case not very conformist to the then predominant Western academic standards.

Still, these different obstacles do not prevent the work from arousing a loud echo in the African progressive left. Certainly, Cheikh Anta Diop first of all represents an ideal, an apparently successful alliance between theory and praxis.[25] But, in fact, rebuffed by the négritude of Senghor, the African intellectuals of the years 1950–1960 are in search of a "Black and militant" ideology. Marxism is "available"; surely, their training is too weak to produce an original and coherent theoretic thought for that moment in time.[26] Besides, Senghor's thinking on the principal themes of Marxism, and their instrumentation in the framework of négritude, contribute to clouding the vision of these intellectuals. Furthermore, the attempt by Majhemout Diop ends up only by producing an effect of dogmatism, of sclerosis, indeed, of caricature.[27] What remains, then, are the theses of Cheikh Anta Diop, which are more comfortable regarding the emancipatory battle of an Africa that is living the destabilization of its values. What Cheikh Anta Diop proposes—to an intelligentsia strongly attracted by an ultimately rather vulgar Marxism but also alarmed by the possible consequences of its choices—is a reading whose interest is obvious. Thierno Diop says it so well:

Cheikh Anta Diop, although he never declared himself a

25. A. A. Dieng, Les problèmes de la philosophie en Afrique, 94.
26. Ibid., 94–114.
27. M. Diop, Contribution à l'étude des problèmes politiques en Afrique noire.

Marxist, had the courage to take a step in the path traced
by the founders of historical materialism in order to throw
light on the civilizations until then considered marginal to
the history of humanity.[28]

In doing so, Cheikh Anta Diop can be retrieved by an African left, not
only to be reassured to be relieved of an original quest through Marxist theory but also to find a counterweight to négritude and to the
federalism of Senghor. If, very simply, that Eurafrica so dear to Senghor is too ambiguous not to stabilize, through opposition, the Negro-
African Federation advocated by Cheikh Anta Diop (even if the latter
much resembles a cartelization of the future Leaders of State),[29] this
is not true for négritude. For both Cheikh Anta Diop and Senghor
depart from the will of a militant revalorization of the "Black race"
confronting the West. Of course, Cheikh Anta Diop presents négritude as a psychoaffective response, an easily chilled withdrawal by a
dominated culture, while his own approach would be scientific.[30] Are
we then dealing more with the choice of the means than with the
finality of the demonstration? And even if that is the case, what about
the accusation of plagiarism brought against Senghor by Cheikh Anta
Diop?[31] In reality, Cheikh Anta Diop will never totally erase the impression that he represented a négritude of good alloy, more acceptable in a context of anti-imperialist struggle. Besides, this ambiguity
is raised by Babacar Diop and will be fought by Obenga more than by
Cheikh Anta Diop himself.[32] That the trouble persists is indicated by
the words of Senghor himself in a preface to an issue of the journal
(*Ethiopiques*) published by the Senghor Foundation. In this special
issue devoted to Cheikh Anta Diop, Senghor says, "He [Cheikh Anta
Diop] has devoted his life to defending, better yet, to making Négritude known."[33] This heavy homage shows that the work of Cheikh
Anta Diop passed from the status of a replacement ideology for a left
in search of mobilization to a status that, more than usual, sanctified

28. T. Diop, "Statut du marxisme en Afrique: Le Sénégal" (Master's thesis of the
Qième Cycle, Paris I, 1978–1979.

29. Mbengue, *Histoire et projet politique dans l'oeuvre de Cheikh Anta Mbop,*
89–90.

30. C. A. Diop, *Civilisation ou barbarie,* Paris: Présence Africaine, 277–281.

31. The notion of plagiarism in Cheikh Anta Diop was one of the themes of the
April 1982 symposium, especially the difference between plagiarism and borrowing.

32. B. Diop, "L'identité culturelle dans l'oeuvre de Cheikh Anta Diop," *Ethiopiques* 4,
no. 12 (1987): 37–42.

33. Léopold Sédar Senghor, "Preface" to the special issue on Cheikh Anta Diop,
Ethiopique 4, no. 12 (1987).

the left/right gulf. This breakaway from the territory of the African left first appeared with the failure of the ideological models of nationalist inspiration in the 1980s; it was to be prolonged the day after the disappearance of Cheikh Anta Diop.

In fact, the nationalist plan of the Independences has, in the course of the years, become corroded by its continued dependency on the West, of which the tutelage of the coupling IMF-World Bank is only the aspect of the 1980s. The permanent economic crisis is thereby doubled by a political crisis. Like other countries—Ethiopia, the Sudan, Chad, Zaire, and so on—Senegal sees its unity disturbed by phenomena such as the separatism in Lower-Casamance, or by the impasse of a fake multiparty system. The citizens born since 1950 (the majority of the population) have a hard time believing that their elders have known worse. On the contrary, they see that, instead of having become strengthened by an anti-imperialist perspective and practice, nationalism becomes more and more a rhetorical discourse that serves both to legitimate the regime in place and to defend against the disintegration of countries that are deeply divided.[34] The nationalist ideology thus suffers general discredit. Youth turns away from it more and more in favor of individualism, Islam, or iconoclastic activism. To them it seems that Cheikh Anta Diop is too indulgent for the responsibilities of the present-day situation. Especially the young Senegalese have not understood his attitude after Senghor's departure: the refusal of a direct confrontation with Abdou Diouf and Abdoulaye Wade and a very moderate electoral campaign at the time of the elections of February 1983 have left an impression of indecision, indeed, of an ill-placed paternalism, and he seemed to respond very little to the expectations of public opinion.[35] These fissures in the politico-ideological stature of Cheikh Anta Diop were visible on his scientific pedestal. And thus, in April 1982, young Senegalese researchers organized a symposium around his work at which they initiated a scientific dialogue until then nonexistent. Even though the majority of his partisans confused this initiative with proceedings instituted against Cheikh Anta Diop by "pretentious juniors," it was the expression of a legitimate scientific curiosity that at last dared to

34. J. S. Saul, "Ideology in Africa: Decomposition and Recomposition," in *African Independence: The First Twenty-five Years*, ed. G. M. Carter and P. O'Meara (Bloomington: Indiana University Press; and London: Hutchinson 1985), 301–329.

35. In the eyes of many observers, Cheikh Anta Diop is the great loser of these elections, despite a worthy campaign that appealed first to the intelligentsia, but that was ill-adapted to the impassioned circumstances created by a slanted multipartyism.

depart from a nonunanimist position.[36] Once this momentum had been given, the questioning of the work of Cheikh Anta Diop became a regular and public approach. From here on in, it is summoned to speak its truth or its truths. When the great man disappeared in February 1986, the rhythm had caught; since then those questions addressed to Cheikh Anta Diop that had remained unanswered have converged to feed a critical reading of an oeuvre ossified by the shadow of its author.[37] The exchanges of 1982 dealt notably with the relationships between African civilizations and others (the question of cultural diffusion), the relationships between modes of production and revolutions, the relations between science/metaphysics and, finally, the problems of genre in Africa. Some speakers blamed him for lacking articulation between internal and external factors in the study of the development of the civilizations, others for his very elastic distance with respect to Marxism, still others his complacency with regard to both the revealed religions and his refusal of a possible African revolution. The majority of these themes would be taken up again later in a series of critical readings. In 1983, Babo Nebila charged Cheikh Anta Diop with having composed an ideological work rather than a scientific one, by showing the idealism of his position on class. Still in 1983, the economist Amady Aly Dieng published a work in which he reproaches Cheikh Anta Diop for his silences on the cultural regression of Black Africa, his total acceptance of the vitalist theses of R. P. Tempels, the homogenization of Africa, the substitution of the "pharaonic miracle" for the "Greek miracle" that he fights, and the refusal of the debate around African philosophy. The process ended for a moment in 1984–1985, as if to spare the man who was the target for certain political disappointments such as the astonishingly tight score of the elections of February 1983, the split of his party, or also the blockage of the national dialogue. His disappearance in February 1986 reopened the questioning. And it is thus that Mbengue tried to retrace the elaboration of the plan of Cheikh Anta Diop,[38]

36. Symposium on the work of Cheikh Anta Diop organized by the Association des Historiens du Sénégal and by the Editions Sankoré, Dakar, April 1982. The papers, unfortunately, have not yet been published.

37. Dieng, A. A., "R d'un bilan critique"; R. Diongue, "Contribution à l'étude du concept de 'conscience historique' à travers l'oeuvre de Cheikh Anta Diop" (Masters thesis, Department of Philosophy, Faculté des Lettres, Université de Dakar, 1986–87; Mbengue, *Histoire et projet politique;* Nebila, B., "L'idéologie dans l'oeuvre de Cheikh Anta Diop" (Master's thesis, Department of Philosophy, Faculte des Lettres, Université de Dakar, 1982–1983).

38. Mbengue, *Histoire et projet politique.*

while Racine Diongue defended the majority of his theses, not from a unanimist point of departure but rather by departing from a scientific reading.[39] Certainly, apart from Amady Aly Dieng, these authors are not experienced researchers, but the value of the papers leaves us to believe that from now on the shadow—that has always prevented a critical and objective analysis from flourishing—will finally grow blurry. The dispute between idealists and materialists, in order to appropriate Cheikh Anta Diop, no longer has any meaning since the work has escaped from the territory of a left that has become more and more reticent in his regard. This demythification on the level of the social sciences corresponds, paradoxically, with a sanctification on the public level. The heavy homage from the men and the institutions that had ostracized him has often been assimilated by the Senegalese regime, happy to find a monument that might overshadow former President Senghor.[40] Taking priority around the remains of a man who was a solitary person, the quarrels cut short the different initiatives that tend to systematize the discussion on the work of Cheikh Anta Diop. This paradox is apparent only because for the social sciences nothing is more irritating and stimulating than the deification of a scientific or a simply human work.

39. Diongue, *Contribution.*
40. Diouf, M., "Mémoires, représentation et légitimité politique au Sénégal: 1960–1987" (paper delivered to colloquium on Mémoire, histoire et représentation historique dans les pays d'expression française, Quebec, October 1987).

Myth, Epic, and African History

seven

Lilyan Kesteloot

In the Western civilizations, the myth and the epic are normally considered very worthy literary styles—although out of date, indeed archaic—but without any real interest for historical research.

Historical research has always sought support from the written document, has always preferred the chronicle to the legend, the scholar to the troubadour, and this tendency has only become more strongly entrenched in the course of the centuries. So much so, in fact, that it would not occur to a single historian to mention the *Chanson de Roland* or the *Niebelungen* as a source for the history of Europe of the High Middle Ages.

The situation is very different for Africa. Some of the (enlightened) colonial governors were busy collecting the oral traditions; Maurice Delafosse, Charles Monteil, and Gilbert Vieillard had already understood that these legends held a content precious to the history of this "continent without history," as it was still defined in that era. Then, with the Independences, the African historians took over and vigorously confirmed the value of these discourses as a privileged source of African history, which remained to be transformed. With this goal in mind,

136

the vast project set up by UNESCO[1] thus brought together the African researchers who used the oral texts in great abundance, texts of which they were frequently the first to make recordings; it must be added that they did not ignore the other sources, such as the documentation by Arabic travelers, the Sudanese *"tariks,"* the connections between the geographers and the European missionaries, and even the ships' logbooks of the captains and the account books of the merchants.

But, nevertheless, one wonders why so much credit is given to the African oral narratives and whether they do truly deserve it. Is it not a question of misused nationalism on the part of Africans? This is an argument that is rarely articulated, but that is hinted at by many a Western academician.

This essay, then, is an opportunity for us, who have often heard these hints, to respond to them once and for all.

It must first be understood that in the African societies of the African Sahel, myths and epics have the status of "true history," as opposed to the tales that are "lies of the evening" (*mensonges du soir*).

The epics especially—over and above their particular literary characteristics such as hyperbole, lyricism, songs of praise—are corroborated by the chronicles on the same subjects, which also are orally transmitted and thus held to rather strict limitations as far as the possibility of "invention" is concerned. Thus, a chronicle on the foundation of the Bambara Kingdom of Ségou (seventeenth century) will differ from the epic by the same name in only one or two precise points: the initiatory stay of Biton Koulibaly with the gods of the river Niger, and the stages of the conquest of power.

Naturally, the epic stresses the miraculous elements while eliminating or attenuating the violent ones of the successive coups d'états of the future king of Ségou.[2]

But otherwise it contains what is essential: the marginal status (both as hunter and as stranger) of Biton in this (then) fertile and agricultural region: his "election," a mystery, to the chieftaincy of his village; and the establishing of an armed band, the "tondyons," which will soon become a kind of regular experienced army, the instrument of the growing power of Biton who will force the neighboring villages and countries to pay him taxes, the clear sign of their dependence.

1. Published by UNESCO and Présence Africaine. *Histoire de l'Afrique.*
2. See Kesteloot, "Mythe et histoire dans la fondation de l'empire de Segou," Bulletin IFAN 3–4 (1978).

Whatever the present versions of the epic may be and whether it consists of two or of forty pages (depending upon the gift of speech of the "griot" who recites it), this same basic information will be there.

But if the narrative is more extensive, there is the chance that it will also give more details, such as the families present, the names of the conquered villages and of their chiefs, the names of the allies of Ségou, those of its enemies, with exact details of the wars undertaken by Biton at Karta, at Kong, all the way up to Timbuktu "where the long-haired Moors are" (*chez les Maures chevelus*).

In this way, by accumulating chronicles and epic versions of the same period, one gets closer and closer to a reconstruction of the facts that will not be very far removed from the historical truth.

And this is not really very surprising, since both griots and traditionalists share the goal of conserving and enlarging the political history of their country. Then one might still wonder whether they really succeed and how?

It must be understood also that the function of the narrator griot is a profession. Belonging to a hereditary and inbred caste, the griot undergoes an apprenticeship of about ten years, during the course of which he studies with his father or his uncle the whole repertory, which includes the episodes of the royal epic, the genealogies, the emblematic figures of each of the heroes, the great families, the great battles, as well as the great griots who were present at all these events. Since there are no written documents, the young griot memorizes lists of names, codified songs, and the diagram of the adventures, a kind of abstract manual. At the same time, he learns the art of developing them, embellishing them, of filling them out with proverbs, ruminations, digressions, depending upon the audience and his imagination. And, finally, he learns to put them to rhythmical accompaniment of a kora (or a ngoni, or a xalam, or a hoddu). The master will check his apprentice and correct him if necessary, sometimes even to the day of his own death. Thus, there are griots who are so old they can hardly speak anymore, but who insist on attending the performances of their successors, and who will fill in the gaps or continue to correct them (if the occasion arises) to the greatest advantage of the modern researcher, who can thus grasp the procedure in its very operation.

This oral knowledge and its transmission are thus not left to chance; at the least, they guarantee a technique handled by professionals and (in general) controlled by the notables of the kingdoms mentioned or their descendants. This in contrast to the tale, which can be told by anyone—man, woman, or child—and which is subject to all sorts of transformations. The transmission of the myths is perhaps even more codified and limited than that which rules the epic narratives.

The myth of Wagadou, for example (ancient Ghana, third to eleventh centuries), is known by every Soninke because it plays the role of charter, dogma, and history all at the same time. But the details of this myth and its religious and political layers cannot be divulged except by a few authorized initiates. And its deciphering (for the myth is first of all a symbolic narrative, therefore a mask that must be interpreted in order to obtain the historical truth that it both hides and reveals) can only be verified by these initiates, since ordinary people are not aware of the exact events the myth hides or transfigures.

Thus, the myths of migration, the myths of the foundation of kingdoms or dynasties—Tekrour, Soundiata, Ségou, Ndiadiane Ndiaye (Wolof), Daman'guile (Diawara), Mamba Koto Sane, or the three daughters of the Mande (Gabon)—the myths of people's dispersion and the end of a reign (Wagadou, Kusa), and the more localized myths of the founding of villages are as many authorized sources for the historian and deserve (as much as the epic) a sustained investigation, which will frequently resemble the kind that is implemented in a puzzle or a detective story!

However, one may still ask, If the myths and epics of our feudal societies are real witnesses of African history, up to what point are they reliable witnesses, and how can their gaps and their biases be evaluated?

For surely our narratives cannot be taken literally. Epics, even if the events are pretty faithfully recorded, throw some Manichaean lights on them: there are always the good and the bad (just as in the Western epics), and the good is always on the same side as the storyteller or his ancestor.

Thus, we note in the dozen epic narratives of Soundiata presently transcribed and translated a rather large structural identity (stages and principal facts), regardless of from what region each narrative hails: Kita, Bamako, Kela (Mali), Fadama, Niani (Guinee), or Banjul (Gambia).

And one may successfully and extensively explore details of specific events taking this common skeleton as a point of departure, for the versions become progressively impoverished as one distances oneself from the places of origin (Soundiata), while the most detailed nar-

ratives are those that border directly on the heartland of the ancient
kingdom.

On the other hand, as far as the characters are concerned, we will
note a stereotyping that removes all credibility from these very historical players: Soundiata, the king and administrator of justice; Soumahoro, the dreadful sorcerer; Sogolon, the prototype of the devoted
mother; her co-wife, the prototype of the evil stepmother; the Tira-
maghans and Fakoly, the valiant captains of a flawless prince. Heroic
values are on the side of the good cause (that is to say, of the Mandingo); treachery, cruelty, black magic are the lot of the Soussou (that
is to say, of the vanquished).

The recent controversy that followed upon the more subtle version—which a Wa Kamissoko[3] consented to give to Youssouf Cissé
(CNRS)—allows us to get an inkling of the *manipulations* (with respect to political opportunism) to which the griots could have submitted history.

Indeed, Kamissoko began to evoke the character of Soumahoro and
the reasons for his war against the Mande States in a very different
manner from the versions of Kela-Kangaba. According to him, in an
earlier time Soumahoro had approached the little kings of the region
with the idea of having them stop the slave trade that was decimating
the populations that were raided for this purpose (thirteenth century).
The Mandingo kings answered him with contempt, under the pretext
that Soumahoro was nothing but a blacksmith. It was only thereafter
that the king of the Soussou decided to go to war and subsequently
conquered their lands. Hence the coalition against the "invader."

It is certain that such a version changes the Manichaean epic vision
completely, to the extent that Soumahoro is explained not through
vile ambitions but through honorable motives.

This forces the observer to revise a certain number of judgments
that used to be considered well-founded through traditions that
agreed with each other. It is also true that the dissenting griot hails
from the former Soussou kingdom and consequently has both a different viewpoint regarding Soumahoro and other information than
have his colleagues who hail from Niani. For the researcher, then,
Kamissoko's version renews the survey, and the epic that took the
place of history (apart from some miraculous details) must now be
corrected seriously, especially where the controversial points are
concerned.

3. Published by Editions Karthala, Paris, 1988.

In addition to the extreme simplifications and the biases of the griots, there is another phenomenon that mutilates the historical truth in the epic or mythical narratives: these are the silences. Indeed, it is a rule that the griot will not tell everything, that every royal story have its secrets (conspiracies, betrayals, adulteries, assassinations), and that only one censored version be made public. In this way, Djibril Tamsir Niane, while inquiring about the version of the Soundiata that we know, obtained the trust of the traditionalist who told him a great deal more about the story under the seal of secrecy, of course. As a result, the researcher was happy, but the historian could neither speak nor publish, which is cruel! There are truths that kill, and this Niane knew well enough not to dare to disobey. In fact, is this not what happened to Wa Kamissoko, whom the griots of Kela reproached for having "spoken too much"—and who died two or three years later?

If it is, then, not without danger that one delves into the depths of the African historical traditions, it will be noted with this example that the epic and history are truly not to be dissociated, that for the traditionalist griots the epic is basically that part of history they have agreed to retain while at the same time they understand that they know facts they have agreed not to divulge.

On the whole, this is a very political (and also a very elitist) concept of history that connects with the gerontocratic concept of knowledge in our traditional societies, which contributes to reinforce their non-egalitarian structure.[4] These, then, are the kind of limitations that the epic or myth impose on historical research.

Limitations both strict and vague? Yes, for, in fact, they are not immediately distinguishable, and one can wander for a long time between pseudocertainties and imitation information before coming up against either an unbreachable wall of silence or a revelation that must be kept quiet, even if that weakens an entire part of the official story.

There are, of course, other handicaps that are due to the very nature of memory and orality. No matter how faithful, how finely tuned it may be, memory has its limits. It is inevitable that things be forgotten and confused. The griots forget names in the genealogies, sometimes skip one or two generations in the most ancient successive stages of a dynasty, sometimes confuse the family relationships or those of al-

4. See the thesis of A. Bara Diop, *La société wolor: Les systèmes d'inégalité et de domination* (Paris: Editions Karthala, 1981).

liances; they make no mistakes around battles or the protagonists or the starring roles, but mistakes do occur in the secondary roles.

Finally, they are always very vague where it concerns indicating time periods: never a date, but an approximate naming of a period—before such and such an invasion, after this or that famine, in the year that a certain phenomenon occurred (flood, drought, locusts, raid, pilgrimage of such and such a king). Moreover, the dating of a narrative does not seem to have any importance for them; the myth is habitually set in an indeterminate era, deep in the past: "[I]t is very long ago, in the old days, in the time of our ancestors . . . " As for the epic, it is situated by itself, the different reigns themselves forming the time reference—"in the time of king Amari Ngone Sobel," "at that time, king Nare Maghan Keita"—everyone is supposed to know, no need to be exact!

Finally, there are universal limits to points of view. We have seen an example of this for Soundiata. There is another one, more obvious and closer to us such as the opposing points of view of the supporters of Lat Dior and those of Demba War in the battle of Derkhele, which marked the fall of the Wolof kingdom of Kayor. Certain griots state that Lat Dior was betrayed by Demba War, that it was because of this betrayal that the Kayor succumbed to the blows of the French at the end of the nineteenth century; other griots say that Demba War did not betray but rather took revenge (and rightfully so) on his "ward," Lat Dior, who had demoted him from his functions as supreme chief of the Tieddo army. To each his truth, which has less bearing on the (irrefutable) facts than on their interpretation.

As I have said, these limitations are universal, for even in our modern history, even in Europe or elsewhere in the world, everyone has his own way of telling common history. For example, the last war: it is certain that it is not interpreted in the same way in Germany or in Japan as in France or the United States. Even if the facts are undeniable (one group was conquered, the others were conquerors), let us rest assured that the reasons given on one side are not identical to those of the other, that the notions of right or wrong are not presented in the same way. Let us also remember the interpretation of the Napoleonic "epic" in the French schooltexts and the one offered by their English, Prussian, or Russian neighbors.

African history, throughout its epic vehicle, does not escape the rule: each national entity has its own point of view of the events, each pressure group in this nation also has its champions, its choices, its interests that modify its judgments of history, that condition its interpretation of the facts, that bend the manner in which these are told, deformed, disguised.

Facing the different versions of the same epic, the historian is thus confronted with different, sometimes contradictory opinions and finds himself forced to practice historical criticism—and particularly criticism of testimonies—with as much rigor as he has learned to use on archives and written documents.

Every day the modern history of Africa is made in this manner. Each African thesis of history is supported today by these oral traditions, of which the epic and the myth are choice pieces. Every thesis builds, by restoration, a section of Africa's past: the thesis of Professor Bathily on the kingdom of the Galam, the thesis of Professor Oumar Kane on the Denianke kingdom, the thesis of Melle Fall on the kingdom of Baol, Tierno Diallo's on that of the Toorobe, Professor Kaba's on the Gabou, and so on. Not to be forgotten is the one by the late Professor Yves Person, who was the first French academician to build an entire scholarly work on the oral traditions around Samory.

I shall conclude this brief outline with a comment by historian Joseph Ki-Zerbo:

> The oral tradition is still much discussed as historical source, although less and less . . . in privileged cases and with an appropriate, methodological approach, it does offer the same degree of certainty that one normally expects from historical knowledge.[5]

5. Ki-Zerbo, *Histoire de l'Afrique noire* (Paris: Editions Hatier, 1972), 17.

part three
Alienation, Voices, and Writing

eight

Alienation and Disalienation: Themes of Yesterday, Promises of Tomorrow

Richard Bjornson

Alienation implies displacement from a normal or natural state of being. One of its meanings in French is madness, and since the beginning of the twentieth century it has often been regarded as the characteristic pathology of the Western world. For Léopold Sédar Senghor and other négritude writers associated with the founding of *Présence Africaine,* alienation was a principal cause for the malaise from which Euro-American society was suffering; more important, it was the condition that afflicted Africans who had become estranged from the values of traditional culture. In either usage of the term, the assumption was that alienation is a negative quality and should be eliminated. According to Senghor, for example, Africans could contribute to the disalienation of the West by sharing with it the humanizing perspectives of their own culture, and they themselves could overcome alienation by acknowledging their rootedness in this culture. A revalorization of African culture resulted from the initiatives of Senghor, Alioune Diop, and others involved with *Présence Africaine,* and it played a crucial role in the awakening of Black consciousness throughout the world.

This revalorization of African culture, however, is in many ways the product of alienation rather than the repudiation of it. Senghor was able to articulate his theses about African emotivity, rhythm, symmetry, and sense of community precisely because he had distanced himself from the specific cultural practices of the Serer and viewed them from the vantage point of a highly educated Frenchman who could compare them with analogous practices from other parts of the continent. The alienation that enabled him to acquire this vantage point was not entirely negative; in fact, it might well be argued that alienation in one form is a prerequisite to the human mind's movement toward knowledge. To achieve new insights, people must at least momentarily distance themselves from their present state of consciousness. If they refuse to do so, they will remain imprisoned in a static configuration of ideas and assumptions. By adopting a perspective that is other than the one they presently hold, they are estranging themselves from themselves, but they are not necessarily repudiating their identity. On the contrary, they may be reconstituting that identity in light of new knowledge and expanding horizons. Viewed in this way, alienation is one stage in a process that makes progress and heightened awareness possible. Those who launched *Présence Africaine* in the late 1940s were deeply involved in this process.

They themselves had undergone a double alienation. As a consequence of having attended French schools, they had adopted many European values that were incompatible with traditional African beliefs. They had also distanced themselves from the French attitudes that were supposed to have been conditioned into them by the schools. At the center of this dual alienation is the French doctrine of assimilation. Since the late nineteenth century, the French had vacillated between two opposing policies toward the people of their African colonies: the treatment of them as inherently inferior beings who should be forced into complying with French plans for the exploitation of their African territories, and the consideration of them (or at least the most talented among them) as potential future citizens of a French empire that would be based upon a shared language and a shared European culture. Often, both policies were applied simultaneously in the colonies. The second or assimilationist stance ultimately prevailed, particularly after the Second World War, but the assumption behind both policies was essentially the same. In either case, the French were assuming that the colonization of Africa represented the arrival of a morally and technologically superior civilization in an area inhabited by people who have been living in a state of barbarism for thousands of years.

Those who, like Senghor, benefited from the assimilationist doctrine were confronted with a serious dilemma. French culture presented itself as the guardian of a universally valid conception of human nature. Moral standards and legal rights were presumably based upon the rational application of it. But when they sought to extend this conception of human nature to Africans, they were rebuffed by the very people who claimed to be civilizing them. Furthermore, they sensed that their own cultures embodied values just as universal as those of Europe, and they became convinced that they could not renounce such values without repudiating a part of themselves. The négritude movement was thus both a product of the assimilationist doctrine and a reaction against it. The ambivalence of this situation deeply marked the works of négritude writers like Senghor, but the process of alienation that it implies actually led them to a heightened state of awareness that has remained at the center of Francophone African intellectual debates since the late 1940s.

This process, however, is also evident in the works of African writers from the previous generation, writers who accepted the assumptions behind the assimilationist doctrine but rejected that part of it which denied validity to all African modes of thought and behavior. A remarkable example of this mentality is Paul Hazoumé, one of the early sponsors of *Présence Africaine*. Along with Senghor and Alioune Diop, he presided over the First International Congress of Black Writers and Artists at the Sorbonne in 1956. For Hazoumé, there was no contradiction between his respect for African traditional values and his support for the civilizing mission of French colonialism. His synthesizing worldview, which found expression in his long historical novel *Doguicimi*, provides a good example of how the dual alienation process can produce a heightened level of awareness. It also reveals the latent contradictions of an assimilationist stance that subsequently became the psychological ground for the further alienation that was experienced by the generation of Francophone Africans who began to publish their works in the 1950s and 1960s.

The principle subject of *Doguicimi* is the group consciousness of the Danhomé; however, Hazoumé felt an extraordinary ambivalence toward the people who had dominated a large part of present-day Benin for more than 250 years. Having attended Catholic mission schools and the Teacher Training School in Saint Louis (later transferred to Gorée, where it became known as the Ecole William Ponty),

Hazoumé had internalized Christian moral standards and French intellectual values that predisposed him to condemn the human sacrifices, the slave raids, and the arbitrary injustices for which the Danhomé had become notorious in nineteenth-century Europe. As a civil servant, he believed in the French imperial ideal and was convinced it had brought peace to his country. Furthermore, like the Sotho writer Thomas Mofolo who devoted his epic masterpiece to the legendary Zulu leader Chaka, Hazoumé was not a member of the ethnic group about which he was writing. On the contrary, he was from the kingdom of Porto Novo, a major rival of the Danhomé for over a hundred years. Although Adja languages are spoken in both areas, tensions between them persisted well into the independence period. In other words, Hazoumé had reasons for depicting the Danhomé in a negative light.

However, when he became a teacher and school director in Ouidah and Agbomé, the capital of the former kingdom of Danhomé, he was fascinated by the customs of the people and began to collect the oral histories and ethnographic materials that he later drew upon in writing *Doguicimi* and a prize-winning monograph on the blood oath. Despite his identification with Porto Novo, his Christian moral values, and his acceptance of French culture as a norm of civilized behavior, he could not help but admire the nobility, the courage, the deeply religious sense of life, and the highly successful administrative structure in a kingdom that had established itself as one of the most powerful in the history of West Africa. Having read Europeans' accounts of Danhomé, Hazoumé felt they had completely misunderstood the human reality behind the society he had come to know so well. *Doguicimi* is his attempt to convey a sense of that human reality. In seeking to reconcile his conflicting attitudes toward the Danhomé, he projected into his novel a worldview that combines French ideals of freedom and justice with traditional African concepts of wisdom and nobility.

In the novel, Hazoumé establishes three main points of focus: the woman Doguicimi's heroic struggle to remain faithful to her conception of herself in the face of extraordinary obstacles, King Guézo's attempt to act wisely and humanely in a cultural setting that often obliges him to sanction cruel and irrational practices, and the historical reality of Danhomé as a social and moral entity. The two main characters in the novel embody the virtues and ideals of an entire people, and the drama of their lives unfolds against the meticulously detailed background of a society at a crucial turning point in its evolution. Although the people of Danhomé still adhere to a rigidly defined traditional way of life, both Guézo and Doguicimi glimpse the possibility of a new society based on knowledge, compassion, and justice. The real question is whether Danhomé can retain its African identity while altering its customs enough to survive in a rapidly changing world.

When Doguicimi, angered by the capture of her husband Toffa in a military campaign he had opposed from the beginning, publicly insults Guézo, the king spares her life, much to the astonishment of everyone present. Her outburst constituted a blasphemy that was immediately punishable by death, but as Guézo later explains to his son, the Vidaho, Doguicimi's words were uttered out of passionate loyalty, and they reflect a nobility and courage that should be held up as an example to the people. On another level, Guézo perceives in Doguicimi the female equivalent of his own wisdom and strength. Although he regrets not having selected her as one of his own wives, he refuses to seize her for his harem because he recognizes the consequences such an act would have for the future governance of the kingdom. In contrast, the Vidaho demonstrates his unworthiness to succeed his father by refusing to sublimate his desire for Doguicimi and by seeking to force her into complying with his wishes. In a context characterized by such corrupt impulses, Guézo illustrates an ideal of kingship—the exercise of power with wisdom.

Like him, Doguicimi has a sense of honor that arises from the knowledge of having acted in accordance with an ideal that transcends selfish desire. In her case, the hallmark of her character is an absolute fidelity to the man she loves. It initially blinds her to Guézo's nobility and prompts her to blaspheme him in public, but it also inspires her with the courage to repulse the Vidaho's advances and to withstand the suffering that is imposed on her. Upon first marrying her, Toffa had given her the name Doguicimi, which means "distinguish me" or "do me honor," and when she learns that he had been killed in captivity, she insists upon being buried alive with his skull. Her willingness to die and accompany him to the land of the spirits does do him honor, but it also testifies to an extraordinary human capacity for shaping one's life according to a passionately held ideal. This final act of courage also reaffirms the possibility of heroic behavior in a world that is often hostile to it.

The final chapter of *Doguicimi* is entitled "A Danhomé Victory,"
although the kingdom's military victory actually occurred in the previous chapter. The only victory in the last chapter is Doguicimi's de-
fiance of death in the defense of her ideal, and, by using the term in
this context, Hazoumé is suggesting that Doguicimi's heroic gesture
is a victory for Danhomé in the sense that it symbolically preserves
the true nature of people struggling to cope with a corrupt and changing world. In one of her extended monologues, Doguicimi hopes that,
if the French make Danhomé part of their colonial empire, they will
not destroy what is good in the kingdom. From Hazoumé's point of
view, this goodness resided primarily in a commitment to the common welfare, a sense of personal dignity, an integrity associated with
institutions like the blood oath, and a profoundly religious respect for
the ultimate mystery of life. He was convinced that such qualities
offered a more viable basis for modern African society than did the
acquisitive individualism of Europe.

Yet *Doguicimi* is as much a critique of traditional Danhomé as it
is a eulogy to it. Superstitions are depicted as an ineffectual way of
coping with reality. Human sacrifices are wanton and cruel. Wars and
slave raids constitute an extraordinary waste of human potential.
Against this background, Hazoumé unequivocally proclaims his allegiance to the ideals that French colonialism had brought to Africa:
the Christian principle of universal love, a respect for individual
rights, the scientific approach to the solution of practical problems,
and the goal of peace among warring peoples. Guézo and Doguicimi
intuitively adopt these ideals long before the French actually assume
control over the kingdom of Danhomé. Both abhor the futility and
gruesomeness of the popular human sacrifices. Both aspire to kindli-
ness and justice in their dealings with others. In a sense, they are
Christians before the arrival of European missionaries. Doguicimi
thus presents the African potential for greatness while drawing attention to the fetters that could prevent the realization of this potential.
The worldview that enables Hazoumé to depict reality in this way is
essentially an assimilationist one that has been expanded to encompass a reaffirmation of positive features in traditional African culture.

The assumptions behind such a worldview were widespread among
the founders and early sponsors of *Présence Africaine,* but they were
increasingly called into question by the generation of younger Africans who studied or worked in France during the 1950s and 1960s.
Although many of them wrote for the journal and acknowledged

the magnanimity of Diop, they tended to reject the assimilationist views of men like Hazoumé and Senghor. Even Ferdinand Oyono, whose humanistic inclinations are not altogether different from theirs, devoted all three of his novels to a critique of the assimilationist position.

The young Toundi in *Une vie de boy* and the old man Meka in *Le vieux nègre et la médaille* accept the false promises of the assimilationist dream at face value and suffer as a consequence of their naiveté; both are eventually forced to recognize the folly of having believed they would "become somebody" in colonial society by trusting the ideals that were adduced to justify the French presence in Africa. In contrast, Aki Barnabas, the autobiographical narrator in *Chemin d'Europe*, is fully aware of the duplicity behind colonialist rhetoric, but he cynically determines to manipulate it for his own benefit. The irony is that he succeeds where Toundi and Meka fail, although he pays for his success by becoming as hypocritical and emotionally sterile as the Europeans he is emulating. All three of these characters pretend to be someone other than they are, and whether they embrace the assimilationist dream or merely exploit it for their own purposes, they must continually flee from an awareness of the truth to avoid the knowledge that they are living a lie.

The underlying worldview in all three novels differs considerably from that in *Doguicimi*. Whereas Hazoumé held out hope for a fruitful synthesis of African and European cultural values, Oyono presents both traditional and modern attitudes as corrupt in a harsh world that is governed by relationships of power and does not reward people according to their merits. If Hazoumé sought to restore a balanced perspective upon traditional society, Oyono felt compelled to rip the veil of hypocrisy from all artificial distinctions that obscure the humanity of Africans and foster their victimization. When these distinctions are internalized, as they are in Oyono's novels, this victimization becomes a self-victimization. Only after being unjustly arrested and beaten do Toundi and Meka gain insight into the true nature of the colonialist system and renounce the illusions that bound them to it. Yet traditional society hardly offers them a viable alternative. The compassionate solidarity of their fellow Africans and Meka's ability to participate in shared laughter do offer solace in the face of absurd conditions they cannot change, but both characters remain profoundly alone at the end of their stories. What enables them to confront their fate with dignity is the intellectual penetration that allows them to accept the truth about themselves. If there is a cardinal virtue in Oyono's first two novels, it is the ability to perceive the reality behind deceptive appearances.

Barnabas, the major character in Oyono's third novel, is in many ways more pathetic than either Toundi or Meka, for he consciously repudiates his most human qualities and never realizes how the colonialist system has distorted his mentality. In fact, the very existence of such a mentality is an implicit condemnation of the society that engendered it. Reacting against the shame he feels at being associated with a father who has allowed himself to be duped by the false promises of missionary Christianity, Barnabas decides to act as Europeans do—solely out of his own self-interest—and not according to their stereotyped notions about how Africans should act. The first three positions he occupies after leaving home expose him to three facets of European culture: Christianity at the seminary where he enrolls in the hope of furthering his secular career, commerce at the Greek firm that he serves as a solicitor, and romantic love at a white man's house where he is employed as a private tutor for an eight-year-old girl. In each of these situations, he represses the shame he would feel if he admitted what he was actually doing, and he internalizes the cynicism behind the benevolent-seeming rhetoric of French colonialism. Traditional society offers him no viable options, for as it is portrayed in *Chemin d'Europe*, it is stagnant, corrupt, and dominated by senile older men. Ultimately, Barnabas achieves his goal of living in France, but he does so by presenting himself so persuasively as a good Christian that an evangelist group sends him there. In other words, as long as he thinks they might give him what he wants, he is prepared to play any role they expect him to play. By the time he recounts the story in the novel, he has become a shallow and hypocritically self-centered individual.

Within the context of Oyono's novels, the French doctrine of assimilation presents Africans with two equally untenable alternatives. If they accept its promises at face value, as Toundi and Meka do, they will be exploited and eventually confronted with a denial of their own humanity. If they adopt the self-serving attitudes behind the colonialist rhetoric, they will, like Barnabas, lose touch with what is most valuable in themselves. According to the worldview that Oyono projected into these works, intellectual penetration and a recognition of the common humanity beneath artificial social distinctions are the most important virtues in a milieu where neither traditional African values nor French colonialist rhetoric provides an adequate basis for forging a stable sense of identity. If Hazoumé and Senghor supported a synthesis of traditional and modern values within the framework of an essentially assimilationist position, many writers of Oyono's generation became alienated from this position and began to call it into question.

A broad spectrum of attitudes flourished in the Francophone African literature of the 1950s and early 1960s. It ranged from the négritude-influenced ideas in works by writers like Camara Laye and Cheikh Hamidou Kane to the socially engaged ideologies of Ousmane Sembène and Mongo Beti. Oyono's perspective is only one of the many that found expression at this time, but it is characteristic in the sense that it represents an alienation from a worldview that was widespread among writers of the previous generation. This alienation would become even more evident in the anti-négritude polemics of Stanislaus Adotevi, Paulin Hountondji, Marcien Towa, and others during the 1970s. The point is that each stage in the evolution of Francophone African intellectual life has proceeded out of the urge to go beyond an existing stage of consciousness. This "going beyond" necessarily involves a type of alienation because it implies the adoption of a viewpoint other than the one that has been held before. This new viewpoint incorporates the old one and ultimately becomes the ground that calls forth further alienations.

Such a dialectical process is inherent to the progression of thought, and *Présence Africaine* served as a catalyst in this process for nearly three decades. The négritude philosophy of men like Hazoumé and Senghor was a part of this process, as were the anticolonialist novels of writers like Oyono during the 1950s and 1960s. In both instances, Francophone intellectuals were addressing problems of crucial concern in the struggle to liberate the African consciousness from the shackles that European colonialism had placed upon it. The journal's present crisis reflects a general indecisiveness among contemporary African intellectuals about the direction in which this dialectical process should now move. The problems are no longer the same as they were forty years ago, and the solutions proposed for coping with the identity question and with colonialist oppression are no longer adequate in the face of massive poverty, rampant corruption, and neocolonialist exploitation. If *Présence Africaine* is ever again to play the crucial role it once played in the intellectual life of Francophone Africa, it will have to become open to the expression of a new alienation—an alienation that goes beyond the present state of consciousness and addresses the real dilemmas of contemporary Africa.

WORKS CITED

Hazoumé, Paul. *Doguicimi.* 1938. Reprint. Paris: G.-P. Maisonneuve et La-
    rose, 1978. Translation: *Doguicimi.* Washington, D.C.: Three Conti-
    nents Press, 1990.
Oyono, Ferdinand. *Une vie de boy.* Paris: Juillard, 1956. Translation. *House-
    boy!* London: Heinemann, 1975.
———. *Le vieux nègre et la médaille.* Paris: Juillard, 1956. Translation. *The
    Old Man and the Medal.* New York: Humanities Press, 1968.
———. *Chemin d'Europe.* Paris: Juillard, 1960. Translation. *Road to Europe.*
    Washington, D.C.: Three Continents Press, 1989.

nine

Présence Africaine: A Voice in the Wilderness, a Record of Black Kinship

Mildred A. Hill-Lubin

Upon the death of Alioune Diop, *Présence Africaine,* in homage, characterized its founder and longtime editor in the following manner:

> The entire life of Alioune Diop, an African from Senegal, philosopher and man of action, was the sign of a double alliance. Firstly, the alliance of black people between themselves; secondly, the alliance of the latter with other people of the World.[1]

Présence Africaine: The Cultural Review of the Black World represents only one of the paths that Diop, and associates, forged in order to promote solidarity among African peoples all over the world. Yet, in the editorial policy of the journal, Diop declares that the periodical is "not under the bidding of any philosophy or political ideology."[2] Furthermore, an examina-

1. "Homage to Alioune Diop," *Présence Africaine,* nos. 117–118 (1981): 10–11, esp. 11.

2. Alioune Diop, "Niam n'goura ou les raisons d'être de *Présence Africaine,*" *Présence Africaine* 1 (November–December 1947): 7–14, esp. 7. Repeated in English by Jacques Rabemananjara in a speech, "Fortieth Anniversary of the Review," *Présence Africaine* 144 (1987): 11–17, esp. 13.

tion of its issues reveals a conglomerate of diverse views which ofttimes challenge the primary assertion. Nevertheless, since its founding in 1947, *Présence Africaine* has survived as a strong voice projecting a vision of Black unity in an intellectual and political climate
which has not encouraged such a pursuit.[3] It is a mirror of the ambivalence, confusion, and caution that encompasses this subject. In
spite of attempts to be a democratic forum, its major objective is summarized in its title. The Société Africaine de Culture (SAC), an organization founded eight years after the journal, became the organ that
permitted Diop and colleagues an even greater opportunity to articulate and advance this concept through conferences, festivals, publications, and personal contacts. While we will devote some time to an
overview of the accomplishments of *Présence Africaine* to strengthen
or—should we say—create a bond linking Blacks internationally, the
focus of this paper speaks to the present and the future. It calls for a
continuation of the original aim of the journal: to provide a platform
for a dialogue among Blacks, both in Africa and the Diaspora; but its
new direction should be to stimulate as well a debate between contemporary Black scholars and, initially, that long list of unacknow-
ledged, unsung, almost-never cited Africans who, against all odds,
invented African Studies. These are the early Black writers. Most had
to print their works at their own expense, or be published by or, perhaps, only receive mention in *Présence Africaine.*

The proposal recommends an expansion and modification of one
made by my colleague, Olabiyi Yai. Upon entering the new long-term
argument on African philosophy, this linguist and scholar of Yoruba
urged a similar debate between "contemporary African philosophers
trained in Western schools and the other African philosophers 'exhumed' from the depths of African history from the Egyptians to the
present day."[4] This new appeal is not limited to Africans only on
the continent, as Yai suggests, but to Africans all over the world. It is
not restricted to "philosophers" but is open to Africanists in every
field. For as Lucius Outlaw, an African-American philosopher, in a

3. We should note that in the United States there are three other journals which
have similar aims and were in existence during this period. They are *The Crisis: A
Record of the Darker Races* (New York: Crisis Publication, 1910 to date); *The Journal
of Negro History* (Washington, D.C.: Association for the Study of Negro Life and History, 1916 to date); and *Phylon: The Atlanta University Review of Race and Culture.*
(Atlanta: Atlanta University, 1940 to date).

4. Olabiyi Yai, "Theory and Practice in African Philosophy: The Poverty of Speculative Philosophy," *Second Order: An African Journal of Philosophy* 6 (July 1977):
3–20, esp. 12.

more recent discussion, writes, "These struggles in philosophy these efforts are but part of larger local and international world-historic struggles on the part of African peoples."[5] Therefore, it is imperative that today's researchers begin with the "dead" Africanists who challenged, questioned, and recorded; but, virtually, have been ignored. In studying their efforts, we may be immensely enlightened about the nature of being African and the necessary means for African people to be equal partners in the world.

Need I state that this recommendation is not racist. It does not prohibit others from engaging in this endeavor. It maintains the position of *Présence Africaine.* It is open to all persons who wish to help "*us* define African originality," but it reserves a special obligation for Blacks:

> Our task is to encourage national cultures, the awakening of African consciences, constructive activity and the free circulation of ideas among African peoples—sound the alarm and make known the dangers in the political, economic, social and cultural spheres.[6]

Blacks will talk to each other while simultaneously permitting the rest of the world to know more about African peoples. Others may enter the discussion but from an African perspective. It becomes even more urgent and appropriate that Black intellectuals continue this process that their predecessors began. The search persists for the means to liberate Black people in order for them to move confidently and creatively into the future. Neocolonialism, where Blacks oppress Blacks, demands a counterforce. Moreover, at this period, there is a greater number of individuals trained in the academies of the West and educated in the African experience of living able to participate in the debate. In discussion with each other, both the living and the dead, Africans should be the ones to define themselves and determine their destiny or destinies. Finally, Blacks must construct and transmit a system of thought that will include truths about Africa and African peoples.

The Collective Voice of the Black World

We shall have more to say about this new direction, but let us briefly note the achievements of *Présence Africaine* and the resources it offers for the journey of African people into modernity. Although there has been caution on the part of everyone not to be too broad or

5. Lucius Outlaw, "The Deafening Silence of the Guiding Light: American Philosophy and the Problems of the Color Line," *Quest Philosophical Discussions* 1 (June 1987): 39–50, esp. 48.

6. "Foreward," *Présence Africaine* 1–4, new series (1955): 8–10, esp. 9.

bold in arguing commonalities and kinship among Black people, from its beginning this publication has represented the collective voice of the Black World. The journal began as a Francophone document but is now a bilingual publication in English and French and accepts articles in other languages used by African peoples. In its inaugural issue, French intellectuals—André Gide, J. P. Sartre, and others—lent support to the new venture begun by their Black colleagues. Most often associated with the writers of négritude and culture, the review leans heavily on literature and the arts; but politics, economics, and education receive considerable mention. Early editions carry essays and poems by Aimé Césaire, Léon Damas, Jean Price Mars, the Caribbean members of the aforementioned literary group, along with works by their African counterparts, Léopold Senghor, Bernard Dadié, David and Birago Diop, and Jacques Rabemananjara. What is so strikingly noticeable, however, is that in its first issue there is a poem in English, with a French translation, "The Ballad of Pearl May Lee," by the Black American poet Gwendolyn Brooks.[7] Interesting, also, is that although Brooks received the Pulitzer Prize for poetry in 1950 and has published fifteen volumes of poetry and a novel, she does not reappear, according to the two guides that index the periodical up to 1976.[8] Also included in the initial volume is the first part of Richard Wright's excellent novella, "Bright and Morning Star," but as "Claire étoile du matin," the French version.[9] Wright and Césaire are also listed as members of the Comité de Patronage.

The first five issues contain articles by Black Americans, but most are French translations. In number 6, however, several pieces appear in English. Most notable is an essay by the sociologist E. Franklin Frazier. In "Human, All too Human," an excerpt from *The Negro Family in the United States*, Frazier introduces the historical argument that New World Blacks retained little of their African heritage, and their social behavior reflects their experience in the United States.[10] In this same volume, Wright presents six pages of American

7. Gwendolyn Brooks, "The Ballad of Pearl May Lee," *Présence Africaine* 1 (1947): 113–119.

8. Femi Ojo-Ade, *Analytic Index of* Présence Africaine *1947–1972* (Washington, D.C.: Three Continents Press, 1977); and Jacques Howlett, *Index alphabétique des auteurs et des matiéres, 1947–1976* (Paris: Présence Africaine, 1977).

9. Richard Wright, "Claire étoile du matin," trans. Boris Vian, *Présence Africaine* 1 (1947): 120–135.

10. E. Franklin Frazier, "Human, All Too Human," *Présence Africaine* 6 (1949): 47–60.

Negro folksongs. In addition, in English are two poems by the academic and poet, Samuel Allen, who is well-known for a later piece defining the reaction of Black Americans to négritude.[11]

Through the years, the pages of *Présence Africaine* disclose numerous articles on the culture and politics of Blacks in the United States. Entries by and about African-American intellectuals and activists appear. Alain Leroy Locke, W. E. B. Du Bois, James Ivy, Horace Mann Bond, Julian Bond, Sonia Sanchez, Harold Cruse, Langston Hughes, Ted Joans, and Leroi Jones (Amiri Baraka) are among the cast. Chick Webb, Louis Armstrong, Alain Locke, Dr. Charles S. Johnson, Richard Wright, Langston Hughes, Malcolm X, and Martin Luther King, Jr., receive homage. Contemporary African-American writers are also finding space in the journal. In 1988, a review of *Beloved* (1987), a novel by Pulitzer Prize winner Toni Morrison, and an interview appear. In the same issue, there are tributes to the late James Baldwin.[12]

Blacks in the United States are not the only Diaspora contributors and subjects. Haiti commands considerable attention. There is a special edition dedicated to the Black poets of Haiti (1951). Its art, especially its painting, gains recognition. René Depestre, Jacques Roumain, F. Morisseau-Leroy, Jacques Alexis, and Maurice Lubin serve as the ambassadors of Haitian culture. The Brazil and Cuba connection achieves visibility through articles on art and, in more recent issues, on race and nationalism. Nicolas Guillen, the Cuban poet, strengthens the linkage with two poems and elegiac notes to the Haitian, Jacques Roumain, and to the Black American poet Langston Hughes.[13]

To further its goal of promoting kinship and consciousness among African peoples, *Présence Africaine* organizes other activities. It arranged two conferences for Black writers and artists and two Black World festivals of art. The proceedings and precolloquium papers of these events appear in the journal; special issues bring the findings and resolutions of these conferences. The First International Congress

11. Samuel Allen, "A Moment Please," and "Sonnet," *Présence Africaine* 6 (1949): 76–77. See "La négritude et ses rapports avec le noir américain," *Présence Africaine* 27–28 (August–November 1959) 16–26.

12. See Christina Davis, "Interview with Toni Morrison," and "'Beloved': A Question of Identity," *Présence Africaine* 145 (1988): 141–156. See also "Tributes to James Baldwin," *Présence Africaine* 145 (1988): 182–194.

13. See Nicolas Guillen, "Mau-Mau," trans. Claude Couffon, and "Mau-Mau," trans. Christopher Hancock, *Présence Africaine* 1–2 (April–July 1955): 109–112. See also "Elégie a Jacques Roumain," *Présence Africaine* 4 (October–November 1955): 64–69; "Le souvenir de Langston Hughes," *Présence Africaine* 64 (1967): 34–37.

of Negro Artists and Writers was held in Paris in 1956 and the second in Rome in 1959. The Diaspora was well represented. At the first congress of writers, the United States delegation consisted of Richard Wright, Horace Mann Bond, John Davis, William Thomas Fontaine, James W. Ivy; and Mercer Cook, James Baldwin, and Chester Himes from time to time attended the sessions. Among the representatives from the Caribbean were Aimé Césaire, George Lamming, Jean Price-Mars, Jacques Alexis, and Albert Mangones. Although the two writers' conferences were successful in bringing the international Black literary community together, the Société Africaine de Culture decided that something had to be done to discover the "real" African artists "who *live* their art much more than *theorize* about it."[14] Furthermore, it was believed that these artists from all over the world needed to come together to present their display of talent to each other, on one hand to bolster their own confidence regarding their creativity, and second to demonstrate to the rest of humanity the art and cultures of African peoples. Thus, the two Black World festivals of art, one in Dakar in 1966 and the second ten years later in Lagos, Nigeria, have done more to establish a basis for cultural unity than any of the other activities. Of immeasurable worth have been the precolloquia which attract scholars and activists of the Black World to explore strategies for solving the problems of Africa and for more effective means to disseminate the information. Société Africaine de Culture, usually in cooperation with some other organization, continues conferences, forums, exhibits, seminars, symposia for small specialized groups; the proceedings or findings of these meetings are reported in *Présence Africaine.* The "Colloquium on the Black African Family," held 6–10 April 1987 in Yaoundé is an example. The proceedings were recorded in issue 145 in 1988.

The organization has published a steady stream of significant books since 1949. Many of them emphasize the total Black community: *Le monde noir* (1950), *L'art Negro* (1951), *Nouvelle somme de poesie du monde noir* (1966). Special issues of the journal focus on values and manifestations: *Negro-African Cultural Identity* (1977); concerns: *Apartheid* (1978) and an update, *L'Afrique du Sud Aujourd'hui* (1986). Having been present at the birth of the Organization of African Unity (OAU) at Addis Ababa in May 1963, *Présence Africaine*

<hr>

14. Alioune Diop, "From the Festival of Negro Arts at Dakar to the Lagos Festival," *Présence Africaine* 92 (1974): 9–14, esp. 10.

published in its *Cahiers Présence Africaine* a special number reproducing the speeches of the Heads of State and Governments who assisted at the birth. In 1988, the journal, to celebrate the twenty-fifth
anniversary of this organization, dedicated an issue and presented an
editorial expressing its continued hope that the goal and dream of the
founders will be brought to a successful conclusion, that Africa will
"reconquer her own identity in all domains." The bookstore is a
meeting place for Africans and Africanists who travel to Paris.

In 1960, as a response to the increasing number of Anglophone
readers and a desire to inform them of past scholarship concerning
African peoples, *Présence Africaine* republished certain articles in
English, which previously had appeared in French, particularly the
proceedings of the two writers' conferences. In 1967, the bilingual
edition began. As political independence came to the continent, many
new subjects and new voices emerged. This freedom contributed to a
literary breakthrough which resulted in a rapidly growing body of
written literature. Political issues and matters associated with forming new governments and nation-states demanded attention. Besides
the creative writers, a generation of scholars, critics, and intellectuals
from all over Africa joined the ranks of contributors on literary criticism, the question of African languages, and aspects of traditional
culture. Chinua Achebe, John Pepper Clark, Pathé Diagne, Lamine
Diakhate, Amady Dieng, M'Bella S. Dipoko, Abiola Irele, Ibrahima
Baba Kaké, Iwiye Kala-Lobe, Ali Mazrui, Englebert Mveng, Georges
Ngango, Kwame Nkrumah, Julius Nyerere, E. N. Obiechina, Alfa
Ibrahim Sow, Charlyne Valensin, and Paulin Vieyra added other dimensions to the journal. Beginning in the late sixties and seventies, a
new group of scholars appeared: Paulin Hountondji, Eboussi Boulaga,
L. Keita, Barthelemy Kotchy, Oruno Lara, Theophile Obenga. Hountondji and Boulaga inspired a discussion of another topic, African
philosophy, which has generated a lively international scholarly exchange that has continued for a decade, produced several books on
the subject, and possibly led to the development of departments of
philosophy in a few African universities. Although women as contributors and subject have not been well represented, this situation is
changing. In 1987, a complete issue was devoted to *La femme noire
dans la vie moderne.*[15] Maryse Condé, a major female novelist from

---

15. *La femme noire dans la vie moderne: Images et réalités, Présence Africaine*
141 (Paris: Présence Africaine, 1987).

Guadeloupe, has been a regular reviewer and discussant on African
and Black female writers since the seventies.

Voices—Cross-Currents

Adhering to its open policy, *Présence Africaine* has consistently
provided a platform for the multiplicity of ideologies and ofttimes
conflicting currents of thought that Blacks have espoused in their
attempts to define themselves, affirm their identity, reclaim their
history and heritage, and forge paths to freedom. The négritude movement, described most often as a cultural and literary phase, represents
only one of these stirrings. According to the *Présence Africaine Index*, by 1976 twenty-two entries explained, denounced, elaborated
upon, or proposed to relate the concept of négritude to the contemporary African situation. Senghor, the spokesperson, had submitted
four articles. It is significant to note that African personality, defined
as the Anglophone version of négritude but not as controversial, has
produced twenty-six articles. What seems most unusual, however, is
that the movement which is considered to be the foremost political
articulation of African unity, Pan-Africanism, does not warrant a
separate heading in Howlett's *Index*.[16] A report from the 1966 Dakar
Festival also states, "The majority of the Founders of *Présence Africaine* in Paris were unaware of many of the Pan-African meetings."[17]
In the light of the objectives of the journal and the entire organization, this phenomenon raises questions and relates to the thesis of
this paper.

If there has been any group determined to foster solidarity among
Africans, it has been the Pan-African movement. Although the concept has its historical roots in Africa, its formal beginning and name
originated outside the continent. Unlike négritude, it was led primarily by Africans of the Diaspora. Henry Sylvester Williams, who called
the first congress, George Padmore, and C. L. R. James were from
Trinidad, and W. E. B. Du Bois was from the United States. The latter, a man of letters, a historian, sociologist, politician, and activist
played an instrumental role in continuing the five Pan-African conferences held between 1900 and 1945. Through these congresses, especially the second one, Du Bois is credited with paving the way for

16. Although Howlett does not have a Pan-Africanism category, Ojo-Ade in the
Analytic Index provides one with thirty-four entries. Many are the same articles in
English and French.
17. A. Diop, "From the Festival of Negro Arts at Dakar to the Lagos Festival," 9–14,
esp. 9.

African independence.[18] The fifth gathering marked the greatest representation and participation from the continent with Nnamdi Azikiwe of Nigeria, Kwame Nkrumah of Ghana, and Joma Kenyatta of Kenya as delegates. Tremendously influenced by the Pan-African philosophy, the three returned home and agitated for self-determination for Africa. Later, as heads of their respective countries, they tried to implement Pan-African policies.

Reported in the journal, the Sixth Pan-African Conference marks a milestone in illustrating the diversity, complexity, and ambivalence that accompany the political concept of African unity.[19] The first held on African soil, the sixth conference convened in June 1974 in Tanzania. The intent of the meeting was to renew the Pan-African tradition after its twenty-nine-year eclipse. Instead, it ushered in to the debate the Marxist, socialist theories which now provide the greatest tension for achieving solidarity among Black peoples. One of the opening speeches, given by President Nyerere, host of the conference, set the tone. In it, he asked the group to reject the idea of liberation based on race or geography; instead, he argued for liberation of all oppressed peoples throughout the world. While he admitted that "racialism" still existed and that the need for African people to unite is still important, he pleaded for Africans to play what he termed their "full part as world-citizens." He urged the participants to shake off the mental effects of colonialism and discrimination and promote the rights of all the world's citizens for an equal share of the world's resources.[20] This congress produced a resolution on Pan-African culture; but it stressed the exclusion of "all racial, tribal, ethnic, religious or national considerations"; it embraced the cause of all oppressed peoples of the world and opposed all reactionary forces throughout the world.[21]

When African unity is discussed today, it is usually in reference to the nation-states on the continent and, even then, with considerable doubt. The Organization of African Unity (OAU) was to provide direction, but it has been relaxed in its efforts. Even as the concept relates to nationalism, the argument is that it is difficult to achieve even in one state because of group and ethnic rivalries and the impact

18. John Henrik Clarke, "Two Roads to Freedom: The Africans and the Afro-Americans Long Fight," *Présence Africaine* 66 (1968): 157–164, esp. 161.

19. "The Sixth Pan-African Congress," *Présence Africaine* 91 (1974): 177–236.

20. "President Nyerere's Speech to the Pan-African Congress, June 19, 1974," *Présence Africaine* 91 (1974): 193–203, esp. 203.

21. "The Sixth Pan-African Congress," 219.

of colonialism.[22] Nevertheless, it is agreed that though Africa has essentially achieved political independence, contrary to expectations it has not brought an appreciable improvement in the lives of the masses. While all admit that racism is not dead, and is most visible in South Africa with its policy of apartheid, most theorists resist relating the problems of Africa to race and geography. They link them to oppressed and exploited people worldwide and insist that Black people must unite with the others to achieve freedom.

This position of becoming a citizen of the world is not too alien from the one *Présence Africaine* has always maintained. It affirms that Black unity would lead to world unity. Diop explained:

> The essential objective is to promote African Studies in order to favour among Africans, the deeper realization of their own cultures, and also to draw the attention of other continents to the interest which is presented in the modern world by the study of African mind and African nature. The broadcasting of knowledge bearing on Africa will be a decisive factor of mutual comprehension and of cooperation between peoples.[23]

Senghor is known for the belief that identification and knowledge of Negro-African values and culture contributes to Universal Civilization.[24] The problem, then and now, is that because of racism, slavery, and colonialism, Black people must rediscover, reconstruct, define, and reclaim their history and their culture as well as assume responsibility for transmitting this information to the rest of the world. Of equal importance is the recognition that this knowledge can give Blacks the power and direction required to plan their future and to act.

A Return to the Roots

This brings us to the main part of the discussion, the future of *Présence Africaine*. The subject provokes many questions. It has been suggested that perhaps the journal may be neocolonialist.[25] Is it re-

---

22. See S. K. Dabo, "Negro-African Nationalism as a Quest for Justice," *Présence Africaine* 107 (1978): 57–92; and J. Sorie Conteh, "Culture and National Development," *Présence Africaine* 107 (1978): 202–206.

23. "The Speech of Alioune Diop, International Congress of Africanists," *Présence Africaine* 67 (1968): 202–208, esp. 202–203.

24. Léopold Sédar Senghor, "Négritude et civilisation de l'universel," *Présence Africaine* 46 (1963): 8–13.

25. Louise Fiber Luce, "Neo-Colonialism and *Présence Africaine*," *African Studies Review* 29 (March 1986): 6–11, esp. 11.

ally? Is it outdated and unable to contribute any further toward solutions of the problems of Africa? While Africa has been its central concern, its subject and source, the question is whether only individuals living in Africa should be the determiners of the future of the continent. Furthermore, most of the articles published have emphasized culture. One can ask, Is culture sufficient to liberate exploited and oppressed people?

The answer must be: when we talk about African liberation, it has to be for African peoples everywhere. Apparently, the founders of this journal recognized this fact. Therefore, the struggle must include all Africans who so define themselves. One could insist as the Marxists or the liberals that the fight should involve the oppressed everywhere. But just as *Présence Africaine* welcomed the encouragement and support of the French intellectuals (Gide, Sartre, and others), contemporary Black Africanists also can appreciate the contributions of non-Blacks in their continued quest for cultural, economic, and political liberation. There is, however, a special role for the Western-trained Black Africanists: they must be the facilitators. As stated earlier, there must be a continued dialogue which will begin as a debate between modern researchers from Africa and the Diaspora—and we stress the international collaboration—with Africans of the past who began the written history. We agree that the boundaries should be enlarged to involve figures of wisdom from the oral tradition and the ordinary people as a way of gathering and confirming the data. The significance here, however, is on one hand to build on a tradition; but on the other to reconstruct a system. Since this journal has served as a forum to present the collective voices of Africans in the past, I suggest that it continue. In its new role it will function as a resource to initiate this debate as well as be the major recorder and reporter for the findings. This does not mean that materials will not be published elsewhere, but it will insure that this publishing house shall become a center of African thought. Consequently, the notion that it is now a marginal publisher that prints only those who cannot mainstream will die.[26]

For many reasons, such a goal is most appropriate for the future of this periodical and for Black scholars all over the world. As V. Y. Mudimbe points out,

> Since the 1960's African theorists and practitioners, rather
> than confiding in and depending on "big brothers" have

26. Ibid., 10.

tended to use reflexivity and critical analysis as a means
for establishing themselves as "subjects" of their own
destiny and becoming responsible for the "invention" of
their past as well as the conditions for modernizing their
societies.[27]

I would argue that there have been Africans with similar deter-
minations who predate this period. These are the men, and a few
women, usually a combination artist and scholar, dedicated to expressing the history, philosophy, and values of African people and
committed to improving the community. One person could be the
poet, historian, anthropologist, politician, sociologist, and minister.
Although such individuals existed in Africa, because of historical factors the majority of them belong to America. Because they and their
works have not been acknowledged or respected in the institutions in
which most present-day Africanists were schooled, they are not well-
known nor are their writings investigated. All of these persons are
not published in *Présence Africaine*, but they are cited. Thus, it becomes the responsibility of Black intellectuals to trace and study
their own scholarly and academic history and development.

Another factor which should enhance and strengthen this investigation is that there are many more intellectuals or educated people
around who could participate in the exchange than there were in
1947. Whether they live in the United States, Nigeria, Haiti, Jamaica,
Mali, Senegal, Paris, London, or Toronto, or whether they write in
English, French, or another language, they all share in the double
heritage of Africa and the West. In other words, we have been Blacks
in primarily Euro-American institutions of learning. We were taught
to accept the research methods, conventions, academic rules, and systems of thought. Furthermore, many who at one time probably could
have published only in *Présence Africaine* now have mastered the
techniques so well that they have access to other journals that are
considered a part of the establishment. Not only are the works of
these illustrious colleagues appearing in Western publications, but
some individuals hold positions in many of the prestigious universities and societies where research and scholarship receive high priority
and recognition. It is time for these academics to raise questions regarding the contributions and findings of these lost Black scholars and

---

27. V. Y. Mudimbe, "African Gnosis: Philosophy and the Order of Knowledge: An
Introduction," *African Studies Review* 28 (July–September 1985): 149–233, esp. 206.

researchers. There are other contemporary researchers, mainly in Africa, who are not completely dependent upon the West for validation of their research. It, then, becomes even more of an obligation for these scholars to begin this task of unearthing and examining the works of these early writers. In the current debate concerning an African philosophy, one group holds that there can be no philosophy without a recorded discourse for reflection.[28] We now offer this body of material.

As I have indicated earlier, many may be unfamiliar with these persons and their contributions. But even more tragic is that there are Africans who know but have been conditioned to see these resources as inferior. Therefore, they follow the majority and ignore these ancestral figures and their legacy. The works of these individuals are hardly ever cited in the research. Yet, African scholars devote reams of paper, produce volumes of books and numerous articles, either criticizing or supporting the publication of a Euro-American. P. L. Tempels, *La philosophie Bantoue* (1945), has produced an exhaustive amount of criticism. Currently, Martin Bernal, *Black Athena* (1987), is receiving considerable attention.[29] Yet, he writes of a George G. M. James, a Black professor at a small college in Arkansas, who has written a book entitled *Stolen Legacy: The Greeks Were Not the Authors of Greek Philosophy But the People of North Africa, Commonly Called the Egyptians*—a pretty long title, but it describes a similar position that Bernal propagates. The small volume of James appeared forty-four years earlier. Few know of *Stolen Legacy* and even fewer of George G. M. James.[30] Should we in the phrase of another one of these forerunners refer to this situation as "the crisis of the Black intellectual"?[31] May I hasten to add that a small number of contemporary scholars have given some recognition to these early researchers.

28. Paulin J. Hountondji, *African Philosophy: Myth and Reality* (Bloomington: Indiana University Press, 1983), 66.

29. Martin Bernal, *Black Athena: The Afroasiatic Roots of Classical Civilization, Volume I: The Fabricator of Ancient Greece 1785–1985*, (New Brunswick, N. J.: Rutgers University Press, 1987). A review appears that supports this thesis in *Présence Africaine* 145 (1988): 196–199, esp. 197.

30. George G. M. James, *Stolen Legacy: The Greeks Were Not the Authors of Greek Philosophy But the People of North Africa, Commonly Called the Egyptians* (New York: Philosophical Library, 1954). See discussion in Bernal on the difficulty of securing a copy of this book (435 and 506).

31. The reference is to Harold Cruse, *The Crisis of the Negro Intellectual* (New York: Morrow, 1967). The book is an indictment of the Black intellectual in America.

Most, however, have been African-Americans.[32] I am not the only one calling for a serious study of the works of these figures. Outlaw makes a similar appeal: "A major part of our efforts involve securing the appreciation, as works of philosophy, of the writings and contributions of a host of stellar black intellectuals and activists."[33]

The Voices of the Ancestors

Who are these individuals? It is impossible to cite all of them. Jacob Carruthers has divided these defender-philosophers into three categories. The first he labels "the old scrappers," persons who "without any special training, but a sincere dedication to ferreting out the truth about the Black past and destroying the big lie of Black historical and cultural inferiority, took whatever data were available and squeezed enough truth from them as circumstances allowed." The second group, educated in Western scholarship and possessed with a desire to prove their worth as scholars and the worth of Blacks as human, include George Washington Williams, W. E. B. Du Bois, John Hope Franklin, and Ali Mazrui. They have "argued only that Blacks had a share in building the Egyptian civilization along with other races"; the third, an extension of the "old scrappers" but who have "developed the multidisciplinary skills to take command of the facts of the African past which is a necessary element for the foundation of an African historiography." According to Carruthers, these include Cheikh Anta Diop, Ben Jochannan, and Chancellor Williams.[34] "Defender-philosophers," "sincere dedication to ferreting out the truth," and "multidisciplinary skills to take command" embody qualities that African scholars should have.

To serve as a concrete example, we could select one of the above or another such as William Leo Hansberry or Carter G. Woodson; instead, let us use one of the scrappers, one who is still alive, *John Henrik Clarke.* He is chosen not only because he is worth studying in his own right but because he has been a major contributor to *Présence Africaine.* Clarke has devoted a lifetime of research and creative abilities, talents, and concerns to discover and write about Africa and her

32. John Henrik Clarke, "African-American Historians and the Reclaiming of African History," *Présence Africaine* 110 (1979): 29–48; Joseph E. Harris, "William Leo Hansberry, Pioneer Afro-American Africanist," *Présence Africaine* 110 (1979): 167–174; Lorraine A. Williams, ed., *Africa and the Afro-American Experience: Eight Essays* (Washington, D.C.: Howard University Press, 1977).

33. Outlaw, "The Deafening Silence," 48.

34. Jacob Carruthers, ed., *Essays in Ancient Egyptian Studies* (Los Angeles, 1984), 34–35.

children. Similar to his African counterpart, Cheikh Anta Diop, after considerable struggle he has achieved a degree of recognition in academic circles. By 1976, he had authored thirty-six entries in *Présence.*[35] They comprise such topics as "The Impact of the African on the New World," "Ancient Civilizations of Africa: The Missing Pages in World History," "Two Roads to Freedom: The Africans and the Afro-Americans Long Fight," "Toussaint Louverture and the Haitian Revolution," and book reviews on practically every significant book published about Africa during this period. A 1988 contribution and a valuable one is a long piece, "Pan-Africanism: A Brief History of an Idea."[36] One of the most promising essays in the light of this proposal is "African-American Historians and the Reclaiming of African History."[37] Clarke presents not only the results of the efforts of these researchers as they rewrote world history to include the truth about Africa, but he concludes with a lengthy bibliography listing all of these persons and their works, an invaluable resource for those who wish to begin this investigation and exploration. Among those names he includes are Edward Blyden, William Leo Hansberry, St. Clair Drake, Alain Locke, Dorothy Porter, Benjamin Quarles, Joel Augustus Rogers, W. E. B. Du Bois, George G. M. James, and Carter G. Woodson. Clarke and his contributions to Western and African intellectual thought deserve study. A concerted and dynamic engagement into the work and lives of all of these multitalented personalities would uncover, I believe, a wealth of illuminating information.

Let me suggest a few areas. One is methodology. One of the criticisms that has been waged against *Présence Africaine* is that it has not been selective or critical; it attempts to treat everything and lacks a position.[38] One could answer that it has only adhered to its original editorial policy, that of accepting all articles about Africa, provided they are adequately written and antiracist and anticolonialist. On the other hand, we may be observing an alternative worldview, a different perspective for organizing the universe. Theorists often write that African people look for synthesis rather than analysis, a harmonious working of all the parts rather than a separation and study of the pieces. These early writers suggested for our consideration have been interdisciplinary in their approach and generalists as scholars. It is

35. See Clarke in Howlett, *Index,* 45–47.
36. John Henrik Clarke, "Pan-Africanism: A Brief History of an Idea," *Présence Africaine* 145 (1988): 26–56.
37. See Clarke, "African-American Historians," 29–48.
38. Luce, "Neo-Colonialism and *Présence Africaine,*" 10.

significant to note that, increasingly, modern Africanists are adopting this interdisciplinary method, regardless of the discipline. The assumption that the early Black writer, out of necessity, had to be "the multiple man" may be a false one. This multifaceted role may be a challenge for modern scholars.

Second, the matter of tone, many of the writings by these early thinkers are classified as not scientific in their approach, that the findings are emotionally inspired rather than scientifically proven. It is probably true that the works of these authors are heavily laden with feelings. After all, they are documents of people struggling for life, struggling to reclaim and vindicate the history of Africa and affirm their existence. Their results reflect the pain, hurt, and frustration of people who have been denied their culture. Why shouldn't their scholarship contain the total condition of their humanness? Should one expect the oppressed to sound like the oppressor? The slave narratives do not read like the nineteenth-century accounts of slavery written by whites, nor does a novel by Chinua Achebe resemble a work by Joyce Cary.

Third, content, knowledge, enlightenment; having been denied access to any information about Africa or having been provided many untruths, distortions, and lies, these early scholars had to conduct their own searches, interpret their own data, and make their own conclusions. On the other hand, they were at a disadvantage, but on the other, as we are discovering, unassimilated people preserve and retain more of their old culture. Even if the works of these writers cannot provide primary information about Africa, they can be studied for the manner in which Africans responded to obstacles.

Finally, in the area of commitment, most of these commentators held a Pan-African perspective which was not limited to the solidarity of Black people in Africa but included Blacks all over the world. They also recognized that without establishing human dignity and confidence about one's self and one's culture, one would not be able to perform in the larger arena. They were devoted to creating a just and equitable world and to giving power to Black people.

Therefore, we need Blacks to analyze as well as criticize the works of Blacks, especially our academic foreparents. Such must be the task of the Black intellectual who has had the academic training of the scientific community, the experiential knowledge of having lived as an African, and the dogged determination and confidence to provide the leadership for advancing Africa and African peoples into the modern world. They can use their African heritage and their Western legacy to merge into better and truer selves and, in turn, inspire and initiate projects that will lead to the reconstruction and empowerment of Africa and the cultural, political, economic, religious freedom for all African people and, simultaneously, for all people.

Over forty years ago, *Présence Africaine* began to pave the way for this movement into the future. It has remained steadfast to its goal, in spite of the other plurality of proposed routes. The journal still stands committed and available to offer the needed impetus and resources to help African people throughout the world accomplish the task of bringing Africa and Africans into full and equal participation in world affairs.

Harlem Renaissance and Africa: An Ambiguous Adventure[1]

Elisabeth Mudimbe-Boyi

ten

Et il faudrait revenir du côté de Papa Longoué.
Tout ce que nous avons oublié. L'Afrique. La mer.
Le voyage.[2]

Edouard Glissant,
La lézarde, p. 197

. . . puisque la mer avait brassé les hommes venus de si loin et que la terre d'arrivage les avait fortifiés d'une autre sève.[3]

Edouard Glissant,
Le quatrième siècle, p. 285

The major themes of the Black literature from Africa, America, and the Caribbean are very often linked to the social and historic contexts. But the transformation of these contexts does not necessarily diminish all the value of the literary works that actualize them. It shows, rather, the need for a literary history, textual analysis, and commentaries that, thus, can keep alive these contexts and topical works in different times and contexts.

The historic process, like a tragic play, consists of strong and weak periods. Seen in this light, the 1920s are a marking point in the cultural history of the Black world. First of all, they coincide with the writings of the African-American intellectuals—such as Alain Locke, Carter Woodson, William Du

1. A first version of this article was published in *Présence Africaine* 147, no. 3 (1988): 18–26.
2. "And one should come back to Papa Longoué's way. / All that we have forgotten. Africa. The sea. / The voyage" (E. Glissant, *La lézarde* [Paris: Editions du Seuil, 1958]).
3. " . . . since the sea had churned and shaken those who had come from so far away and the land where they arrived had fortified them with another sap" (E. Glissant, *Le quatrième siècle* [Paris: Editions du Seuil, 1964]).

Bois—who by their action encouraged a new awareness that formed the basis for a literary and artistic renewal: the Harlem Renaissance. Also, it is from America that the great Black outcry comes (with repercussions elsewhere) in the négritude movement in Africa and the Caribbean.[4]

The literature of the Harlem Renaissance claimed to be a Black literature, and it proved itself to be so through its quest for racial and cultural roots that will lead it back to Africa. It also desired to assert a Black identity in the heart of the American culture; it explicitly wished to revalorize the history, the culture, and the unique experience of the African American. But at the same time this literature was eminently American literature, because it was the spiritual and ideological expression of a specific group in American society whose material conditions of existence it reflects.

Thus a double belonging—at one and the same time racial and sociopolitical, Black and American—sheds light on the themes of the Harlem Renaissance and of the literary production of the following decades, during which it remains closely linked to the different moments of awareness and of the cultural and political Black revindication. Linked to the growth of consciousness, a written literature that reflects the African-American experience progressively replaced a conventional literature that gave simplified and stereotyped representation of the African American. Up to that point, one had to read the condition of the Black, especially in the oral literature—for example, in the Negro spirituals,[5] whose poignant lyrics tell the anguish and the bitterness of the uprootedness and exile.

> Sometimes I feel
> Like a motherless child
> A long way from home, a long long way from home.

In the search for origins and roots, for a "mother" and a "home," the Black writer attempts to reduce his anguish and put an end to the alienation of the industrial society. This return to the sources is a

---

4. Lilyan Kesteloot, *Les écrivains noirs de langue française: Naissance d'une littérature* (Bruxelles: Solvay, 1963); M. E. Mudimbe-Boyi, "African and Black American Literature: The Negro Renaissance and the Genesis of African Literature in French," in *For Better or for Worse: The American Influence in the World*, ed. A. Davis (Westport, Conn.: Greenwood Press, 1981), 157–169; M. Fabre, "*La Revue Indigène* et le mouvement nouveau noir," *Revue de Littérature Comparée* (1 January–March 1977): 30–39.

5. See Houston Baker, Jr., *Black Literature in America* (New York, McGraw-Hill, 1971), 3–5.

necessary itinerary in the quest for identity and for the reconstruction of the past. In this context Alex Haley's book, *Roots,*[6] becomes particularly significant; in it he undertakes the reconstruction of the genealogy of his family going back six generations to his African ancestor, Kunta Kinte. Margaret Walker's *Jubilee,* Toni Morrison's *The Song of Solomon,* and Paule Marshall's *Praisesong for the Widow* similarly illustrate the interest for the past and, on the level of literary creation, they testify to the importance of memory as the reverse side of a cultural amnesia.

The recovered identity consecrates the reunion with Mother Africa—until then an African unknown—that the writer will recreate and celebrate. What one could stress here are the different pathways followed by the African and the African-American writers in their itinerary of return to the sources. For the African writer, even after contact with a foreign civilization, the Africa that he promotes is also a romantic Africa and, undoubtedly, an idealized one. But it refers to a concrete context, one that can still be found and put in contrast with the writer's representation, even if the traditional elements put in motion have today lost all or some of their significance for the urbanized African. Thus, one could refer to traditional Africa as recreated in such works as *Doguicimi* by Paul Hazoumé, *Le chant du lac* by Olympe Bély-Quénum, *Le crépuscule des temps anciens* by Nazi Boni, *L'enfant noir* and *Le regard du roi* by Camara Laye; one could also refer to the exemplary heroes described by Djibril T. Niane and Seydou Badian: Soundjata and Chaka. If the evocation of the elements of the traditional culture, myths, legends, rituals, and ancient heroes is the fruit of a certain nostalgia in the face of a new world and its demands, then it refers, despite everything, to relatively recent realities that either still exist in one's memory or are made into a reality by a real background—namely, that of childhood—of a village where one could have lived or that one might even be able to find again in ethnological studies.

On the other hand, the Africa of the writers of Harlem Renaissance is an imaginary and imagined Africa. It is more a mythical and legendary representation than a geographical reality. And, generally speaking, both among the major writers of the movement and the minor writers, this Africa offers a mysterious charm, surrounded by a halo of beauty, grandeur, and nobility. It is linked to the sun, the for-

6. Alex Haley, *Roots* (New York: Doubleday, 1976).

est, the moonlight, the sound of the drums and the dance. In his poem, *Heritage*, Countee Cullen evokes the African forest filled with smells of spices, populated with birds and snakes, the pagan gods, the irresistible call to dance in the tropical night, like a frenzied invitation to love. And the Africa to which he aspires remains an exotic mystery for him. And so he asks himself:

What is Africa to me:
Copper sun or scarlet sea,
Jungle star or jungle track,
Strong bronzed men, or regal black
Women from whose loins I sprang
When the birds of Eden sang?

In turn, Langston Hughes, in *African Dance*, celebrates an Africa of deep nights, pierced by the breaking of the sounds of the drum and the noise of the dance. Fascinating and attractive, yet mysterious and far away, Hughes's Africa in *Afro-American Fragment* is:

So long,
So far away
Is Africa
. . . .
Subdued and time-lost
Are the drums—and yet
Through some vast mist of race
There comes this song
I do not understand
This song of atavistic land . . .

B. B. Church, in his poem, *Africa*, glorifies an Africa whose beauty is similar to a sapphire, to an emerald from the ocean and bathing in the moonlight. L. Alexander, in *Enchantment*, recalls the spellbinding magic of Africa and the majesty that it shares with the wild beasts that live there.

Other writers such as Jean Toomer, in *Conversion*, weep desperately over the Africa that is dispossessed, torn away from itself.

It is because they feel alien and exiled that the African-American writers so passionately celebrate Africa: mother, haven of peace, paradise lost. It is because the "American Dream" is not for them that the Black poets of America create for themselves an idyllic Africa, a land of dreams, as balm for their nostalgia as uprooted and rejected ones. With bitter irony, moreover, Langston Hughes writes in his poem *Let America Be America Again*:

(America never was America to me.)
. . . .
(There's never been equality for me,
Nor freedom in this "homeland of the free")

Furthermore, in modern technological and industrialized American society, man has been reduced to a cog, as Claude McKay evokes in *The White City*. How to live from then on?

Thus, then, the theme of a return to Africa becomes clear: Africa becomes the symbol of a haven of peace wherein beauty, love of life, and harmony reign.

And present-day America, where things, animals, and people have lost their vitality, makes the nostalgia for lost Africa even more intense. The image of an inhuman America, loveless, cold as the metal of its skyscrapers, is at the center of the poem, "New York," by Léopold S. Senghor in the collection called *Ethiopiques*. New York is the symbol of America with its "eyes of metal blue" and its "smile of hoar frost," its "artificial hearts"; New York, where there is

Pas un rire d'enfant en fleur . . .
Pas un sein maternel, des jambes de nylon. Des jambes sans
    sueur ni odeur.
(No laughter of children in bloom . . .
no motherly breast, nylon legs. Legs without sweat or smell)

And the Senegalese poet appeals to Africa, source of life and love, to revitalize and regenerate America:

New York! je dis New York, laisse affluer
    le sang noir dans ton sang
Qu'il dérouille tes articulations d'acier,
    comme une huile de vie . . .
(New York! I say New York, let Black blood
    flow into your blood
That it remove the rust from your steel articulations,
    like an oil of life . . .)

It is in this regenerative sense that the Black writers, by contrast, call for a warm, maternal, security-providing Africa. In Claude McKay's novel, *Home to Harlem*, Africa is represented by a cabaret in the heart of Harlem, that bears the significant name of "Cabaret Congo." It is the place where Jack, a Black soldier returning from war, stops a moment in order to be completely permeated by the air of his native country which he has just found again. For him, the "Cabaret Congo" makes the return to the motherland concrete.

It appears, then, that the representation of Africa in the literature of Harlem Renaissance is more the symbol of a lost paradise, the expression of the wish to find it again. Africa thus becomes a mythical place,[7] a dream that replaces the inaccessible "American Dream," a dream that allows an escape from the harsh realities of life in a society in which one is a stranger to others and to oneself.

The perception of Black literature as an American literary production does not mean that it has no links with the other Black literatures, especially with those of the francophone Black world. In the decade following the 1920s, there was among the African-American, Caribbean, and African writers a new common awareness of the racial issue, translated in a protest literature bearing testimony to the political and social contradictions specific to each community: colonization, cultural assimilation, racial segregation. It demonstrates that despite linguistic and geographical differences a racial solidarity and identical situation—Black and oppressed—could momentarily unite all Black people. This is what Jean-Paul Sartre mentions in his famous *Black Orpheus:*

> But, if the oppression is a common one, it is patterned after historical and geographical conditions. The black man is a victim of it, inasmuch as he is black, in his role as colonized native or as a deported African . . .
> . . . He is black. Thus he is held to authenticity. Insulted, enslaved, he redresses himself; he accepts the word "Negro" which is hurled at him as an epithet, and revindicates himself, in pride, as black in the face of white.[8]

If there is an influence that comes from the United States, a relative similarity between the condition of American Blacks and African Blacks, then there are also rather significant peculiarities and differences.

An attentive reading of the works of the Harlem Renaissance reveals a certain ambiguity that is characteristic of this movement. Indeed, those who prepared the Renaissance—A. Locke, W. Du Bois, C. Woodson—and others, wanted both to give back to the Black

---

7. See *Notre Librairie* (November–December 1984) issue on African-American writers and Africa. See Amara Diarra, "L'image de l'Afrique dans la poésie afro-américaine contemporaine," *Notre Librairie* 77 (1984), 75–83; the representation of Africa in contemporary Afro-American poetry is quite similar to that of the Harlem Renaissance.

8. Jean-Paul Sartre, *Black Orpheus,* trans. into English by S. W. Allen (Paris: Présence Africaine, 1954).

man his identity and his dignity and to bury "the former Negro."
The Harlem Renaissance claimed to be a new birth, a revalorization of the Black man, his affirmation as a subject and an autonomous being: a "new Negro." Yet, the image of Harlem (as it comes
across throughout the writings, poems, and novels of the period) is
that of a place of night pleasures, of a change of scenery for souls
in search of "primitivism." It suffices to refer to poems such as
Harlem Dancer by C. McKay, as well as *Minstrel Man, Boogie Dream,*
and *Harlem Night Club* by L. Hughes. As Hughes puts it, Harlem
had become the place "where now the strangers were given the
best ringside tables to sit and stare at the Negro customers—like
amusing animals in the zoo."[9] Harlem "by night" in some way
perpetuates the image and the stereotypes of the Black entertainer:
the blues singer, the dancer, the prostitute. The White clientele that
filled the Harlem cabarets and nightclubs seemed to look for and to
find in these shows enough to satisfy its appetite for "primitivism,"
in the sense it was popularized at that time by Carl Van Vechten
with his novel, *Nigger Heaven*.[10] In this novel, Black life is represented by Harlem: it consists of barbarous rhythms, spellbinding
music, sensuality. And, in Van Vechten's generous intention, the
Black man is at the opposite end of American life dominated by
technology and intellectualism. The Black is nature's child, creature
of instincts and emotions in their pure state, uncorrupted by technical civilization. This exotic vision of the Black as presented by Van
Vechten was violently denounced by some Black intellectuals, such
as W. E. B. Du Bois. However, others—such as James Weldon Johnson
and Wallace Thurman—applauded the publication of Van Vechten's
novel which very quickly became a best-seller. In his autobiography, Hughes recalls with bitterness and pain the circumstances that

9. Langston Hughes, "When the Negro Was in Vogue," in *The Big Sea: An Autobiography* (New York: Thunder's Mouth Press, 1986), 225.
10. One finds in Van Vechten and in Hughes's benefactor the same generosity in
supporting and working for the promotion of Black artists. But despite their generosity
and their conception of a "positive" primitivism, they remained somehow unconsciously and unwillingly caught in the dominant stereotypes of their society. See D.
Lewis, *When Harlem Was in Vogue* (New York: Knopf, 1981), 156–197. For Hughes's
benefactor "she felt that they [the Negros] were America's great link with the primitive, and that they had something very precious to give to the Western world. She felt
that there was mystery and mysticism and spontaneous harmony in their souls, but
that many of them had let the White world pollute and contaminate that mystery
and harmony and make of it something cheap and ugly, commercial and, as she said,
'white' . . . " (*The Big Sea*, 316).

brought him to break up with his White benefactor lady from Park Avenue:

> She wanted me to be primitive and know and feel the intuitions of the primitive. But, unfortunately, I did not feel the rhythms of the primitive surging through me, and so I could not live and write as though I did. I was only an American Negro who had loved the surface of Africa and the rhythms of Africa—but I was not Africa.[11]

Still, the actors who nourish the Harlem shows—despite their laughter, their dances, and their songs of joy—carry deep inside their tragic ambiguity: a suffering hidden behind the social function of entertainer, destined to please the gaze of an audience who has reduced them to the status of the object to be exhibited and stared at.

So is the woman dancer of *The Harlem Dancer* by Claude McKay who shows off her exotic beauty, but whose spirit is elsewhere.

> She sang and danced on gracefully and calm,
> . . . .
> The wine-flushed, bold-eyed boys, and even the girls,
> Devoured her shape with eager, passionate gaze,
> But looking at her falsely-smiling face,
> I knew her self was not in that strange place.

The poignant complaint of *Minstrel Man* by Langston Hughes expresses the same theme of ambiguity:

> Because my mouth
> Is wide with laughter
> And my throat
> Is deep with song
> You do not think
> I suffer after
> I have held my pain
> So long.

These examples echo Paul Lawrence Dunbar's tragic poem, *We Wear the Mask:*

> We wear the mask that grins and lies,
> It hides our cheeks and shades our eyes . . .
> . . . .
> We smile, but, O great Christ, our cries
> To thee from tortured souls arise.

11. Hughes, *The Big Sea*, 325.

A similar ambiguity underlies the representation of Africa simultaneously celebrated and molded in the reducing weight of stereotypes. One can see the evocation of Africa as a literary theme—which might be related to the needs of escaping from industrial America—embodied in the taste of that period for "primitivism" and exoticism.

On the whole, the image of Africa conveyed in the Harlem Renaissance poetry conforms to that of a "primitive" Africa according to classical exoticism: the sun, the jungle, wild animals, the drumbeat, dance, but also beauty, purity, and innocence. It turns out that the African-American writers, despite their desire to celebrate Africa, integrated into their imaginary the clichés and the stereotypes of their society, popularized furthermore by the movies and the comic strips. Speaking of the exotic landscape, Bernard Mouralis writes:

> The writer who resorts to this [exoticism] thereby already indicates what separates him from his original background and this indication very often seems like a true questioning . . . leading to a displacement or a reversal of some values that were current until then.[12]

By turning toward Africa, African-American authors are willing to distance themselves somehow from the dominant American culture. For them, the exoticism and the primitivism of Africa are improvements, not disparagements. They are an answer to the appeal of the sources, a new way in which to perceive and identify with Africa. Traditionally represented by the mainstream as the continent of barbarism and of all that is primitive, Africa was for a long time rejected by the African-American. In the Harlem Renaissance poetry, though, it is an attractive and likeable primitivism that has permitted Africa to preserve the very qualities that industrial America has lost: beauty, harmony of man with nature, spontaneity. It is thus a revalidation of Africa that goes hand in hand with a rehabilitation of the color Black: formerly rejected and despised, from now on accepted and celebrated, as in L. Hughes's poems *My People* and *Me and My Song*. Rather less known today is the poem by Waring Cuney, *No Images*, that sings of the discreet beauty of the Black woman:

> She does not know
> Her beauty,

---

12. Bernard Mouralis, *Les contre-littératures* (Paris: Presses Universitaires de France, 1975), 71 (our translation).

> She thinks her brown body
> Has no glory.
>
> If she could dance
> Naked,
> Under palm trees
> And see her image in the river
> She would know . . .

From a sociohistorical perspective, the Harlem Renaissance remains a striking fact, in spite of its ambiguities. Indeed, it constitutes
the first explicit recognition by Black intellectuals of racial and cultural bonds between Black America and Africa, it is a statement for
the revalidation of Africa and its past.[13] At the same time, the reunion
with Africa offers an answer to the anxious question marks of the
uprooted and the exiled: Who am I?

As represented in the poetry of the Harlem Renaissance, the image
of Africa and that of Harlem by night express the dual reference of
the African-American poet and the complexity of his discourse. Without being in itself ambiguous, this discourse nevertheless reveals the
ambiguous situation of the one who generates it: he is both outside
and inside at the same time. Despite himself, he is sometimes the
Self vis-à-vis Africa (and thus the point of departure of the discourse
and the gaze) and sometimes the Other vis-à-vis the dominant American culture (for which he is the object of the gaze and the discourse).
His glance at the Other, like that of the spectators in the Harlem
nightclubs, represents a vision from the outside that dreads the difference of the Other (even when it is attractive), not for itself but in
reference to its own environment. It is on good grounds that Mouralis
states that

> the exotic discourse can only be developed on the condi-
> tion that the Other not be considered an absolute . . . The
> Other thus has not an autonomous existence since he does
> exist only in terms of our society, our preoccupations or
> our fantasies.[14]

13. The "emigration movement of the XIXth century, with Martin Delany, speaks
of Africa as 'fatherland.' But the link and return to Africa was intended as a missionary
project: to evangelize and regenerate Africa, that is, to take her from her primitiveness." See M. Bergahn, *Images of Africa in Black American Literature* (Totowa: Row-
man and Littlefield, 1977), 42–62.
14. Mouralis, *Les contre-littératures*, 404.

Thus it appears that the discourse or the representation of the Other, whatever its producing center or its point of departure, always emerges from a cultural and historical locus. In the study of Black literatures, this place of emergence cannot be neglected, for it is that which basically establishes the unity, but also the diversity and the originality of the literary creations and experiences from the Black diaspora.

If the Dead Could Only Speak! Reflections on Texts by Niger, Hughes, and Fodeba

Bernadette Cailler

In *Césaire entre deux cultures,* Zadi Zaourou compares texts of the great Bété poet Madou Dibero with Césaire's *Cahier d'un retour au pays natal* and demonstrates that the *Cahier* has retained an African "oral" dimension. According to Zadi, this text suggests that the "African poem" eludes the disorder of the signifier as well as the tyranny of the signified. For example, the phrase *au bout du petit matin* ("at dawn's end") operates simultaneously at the level of symbolic function and at the level of rhythmic and narrative functions.[1] If Zadi's analysis is correct, its implications for the cultural contexts he is considering may be summarized as follows: to study form is to witness the birth of meaning; "poetic" speech, whatever its object (whatever its subject matter), cannot be useless—there is no such thing as mere play with words; these contexts virtually preclude the development of notions of distinct boundaries between the epic (narration that fills "time"), the dramatic (voices, gestures that fill

1. Bernard Zadi Zaourou, *Césaire entre deux cultures: Problèmes théoriques de la littérature négro-africaine d'aujourd'hui* (Dakar and Abidjan: Les Nouvelles Editions Africaines, 1978).

"space"), and the lyric (breathing, cries, songs, attempts to bring movement, in its spatio-temporal dimension, to a halt).

We can trace this tradition in Paul Niger's "Je n'aime pas l'Afrique" and Langston Hughes's "Let America Be America Again"; many other texts by Afro-New World writers—to borrow Dathorne's useful term—would doubtless provide equally convincing evidence.[2] The texture of Keita Fodeba's "Chansons du Dioliba," at first glance quite different, proves closely related to that of the first two poems, as we shall soon see.[3]

In Niger's poem, the recurring syntagma "je n'aime pas l'Afrique" ("I do not like Africa") indicates both the issue at stake and the sequential and rhythmic itinerary to be followed as the poet weaves a meaning-bearing form (*la forme du sens*).[4] The modulations of the syntagma within the narrative framework create at once a geohistorical dimension (in which the Judeo-Christian myth intervenes), a many-voiced drama, and a lyric song of pain through which, in the end, hope emerges. The poet's chosen theme, one individual subject's disaffection vis-à-vis a certain Africa, is at once embodied, carried out, and transformed by the deployment of the text's phonic substance. The title finds its antithesis in the declaration of an Other whose discourse is reported by the first person narrator: "'J'aime ce pays,' disait-il. . . ." ("'I love this country,' he used to say. . . ."). The landscape depicted here is that of a subdued and exposed country, some of whose inhabitants nevertheless stand tall. The speaker announced by the title, whose voice is presumably reporting the first segment of the other's speech, takes the floor again by repeating the basic phrase in a slightly modified form: "Moi, je n'aime pas cette Afrique-là" ("*I* do not love that Africa"). The emphasis on the subject announces a figure of authority, a voice that knows what it is talking about. The definite article of the title that placed Africa in a nebulous zone—an ironic reminder, perhaps, of all the wholesale, stereotyped rejections of the African world—gives way here to the demonstrative *cette . . . là*, a concise way of situating the discursive theme in a particular spatiotemporal context. The anaphora "l'Afrique" serves to

2. Paul Niger, "Je n'aime pas l'Afrique," *Présence Africaine* 3 (1948: 432–40); Langston Hughes, "Let America Be America Again," *Présence Africaine* 59 (1966): 3–5. Oscar R. Dathorne, *Dark Ancestor: The Literature of the Black Man in the Caribbean* (Baton Rouge and London: Louisiana State University Press, 1981).

3. Keita Fodeba, "Chansons du Dioliba," *Présence Africaine* 4 (1948): 595–598.

4. This familiar expression is from Paul Valéry, *Oeuvres* (Paris: Editions Gallimard, 1957), 668.

sum up what the other loves, allowing the principal narrator's statement to be affirmed by negation. The discourse of the negating voice
includes in its own vision of a rejected Africa the vision transmitted
by *other* voices, by a discourse that is *other*. Moreover, the poet's
skillful enumeration, his direct juxtaposition of distinct tableaux,
confers an ambiguous dimension on the statement that closes this
section: "l'Afrique des Paul Morand et des André Demaison" ("the
Africa of men like Paul Morand and André Demaison"). One wonders
to what extent the tableaux evoked may be the products of texts by
these writers.

The transition to the next section, in which God is the principal
actor, is achieved by a repetition of the basic syntagma, without the
now-superfluous emphasis on the "I." God's action is inscribed first
of all in an act of omission, a forgetting (God's plan left Africa out),
then in the "civilizing" enterprise where Church and Society converged, in a massacre whose victims were mostly Africans. The Africans' repeated immolation was intended to pay for the salvation of
the other half of the world; theirs is the race of victims whose blood
is to allow the earth to bear fruit. God's action can thus be said to
grow out of a Word ("in the Beginning was the Word . . . "), in a
dual sense, for the text refers to the Scriptures, but God's voice also
speaks directly: "I'll show them what peace is, their fucking Naza-
rean peace. . . . " The narrator's sacrilegious intent is unmistakable:
God's word is obscene. In counterpoint, we have the marginal figure of
Melanie saying her prayers, an old servant whose consciousness has
been alienated.

The three final sections of the poem develop as follows. In a first
phase, the narrator's voice asserts itself once again in the mode of
refusal and negation, through the anaphoric evocation of "a certain
Africa," in an enumeration framed by the basic proposition. Then the
rejecting voice takes an inquisitorial turn and becomes a conscientious objector: "What will you answer your God on Judgment Day?"
Here an addressee appears for the first time in the text; the narrator
embarks upon a dialogue with a familiar "you," an other whose identity nonetheless remains vague.

Then, once again, the narrator allows God to speak directly, this
time freed from the obscene caricature to which the preceding Word
had reduced Him. The shift from the biblical reference—"What have
you done with your brother?"—to the question "What have you done
with my people?" establishes the suffering and betrayed people as
God's own. Soon the voice of the first-person speaker takes the place

of the questioning and accusing voice of God: it is no longer God who is demanding a response but rather that first-person speaker himself. The anguish conveyed to the reader is finally, unmistakably, that of the text's principal voice. The speaker questions a God who has been his own. This God leaves his questions unanswered, but the speaker rejects His silence. The accuser's reference to "a God yet unknown" implies that there is a divine message yet to be discovered.

The poem's final section gives voice to Africa itself: here is the voice that, once proffered, takes on exclusive authority. This voice is substituted henceforth for the subverted and rejected voice of the speaker "who loves this country," for the voice of the narrator "who does not love that Africa," and for the voice of God who had "forgotten" Africa and then let it *whiten* in the sun.[5] Similarly, we can take the addressee—whose presence is manifest in the imperatives and questions put forth by the voice "that does not love Africa" ("do not answer him . . . ," "listen . . . ," "do you love adventure . . . ")—as a condensation of all those to whom this poem might have been, or might yet be, addressed. This addressee is finally called "friend," a term that emblematizes the dream of reconciliation elaborated toward the end of the poem. The shift from the singular and familiar *tu* to the plural and/or formal *vous* unmistakably evokes the growing multitudes to be incorporated into the community that is awaited but not yet achieved.

In this poem, an appeal to the discourse of Africa is made in at least three ways: first, through the text's form, where meaning is elaborated on the basis of a rhythmic structure organized around, or with, or against, a basic proposition; second, through the technique of the voice that constructs, deconstructs, and reconstructs the "real"; and finally through the "initiation" to that inexpressible "something" borne by Africa, an awakening promised to our "questing souls." The poem's final section evokes dance and could easily be recited by dancers. Its closing words offer an optimistic vision of a fertile continent on the move.

Langston Hughes's poem also presents its basic proposition in its title: "Let America Be America Again." It is clear at once that Hughes's approach is in some sense the inverse of Niger's. The title suggests that America *was* America once upon a time, that there was once an America one could love. The antithesis of this assertion is not long in coming. Corresponding to the first poem's modulations

---

5. Here I am paraphrasing a passage from the poem.

on its basic proposition, here we have a repeated negative statement: "America never was America to me." This declaration and his variants are set in parentheses at three different points; this fact raises a question as to the speaker's identity. It may be that the reader is witness to the conflict of a consciousness that is on the one hand echoing the popular invocation of all those nostalgic voices that "remember" better times, and on the other hand resisting the seduction of the collective tendency out of a private feeling that, here, "again" has no meaning whatsoever.

The only lines in the text not set in italics are the following: "Say who are you that mumbles in the dark? And who are you who draws your veil across the stars?" As a result, the reader may well see in lines like "Let America Be America Again" less a song of liberation than the sign of the obsessive presence of an insidious discourse (the installation of an invading ideology) that the first-person speaker's alter ego is trying, in flashes of lucidity, to eradicate—the same alter ego that is bracketed in the "official" discourse and is attempting, in a new awareness, to bring a new discourse to light. In this reading, lines like "America never was America to me" would be opposed to everything that follows the two lines quoted above: "Say who are you. . . . "

This second section proceeds from the starting point of the anaphora "I am" and culminates in the assertion: "I am the people. . . . " Just as in Niger's poem the discourse that follows has to be that of "Africa," in Hughes's text the discourse that is already succeeding in having its say in the poem—starting from vague murmurs uttered in the dark and going beyond then—is the discourse of all: the perpetually hungry multitude. The conjunction of the singular "I" with the ambiguous plural "people" (achieved by the copula "am") confers on this new "I"-narrator an unmistakable collective dimension that is undoubtedly necessary for the expression of a tragedy that persists on a massive scale: " . . . The millions on relief today! . . . /The millions who have nothing for our pay?" Even as the reader grasps the paradox of the following lines where "again" and "never" appear in opposition—"O let America be America again—/ The land that never has been yet"—the full meaning of the paradox is deferred: on the one hand we have the declaration of "the land that's mine—the poor man's, Indian's, Negro's, ME—/ Who made America . . . ," and on the other hand the resolution "We must take back our land again." The irony in these two lines finally takes on its full force: the idea of a land that does not belong to those who work it flies in the face of

common sense. Even more strikingly, the appearance of the metaphor—"The land that's . . . ME" (not only does the land belong to me,
it is of one substance with myself)—describes a milieu in which
workers' oneness with their landscape, as well as their mutual responsibility for each other, is crucially important. The resolution
offered by the rebel voice in the concluding stanza espouses the fundamental terms, the very leitmotif, of American democracy: "We, the
people . . . " A terrible lesson for one and all: let's take ourselves at
our word, and the American dream will come to be.

In Hughes's text, we may see a symbolic appeal to a Word (*Parole*)
belonging to America = land = people, comparable to Niger's appeal to
the word of Africa = land = people; and in Hughes's case, too, several
factors contribute to this elaboration of an appeal to the word of the
people: a specific rhythmic structure that is almost incantatory; the
use of an introspective voice that turns outward and becomes demanding (on its own behalf and for others); and the ultimate vision of
a redemption, a rite of passage toward a new "we." And once again
the reader is witness to the fusion of a narrated history, a drama en-
acted by clandestinely collective voices, a lyric song rooted in pain
that endures as homage to the strength of the living.

The third work we shall consider is Keita Fodeba's "Chansons du
Dioliba" ("Songs of the Dioliba"), which takes its title from the Ma-
linké name for the Niger river. In terms of surface form, this text
appears quite different from the two we have been examining; however, its underlying thrust is the same, as the reader quickly discovers. Thus (for example) its lyric, dramatic, and narrative modes are
not compartmentalized as distinct "genres" but rather are united in
the poem's vocal and musical (and even gestural) expression. Moreover, the human need for an alliance with the earth and its waters
asserts itself here as knowledge, wisdom, and promise of life. The
poet's technique demands a particular effort of imagination on the
reader's part; indeed, the text printed on the page is no more than a
pale reflection of the piece in its "African" production. First of all, the
text is intended to be sung, to undergird "song." (In Africa, it would
seem, there are no strict dividing lines between what is said, recited
to music, and sung.)[6] Second, the backdrop for the production of these
songs ought to be a village square, according to the author's own in-

6. See Paul Zumthor, *Introduction à la poésie orale* (Paris: Editions du Seuil, 1983),
chap. 10. In presenting his text, Fodeba mentions the use of a *guitar*. There is no doubt
that he had a *kora* in mind and that he is courteously addressing himself to readers
who may be uninformed about African stringed instruments.

structions: " . . . the public square of a village, with its tree under
which people gather to talk, its water jars, its old men lying on
mats in the shade, its starving dogs . . . " Finally, each lyric segment, linked to the next by a kora, is directly addressed to the river
Dioliba, which becomes the fount of speech itself. In this respect,
Fodeba's poem seems to go a step beyond the two others we have
considered. For Niger and Hughes, the people = land is made to *speak*
so as (once again) to *be*. For Fodeba, the fecundating existence of the
earth or the river is in no way displaced or bracketed; no explicitly
didactic strategy intervenes. The earth—past, present, and future—
is the origin and mistress of all speech and all life. Here the poet
leaps (and the leap is lyrical, to be sure, but not imaginary in a fan-
tasmatic sense) right over the periods of colonization, oppression,
denaturing, drought, and sterility. These grueling negative realities
are not merely marginalized by the singing voice; they do not even
pass the singer's lips (except for one brief reference near the end to the
treaty of Kignébacoro between the whites and the Almany Samory,
and one allusion to the Senegalese Sharpshooters [*Tirailleurs Séné-
galais*].) The unmistakable ironic dimension of the poet's stance cannot be dismissed; in any event, here we have a resounding act of faith
in the African land. From one song to another, praise for the river
Dioliba bursts forth as if it were arising from all segments of the
population: farmers, children, fishermen, hunters, canoe paddlers,
and all the rest.

Moreover, the lessons taught by the river provide a wealth of information concerning the maintenance of life and harmony among
human beings. Water belonging to one group may also belong to another: "Without any distinction whatsoever, you have been able to
satisfy all the regions of Manding." At the same time, the rational use
of local resources and the need for irrigation are evoked a number of
times in the simple and direct language so characteristic of Fodeba, a
language whose resonances always suggest potential actions. Let us
take the following passage, for example:

If Kankan has a monopoly on rice-growing,
Credit is due your generous brother the Milo.

Or this one:

The Menien region, which has suffered so badly from
drought in the past, is regaining its freshness today because
you have consented to send it the turbulent but inoffensive
stream Koba.

The song's primary role is to praise, yet from beginning to end it also provides useful knowledge for daily life. Fodeba's singer ultimately reminds us that no one knows the people's history better than the river Dioliba. It has witnessed countless moments of African history; it has played a role in battles and treaties; it has even marked off frontiers. The Dioliba knows. We must address ourselves to the Dioliba if we are to learn.

The closing song proposes a productive international sharing of the waters in a spirit of disinterested mutual aid, which is the only kind of aid that has absolute meaning ("le seul qui, absolument, signifie"). The appeal grows out of a lesson learned by contemplation, by the cultivation (as one cultivates the earth and as one cultivates relationships) of the native landscape: by its very nature, water flows and nourishes. Poetic speech has the same nature: the pen name chosen by the Guadaloupean poet Albert Béville (Paul Niger) seems to symbolize the powerful link that exists among these three texts in their various potential significations. One of them reminds us that the river of poetry maintains intimate, inextricable, and wholly compromising relations among living people, upstream and down: relations of life and death. The Martiniquan writer Edouard Glissant put it particularly well in an essay devoted to his friend Paul Niger:

> The signification (the "history") of the land, or of Nature, is the revealed clarity of the process through which a community cut off from its ties or its roots . . . begins little by little to *suffer* the land, to deserve its Nature, to know its country. The search for meaning brings this clarity to consciousness. The ardent struggle toward the earth is a struggle within history.[7]

Are these words from the dead? In the second part of this essay I shall attempt to assess the actual or potential presence of these three texts in two different settings: the academy (particularly in the United States) and Présence Africaine (both the publishing house and the journal, with reference to how it might—and perhaps should—research and act in the future, particularly in the context of formal education). This subject deserves a whole book of its own; I can only sketch in some broad outlines here.

In the first place, our three texts need to be situated in the historical and social context of the period in which they were published in

---

7. Edouard Glissant, "En souvenir du fleuve Niger," *L'intention poétique* (Paris: Editions du Seuil 1969), 196.

Présence Africaine. Niger's text and Fodeba's both appeared in 1948, only a short time after *Présence Africaine* was founded. Langston Hughes's poem, published in that journal in 1966, had appeared in the United States much earlier; Hughes was the first author chosen by the *International Workers Order* for its newly established literary series in 1938. This was a time when American labor groups were attempting to break into the arena of "culture," a period strongly marked by the recent Depression and by foreshadowings of the Second World War.[8] This was also a time (as we hardly need to stress) when Parisian—especially Afro-Parisian—circles were taking an intense interest in the artistic productions of Black Americans. By the time the other two texts appeared after the war, independence movements in Africa were under way but had a long way to go. The Antilles region was undergoing "departmentalization," a state of "overly successful colonization" (to paraphrase Glissant's ironic language): the Antilleans found themselves with a "cord" around their necks, a stronger version of the "cord" that had linked these regions to France in 1635.[9] The position of Antillean intellectuals could hardly have been more ambiguous. Niger, an administrator with credentials from the Ecole Nationale de la France d'Outre-Mer, for example, went off to "serve" in Africa; at the same time he was a cofounder of the Antillo-Guyanese front[10] and an ardent proponent of autonomy. A member of the Executive Committee of the African Cultural Society, Niger had participated as early as 1942 in the "terrible, painful years during which Présence Africaine was being born."[11] As for Fodeba (who was director of the Guinean ballet before becoming Minister of the Interior under Sékou Touré), we know that he was destined to disappear in the tumult. There is a sad irony in the chapter of Frantz Fanon's book that takes a passage from Sékou Touré as its epigraph, a

---

8. Langston Hughes, *A New Song* (New York: International Workers Order, 1938). See Michael Gold's introduction to this volume: "It is altogether fitting that the International Workers Order, a fraternal society serving the American people of all races and nationalities, should have chosen this poet as its first author in a series of literary pamphlets for the people . . . American labor has at last entered the field of culture, so long deemed the private property of the upper classes. In New York, several trade union theatres are teaching new lessons to jaded and cynical Broadway. In Detroit, the auto workers union has published a novel by Upton Sinclair in an enormous edition."

9. Edouard Gillant, *Malemort* (Paris: Editions du Seuil, 1975), 190.

10. The Front was dissolved by General de Gaulle's decree in July 1961.

11. See the note of homage published by Présence Africaine in its journal when the poet's death was announced, following an article by Césaire entitled "Deuil aux Antilles," *Présence Africaine* 42 (1962): 221.

chapter in which Fanon demonstrates the value of a well-known poem by Fodeba in the context of the national culture.[12] To be sure, it is to the credit of Présence Africaine that it has counted writers of this stripe among its collaborators, writers as prolific in action as in words, remarkable representatives of a multilingual diaspora presented by so many now-vanished voices in the pages of the journal.

And if the dead do speak? Who hears them? And if these dead—Niger, Hughes, Fodeba—could speak today, what else would they say? Would they speak differently? As teachers, we are accustomed to trying to help our students understand that the "universal" value of a writer's themes means that his texts often remain accessible and valid even if their forms are "outmoded." Hence a series of questions. Can we find in these dead writers' texts some element, form, or theme that will not necessarily require of us the overwhelming task of initiating our students? What do our students know of African and Afro-American histories; of the relationships of all these diverse peoples with the West; of their cultures, religions, languages, living conditions; their political, economic, and other problems? What has been the use, and to whom, of the somewhat marginal courses we have added to the curriculum, courses that are rarely required for anyone's diploma? Then, too, we need to consider the forms in which the meanings of these texts are elaborated: are they "outdated" not only for a reader of French or English but for any student of literature? As for the themes (meanings) of these texts, are they "interesting" because they are universal, or are they sadly still crucial in today's African and Afro-American contexts? Without much exaggeration at all, I can assert that I myself, an assiduous reader, remain the greatest beneficiary of the long hours of work spent preparing and presenting my classes. The African presence has truly nourished and educated me. It remains largely foreign to my students' milieu. Indeed, in today's environment, it has become exceedingly difficult to convey the idea that the patient study of texts is a precious investment under any circumstances. And yet, as teachers, what are we doing to resist or change this environment? What strategies are we using to reintroduce important texts—and the notion of the importance of texts? At the same time, the core of French studies (the study of France) has retained importance with respect to the nebulous Francophonic mass, and this fact has led to one very

12. Frantz Fanon, "Sur la culture nationale," *Les damnés de la terre* (Paris: F. Maspéro, 1968), 141–165. The reference is to the poem entitled "Aube africaine."

simple observation: the African presence is dismissed. The fact that our libraries have all the back issues of *Présence Africaine* on their shelves is irrelevant. What is worse, in courses on contemporary French culture or courses in French civilization that have a "historical perspective," France's overseas relations—its past and present political and cultural ties—are most often presented too rapidly or, worse, prejudicially; it seems safe to state that such basic questions are left largely untouched by too many course instructors. As for courses on "Francophone cultures," unless they can convey a sense of the history of the problematics of the subject, their intellectual and human value is likely to be minimal.

I am led to make a harsh observation that I shall not attempt to soften: in my own academic context—which is doubtless above average with respect to research facilities for students as well as in the caliber of its student body—the discourse of the writers of Présence Africaine has hardly begun to be born. Here I must be schematic. If the African "humanities" suffer from the precariousness afflicting literary and artistic studies in general today, they suffer even more seriously from a cultural prejudice that is endemic in the university setting. The number of inane remarks that can be overheard in the ivory tower could fill a number of books; the first steps toward even a minimal understanding of African cultures have yet to be taken. There is one source of comfort for those of us who are often marginalized: if, in an ironic historical twist, Africans today are much better informed about Europe and the West in general than are the vast majority of Westerners about Africa, then those Western teachers and students who do take an interest in Africa are well on their way to acquiring a solid education. Believing as I do that if we are to change entrenched ways of thinking, then we have to change basic structures, I should like to see all French departments require truly interdisciplinary courses, parts of which would focus directly on the French "invention" of Africa. I should also like to require all French majors to pass an exit examination that would include substantial material on the history and civilizations of "Francophone" groups and nations. The best way to avoid decentering France is, of course, to maintain the largely unquestioned dichotomy between "French" and "Francophone"; we all know twentieth-century specialists who have never read a line of Césaire, Kateb, or Tchicaya U Tam'si.

And if the dead could talk? What else would they say, and how? I am firmly convinced that the little-known texts published by Présence Africaine are useful and necessary. But the question needs to be

considered on another level as well, that of the relation of these texts
to certain contemporary political, economic, and cultural situations,
and to various linguistic, aesthetic, and critical questions that ought
to engage the attention of many intellectuals today, especially those
who are concerned about the future of Présence Africaine.

As we have seen, the three texts examined in the first part of this
study constitute an appeal to the discourse of Africa/America =
people = land on several levels. These texts well might serve as the
starting point and reference point for an interdisciplinary course covering three major topics: (1) a study of the tortuous and supremely
ambiguous paths along which a discourse about Africa has been
elaborated by non-Africans but also by Africans and (to borrow Jahn's
often-criticized but still useful expression) by neo-Africans, a study
that would obviously include an investigation of relationships to imported religions; (2) a study of the relationships between on one hand
"development" and on the other hand popular action (discourse) or
the absence thereof; (3) a study of the relationship of these texts to
the languages of a present and future aesthetics. This multidimen-
sional work should ultimately lead scholars to reflect on the conditions under which African "subjects" can have their say, in diverse
settings and circumstances. This last topic for reflection might well
suggest new directions for the future work of Présence Africaine.

Four texts in particular strike me as useful background material for
such a project: V. Y. Mudimbe's *The Invention of Africa: Gnosis, Philosophy, and the Order of knowledge; Achille Mbembe's Afriques
indociles: Christianisme, pouvoir et état en société post-coloniale;
Food in Sub-Saharan Africa.* ed. Art Hansen and Della E. McMillan;
and Edouard Glissant's *Le discours antillais.*[13] A careful study of
these four works suggests a number of important observations.

13. V. Y. Mudimbe, *The Invention of Africa: Gnosis, Philosophy, and the Order of
Knowledge* (Bloomington and Indianapolis: Indiana University Press, 1988). Achille
Mbembe, *Afriques indociles: Christianisme, pouvoir et état en société post-coloniale*
(Paris: Editions Karthala, 1988), and *Food in Sub-Saharan Africa*, ed. Art Hansen and
Della E. McMillan (Boulder, Colo: Lynne Rienner Publishers, 1986); Edouard Glissant,
Le discours antillais (Paris: Editions du Seuil, 1981); *National Data Book and Guide
to Sources: Statistical Abstract of the United States, 1988,* U.S. Department of Com-
merce, Bureau of the Census, 1988 (Washington, D.C., 1987). I would add the issue of
Le Monde Diplomatique of 22 May 1988 that includes an article by Pierre Dom-
mergues, "La fin du rêve américain?" and bibliographical notes. The annual *Statistical
Abstract of the United States*, published by the U.S. Bureau of the Census, is invaluable for making observations and comparisons on social and economic topics.

Any simplistic dichotomy between the colonial and post-colonial periods or between "tradition" and "modernity" can only have negative consequences for the future in the African and Antillean contexts. (2) The capacity of the Christian and Muslim religions to function in such a way as to promote the public welfare must be called into question. (3) A large number of post-colonial societies are (as Mbembe puts it) discipline-based societies in which ideological and physical control has had—and continues to have—a devastating effect on the well-being of their citizens. (4) A considerable number of citizens of these societies make their escape, either by going into exile, by rejecting any responsibility for the prevailing conditions (the Pontius Pilate position), by developing cynical coping mechanisms, or by finding *symbolic* creative outlets (this symbolic creativity has positive as well as negative aspects; Mbembe speaks of a historical capacity for indocility, while Glissant discusses creolizing manipulations). (5) Whatever natural catastrophes and problems of climate they face, whatever problems they have inherited from the system of colonial exploitation, the greatest difficulties encountered by the majority of Africans today in the areas of food and living conditions are above all related to political questions; while the principal victims remain food-growers and women (women being often involved in agricultural production), these groups are rarely consulted (see especially Asante, Lemarchand, and Spring in *Food in Sub-Saharan Africa*), no matter what governmental ideology prevails (see Lemarchand).

Let me observe briefly here, too, that while Glissant's analyses of the current Antillean situation corroborate those Béville (Paul Niger) published in an article in *Présence Africaine* in 1960[14]—Glissant's prognosis for Antillean well-being in the framework of departmentalization being decidedly unoptimistic—the hopes Béville expressed for Africa in the same article have fallen far short of realization. As for the situation of Afro-Americans in the United States, recent studies show stagnation, if not lost ground, with respect to the progress that had been hoped for.

Mudimbe's excellent synthesis allows us to link that set of reflections on the avatars of African discourse both to the broadened sense that implies a close dialectic between speech and action, and also to the consciousness that no discourse can completely rid itself of con-

14. Albert Béville (Paul Niger), "Problèmes des pays sous-développés, *Présence Africaine* 32–33 (June-September 1960).

straining structures, even if the speaker intends to challenge these
structures—no matter how powerful the challenge. In the perspective
of an aesthetics to come (producers and consumers of discourse alike
are implicated here), the remarks Mudimbe borrows from Verhaegen—
who was echoing Gutierrez in turn—seem to me to strike home. In
the following text, I propose that we read the word "aesthetic" instead of (or rather in addition to) the word "theology":

> Three characteristics will mark the new African theology:
> it will be *contextual*, in other words, stemming from the
> life and culture of African people; it will be a theology of
> *liberation* because the oppression is not to be found only
> in cultural oppression but also in the political and eco-
> nomic structures; it should recognize the place of *women*
> as a vital part of the struggle for liberation and the struggle
> against all forms of sexism in the society and in the
> church.[15]

The African aesthetic will be contextual, liberating, and resolutely
feminist. Recalling the three texts we examined at the beginning of
this study, the reader will undoubtedly be capable of appreciating the
"modernity" of these texts, at least in certain respects. Their value
seems to me to go well beyond the interest one may take in African
and neo-African cultures. They offer the opportunity—within the
context of an interdisciplinary course—to discuss the place of such
texts in a curriculum of comparative literature where, among others,
the problem of genre would have to be confronted, along with the
problem of the relation of oral production to writing and the relation
of literature to life (see the opening paragraphs of this chapter). It may
be that the texts we have been considering will prove to be still more
"modern" than they first appear. The creative dispersal that has led
in the West to what Glissant calls the crumbling of the bad faith that
lies behind denials that, on one hand, all great literature leads the
reader to reflect on political and social questions while, on the other
hand, any rigorously textual analysis can only be *contextual*, the false
problematics in which the relations between "creator" and "critic"
are discussed—all these questions could be reexamined in the light
of texts such as Niger's, Hughes's, and Fodeba's. Such texts may also
lead readers to reflect on the crisis currently being experienced by

15. B. Verhaegen, "Religion et politique en Afrique noire," *Religions Africaines et Christianisme* 1 (1979): 179–194 (Kinshasa: Faculté de Théologie Catholique). Mudimbe quotes from 179.

civilizations based on the "book": civilizations of the *Book* (the Bible, the Koran), civilizations of the *Father* (conqueror/male/author), civilizations of *writing/reading*. Our texts could even open the way to a discussion of the much debated *subject* who, though he or she may not be able to control "meaning," cannot wash their hands of it: who speaks and who sees, in what language, for whom, why, and how? Who suffers, who dies, and who shall live? In addition, these texts should make it clear that from now on all work with literature needs to be undertaken from the perspective of comparative culture, even within a single language. However, it should be noted that (aside from some allusions on Niger's part to the oppression of woman in the colonial context) woman's presence, her tragedy, her rebellions, her *endurance*, are not evoked in the three texts in question; their liberating dimension is correspondingly reduced.

Présence Africaine might go still further, it seems to me, in this triple struggle for a contextual, liberating, and feminist aesthetic, an aesthetic not so much cut off from those that reigned in the past in the colonial and postcolonial contexts (or, in the United States, in the period when the struggle for civil rights had not yet been won), as it is an aesthetic that has to be elaborated within a network of complex, shifting relationships, a network that scholars will increasingly have to investigate from all angles. Let us repeat that this aesthetic cannot make a useful contribution to future civilizations without a decoding, a welcoming, an organic integration to the whole, of *marginal* discourses—discourses that have appeared marginal because they have been largely ignored, but that belong in fact to the majority. These discourses are often couched in languages unknown to most readers of *Présence Africaine:* languages that belong to tellers of tales, village poets and musicians, but also to farmers, artisans, fishermen, clerks, shopowners, workers, to the physically handicapped and the mentally ill, to the unemployed, to beggars, solitary thinkers, dissident visionaries, to women, literate or not. There is no doubt that the role of African intellectuals is of primary importance in this promotion of marginal discourse, for in the vast majority of cases they alone hold the key to the languages, the sensibilities, the *forms*—in all senses of the term. A discourse by African "subjects" cannot help but follow that route henceforth, establishing its own legitimacy and impact. I am thus suggesting that those who dare to say "I" in the future will have found the means—and the courage which from our protected vantage point can only be admired—to draw aggressively on all the betrayed, humiliated, knowing voices constituting "us."[16] I am thinking, too, of another sort of task, more directly tied to intercontinental university research. It would be useful to have access, in the future, to dossiers bringing us up to date on questions such as (1) the state of language and literature studies (African and other) in schools and universities (in Africa and elsewhere); (2) the state of scientific research in Africa, in diverse areas such as physics, mathematics, biology, sociology, medicine, musicology, and so on. In my own area, literary studies, I confess (for example) that I know nothing about African criticism of non-African literatures. Even where African and Afro-American literatures are concerned, I have relatively little information about insights and trends among African scholars.

A great Congolese poet and collaborator of *Présence Africaine*, who died in 1988, left us powerful and moving words that remain charged with suffering and with experience:

> False suffixes on the roots of my tree
> Give me a bitter ending[17]

Let us imagine that in its future flowerings Tchicaya U Tam'si's tree will no longer have to worry about the authenticity of its suffixes. Let us imagine a time when the root problem will have given way to problems—endless, and largely unexplored—of communication: a vast space, as Glissant might say, of the "poetics of relation."

---

16. Here I am thinking of the last sentence of the short essay Glissant devoted to Niger's work, cited above: "A ceux qui n'ont pas eu de voix eu dont *nous ne saurions être la voix: pour ce que nous ne sommes que partie de leurs voix*" (*L'intention poétique*, 195–197). I have long believed that here Glissant is making an ironic and no doubt subversive allusion to Césaire's well-known statement: "[M]y mouth will be the mouthpiece for the misfortunes that have no mouth."

17. Tchicaya U Tam'si, *Epitomé*, in *Epitomé: Arc Musical* (Honfleur: Oswald, 1970), 41.

In Praise of Alienation twelve

Abiola Irele

The starting point of any consideration
of our perception of Europe and the
civilization we associate with that continent is the observed fact that it is
marked by a profound ambivalence.
This is a quality of emotional response
that we share with other peoples who
have experienced European conquest;
in other words, it is a function of our
historical experience. As we keep being reminded by our writers and our
historians, notably by Chinweizu in
his book, *The West and the Rest of
Us*,[1] the circumstances of African encounter with Europe were especially
brutal. The British Empire was not acquired in a fit of absent-mindedness,
nor lost in a similar attitude of noncha-
lance; much less the French. Modern
imperialism was an act of calculated
aggression; as far as we in this part of
the world are concerned, Obara Ikime
has documented for us, in his book *The
Fall of Nigeria*,[2] the violent process by
which the British colonizer, and especially Lord Lugard (of venerated memory at Chatham House) subjugated the
peoples and societies of the territory
that now make up our modern State.

More generally still, in our historical
relationship with Europe, the master-
slave relationship was exemplified in a
very real sense, with not merely a meta-

1. Chinweizu, *The West and the Rest of Us*
(London and Lagos: Nok Publishers, 1978).
2. Obaro Ikime, *The Fall of Nigeria* (London:
Heinemann Educational Books, 1977).

phorical but a literal significance. We played Caliban to the White man's Prospero, Man Friday to his Robinson Crusoe, as part of a historical drama of slavery, colonialism, and racism.

The consequences of this experience have been unsettling for us in all kinds of ways. The incursion of Europe disrupted traditional societies all over Africa, and in some cases this disruption was so severe as to have turned the drama of colonialism into pure tragedy. Such was the case especially in Central Africa, where the French and the Belgians, particularly those who worked for King Leopold in his Congo Free State—a name that reflects his bizarre sense of irony—wrought such devastation as to have turned the stomach of decent humanity everywhere. These facts require to be recalled, for our resentments carried over from a phase of history from which most of us have only just emerged, and into which a substantial section of the race is still locked in Southern Africa even now; these resentments remain with us extremely vivid.

At the same time, we are conscious of the irreversible nature of the transformations the impact of Europe has effected in our midst and which are so extensive as to define the really significant frame of reference of our contemporary existence. The traditional precolonial culture and way of life continue to exist as a reality among us, but they constitute an order of existence that is engaged in a forced march, in a direction dictated by the requirements of a modern scientific and technological civilization. It also happens to be the case that Western civilization, at least in its contemporary manifestations and circumstance, provides the paradigm of modernity to which we aspire. Hence our mixed feelings, the troubled sense of acceptance and rejection, of a subjective disposition that is undermined by the objective facts of our life. There is something of a paradox here, for the intensity of the ambivalence we demonstrate in our response to Europe and Western civilization is in fact a measure of our emotional tribute; it is expressive, in a profound way, of the cultural hold Europe has secured upon us—of the alienation it has imposed upon us as a historical fate.

The association in our minds of Western civilization with the historical fact of colonial domination and the real discomforts of social and cultural change give to this alienation a wholly negative significance in our eyes. All our modern expression in literature and ideology has developed from a primary concern with the pathology of alienation as inscribed in our experience as a colonized people. It isn't so much the fact that our modern literature has explored the theme of culture conflict that strikes one now as that it has determined a fixation upon this pathology of alienation, and thus conditioned our emotional and intellectual reflexes to the whole subject of our relationship to Europe and Western civilization.

The classic representation of the pathology of alienation is that offered by Cheik Hamidou Kane's novel *L'aventure ambigüe* (Ambiguous adventure). The title of the novel is more than eloquent. The hero, Samba Diallo, is the archetype of the divided consciousness, of the African who suffers in his mind the effects of cultural dispossession. His agony is that of his dual nature, marked by a cleavage rather than an integration of its two frames of reference. As he says in the novel, and I quote:

> I am not a distinct country of the Diallobe facing a distinct occident, and appreciating with a cool head what I must take from it and what I must leave with it by way of a counterbalance. I have become the two. There is not a clear mind deciding between two factors of a choice. There is a strange nature, in distress over not being two.

The very expansion of his vision upon the world becomes for him his dilemma, his existential plight. He is no longer able to relate to the world because that world is no longer coherent, no longer offers him a stable and compact order of values. His suicide at the end of the novel is thus a logical outcome of his spiritual tragedy. But it is significant that Cheik Hamidou Kane contrives an ending in which Samba Diallo's struggle with the concrete world of experience finds a resolution—he is finally integrated into the cosmos, that is, nothingness. For presented in the way in which the novelist has presented the drama of alienation, the choice is, indeed, between being and nothingness in the very perspective of Jean-Paul Sartre's brand of existentialism: between an affirmative being in the world, which confronts all its problems in order to wrest a meaning out of its contingencies, and a withdrawal into meaningless void.

The theme of alienation as an existential predicament runs through all our literature inspired by the colonial experience, in one form or the other. The self-dramatization of Senghor's poetry lends it a pathos and a grandeur with which we are also able to identify, because we accept it as not merely an individual poetic experience but as a transposition into the language of image and symbol of a felt personal experience, which is also representative—as an authentic statement of a general condition. But the writer who seems, in fact, to have engaged our responses most forcefully upon the problem of alienation is Chinua Achebe, especially in his masterpiece, *Arrow of God*, whose impact derives from the writer's profound sense of tragic irony. His quite unsentimental approach to a common theme lends it an uncommon significance and gives it a universal application. For Achebe, history in its broad movement is simply not of man's making; the most we can do is accommodate ourselves to its turns and changes and strive to keep up, as best we can, with its caprices; the image of the mask dancing which requires that we change our positions so as to capture its progress seems to me to summarize his vision. However, Achebe's vision does not deny human freedom, it only acknowledges that this freedom is limited, but that within the narrow confines of its possibilities is infinitely precious. From Joseph Conrad, whom he was later to turn against, largely I believe out of a misunderstanding, Achebe learnt the lessons of a humane pessimism.[3]

When we consider our modern literature in its development, in its themes and preoccupations, and in its orientation, the striking fact is that it offers an image of our experience as one not only of cultural and spiritual disorientation but of moral decline, a situation that is presented as the aftermath of our contact with the West. Implicit in this image is an idea of the past and of our traditional culture as a universe of pure coherence. In Camara Laye's *L'enfant noir* and *Le regard du roi—The African Child* and *Radiance of the King* in the English translations—it is this idea that explicitly commands the narrative structure, point of view, symbolism and the whole tone of both the autobiography and the fiction. In greater or lesser measure, our writers are constantly tempted by, and yielding to, this romanticism; it is not even altogether absent from Achebe's novels, despite his incomparable sense of sobriety. What runs through all this literature is the feeling that it is within our traditional culture that we are happiest, most at ease with ourselves, that there is the truest coincidence between us and the world: in other words, that our identity is located.

The whole movement of modern African thought has been to define this identity. The intellectual reaction to our humiliation under

3. This underlying quality of Achebe's vision is well in evidence in his latest novel, *Anthills of the Savannah,* and his second collection of essays, *Hopes and Impediments,* both published by Heinemann, in London, in 1987. Achebe's reaction against Conrad is contained in the essay "An Image of Africa," included in the latter volume. (1–13).

the colonial system and to our devaluation by its justifying ideology has consisted in affirming our difference from the white man, the European. This conscious effort of differentiation has produced the well-known ideologies of "African personality" and négritude. In Senghor's formulation of the latter, the idea of African identity takes the form of an irreducible essence of the race whose objective correlative is the traditional culture and world concept. This essence is held to confer an inestimable value upon our past and to justify our claim to a separate existence. The whole movement of mind in Black cultural nationalism, from Blyden to Senghor, leads to a mystique of traditional forms of life, whether or not allowance is made for their interaction with European forms of cultural expression. And it is a mystique that continues to exercise a special force upon our minds and sensibility.

I have lived for a good part of my professional life with these ideas, and in presenting them on both sides of the language wall that divides the intellectual world in Africa I have shown considerable sympathy for them. In reality, what I have tried to do, in what I considered to be my privileged position, was to bring together the two streams of our intellectual history so that we begin to see it as a whole. You cannot do that kind of work without striking a relation of sympathy with the ideas of such powerful minds as Blyden and Senghor. Besides, the concept of African personality and its more elaborate variant of négritude represented a genuine attempt to think through the tensions of an especially difficult historical experience to some form of balance. There is no question, therefore, that they were both necessary and valuable. Blyden and Senghor thus deserve an eminent place in the intellectual history of Africa, as indeed of the Black race as a whole.

That said, it is impossible today not to recognize that the concepts they have provided us with have some serious shortcomings, and the feelings they have diffused make for some serious confusions. It is not only in the particulars of their formulation that they can be faulted but in their fundamental presuppositions, and ultimately in the general propositions they hold out for African development.

It is not possible for me here to undertake a detailed critique of the various theories of Africanism that have been propounded; in the case of Senghor's négritude, it is not even necessary for me to do so. The objections to négritude have been advanced by several writers: in the Francophone world, by Franklin, Cheikh Anta Diop, Adotevi, Fanon, and more recently as a part of the debate on African philosophy, by

Marcien Towa and Paulin Hountondji.[4] I have given an account of the
views of these critics of négritude in several articles.[5] On the Anglophone side, we are familiar with the attacks of Mphahlele in *The
African Image*[6] and of Soyinka in *Myth, Literature and the African
World.*[7] You will also find a penetrating critical assessment of négritude in Kwasi Wiredu's *Philosophy and an African Culture.*[8] It is not
always that I find I can accept the terms of the critique of négritude
presented by these gentlemen, and I am especially aware that in the
Anglophone world the views of Senghor have been simplified and perhaps misunderstood; there is a complexity to his formulations which
is often missed. Nonetheless, these are important objections which
have kept alive a necessary debate among us concerning our entire
structure of life and experience, and our destiny in the modern world.
   It is precisely in this spirit that I want to add my voice to this debate, and to develop the critique of cultural nationalism in relation to
the specific problem of our present alienation. And the first point
concerns its refusal of history. I am not sure myself that this is a
correct evaluation of Blyden and Senghor's position, both of whom
seem to me to have a keen sense of historicity, but what is being
attacked in cultural nationalism as a general phenomenon is clear
enough to me. It is the failure to recognize the radical discontinuity
between the precolonial past and the present direction of African
life.The point is that what we perceive as alienation is in fact a much
more serious affair than we recognize; we have all of us, whether edu-

   4. The relevant works are the following: Albert Franklin, "La négritude: Réalité ou
mystification," *Présence Africaine* 14 (1952) (parks); Cheikh Anta Diop, *Nations
négres et culture,* Editions Africaines (Paris: Présence Africaine [1955] 1977) (the critique of négritude is contained in the introductory chapter); Stanislas Adotevi, *Négritude et négrologues* (Paris: Union Générale d'Editions, 1972); Frantz Fanon, *Les
damnés de la terre* (Paris: Maspéro, 1975) (in particular chaps. 3 and 4 entitled, respectively, "Mésaventures de la conscience nationale" and "Sur la culture nationale"); Marcien Towa, *Essai sur la problématique philosophique dans l'Afrique actuelle*
(Yaoundé, 1971); Paulin Hountondji, *Sur "la philosophie africaine"* (Paris: Maspéro,
1977).
   5. See in particular the essay "What Is Négritude?" in my *The African Experience
in Literature and Ideology* (London, 1981; reprinted Bloomington, Ind.: Indiana University Press, 1990).
   6. Ezekiel Mphahlele, *The AFrican Image* (London: Faber and Faber, 1962).
   7. Wole Soyinka, *Myth, Literature and the African World* (Cambridge: Cambridge
University Press, 1976).
   8. Kwasi Wiredu, *Philosophy and an African Culture* (Cambridge: Cambridge University Press, 1980).

cated in the ways of Europe or not, become strangers in our own world. It is an illusion to imagine that the problem of alienation concerns only intellectuals and the Westernized elite; it is, in fact, a global phenomenon, affecting every single individual—in varying degrees it is true, depending upon the particular circumstance of each, but every individual nonetheless. The truth of our situation is that the modern institutions we now operate, the material furniture of our modern universe, the ideas that are making their inexorable way among us, are creating a new context of life and meanings to which every single individual has perforce to relate in one form or the other. More important still, to the same degree that any individual retains his attachment to the traditional culture, to that same degree does he sense the threat to his way of life, the increasing marginalization of the traditional culture. The point is not that the culture does not have a reality for him, it does, but that precisely is the problem; he knows that it is a precarious reality, that the axis of the world in which he is living is shifting from its grounding in the institutions and values of the traditional culture toward a new point of orientation determined by the impact of an alien culture, specifically Western civilization.

The refusal of history in cultural nationalism proceeds from blindness to what Professor Peter Ekeh has described as the epochal character of colonialism in his inaugural lecture delivered from this same forum two years ago.[9] The colonial experience was not an interlude in our history, a storm that broke upon us, causing damage here and there but leaving us the possibility, after its passing, to pick up the pieces. It marked a sea change of the historical process in Africa; it effected a qualitative reordering of life. It has rendered the traditional way of life no longer a viable option for our continued existence and apprehension of the world.[10]

This raises a fundamental issue in any evaluation of the phenomenon of cultural nationalism: the view it promotes that culture is an

9. Peter Ekeh, "Colonialism and Social Structure" (Ibadan: Ibadan University Press, 1980).

10. An awareness of the profound impact of colonialism on our societies and cultures does not preclude a proper estimation of the large measure of initiative which, as J. F. Ade Ajayi has insisted, still remained with us as Africans in the making of our history during the colonial period. See his two essays, "The Continuity of African Institutions under Colonialism," in *Emerging Themes of African History*, ed. T. O. Ranger (Nairobi: East African Publishing House, 1968), 189–200; and "Colonialism: An Episode in African History," in *Colonialism in Africa, 1870–1960*, ed. L. H. Gann and Peter Duignan (Cambridge: Cambridge University Press, 1969), 497–509.

intrinsic value, bound to the natural environment of a people or race and, therefore, determining a natural correspondence between a way of life and a collective identity. This is, of course, the organic view of culture, which found its most powerful expression in Burke's *Reflections on the Revolution in France* and informs the writings of all cultural nationalists of every hue and color, of every age and continent. In Germany, through the influence of Herder, it promoted the notion of *Volkgeist,* and inspired a heady and cloudy romantic nationalism that found magnificent expression in the music of Wagner but also led to the Aryan myth, the consequences of which the world still has to live with even today. I have cited this example simply to point out that cultural nationalism is, to use a cliché, a double-edged sword; to stress one's distinctiveness is to set oneself apart, and this is an attitude that contains equal possibilities both for cooperation and for conflict. It is also a relevant example, for Senghor's négritude drew much of its substance (and overtly so) from the movement of cultural nationalism in France itself, represented by Gobineau and Barrès. The link between this movement and the Fascism of Action Française is well known. I don't want to give the impression that Senghor's négritude was an ideology of aggression; in fact, one of the main objections leveled against it by its radical critics is that it was, in fact, a form of collaboration and accommodation with colonialism.[11] I only want to emphasize the point that the ideas of cultural nationalism have shown a tendency in the past of changing their joyful character, and becoming manifestations of a collective neurosis especially under conditions of stress. European history from the beginning of the nineteenth century up to the Second World War can be regarded, in part, as an illustration of this observation.

The organic conception of culture derives from an excessive valuation of tradition. Its romantic vision of the past confers an ontological status upon the notion of identity and constitutes the abstraction of national culture into its transcendental category. But the movement of thought which culminates at this lofty point proceeds, in fact, from a fallacy—what I'd like to call precisely the "organic fallacy," which derives in turn from a confusion of metaphor with fact. In that metaphor, the dominant imagery is vegetal. The life of societies is likened

11. Indeed, this has been the principal argument against Senghor's formulation of négritude, an argument advanced notably by Irving Leonard Markovitz in his *Léopold Sédar Senghor and the Politics of Négritude* (New York: Atheneum, 1969); and by Stanislas Adotevi in his *Négritude et négrologues.*

to that of a tree, growing slowly and imperceptibly, and sending down firm and strong roots, producing with time the ripe fruits of a settled way of life. But for all its suggestion of growth and vitality, the organic conception of culture is a static conception of the life of societies. It is not surprising that social theories based on it have a powerful element of reaction built into them, as Karl Mannheim has demonstrated in his well-known essay, "Conservative Thought."[12]

I say confusion of metaphor with fact, for when the matter is considered it becomes evident that it is in the very nature of tradition to be vulnerable, to be under constant barrage from the forces of change. If we conceive of tradition as a specific configuration of social relations, of techniques and modes of production, of collective representations and so forth, in short, as the totality of culture as it is actually lived, then it is easy to understand that a modification in any one department will affect the totality. The dynamism of social life puts a constant pressure upon tradition in this sense, shapes and reshapes it over time, until it is no longer recognizable as a specific relation to specific parts within a total structure but simply as an idea. The idea may retain a meaningful correspondence to a present reality and thus serve an integrative function. I take this to be the essential meaning of what Rev. Dr. Munoz has alluded to as the "rationality of tradition" in his essay of that title.[13] But sometimes, as in a time of social revolution, or of rapid social change—in states of pronounced transition—the functional correspondence between the idea of tradition and the actual forces and processes of collective life disappears, and in its place you have a marked cleavage, a pronounced asymmetry. In such cases, the idea of tradition actually becomes dysfunctional, quixotic, in the exact historical sense of the term as derived from the celebrated novel by the Spanish writer, Cervantes. The value of tradition as an idea is thus largely functional and not axiomatic; it is measured by its appositeness to the reality of a living culture and need not have the moral connotations that we often ascribe to it.

To return to the subject of our historical alienation in the light of these observations: the striking thing about our present situation is the discrepancy between the idea of tradition still current among us and the emerging structure of reality in which the fortunes of our

12. Karl Mannheim, "Conservative Thought," in *Essays on Sociology and Social Psychology,* ed. Paul Kecskemeti (London: Routledge and Kegan Paul, 1953).

13. Louis Munoz, "The Rationality of Tradition," *Archiv* für *Rechts—und Sozial Philosophie* 67, no. 2 (Frankfort, 1980): 197–216.

cultural and moral values are now engaged. The discontinuities between the various departments and levels of our social experience
thus make for all kinds of contradictions in the objective spheres of
life and for curious distortions of the personality as reflected in observed behavior.

Let us take, for example, the area of political institutions. Nigeria
is a democratic republic with a written constitution, a legal document which is the source of legitimacy in the modern political system we operate. Yet the territory covered by this document contains
a large number of kingdoms, principalities, city-states, or what have
you, whose authority derives from the traditional political culture
and who have no status whatsoever, formal or informal, in our constitution. All the same, our traditional rulers are encouraged to consider themselves in some special but obscure way to be entitled to the
allegiance of people belonging to their area of traditional authority.
The potential for conflict of this untidy situation has been demonstrated by events which have had tragic consequences in the recent
past.[14]

Let me take another example closely related to the one I've just
cited and which is topical. The controversy that now surrounds the
Land Use Decree centers on the traditional system of land tenure.
The argument that has been advanced for the repeal of the decree is
that land was vested in the past in the traditional ruler who held it in
trust for the rest of the community. What is being urged by those who
use this argument is that we should return to tradition which the
Land Decree is supposed to offend. The possibility that the very logic
of this argument can be turned against them doesn't appear to have
occurred to any of those who employ it. For if the point they are making is that land was socialized in the traditional system, then all the
Land Use Decree has done is to extend this principle to the modern
system by vesting this important economic asset in the authority
which now transcends the traditional within the framework of a plural society. The State governor has manifestly replaced the Oba, the
Obi, the Emir; it is he who is responsible for the economic and social
welfare of those who have elected him into office. The provisions of
the Land Use Decree may well be open to objections but not on the

14. The reference is to the riots that broke out in Kano, in Northern Nigeria, with
serious loss of life reported, following an attempt by the elected governor of Kano to
circumscribe the powers of the emir of Kano; one of the people killed was, in fact, the
political secretary of the governor.

grounds of a reverence for tradition as narrowly defined by those who are agitating against it.[15]

The argument from tradition simply fails to take account of the transformations in our whole political and social order, transformations that reach right down to the intimate aspects of life. This can be illustrated from another example—that of polygamy. The common argument for its perpetuation is that it is not only justified by the African way of life but even dictated by it. This may still be true for the man in the village, but for the civil servant in Ibadan, not only is there no compulsion upon him to marry several wives, the very conditions of his life recommend the discipline of monogamy. The socioeconomic context in which polygamy can function with a minimum of convenience simply does not exist in the urban centers. What is more, anyone familiar with our folktales must know the tensions that polygamy is capable of setting up even within the traditional culture.

This example is not trivial. It illustrates the way in which the notion of tradition can be manipulated for motives that have nothing to do with a genuine respect for the African way of life. This kind of manipulation has attained a remarkable level of cynicism in the politics of some African states—popular attention is diverted to the wearing of leopard skins over the safari suit, the wholesale adoption of indigenous names, the animation of traditional dancing, while the serious business of holding onto power and amassing fabulous wealth goes on elsewhere. In such a situation an attitude of robust skepticism—even more intense in quality than what the late Professor Dudley recommended to us from this same forum a few years ago— seems to me perfectly in order.[16]

One important point emerges from all this: when the notion of tradition is not being invoked to confuse deliberately, it obeys a selective principle. Those who make the appeal to tradition are perfectly willing to enjoy the satisfactions of modern civilization; sometimes even the appeal to tradition is made to insure their unhindered access to its material benefits. This throws a sharp light upon the superficial understanding of tradition and culture that is being fostered among

15. The controversy aroused in Nigeria by the Land Use Decree has subsided somewhat since the reintroduction of military rule in 1984 and the limitations imposed on political discussion as a result.

16. Billy Dudley, "Scepticism as Virtue," Inaugural Lecture, University of Ibadan, 1975.

us by the organization of festivals and the like which do nothing, in their banality, other than rob our indigenous artistic cultures of their poetry and dignity.

The converse of this state of confusion is the spurious Westernization of the national bourgeoisie. Frantz Fanon's celebrated denunciation of this social category in Africa has not lost its relevance in the twenty and more years since it was proffered. The incapacity of the national bourgeoisie to grasp the implications of the process of transition in which we are involved is betrayed by the shallow spirit of materialism that is abroad among us today. We have joined the movement of the "international bazaar," to use an expression by V. S. Naipaul in his book *Among the Believers*, or what Ayi Kwei Arman (in his novel *Fragments*) has represented as a new version of the cargo cult. In Nigeria today, the magical element of this cult is supplied by our much vaunted oil wealth. From it has flowed all the "goodies"—the cars, the furniture, the stereo sets, the champagne, the jewelry, and all the other tinsels of an industrial civilization in which we have no creative part. The depths of the consumer mentality now abroad among us are touched when an adult Nigerian male, affluent, with wife or wives and several children, can find no better use for his Japanese-made video set than to watch blue films, sometimes in the presence of his children. This example suggests a deplorable twist to the prevailing ethos, but it is perfectly in character with the state of moral indolence it has induced in the general society. The idea that there should be a relation between effort and reward has become openly laughable: instant gratification has become the norm.

The moral indolence is well matched by a remarkable intellectual indolence. Outside of a few circles of writers and intellectuals, generally of a radical persuasion—pools of light in a vast area of conceptual darkness—there is no sustained thought in this country, no coherent intellectual, cultural, or moral connection with any scheme of ideas or values, traditional African or Western. The Israelites in exile singing of their unhappy lot likened the sky above them to a sheet of bronze spread over their heads. Matthew Arnold, in his *Culture and Anarchy*, made use of this biblical image to characterize the intellectual climate of Victorian England. Here, I am afraid the intellectual sky above us is made of grosser material: it is not even bronze, but *wooden*.

The situation I have just evoked corresponds to the pathetic aspect of our global alienation. It demonstrates the way in which we are wedged uncomfortably between the values of our traditional culture and those of the West. The process of change we are going through has created a dualism of life which we experience at the moment less as a mode of challenging complexity than as one of confused disparateness. The ideas of cultural nationalism cannot help us out of this agonizing situation, cannot help us to resolve the problems posed by our alienation. On the contrary, they unfit us mentally for the urgent tasks we have to undertake—which we *are* undertaking but in a muddled frame of mind—in order to create a new and viable society. It is of no practical significance now to us to be told that our forebears constructed the Pyramids if today we cannot build and maintain by ourselves the roads and bridges we require to facilitate communication between ourselves, if we still have to depend on the alien to provide for us the necessities of modern civilization, if we cannot bring the required level of efficiency and imagination to the management of our environment. Admittedly, the earlier emphasis of cultural nationalism was beneficial: it had an inspirational purpose which had a point in the colonial period. And if Cheikh Anta Diop to whom I have just alluded is to be understood aright, his appeal to a past of African achievement was not meant as an encouragement to cultural smugness but to greater effort. Unfortunately, that point is lost sight of in the postures we now adopt. It was thus that the pieties of cultural nationalism led to the scandal of our being caught dancing at Algiers in 1969 on the day the Americans landed a man on the moon for the first time.

We may have no business now sending a man to the moon, but we have to cope with the demands of the modern world. We cannot meet the challenges of the scientific and industrial civilization of today by draping ourselves with our particularisms. The resources in ideas, techniques, and in certain respects values offered by our traditional cultures are simply not adequate for our contemporary needs and interests. This is a truism I'd not have ventured to utter if time and again one didn't come up against the simplifications of the cultural nationalists, an example of which I came across the other day. At the end of his textbook entitled *The Social Anthropology of Africa* published by Heinemann, Angulu Onwuejeogwu has placed an epilogue entitled "The Faceless versus the Face." In it, he tells the story of two groups of children, one from the modern urban elite, the other belonging to the rural community. He makes an observation I'd like to quote:

> The children of the new elite did not know that the teapots and teacups which they were using were made of clay,

while all the local children knew this. Indeed, some of them helped their parents to make clay pots and cups and fire them. The children at home could name all the trees around, and talked about the palm trees, banana and yam, while the children of the new elite knew nothing about them. They ate them and that was all. The children from the urban area talked about aeroplanes, television, hotels, birthday parties, fine dresses and shoes. Those at home talked about masquerades, wrestling on the sand, making traps and fishing.

Now, the thrust of our anthropologist's story is in fact tendentious and amounts to a prodigious begging of the question: he proves only what he wants to prove, which is that the traditional culture produces children better adapted for life. But it depends what life: in the village or in the city, in the traditional culture or in the modern culture. Our anthropologist leaves out many issues relevant to his demonstration. If the children of the elite in this story did not know that the teacups they drank from were made from clay, there is obviously something wrong with their education. But the solution is not to send them to the village to learn this—they may, of course, need to go to the village for other reasons—but to reform the educational system so that they can learn this elementary fact at school along with the facts about airplanes and television. As for the rural children, those activities which presumably gave vitality to them must be seen in a context of life in which their chances of survival at birth were very small. *To have vitality, you need to be alive in the first place.* The overriding consideration in any case is that the urban children are, in fact, more prepared for a modern technological civilization, more attuned to the future we envisage for ourselves, whatever the new problems that future will bring—a future indeed in which social anthropology will have become an anachronism in Africa.

My contention is that we need to advance beyond the kind of romantic stuff being peddled by our anthropologist. We need to abandon the self-consciousness that goes with cultural nationalism, to move beyond its positions to entirely new ground. We need a new determination, a new spirit of adventure fired by a modern imagination: a new state of mind that will enable us to come to terms with our state of alienation and to transform it from a passive condition we confusedly endure into an active collective existential project. We need to take charge of our objective alienation by assuming it as an *intention* so as to endow it with a positive significance.

It is pertinent at this point to remind ourselves that the concept of alienation, in its rigorous philosophical form (as opposed to the loose sociological application of the term with which we are more familiar) contains this positive significance. In its formulation by Hegel, from whom the concept has come down to us via Feuerbach and Marx, alienation designates the state of consciousness produced in the dialectic of mind and matter. The adventure of mind in the realm and universe of nature is for Hegel the very definition of history. From the point of view of human existence, what we commonly term "culture" is the result of man's transformation of nature, a result which stands apart from his consciousness but from which these transformations originally flowed. In other words, it is through the active confrontation of matter by mind that culture and thought are produced and that history itself is made possible; it sets in motion the historical process, within which mind undergoes refinement and progresses toward the ultimate perfection of the "Absolute Idea." Culture and thought are thus the objectified forms of mind within the historical process, of primal mind alienated in nature. The state of alienation is thus a condition for the fulfillment of mind, perhaps even for its self-recognition. Like the Judeo-Christian God in the Book of Genesis, the primal mind is not only moved to creation but also to the contemplation of its own work.

I have attempted this summary of Hegel's phenomenology in which the concept of alienation features because it is central to my argument. From Hegel's abstruse dialectics, we can retain the notion of alienation as the principle of all becoming or, more simply, as the moving power of the historical process. In cultural terms, it implies a willed movement out of the self and a purposive quest for new horizons of life and of experience.

In the historical context of present African development, we may now ask, Alienation for what, and in what direction? I will answer that question unequivocally: as a matter of practical necessity, we have no choice but in the direction of Western culture and civilization. If the answer is unequivocal, it is not meant to be taken unilaterally, for I am aware that my answer needs to be hedged round with all sorts of qualifications, some of which, I hope, will become apparent in my conclusion. But for the moment, let me consider one aspect of Western civilization on which there is hardly any dissent as to its importance for us, namely, science and technology. The general consensus is summed up in the expression "transfer of technology" which denotes a current obsession.

But there is a naive assumption underlying the use of this expression, that we can domesticate science and technology by a quick arrangement of rapid industrialization: we buy and install machines, train the manpower, and all will be well. I am even leaving out of account here the problems of capital and finance which come into the question and are far from negligible.

I am afraid this will not do, for there is more to science and technology than machines and their manipulation—there is the scientific spirit itself, which governs the whole functioning of the scientific and technological civilization we now wish to appropriate. It so happens that what we now recognize as the scientific spirit is the product of a whole movement of ideas by which what we now refer to as the West sought to understand man and the universe: the ground for modern science was a matter of historical fact prepared by the development of Western philosophy.

The outstanding good fortune of Western civilization was to have cultivated the deductive method which was elaborated in the philosophy of ancient Greece, and to have made it the foundation for its entire approach to the world. For all the distinction that is commonly made today between philosophy and science, modern science not only owes its existence to the fortuitous development of the deductive method, it is made possible by the application of this method to the universe of phenomena and experience. It is not only in mathematics that this observation holds true, but in all the natural sciences. The very definition of a science is that it is systematic, even systemic, that it displays order in its procedures and in its results. It is not only observation and description that make a science, but the organization of empirical data into an intelligible order. The inductive method is incompletely prosecuted without the final intervention of the deductive; the latter thus subsumes the former. The significance of this for contemporary scientific method, with its emphasis on structure and its recourse to model building, has been stressed by Popper and Kuhn. But it was recognized in the work that served as a manifesto for modern science in its infancy—Francis Bacon's *Novum Organum*, which was conceived, as its title indicates, as a restatement of Aristotle's *Organon*. It is no accident that the great biologist Linnaeus based his taxonomy on the order of concepts of formal logic.

This example will also serve to illustrate the misfortune of African civilization, the inability of our traditional world concept to break free from the prison of the mythopoetic imagination. In Yoruba *ijala* poetry, for example, there is a wealth of information about the fauna and flora of our natural environment which is truly astonishing, but all this information is fitted into an exclusively poetic mode. I understand, too, that the operation of the Ifa corpus depends upon a sophisticated calculus, but nowhere in the culture is this calculus made explicit. This second example points to the real distinction between our traditional worldview and that of Western thought. It is not, as some anthropologists have maintained—and they are well represented in the collection of readings edited by Bryan Wilson under the title *Rationality*[17]—it is not a question of the absence of a rational mode of thought in the one, and its presence in the other, but rather that of its theoretical formulation. It is not rationality as such that distinguished Western civilization but its logic of rationality.

Thus, while we have been content to celebrate the universe, Western man has been engaged in analyzing it as well. This approach bred a tough-mindedness that became a moral value in Europe, and is well expressed in the motto that Leonardo da Vinci adopted for all his activities as both artist and scientist: "ostinato rigore," which can be translated as "stubborn application." That motto was to turn out to be emblematic not only for the internal effort of development in Europe but also for the Europeans' dealings with the rest of the world. From the Renaissance onward, as Europe became increasingly conscious of its power, its civilization assumed an aggressive posture. We are only too familiar with the rest of the story—the political, economic, and human consequences of the European colonial adventure. But there is an aspect that is not sufficiently attended to and which the Italian scholar, Carlo Cipolla, has illuminated with a wealth of fine detail in his book *European Culture and Overseas Expansion*.[18] He points out that the decisive factor in the world supremacy of Europe was the stubborn application of intelligence and skill to the improvement of firearms, ocean-going vessels, and, above all, precision instruments; to the perfection of all these technical resources which finally gave the advantage to the Europeans in their onslaught upon other races, other peoples and nations, other civilizations. The terrible truth of our colonial experience, therefore, is that we were

17. Bryan Wilson, *Rationality* (Evanston, Ill: Harper and Row, 1970).
18. Carlo Cipolla, *European Culture and Overseas Expansion* (Hammondsworth: Penguin Books). See also J. H. Parry, *The Establishment of the European Hegemony: 1415–1715* (New York: Harper and Row, 1966).

victims of the European's developed sense of method. We were over-whelmed, in fact, by the objective force of the deductive people.

Now, there is a Yoruba saying which sums up admirably the moral of the story: *Adaniloro k'oni logbon,* which can be translated into English as "One who causes you injury also teaches you wisdom." The immediate lesson of our recent past of colonial domination can be extended to our contemporary situation. We are still in a position of weakness with regard to the West. If the term "neocolonialism" sometimes has a hysterical ring, it is not meaningless, for it refers to a concrete reality of contemporary international life. I hardly need to stress the point in the present situation of Nigeria today, in which every aspect of our lives is affected by our pathetic dependence upon the West. In a situation where all the ideas and resources we require for a modern economy—for the conditions of daily existence—are still controlled from the West, all loose talk about "transfer of technology" will be of no avail. We cannot do without a thorough-going revolution of the mind.

It is certainly not simplistic to affirm that this revolution can be brought about by an assiduous cultivation and internalization of those values enshrined in the scientific method—organization, discipline, order, and, not least, imagination. Imagination, because the scientific culture involves projection, calls upon qualities of mental resourcefulness which translate, in social terms, into a vision of the future.

The scientific revolution in Europe did not take place in a void but in a dynamic context of political, social and cultural development, and, especially in the eighteenth century, of intense intellectual debate which Paul Hazard has described as "crisis of consciousness."[19] An intellectual like Voltaire was a passionate man: he could feel the changes taking place in his universe on his very pulse. Voltaire typifies the strengths and limitations of his age; the unbounded faith in the power of reason closed to him important avenues of the imagination and of human experience,[20] at the same time, the clarity of his moral perceptions gave meaning to his cosmopolitanism. He had a broad vision of humanity such that he was able to place the European world in the right perspective and to understand that its civilization did not have a monopoly of human achievement. Indeed, his attitude to the medieval past was much like that of the Frasers, the Tylors and

19. Paul Hazard, *La crise de la conscience européenne* (Paris: Boivin et Cie, 1934).
20. Hence what amounts to the dismissal of Voltaire's work by Eric Auerbach in his celebrated work *Mimesis,* tr. W. R. Trask (Princeton: Princeton University Press, 1953).

the Levy-Bruhls of a later century with regard to non-Western cultures.

You may begin to wonder what all this has to do with us. I will answer directly by saying "everything"; by drawing your attention to the Nigerian constitution which came into effect in October 1979. Without the intellectual ferment of eighteenth-century Europe, without the ideas of men like Locke, Montesquieu, Voltaire, and even Kant (in his moral philosophy summed up by the phrase "man as an end in himself"), we would have had a different constitution, perhaps even no constitution at all. At any rate, these ideas are embodied in the legal document which regulates the corporate life of all of us today. Take, for example, the notion of the independence of the judiciary. That notion has come down to us via America, from the principle of the separation of powers enunciated by Montesquieu in his *L'Esprit des Lois*. Notions such as these have become commonplace today, but they were forged in the heat of political and ideological battles fought in Europe. We have entered into the intellectual inheritance of eighteenth-century Europe as regards our political culture simply because its ideas have now become the property of all mankind.

We could do, then, with a broader vision of our humanity than cultural nationalism in its present emphasis proposes to us. If we can accept that the scientific and technological civilization which has come down to us, historically, from Europe can improve the quality of our lives, if we can accept that our modern institutions should be based on political and social ideas articulated elsewhere, there is no reason why we should exclude from our acceptance other valuable areas of experience simply because of their association with Europe. There is no earthly reason why a professor at Ibadan who has mastered the mathematics of, let us say, Gauss, and enjoys the comfort of a Mercedes-Benz saloon, cannot extend the range of his satisfactions to include a Bach fugue. Between all those, there is a historical and cultural, if not a structural, connection, which can be embraced by a single sensibility. In my view, our not altogether hypothetical professor could do with a little more alienation.

Let me refer to another of our proverbs which says that one should not point the left index at one's father's house. Nothing I have said goes against the spirit of that proverb. I have not come to bury our traditional culture under a foolish scorn inspired by an alienated consciousness. Neither have I come to sing the praises of Western civilization, much less to justify its historical aggression upon us and to endorse its ideology of the civilizing mission. As Aimé Césaire has said, "From colonization to civilization, the distance is infinite."[21] Nothing I have said is meant to confirm the White man in his racial and cultural arrogance. The scientific and technological supremacy of Europe was a historical phenomenon that was both particular and contingent, marked by all the vicissitudes of human experience. European civilization did not spring forth fully formed from the brain of a providential God but was shaped over time, often under dramatic circumstances that could well have deflected its course in a direction other than the one it was eventually to pursue.

There are, indeed, interesting parallels between this development and our historical experience and present situation. Like us, the early Europeans were conquered—in their case by the Romans. They were colonized, exploited, and even enslaved. They were later Christianized; I should know something about this, for my Irish teachers did not tire of reminding me that it was St. Gregory, the patron saint of the school I attended in Lagos, who sent the first Christian missionaries to England. These early Europeans were dispossessed culturally, and with time whole populations even lost their indigenous languages—you can't be alienated further than that—so that they began to speak pidgin forms of Latin which have evolved into the Romance language of today. In the all-important area of literacy, they learnt everything from the Romans as, indeed, in other areas such as civil works and architecture. When the fact is remembered that the Romans considered these people savages and barbarians, the later pretensions of European ethnocentrism and racism appear in all their hollowness: as the products of a monumental amnesia.

Some eminent European scholars and philosophers seem to have been acutely affected by this malady. For example, Max Weber, in the introduction to the final edition of his classic work, *The Protestant Ethic and the Spirit of Capitalism*, practically makes the staggering claim that all worthwhile human achievement has been the work of Europeans. The philosopher Martin Heidegger has also affirmed with a dogmatism that goes against all the principles of his discipline that philosophy is, by its very essence, a European phenomenon.[22] But we must be clear what we mean by the word "European" in this context,

21. Aimé Césaire, *Discours sur le colonialisme* (Paris: Présence Africaine, 1955), 10.

22. See Heidegger's *What is Philosophy?* trans. Jean Wilde and William Kluback (New York, 1958); Paul de Man offers a critique and refutation of Heidegger's affirmation in his *Blindness and Insight*, 2d ed. (London: Methuen, 1983).

and whether the ancient Greeks can be considered European in the modern sense of the word. For it seems likely, from what comes through of Plato's personality in *The Republic*, that he would have recoiled from the suggestion that he should live among the ancestors of Weber and Heidegger with the classical Greek equivalent of Frazer's celebrated remark, "God Forbid!"

Joseph Conrad by the way, seems to have been affected much less than the Europeans of his time, despite appearances to the contrary. In *Heart of Darkness*, for instance, there is an evocation of the Thames estuary as it would have appeared to the Romans, this evocation placed in symbolic parallel to that of the Congo river later in the work. This double evocation of two ages of imperialism, far removed in time and place, in Conrad's short novel, makes the point I'm trying to put across here—that of the strange forgetfulness of the European racists and of the historical and moral horror it has engendered both for us and the European colonizer.

The fact remains that the civilization we now associate with Europe was originally a derivation, and as it developed it continued to assimilate elements from other world civilizations. It is surely one of the greatest ironies of history that gunpowder, which later gave Europe such immense power, was originally a Chinese invention.

The contribution of Africa itself to Western civilization is far from negligible. It is now generally accepted that ancient Egypt exercised considerable influence upon the early civilization of Greece. Moreover, African philosophers have made individual contributions to the conceptual elaboration of Western civilization all through the centuries—St. Augustine of Hippo being the most eminent. In our own century, our traditional art and music have provoked a remarkable revolution in Western aesthetics, the effects of which have been more far-reaching than is generally realized. The visual landscape of Europe is still being transformed by the influence of modern art on architecture and technical design, an influence that goes right back to the impact of African sculpture on artists like Modigliani, Braque, Picasso, and Ferdinand Léger. Indeed, modern technology seems to have found in African art its most adequate mode of presentation: the very organization of volume, shapes, and lines in the manufactured objects we all handle everyday has benefited immensely from the absorption of the formal principles of African art into European aesthetics. You only have to compare nineteenth-century designs to those of the twentieth century to realize the simplifying effect of the application of these principles, and the gain in functionality it has effected. (How strange, then, that your ordinary Westernized African cannot suffer the presence of an African mask in his sitting room, side by side with his videorecorder!) We must not forget, too, that African labor and resources went into the building of the material prosperity of the West. In many ways, therefore, we have a claim upon Western civilization, as well as a considerable stake in it, as the instrument for the necessary transformation of our world. It is in our interest to make good that claim, to adopt strategies that will make our stake in that civilization pay handsome dividends. We cannot do this if we continue to be burdened by the complexes implanted in us under colonialism, and which are only intensified by cultural nationalism. If the Japanese had been deterred by the insults constantly hurled at them by the Europeans during the last century, they would not have been where they are today: as we all know, the yellow peril has become with time the yellow paradigm.

Let me conclude these reflections by going back to the essential point of my argument, which has led me to a positive evaluation of the concept of alienation. I have tried to argue with specific reference to our situation that the phenomenon of alienation in its positive aspect is the generating principle of culture, the condition of human development. There is no society, no civilization that has not experienced alienation in one form and to some degree of the other. Our present experience of alienation stems directly from our historical encounter with Europe, and from our continuing relationship with a civilization that, in its present form, was forged in that continent, and which, therefore, holds out a special interest for us. We cannot ignore the fact that the transforming values of contact with this civilization have produced the present context of our collective life, if we are to get a mental handle upon the process of transition in which we are involved. The very tensions and conditions of stress of this process would have been beneficial if they helped to concentrate our minds both wonderfully and intensely upon the nature of our alienation.

The necessary effort of understanding our alienation and coming to terms with it justifies all forms of scholarship devoted to European culture and Western civilization, considered as a totality. Indeed, we have been so involved in this civilization that to consider it as something apart from us is to set it up as an abstraction. Our ancestors may not have been the Gauls, the Saxons, the Visigoths, or what have you, but that is not because we are not descended racially from them but because we know practically nothing about what they did or thought, and it doesn't really matter for us. On the other hand, the Hellenic and Roman civilizations have a direct significance for us, as much as for any European. Indeed, in one particular respect, classical Greek civilization has a more immediate interest for us. Its philosophers were confronted with the same dualism of modes of thought in a context of social change and even of political instability that we are now confronted with, and by grappling at the level of ideas with the real problems of existence which this situation posed for their age, with the difficulties of creating a viable society such as we now experience, they made the conceptual breakthrough responsible in large part for the scientific and technological civilization which defines the modern world.

This reference points to the final significance of my argument arising from my particular involvement with the discipline of modern language studies—the conviction of the universality of human experience on which it is based. To study another language is to assume that you will get to understand it, and in the perspective of modern language studies that the culture it reflects can speak to your mind and imagination in ways which may be different from those of your original culture but which can still be meaningful to you. In fact, all human history confirms this assumption: language and culture know no boundary, at least not significantly, and the reality of the contemporary world, the "global village" in the expression sent into circulation by Marshall McLuhan and now become current, has tended to reinforce our awareness of a common humanity.

Thus, it is significant that in the Humanities today the dominant trend of scholarship has been inspired by a new universalism, a direct result of contemporary historical experience. The Linguistics of Chomsky, the Structuralism of Lévi-Strauss, and the Semiology of Barthes have no other final objective than to demonstrate the proposition that different languages and different cultures are varied forms of realizations, varied modes of transformation, of a universal grammar and of a universal structure of experience. The philosophical anthropology that informs contemporary scholarship in the Humanities envisages the essential unity of the human mind, no longer in terms of its rational function but from the point of view of its faculty of symbolization.

The notion of the universality of human experience does not, however, imply uniformity—quite the contrary—but it does mean that cultures maintain their dynamism only through their degree of tension between the particular and the universal. Alienation, in this view, cannot mean total loss; the fulfillment it promises resides precisely in the degree of integration it helps us to achieve. In its creative potential, alienation signifies the sensitive tension between the immediate closeness of the self and the reflected distance of the other.

part four

Philosophy and the Practice of Everyday Life

Inventing an African Practice in Philosophy: Epistemological Issues

K. Anthony Appiah

> By "African philosophy" I mean a set of texts, specifically the set of texts written by Africans themselves and described as philosophical by their authors themselves.
> Paulin Hountondji[1]

Introduction

It is surely up to us: we Africans, who have inherited from our various trainings the European title "philosopher," who have now acquired the institutions of a postcolonial academy, who are trying to make up our minds as to what we should be doing with that title, those institutions. It is up to us, as Paulin Hountondji has insisted, because Africa is

> above all a continent and the concept of Africa an empirical, geographical concept and not a metaphysical one[2]

and, one might add, philosophy is an historically determinate institution, whose shape is the product, on the one hand, of the purposes and beliefs, (the interests, in short) of a Western academy that institutionalized a profession of philosophy in the Enlightenment, allowing it (and not, say, what we now call "physics") to inherit the most dignified of the titles of humanism; and, on the other, of the contingencies that have shaped specific philosophi-

1. Paulin Hountondji, *African Philosophy: Myth and Reality* (Bloomington: Indiana University Press, 1983), 33.
2. Ibid., 66.

cal contributions—Kant's infatuation with a certain technical vocabulary, Hegel's Prussian nationalism, Wittgenstein's rhetoric.

It is up to us, then, now that we wield the title (or are burdened
with it), to ask what we can do with these institutions; up to us if we
choose to stop asking whether there is an African philosophy because
we have discovered something for ourselves to do.

And yet, at the same time, it is, of course, not to us at all, we do
not determine the material conditions that shape the crisis of the African university. In the context of the book famine, of the continuing
centrality of faculty trained in Europe and the United States, of the
unavailability of many of the resources—xeroxing, computers, sometimes even paper—on which modern intellectual life depends, there
are many threats to the development of autonomous traditions of
scholarly work.

The most important consequence of this situation is the aggrava-
tion of the already too-ample intellectual dependency of Africans and
African institutions on the institutions of the West; and it is surely
an intolerable state of cultural affairs that some of the finest—and
certainly the best-funded—work in the African humanities (much of
it by displaced Africans) continues to be done outside the continent.[3]

In this situation, it seems to me, there are reasons for developing a
notion of African philosophy, not as Hountondji's philosophy "by Africans themselves"; nor simply, as others have proposed, as philosophy *in* Africa, either: but rather as philosophy *for* Africa. And to
make sense of his idea we must inquire into what it is that Africa
now needs of her intellectuals (which is to say, intellectuals who are
for her); and which parts of that need a training in "philosophy" can
supply.

This is a thoroughly practical question: it is likely to have a messy
and multiple answer. It will be best, therefore, I think, to treat it
slowly, practically, piecemeal. And so I propose to proceed by examining one question in the space of questions that surrounds this practical question in the way that the philosopher's training makes
inescapable: namely, by exploring the grounds of the possibility of a
certain project: that of challenging the cultural hegemony of the me-
tropole through an engagement with its concepts grounded in African
systems of thought.

3. I have discussed this question a little further in "Thought in a Time of Famine,"
a review of *An Essay on African Philosophical Thought* by Kwame Gyekye (*Times
Literary Supplement*, 29 July–4 August 1988).

What Is an African System of Thought?

We should complicate, first of all, the notion of an African system of thought. Hountondji has already established, through his critique of unanimism, a double rejection both of the preposterous idea of one African system of concepts and of the astonishing notion that we should expect unanimity in belief within each African society. The distinction between concepts and belief—even if it is one whose absoluteness has been challenged by Quine and Wittgenstein—is of crucial importance here. While the conceptual resources available through a certain language are the shared property of a society, the beliefs that can be expressed with those concepts need not—in general, will not—all, or even mostly, be shared. So we would think of African intellectual lives as various, both within and between societies, with arenas of contestation, private reservations, sectional, for example, gendered or class-based modes of understanding; at the same time both allowing that the conceptual resources of a certain ethnic or social group, constituted and constitutive of their cultural practices, must be common property, *and* recognizing that the beliefs of different actors—even on central questions—may differ.

What we should not do, however, having distinguished concepts and beliefs, is to replace the sentimentalities of unanimism about belief with a sentimentality of original authoctonous concepts: by African concepts, I mean those concepts left to us in Africa now—and that means after our first century of close interaction with European cultures. What is left to us now includes our modern identities as citizens of new states, a taste for Michael Jackson and Jim Reeves as well as for Fela Kuti or King Sonny Adé, respect for Aspirin as well as for juju, for Methodism or Catholicism or Shia Islam as well as respect for the ancestors. African intellectuals (Christian priests, academics, teachers, novelists) are not less African than African peasant farmers; even if, as some of us think, the former sometimes show an unjustified contempt for the latter. Grounding oneself in Africa, in short, is grounding oneself in the present, not the past; and it is in that present that the issues I want to raise arise.

Conceptual Relativity

Perhaps part of what I want to argue is obvious: for what I want to say, first, is that philosophy is always "local," which is to say, always someone's, somewhere, somewhen; that its conceptual materials are always relative to some historical community from which it speaks; that there is always some contextually specific determination of the "we" for whom the philosopher—the intellectual—speaks. But I want also to argue, I hope less obviously, that, from an epistemological perspective, we should celebrate this essential positionality: for as I shall try to show, we have reason to hope that a conversation among discourses, between occupants of this position and that, offers the best hope that we shall create *as a species* the rich intellectual landscape that is essential if we are to understand our universe and our place in it. The multiple discourses of humankind, brought, now, by history into mutual consciousness, are not a Babel but a chorus.

I need hardly say that this hopeful image of pluralism is one that has been discovered over and over again in our century in different dimensions of culture, across wide political divergences: recall the Maoist slogan "let a hundred flowers bloom" while remembering also T. S. Eliot's "although it is only too easy for a writer to be local without being universal, I doubt whether a poet or novelist can be universal without being local too"[4]; or—most resonant for us—the ·powerful words of Aimé Césaire:

> Ma conception de l'universel est celle d'un universel riche
> de tout le particulier, riche de tous les particuliers, appro-
> fondissement et coexistence de tous les particuliers.[5]

But there are bars to accepting this vision, for one who inherits the philosophical tradition to which I belong. For, generally, the relation between the conceptual worlds of different cultures, institutions, or traditions is seen—in what Wole Soyinka has suggested is a distinctively Western way[6]—as one of combat (at least when it is not one of mutual irrelevance); and, more specifically, in recent Anglo-American philosophy, a powerful case has been made for the view that systems of concepts—conceptual schemes—can address each other only at the price of being, in the end, the same.

This case, as made by Donald Davidson—in a presidential address to the American Philosophical Association some fifteen years ago—against what he calls "The Very Idea of a Conceptual Scheme," has been powerfully influential, even if often opposed. It centers on an

---

4. Eliot is cited on p. 106 of Chinweizu, Onwuchekway Jamie, and Ihechukwu Madubuike, *Toward the Decolonization of African Literature* (Enugu: Fourth Dimension Publishing Co., 1980).

5. Cited by V. Y. Mudimbe, *L'odeur du père* (Paris: Présence Africaine, 1982), 14.

6. Robin Horton has used the term "adversarial" to contrast this Western approach to argument with what Wole Soyinka calls the "accommodative" style of many traditional cultures.

approach to such questions that begins with the notion that conceptual schemes would be, if they were anything, essentially linguistic; argues that to recognize two languages as in competition for the same world (and thus potentially conflicting) we must be able to translate them; and proceeds to show that translation is impossible unless we find in the translated language the conceptual structure of the metalanguage of translation.

I am not concerned here to argue with the internal logic of Davidson's position.[7] Rather what I want to point out is that it has a certain presupposition: namely, that conflict between ways of thinking about the world is a matter or propositions with mutually contradictory truth-values. It is not essential to this view that the issue be drawn, as it is by Davidson, in terms of (natural) languages; what is crucial is the idea that conceptual competition—and this might be competition not among sentences but among beliefs—can only be competition for the truth.

Davidson does not, at least in his published work, find difficulty with the idea that different people or cultures might care about different things, so that to live with one person or in one culture rather than another would require us to choose between ways of ordering desire. To the extent that Davidson—or more interestingly, since we hardly care about his specific biography, a major tradition in Anglophone philosophy—inherits a positivist conception of value, this acceptance of a relativism of desire will entail a relativism of values.

But suppose we give up the positivist conception of fact and value as radically ontologically distinct: giving up thinking of the former realistically, and the latter as at best a fiction, at worst a lie. Suppose we recognize the interest-relativity of the discourse of the factual;[8] then, I suggest, we shall have to take a more complex view of the relations between faculty discourses; a view that allows them to compete in more ways than for the truth. And once we have recognized *this*, we shall have space for the idea that different—even, in some sense, competing discourses, ways of thinking—can be put to use by the same people *for different purposes*; and that the availability of a plurality of discourses is a resource for the human community.

I think this is an attractive, even an exalted, vision: but, since I am

7. That has been done, for example, by Kendall Walton in, "Linguistic Relativity," in *Conceptual Change*, ed. G. Pearce and P. Maynard (Dordrecht: Reidel, 1973); and Richard Rorty, The World Well Lost," *Journal of Philosophy* 69 (1972).

8. Just as we might insist, for other purposes, on the fact-dependency of the discourse of value.

a philosopher, I must *argue* for it. And to do so I propose to begin at the heart of Western intellectual culture, with the natural sciences. If you share my excitement in the vision, I am sure you will bear with me as I muster my materials.

The Argument

To begin with, I wish to borrow and then modify Habermas's notion that an area of inquiry is partially constituted by a characteristic range of interests.

As is well-known, Habermas accounts for the distinction that Dilthey had sought to establish between the *Naturwissenschaften* and the *Geisteswissenschaften,* by arguing that each kind of knowledge is constituted by a distinct kind of interest. The natural sciences are rooted in a "knowledge-constitutive interest in possible technical control,"[9] while the knowledge-constitutive interest of the Geisteswissenschaften is "practical."[10] There are many problems with this line of thought: the distinction between a "practical" interest in mutual understanding and a "technical" interest in control is far from clear, for example; nor is it clear how these differences in interest "constitute" a field of inquiry; or that we should seek to understand differences between domains of knowledge at the perilous level of abstraction at which natural, social, and critical knowledge are supposed to be differentiated. But the idea that *interests* play a role in the constitution of areas of inquiry or of the institutions we call "disciplines," while already less specifically Habermasian, is surely something we can borrow.

"Interest" here should carry both its senses: the sense in which it contrasts with disinterest and the sense in which it contrasts with a mere lack of epistemic engagement. But what should immediately draw our interest is the question, What is it for an interest—in any sense—to *constitute* an area of inquiry or a kind of knowledge?

And here, I believe, we can draw on some recent work in the philosophy of psychology and the philosophy of physics. First, take an example from psychology. It has been argued by many recently— among them the same Donald Davidson—that in understanding people as intentional systems—as having the beliefs, desires, intentions, and other propositional attitudes of commonsense psychology—we make a certain projection of rationality. We ascribe beliefs

9. J. Habermas, *Knowledge and Human Interests*, trans. Shapiro (London, 1972), 135.
10. Ibid., 176.

and desires to people in such a way as to "make-rational" their acts. The details here are not important for what I want to say now: the crucial point is that it is also acknowledged that it is simply false to suppose that agents are generally (indeed, ever) rational. If this line of thought is correct, then, our psychological theories are at best implicitly conditional upon a false presupposition, at worst inevitably false.

At this point it is usual to mention "idealization." As Fodor has often insisted, we should not make methodological demands of psychology that cannot be met by chemistry and physics. And so, the argument goes, since it is clear that, for example, ideal gas theory is still held to be usefully explanatory because "approximately true," why shouldn't we hold that rational psychology is useful because roughly correct also? But the crucial point here, one that often gets missed, is that what is being offered is an argument in defense of a theory that is acknowledged to be false: for, if I may be permitted an aphorism, being approximately true is just a special way of being false.

The same sort of problems arise for physics if, as Nancy Cartwright has argued, most of the laws of physics are false and known to be so. Here, too, idealization is common; and here, as in psychological theory, the notion of approximate truth has been driven very hard. I am sure that some notion of approximate truth is needed to handle the case of psychological theory or the theory of lasers: but, as Cartwright says (apropos idealization in physics):

> In calling something an idealization it seems not so important that the contributions from omitted factors be small [gloss: so that the theory is approximately true], but that they be ones for which we know how to correct. If the idealization is to be of use, when the time comes to apply it to a real system we had better know how to add back the contributions of the factors that have been left out . . . either the omitted factors do not matter much or we know how to treat them.[11]

There are, then, two major sources of idealization: one is approximate truth, the other is what we can call *truth under idealized as-*

11. N. Cartwright, *How the Laws of Physics Lie* (Oxford: Oxford University Press, 1983), 111. (The idea of ignoring factors for which we know how to account is a very old idea: consider Anselm's discussion of the existence of God *remoto Christo*. Here, removing Christ from the picture is plainly not meant to be a trivial move, a move that leaves the world "approximately" as it was. But the point of considering whether we can prove the existence of God, *remoto Christo*, is that Anselm is clear enough that he knows "how to add back the contributions of the factor[s] that have been left out.")

sumptions. Thus, in the case of ideal gas theory, the theory may be horribly inaccurate in its handling of a case—a large molecule gas at high temperature, even though, if the explicitly counterfactual assumptions of the theory—that the gas is composed of frictionless, perfectly inelastic point masses—were true, the theory would indeed (in some sense) give the right answer.

Now the crucial point in each of these cases, whether the issue is approximation or idealized assumptions, is that the question whether we count the theory as false *simpliciter* or approximately true is a question of *judgment,* a question that may legitimately depend on our interests (in both senses). A chemistry whose practical focus is on the development of industrial dyes might, say, accept the idealizing assumption that filtered river water is H_2O; a chemistry interested in energy regulation at the cellular level probably could not. And as for "approximate truth," "good enough" in the theory of the laser is "good enough to build a laser that does its job."

So, we learn from recent philosophical psychology and philosophy of physics that our theories are best conceived of as idealizations, and that this means they are both (in some sense) approximately true and conditional upon false assumptions that simplify the theoretical task. Interests constitute areas of inquiry in part by determining what sorts of falsehoods are tolerable. And given that this is so, there is the inevitable possibility of a dimension of theoretical criticism that challenges not the claim of a theory as an idealization but, rather, the interests by which that idealization is judged adequate. We don't need to keep hold of purely disinterested reasons for idealizing anymore than we can insist on *un*interested ones. An idealization is a useful falsehood: if we manage disinterest, uninterest will leave us simply rejecting idealization (and thus theory) altogether; useful always means "useful for some purpose."

I would only want to add to this picture a recognition of the fact that the interests that drive theory will change—are suitable objects of historical inquiry; that they are often unlikely to be explicitly articulated, even where they are articulable; and that, in one of those many subtle dialectics that inform historical process, the ways in which they change may themselves be driven by the very theories they constitute.

The Theory of the Person

Let me now pursue my argument through a specific case: that of the different concepts of the person of different societies. It is a useful example not least because we have available to us a good deal of recent African discussion of African concepts of the person. It will be clear already what the argument is that I need to make: I must argue that the interests that are served by the discourse of the subject—the conceptual world within which we understand what we call the "person"—in different societies may be different. And then, precisely because the guiding interests may be differently rooted, a simple equation of terms that occur in two such discourses entails a conflation of different meanings.

Let me proceed, then, by sketching in a general way the theoretical economy of the subject; the kinds of interest and the kinds of theory whose interaction results in the theories about people and how they function that belong to what I will call folk psychology.

The basic thought is this. A person is, first of all and fundamentally, what each of us is for ourselves. Our theories of the person are connected in the most direct possible way with what Habermas rather bloodlessly describes as a "practical" interest in mutual understanding; in other words, as one might more humanely express the matter, by our concern to live intelligibly in community with other agents who are, first of all, lovers, families, and friends, and then, colleagues, officials, traders, healers, strangers, and so on. This practical interest requires us to be able to articulate our own behavior in relation to theirs, and this we do through our understanding of them as having beliefs and intentions—in short, as reasoning—and also as having passions and prejudices—in short, as always potentially unreasonable. But the very theories that make this possible themselves provide terms, ranging from the most neutral—*belief*—to the most affectively inflected—*love*—which themselves come to constitute the objects of our projects: if I love you, I may want you to hope that we shall see the end of *apartheid* in this century; to fear that this is too much to hope for. So that here is an instance where a primary interest in the coordination of behavior may lead to a theory that itself then plays a part in determining a further interest in developing the theory—which is only to say what we call our understanding of each other—in new directions.[12] In particular, in some—but not, apparently, all—societies a crucial moment in the development of the language of the subject comes when agents, whose subjectivity is, of

12. You will notice here how I have been driven to narrativize this theoretical point as if these different interests, which we can presume developed historically in tandem, in fact, came in succession. But to tell the tale without this misleading temporal implication is a feat beyond my narrative capacity.

course, dialectically constituted with the theory, come to focus their interest on, as we say, themselves. What recent Anglo-American literary history calls "self-fashioning"—a process we already know to occur in radically different ways in different societies and times—is exactly the sort of possibility that the view I am developing intends to make intelligible.

It is a determining fact of philosophical anthropology that once there exists a human community possessed of the materials for mutual theoretical understanding it develops practices—which is to say, common activities coordinated and understood through that understanding, which constitute them as a society: as having families and relationships, marriages and alliances, and, of course, in the end, social stratifications and contradictions determined by the conditions of scarcity that led Hobbes to his pessimistic conception of human potential and Marx to his materialism. And, more to our current purpose, that these social facts themselves become the objects of belief, of repulsion, and of desire.

The point of this story is twofold: first, to indicate the complexity of the interests that guide our understanding of each other; second, to indicate that social facts themselves become the objects of that understanding through our recognition of them as the objects of our psychological attitudes and thus, in particular, make possible new interests by which the development of our understanding may be driven.

Let me call the body of propositional belief dialectically constituted by these developing interests "folk psychology"; it is not everywhere the same; nor, certainly, everywhen. The literature on the psychological theories of classical Greece or Yorubaland, or the history of "possessive individualism," or the economistic rational psychology of the utilitarians, or of Freudian psychoanalytic theory is a catalogue of its varieties. And the story I have been telling is meant to persuade you that it is a foolish question which of these theories is truest or even true; for to adhere to one of these visions is not simply to see the world and your fellows a certain way but to live a certain way, to care about certain things and not about others, to admire not this but that. The complex dialectic of interest and theory in each social formation engenders its own tolerable falsehoods.

Suppose you have followed me so far. Then you will surely grant that it is at least an open question whether the interests through which the discourse of the subject has been constituted and reconstituted in a continuous dialectic with folk-psychological theories in one society will be close enough to those of some other society for us to be able simply to translate from one theory to the other. Each theory will be partly constituted by the form of life of those whose theory it is; and the contention between them will not simply be between different beliefs about people but between hopes for human life. And if this be true, then to explore different views of the person will be to explore and counterpose different possible modes of human existence; and to choose among them will be to explore the potentialities of human life. Such a comparative project will be one that requires contributions from many societies, while seeking to make available to each society an understanding of the modes of experience, feeling, and belief of other societies: and it will enrich our understanding of ourselves, wherever we live and move and have our being, just as it enlivens our understanding of others.

Envoi

We have already become accustomed to the idea that Africa is one of the world's remaining genetic treasure houses, and that the invasion of the monoculture of crops developed by Western technology risks depriving us of this treasure. I would like to propose that Africa is also a cultural treasure house—a treasure house of ways of understanding, ways of living, forms of human creativity—and that her relentless incorporation in the intellectual economy of the West puts us in danger of losing—in the name of progress—another priceless treasure. And if that is so, then one of the dreams of an African philosophy—a philosophy that, in being *for* Africa and particular will also be *for* humankind and universal—will be to explore our human world with a plurality of Africa visions. My colleague Valentin Mudimbe has expressed this aspiration better than I can:

> Il s'agit donc, pour nous, de promouvoir cette norme
> importante: l'arrêt sur nous-mêmes, ou plus
> précisément, un retour constant sur ce que nous
> sommes avec une ferveur et une attention
> particulières, accordées à notre milieu
> archéologique; ce milieu qui, s'il permet nos prises
> de parole, les explique aussi.[13]

13. From immediately before the citation of Césaire, quoted above, V. Y. Mudimbe *L'odeur du père*, 14.

Recapturing

fourteen

Paulin J. Hountondji

It is from the economists that I borrow
the notion of extraversion, as it functions in the theory of development, in
order to transfer it to another terrain:
that of a sociology of science.[1]

In fact, it seems urgent to me that
the scientists in Africa, and perhaps
more generally in the Third World,
question themselves on the meaning
of their practice as scientists, its real
function in the economy of the entirety
of scholarship, its place in the process
of production of knowledge on a worldwide basis. Are we satisfied or not with
"the way it is going?" As long as we
look upon the problems of scientific research only from the angle of the individual performance and career, we have
nothing or almost nothing to criticize
about the present situation. We will
only deplore, and that is what we cus-
tomarily do, the lack of equipment, the
numerical weakness of research groups
compared to the importance that these
groups have in the industrialized
nations, and other similar weaknesses.
But these quantitative insufficiencies
are not really very worrisome. At most
they would indicate that scientific research is here still in its early stages,

1. This text was delivered as a paper at the
Sixth General Assembly of the Conseil pour le
Dévelopement de la Recherche Economique et
Sociale en Afrique (CODESRIA) in Dakar, 5–10
December 1988, under the title "Recherche et
extraversion: Eléments pour une sociologie de la
science dans les pays de la périphérie."

that it is relatively young compared to that of the great industrial metropolitan centers, and that with time the gap actually will be reduced, to the extent that scientific and technological activity will be developed in Africa. Thus, one would encourage a patience and greater efforts toward higher performance within the framework of the present institutions and of the present production ration.

If we look more closely, however, the problem is less simple. For we must go beyond the quantitative parallels, beyond the performances of a given African scholar taken in isolation, or of a given research team; beyond the competitiveness of a given center or laboratory in order to examine, for example, the source of the equipment and other instruments used, the modalities of the choice of the subjects of research, the social needs and other practical demands from which the subjects chosen proceed, directly or indirectly; the geographical location in which these needs and demands first commanded attention, the real destination of the research results, the place where and the way in which these results are assigned, guarded, capitalized, the way in which they are applied, if need be; the complex links between this research and industry, this research and the economic activity in general—each time asking questions: What purpose does this research serve? Who will benefit from it? How does it insert itself in the very society that produces it? To what extent does this society manage to appropriate the results? To what extent, on the contrary, does it allow these to be taken away?

By considering things from this angle, one will readily notice that the difference (between scientific activity in Africa and that activity in the industrial metropolitan centers) is not only quantitative but qualitative as well, not only in degree or level of development but in orientation and in mode of operation. Research here is extraverted, turned toward the exterior, ruled by and subordinate to outside needs instead of being self-centered and destined, first of all, to answer the questions posed by the African society itself, whether directly or indirectly.

II

I will refer here to a study proposed elsewhere.[2] Scientific activity in the Third World seems to me to be characterized, globally, by its

2. Paulin J. Hountondji, "Situation de l'anthropologue africain: Note critique sur une forme d'extraversion scientifique" (paper delivered at a colloquium around Georges Balandier on Les Nouveaux Enjeux de l'Anthropologie, in Cérisy, France, June 1988. To be published in a collective work under the direction of Gabriel Gosselin.

position of dependency. This dependency is of the same nature as that of the economic activity, which is to say that, put back in the context of its historical genesis, it obviously appears to be the result of the progressive integration of the Third World into the worldwide process of the production of knowledge, managed and controlled by the Northern countries.

It has been observed thousands of times before that, during the colonial period, the occupied territory functioned on the economic level as a warehouse for raw materials, destined to feed the factories of the metropolis. What has been less well observed is that it functioned also, with respect to metropolitan scientific activity, as a provider of raw materials. The colony was nothing other than an immense storage place for new scientific facts, gathered in their crude state in order to be communicated to the urban laboratories and research centers, who took it upon themselves, and were the only ones who were able to do so, to treat them theoretically, to interpret them, to integrate them in their proper place in the system of the totality of the facts, both known and unknown to science. In other words, if the economic activity of the colony was characterized by a kind of industrial vacuum, scientific activity, too, was characterized by a crying theoretical vacuum. The colony lacked laboratories, as it lacked factories. It lacked laboratories in the broadest sense of the word, in the sense that every discipline, whether of the exact and natural sciences, of the social and human sciences, or of other sectors of knowledge, is by necessity developed in the laboratory. All the colony had to do, it was thought, was to build places especially organized and equipped for conceptual work, scholarly libraries or, if need be, that complicated technical apparatus necessary for the transformation of raw facts into verified knowledge—which is called experimentation. On the other hand, the metropolitan laboratories found, in the colony, a precious source of new information, an irreplaceable opportunity to enrich their stock of data and to step up one notch in their research, both through exhaustive and truly universal knowledge and through a practical mastery of the environment.

As a provider of raw materials, the colony was furthermore, as is known, one outlet among others, incidentally, for the products of the metropolitan industry. But what has been less well observed is that it functioned in the same manner with respect to the products of metropolitan scientific research. Thus, one used to find, and one still does, in the Dahomian market (Béninois, as it is called today), "Palmolive" soap made in France from palm oil (which Dahomey produced and still produces), as one found and still finds in another area textbooks of tropical geography, indeed, of the geography of Dahomey, produced in France from data gathered on the site, in Dahomey or in other tropical countries, and treated in the laboratories of the Institut National de Cartographie in Paris. Or in yet another sector there are locomotives, cars, various machinery and equipment that are the result of the technological application of the knowledge accumulated in the urban centers and of its industrial exploitation. The colony was, in its fashion, a consumer of science, as it was a consumer of industrial products, imported products in every case, and perceived as such; products whose origin and mode of "fabrication" the local population knew nothing about and that, therefore, could only appear to them as surreal and not to be mastered, miraculously placed on top of their daily reality like a veneer.

It would be interesting to examine the forms and modalities of this peripheral scientific "consumerism" in detail, to measure its importance, to calculate the relationship or, more precisely, the disproportion between this consumption and the more or less embryonic scientific production, which could provide a precise indication of the degree of scientific and technological dependency in the different countries, or in the different sectors of activity in the same country. It would, furthermore, be interesting to examine the nature and the relative importance of the facts and of the raw information "exported" from the colonies to the central laboratories of research, to compare these facts and this information with the raw materials proper exported from the same countries to the urban factories, and to establish criteria for a close approximate distinction between these two categories of "raw" materials. Such a distinction is not easily made, to the extent that even the raw materials of industry themselves sometimes undergo a "scientific" treatment in the urban center preceding their real transformation.

Finally, it would be interesting to appraise, from a historic and epistemological point of view, what European science owes to the Third World, to appraise the nature and the scope of the knowledge that came forth from the theoretical treatment of this new mass of data and information, to appraise the real working of the new disciplines based on these discoveries (tropical geography, tropical agriculture, African sociology, anthropology, etc.), and the alterations made in the older disciplines through these same discoveries.

This is not the place to resolve these complex problems. It suffices to have noted, at the very least, the real parallel between the functioning of the colony with respect to the metropolitan economic activity and its functioning with respect to the scientific activity; to have noted the very strong analogy between the applied strategies of removal in both cases, that is to say, on the one hand the draining of resource materials, and on the other the draining of information for the purpose of feeding the factories and the universities and urban research centers, all at the same time.

Undoubtedly, this analogy is far from perfect, since, for example, the "draining" of information does not deprive the colony that produced it of this information, while the removal of gold, ivory, and palm or peanut oil materially impoverishes the country that produces it. With respect to our problem, however, this difference is secondary.

There is more. Not only is this difference secondary, not only does the analogy remain very strong between the two forms of removal, but, and this is the bottom line, it concerns two complementary moments of one and the same process: accumulation on a worldwide scale. Scientific activity in general can, in fact, be thought of as a specific modality of economic activity; it is also an activity of production even if the objects produced here are those of knowledge, that is, concepts, intellectual and not material objects. Thus, it was natural that the annexation of the Third World, its integration in the worldwide capitalist system through trade and colonization, also comprise a "scientific" window, that the draining of material riches goes hand in hand with intellectual and scientific exploitation, the extortion of secrets and other useful information, as it was natural, on a different level, that they go hand in hand with the extortion of works of art meant to fill the museums of the metropolitan areas.

III

The period of which we speak has certainly gone by, but it has left its traces. Economically (in the narrow sense of the word "economy"), one can no longer speak of an industrial vacuum, no more than one can speak of a theoretic vacuum in the field of science. The former colonies now have factories and an industrial activity that is sometimes intense, and on a different level they have universities, laboratories, and research centers that are at times very well equipped.

That multiplication of factories, however, has not led, as we know, to an authentic development but rather to a growth without development, to use Samir Amin's phrase. The establishment of assembly lines for automobiles and other industrial units of the same kind continues to obey a logic of extraversion. Neocolonial industry continues

to be defined, on a massive scale, by the needs of the urban middle
class: it aims to produce luxury consumer goods destined for the
privileged few rather than consumer goods for the people. Therefore,
it cannot provide the collective rise in the standard of living of the
broadest layers of the population—which is what development would
really be.

Mutatis mutandis, I personally hold that the peripheral multiplication of the structures of intellectual and scientific production
(universities and research centers, libraries, etc.) far from ending extraversion have had as their essential role up until now the facili-
tating, therefore the reinforcement, of the draining of information,
the violation of what is secret, the marginalization of "traditional"
scholarship, the slow but sure integration of all useful information
available in the South into the worldwide process of production of
knowledge, managed and controlled by the North. In other words,
these structures of scientific production are themselves also, for the
same reason as the assembly lines, structures of import-substitution
which, far from suppressing it, on the contrary, reinforce extraversion, reinforce the dependency of the periphery with respect to the
center.

One can cite at least the following indications of this extraversion:

1. Scientific activity in our countries remains largely dependent
upon the laboratory equipment made in the center. We have never
produced a microscope; this holds all the more for the new equipment today, that is more and more sophisticated and necessary for
today's research that is on the cutting edge. And so the first link in
the chain, the making of the instruments of research, the production
of the scientific means of production, already eludes us.

2. Our scientific practice remains largely dependent upon the libraries, archives, publishing houses, journals, and other scientific periodicals published in the North; more generally, dependent upon
those holding places, locations on conservation and circulation of the
results of research, where the scientific memory of humanity takes
shape, and which remain largely and essentially concentrated in the
North. One must, without a doubt, recognize the enormous progress
that has been made in this respect in the Southern countries for the
last few dozen years. One should unquestionably appreciate, in all its
merit, the intense activity of scientific publishing and editing that
has materialized, here and there, through university annals, various
journals and periodicals, and more and more credible publishing
houses. Still, the progress made in this area is far from having re-

versed the process. Proof for this is the simple fact that these publications continue to find their most numerous and most loyal readership in the Northern countries. Of course, it is not a question of complaint but rather of stating the fact, analyzing it, and sifting out the significance.

3. We are here touching upon theoretical extraversion in its true sense; the fact that the work of our scholars is always known and read more in the North than in the South: the still more serious fact that this circumstance, that at first sight could be considered as purely exterior, is, in fact, still interiorized by our scholars themselves, to the point where they curve the very orientation and the content of their works in determining the choice of the themes of their research as well as the theoretical models applied to their treatment. The Third World researcher, thus, has a tendency to let himself be guided in his scientific work by the expectations and the preoccupations of the European public to which his virtual assistantship belongs.

4. The result, among others, of this theoretical extraversion: research on the periphery bears most frequently on the immediate environment; it remains riveted to the local context, enclosed in the specific, incapable of and not very eager to rise to the universal. At first sight, one might find it contradictory that the centripetal orientation of the research is presented here as a sign of scientific extraversion. One would be more inclined to see, on the contrary, an indication there of a liberation for the researcher from the South with respect to the dominant themes of Northern research, the sign that this researcher gives priority to the questions that are of direct interest to his own society. But the truth is very different: for in the total movement of the history of the sciences, territorial specializations have, once again, been produced by Europe and responded, originally, to the theoretic and practical needs of Europe. The truth is that Africanism itself, both as practice and ideology, is once again an invention of Europe, and that by enclosing himself in it, the African researcher, in fact, accepts playing the subordinate role of a knowledgeable informer with respect to European science. By becoming exclusive and badly mastered, the legitimate interest of the Southern researcher in his own milieu can thus generate dangerous traps. The obsession with the immediate future, the fear of breaking loose, then lead the researcher to scientific imprisonment and keep him away from an essential stage of the process of the totality of knowledge: the production of the theoretical models themselves, the elaboration of the

conceptual schemas that thereafter permit the grasping of the specific as such.

5. But scientific extraversion can have a more immediately practical origin and reach: it can happen that the choice of the field of research is not conditioned only, that is, indirectly determined, by the preoccupations of the European readership, but that it is immediately dictated, without any deviations and any subtleties, by the demands of an economy that is itself extraverted. Until quite recently, agronomic research provided a fine example of this crass form of extraversion, since its work was aimed, essentially, at the improvement of export crops (palm trees [oil], coconut trees, coffee, cocoa, peanuts, cotton, etc.), destined for the factories of the North or the factories of "import-substitution," established here and there in the South, while the food crops, from which the great mass of the local populations lived, were being neglected. Things have certainly made progress since then, but the basic tendency remains: agronomic research often remains largely in the service of a trade economy.

6. The famous *brain drain*, the flight of the brains from the South toward the North, in this context, takes on a new significance: an accidental manifestation of the global extraversion of our economy and more particularly of our scientific activity, it should not be treated as an evil in itself but as the visible tip of an enormous iceberg that we must learn to take into consideration and, if possible, to raise in its entirety. Those who leave are not, in fact, the only ones: those who stay are indirectly caught up in the same movement. The brains of the Third World, all the intellectually and scientifically competent, are rigorously carried by the whole flow of worldwide scientific activity toward the center of the system. Some "settle" in the host countries; others go back and forth between the periphery and the center; still others, caught in the impossibility of managing a move, survive as best they can on the periphery, where they struggle every day, with varying degrees of success, against the demons of cynicism and discouragement, while their eyes remain turned toward the center, for it is essentially from there that come equipment and instruments of research, traditions, publications, theoretical and methodological models, and the entire parade of values and countervalues that accompany those.

7. A minor form of the *brain drain*, scientific South/North tourism, seems an important phenomenon to which little attention has been paid until now. In the normal routine of the researcher from the Third World, the journey remains unavoidable; the researcher must move

physically, leave for the great industrial urban centers, either to perfect his scientific training, or, once his research project is launched,
to pursue it beyond a certain threshold. The question is not whether
such journeys are pleasant or not: undoubtedly, many find them
pleasant, especially at the beginning of their careers; others, on the
other hand, find them oddly repetitive, or experience them as a true
wrenching. This is nothing but a question of personal appreciation
that leaves the true question intact, that of the structural need for
such journeys, of the objective constraints that render *this* form of
scientific tourism inevitable, and that characterize the scientific activity in the Third World in a very particular way.

In saying that, naturally I do not claim to minimize the enormous
scientific advantage one can take from such trips; on the contrary, I
am focusing attention on the fact that these trips remain, under the
present circumstances, the condition sine qua non of that kind of advantage. Under these circumstances, it would also be absurd, everything else being equal, to seek to put an end to scientific South/North
"tourism," which is not a form of tourism at all, as I am trying to
point out emphatically. The real demand lies elsewhere: it must be a
question of changing, of profoundly transforming the present scientific relationships in the world, of promoting a self-centered scientific
activity in those countries that are today peripheral.

I am, furthermore, not ignoring the fact that even in the center of
the system today's researcher cannot remain altogether sedentary, under penalty of slow death, unless it be in the very heart of the center;
there is the center of the center, the absolute pose: the United States
of America which, to the detriment of Northern Europe and Japan, is
attracting the "cream" of the international community of researchers
more and more all the time. However, scientific "tourism" then no
longer has the same significance: the flow of the researchers South/
North is not the result of an internal imbalance in scientific activity
in the secondary capitalist countries; each one of them develops, and
very well at that, an independent, self-centered activity, in principle
capable of surviving by itself. The exodus of its men of science toward
the United States, or for certain disciplines toward Japan, for this
reason, comes from their seeking something "more." With respect to
the exodus South/North, it represents a luxury rather than a vital
necessity.

8. To make this complete, another form of scientific "tourism"
should be examined: the mover North/South. The movement that
brings a researcher from the industrialized nation to a nation of the

periphery never has the same function as the opposite movement. The European or American scholar is not going to Zaire or the Sahara looking for science but only for the materials for science and, if need be, for a terrain to apply his discoveries. He is not going to look there for his paradigms, his theoretical and methodological models, but on the one hand for new information and facts that might enrich his paradigms, and on the other hand for distant territories where, with the least possible risk to his own society, he can perform his nuclear experiments or other types of experiments postulating various degrees of danger.

Entire portions of contemporary knowledge were born from this scientific investment in the South by the North. Out of this have come new disciplines, such as social and cultural anthropology, and different specializations within the previous disciplines. The knowledge thus collected, the knowledge on Africa and the Third World, completely escapes Africa and the Third World but is systematically returned to Europe, repatriated, capitalized, accumulated in the center of the system. Consequently, there is no extraversion in the movement North/South, but a simple tactical detour in the service of a self-sufficiency and of a strengthened technological mastery.

9. Under these conditions, what becomes of the traditional knowledge and knowhow? It is a fact that, in our oral cultures, there exist bodies of knowledge, sometimes very elaborate ones, faithfully transmitted from one generation to the next and often enriched in the course of this transmission. These knowledges of plants, animals, health, and illness, this knowledge of agriculture and the artisans, instead of developing, of gaining in precision and in vigor through the contact with foreign science, have more of a tendency to turn in upon themselves, subsisting in the best cases *side by side* with the new knowledge in a relationship of simple juxtaposition, and in the worst cases possibly disappearing completely and being erased from the collective memory. The integration into the worldwide process of the production of knowledge thus has the effect of marginalizing the old wisdom, indeed, in the worst of cases, of driving them out of the conscious memory of the peoples who, at a given time, produce them.

10. Scientific extraversion shows itself as well by using merely Western languages as languages of science, obliging the Third World researcher to accept the humiliating terms of these languages of foreign origin in order to have access to knowledge and, even more so, to reproduce and extend it. Without a doubt, one must be careful not to exaggerate the inconveniences that result from this situation, or to

fall into the extremes of a Romanticism that would have each language already be, in itself and through itself, the expression of a determined vision of the world, and consequently have the mother
tongue be the only one in which any person can express his true identity. Without a doubt, language should be brought back to its instrumental role and made to comply with the modern demands of a
widened community, in a world where no one, under penalty of asphyxiation, can entirely turn in upon himself any longer. Equally to
be recognized is the antinatural character of the real relationships
that presently exist in certain Third World countries, and particularly
in Black Africa, between the native languages and the imported languages: the factual marginalization of the former to the exclusive advantage of the latter, the relegation of native languages to substandard
languages, indeed "dialects" or "patois," barely good enough to express the platitudes of everyday life, the absence of a daring project of
generalized literacy and the use of native languages as vehicles for
teaching and for research at the highest level, with a real democratization of knowledge as an end.

I will not go any further. These remarks have no other goal than to
indicate a direction of research and to ground its legitimacy with respect to the existing research. They come forth from a well-known
discipline: the sociology of science. But contrary to the usual work in
this field, the study envisioned here could not stop at examining the
functioning of science in the industrialized societies. On the contrary,
it will question specific traits of scientific and technological activity
in the Third World, at the periphery of the worldwide capitalist
system. The final objective is to establish a new scientific and technological politics that, in the end, would allow the collective appropriation of knowledge and of the entire scientific heritage available in
the world by the peoples who, until now, have constantly been dispossessed of the fruits of their labor in this area as in all others.

French Marxist Anthropology of the 1960s and African Studies: Outline for an Appraisal

Emmanuel Terray

fifteen

I would like to make the limitations of the remarks that follow clear from the start: I present the attempt at an appraisal from a personal point of view, and have no inclination to mask what it may contain in subjectivity. Contrary to an opinion that is sometimes held, especially abroad, there never has been a French school of Marxist anthropology. To stay within my own generation, M. Godelier, C. Meillassoux, P. P. Rey, and myself have never formed a group in any way. We were deeply divided, not only in the political realm—with Maurice Godelier belonging to the Communist party and the others to different varieties of the left—but we also were divided in matters of theory, and our divergences did not concern small points of detail but the interpretation of several of the fundamental notions of Marxism. My judgments, therefore, involve only myself, and I take it for granted that the majority of them would not be shared by my comrades.

In order to evaluate the contribution and the success of an enterprise, the situation that provided it with its point

249

of departure should be taken into consideration. At the end of the 1950s, French Africanist anthropology was largely dominated by what might be called the school of Marcel Griaule. The members of this school were above all interested in discourses, representations, visions of the world, and they had a tendency to neglect social organizations and practices. They preferred to have contact with privileged interlocutors without questioning whether they were truly representative. Finally, they clung primarily to tradition and deplored the evolutions that were coming to compromise it. In Great Britain, it was functionalism that dominated. African history—not the history of the contacts between Europeans and Africans but the history of pre-colonial Africa as seen from the inside—was just in its beginning stages, and many professional historians deemed it impossible. Only some isolated voices expressed a conflicting opinion; this was the case with the school of Manchester, in Great Britain, and with Georges Balandier, in France: I will come back later to the influence they had on us. As far as Marxism is concerned, finally, it was barely coming out of its "dogmatic sleep." Jean Suret-Canale had just proposed that, in order to examine the African societies, one draws one's inspiration from the concept of the "Asiatic mode of production," thus hoping to escape the yoke of the five stages enumerated by Stalin. To evaluate our attempt equitably, this situation should be kept in mind.

To make an appraisal of a movement, the ambitions that brought it to life should also be taken into account. For my purpose, I shall distinguish three principal ones present in varying intensity in each of the researchers who participated in the enterprise; the order of my recital of facts is, therefore, not significant.

Our intention was, first of all, to lay the foundation of a science. Of course, this motive was particularly powerful among those who were called the Marxist anthropologists of the second generation, strongly marked by the influence of Louis Althusser. But he also inspired all those of us—more numerous perhaps than they later admitted—who had been seduced by the works of Claude Lévi-Strauss, and notably by *Les structures élémentaires de la parenté* ([1949] 1967; English trans. *Elementary Structures of Kinship* [1969]). What we all rejected, I believe, and always did, in Claude Lévi-Strauss, is the transcendental materialism that he uses as philosophy, the thesis according to which the secret of the structures of kinship relationships or of the myth should be looked for in the structure of the human brain, set up as ultimate subject of culture and history. But disclosing the operation of an unconscious logic from beneath the chaotic diversity of appearances was what Marx had already done for the "bourgeois" economy and society, and was what Lévi-Strauss, too, had succeeded in doing in the field of kinship relationships. Supported by the knowledge acquired by each of these, we could hope to go further on the road of a more rigorous knowledge of the so-called primitive societies.

Second, our project was one of criticism. We wanted to dismantle the image that, until the present and from different angles, European ethnology had given of the so-called primitive societies. There we were attacking both the theories of order and balance that seemed to dominate British anthropology and the opposition traced by Claude Lévi-Strauss between "cold" societies and "hot" societies, societies against history, and cumulative societies. This critical concern was especially alive among those of us who had been the students of Georges Balandier, who had shared the preoccupations of his dynamic anthropology, and who, with him as intermediary, had been influenced by the British researchers of the Manchester school and by Max Gluckman, in particular. In this perspective, the themes of contradiction and conflict took on a very special importance.

Finally, our project had a political bearing. In our mind, it was not only a question of taking part in an ideological struggle in the European metropolises by destroying the mystifying conceptions of the primitive societies that were our opposites. Having come to political consciousness during the time of the wars of Indochina and Algeria, we were hoping to contribute to the liberation struggles of the oppressed peoples, on the one hand, by helping the militants who came forth from these peoples to understand correctly the objective conditions of their actions and, on the other hand, by participating more or less directly in this action.

If we reduce it to these initial ambitions, the appraisal is "globally mediocre," to put it bluntly. The term "science," undoubtedly, no longer carries the weight in our eyes that it did twenty years ago. Yet, it was not unreasonable to hope that the introduction of the categories of historical materialism into anthropological studies would lead to a renewal of perspectives, to the opening of original directions in research, to the blossoming of unprecedented problematics, in short to a mutation comparable to the one brought on by structuralism, for example. From this point of view, the results were modest.

Surely, greater attention has been accorded to economic phenomena, but what else should be said? In fact, we first of all remained prisoners, to a very great extent, of the traditional concepts of anthropology and of the definitions that our precursors had established of its objects and its problems. The history of the concept of the mode of production is, in this regard, exemplary; this concept and the elements it combines—producer, means of labor, object of labor, product; real appropriation and control; productive forces and yield of production, and so on—should have allowed the elaboration of models that "represented" the economic base of the so-called primitive societies in all its diversity. But, in this sense, only scattered attempts that very quickly came to a dead end were observed. Most of the time, one was satisfied with defining the mode of production by the juxtaposition of a few general traits concerning a certain type of economy, and thus the concept became an instrument of classification. Losing its analytic capacities, it only served to establish a typology. What classical anthropology used to call "society" was sometimes rebaptized "mode of production" or "social formation," and it was considered that the demands of historical materialism were thus satisfied. In this fashion, the fertility of the concept of the mode of production had been wasted entirely, and it is not surprising that some of us consider it useless and harmful today.

Just as we gave up rigorously using the categories that historical materialism offered us, we most often accepted, without criticizing them, the objects and the problems inherited from classical anthropology. As Jean Copans so rightly observed, even while we were contesting the notion of ethnos or society, we preserved it as a frame of reference for our research. In the same way, we left kinship "relationship" its status of first and irreducible object without wondering if the totality of the representations, the rules, and the practices regrouped in this term were a totality given in the reality or an aggregate reunited by the mere artifice of the ethnologist. In short, while we believed that we were changing the content, we very often changed nothing but the labels.

What is more serious is that we very largely remained dependent upon the traditional explanations of anthropology and, especially, on the functionalist explanation. In the first place, the latter was copiously made to contribute as soon as it concerned specifying the relationship between infrastructures and superstructures. Confronting this task, we wanted to stand aloof from the old theory of "reflection," but this was more often than not in order to replace it by a given variety of functionalism. In other words, we explained beliefs and institutions through the role that we assigned them in the functioning of the organism or the social machine. As I have had the opportunity to write elsewhere, it is the notion of reproduction that was the occasion of this return by dint of functionalism: identified with the repetition of the existing order, reproduction was conceived as a final cause from which the totality of examined structures and institutions would proceed, each one of the latter appearing as the resolution to one of the problems posed by the former.

Through lack of imagination and daring, we thus let ourselves be cornered by a dilemma between dogmatic mechanism and empiricist eclecticism, from which we emerged vanquished in every way. Confronted by the criticism of our adversaries, we hesitated between two attitudes: either we gave up on upholding the fundamental axioms of Marxism—determination ultimately through economics, the driving role of the contradiction of class, and so on—and, by means of variations upon the theme of the autonomy of superstructures, we came back to an eclectic concept of historical causality. Or, we defended these axioms because we were tied to their breaking power, but then we gave a reducing interpretation of it that forbade us any significant thrust in the analysis of politics and ideology.

All in all, what happened to many a generation of Marxists before ours happened to us: we wanted to be innovative and believed we had been so, but without our being aware of it our effort had been eaten at from the inside through the pressure of the dominating tendencies of established anthropology—functionalism, structuralism. We had thus repeated old contents in a different language. When we wanted to take our distance, we had hardly any other recourse than the evolutionist vulgate that still dominated French Marxism.

Hence, on the theoretic plane, the attainments seem to me to be limited. We have been more felicitous, it seems to me, with the critical aspect of our project. After M. Gluckman and G. Balandier, we helped in the reintegration of the so-called primitive societies into the sphere of history. The idea of a "cold society" is hardly accepted any longer, and there are few researchers to continue to assert that the so-called primitive societies escape inequalities, oppressions, exploitations, conflicts.

The idealized images such as those pictured a long time ago by Pierre Clastres in *La société contre l'état* are today widely recognized for what they are: war machines in the ideological struggle in the heart of the Western metropolises. To be more specific, by insisting upon the status of the elders and the tensions that oppose them to their juniors within the lineage societies, we have helped to reveal that which Marc Augé so felicitously called lineage totalitarianism. Similarly, we have rightly called the attention of the anthropologists and the historians of Africa to slavery and shown that the latter could not simply be reduced to the amiable domestic captivity as described by certain researchers of earlier days.

In the realm of methods, we did not question the traditional conceptions and forms of ethnographic work; our materials have been gathered in the course of surveys on the site and conducted according to the customs and rules in force. Specifically, we respected the framework traditionally assigned to these surveys: the ethnic group, the village community. What we did, under these conditions, is to propose a different reading of the material assembled according to the classical procedures. To the extent that, in anthropology as in any other discipline, the production of the facts determines their meaning and their interpretation, the originality of our contribution inevitably had to support the effects of our conformism where methods were concerned.

In the last place, I do not believe that we succeeded in resolving the difficult problem of the relationship between "professional" practice and political practice. To the extent that we ratified—and how else can one act?—the central place that classical anthropology accorded to fieldwork in the practice of our profession, we ran into insurmountable obstacles.

Indeed, the political situation in the countries where ethnologists generally work is such that, on the one hand, the researcher inevitably seems more or less directly linked to those in power, and, on the other hand, he must respect a minimum of political "neutrality" if he wishes to pursue his work over a relatively long period of time without risking expulsion and the prohibition from entering certain areas. The attempts at elaborating a militant practice on the site have, to my knowledge, all ended in failure: the stage of workers confronting the crassest bureaucratic oppression has never been passed. To compensate for these failures, some, accepting the split between professional life and political action, have respected the demands of neutrality in the former, or at the very least the demands of prudence, and on the other hand became involved, more or less intensely, in a political organization, but without then acting on behalf of their specialty. Others have made more or less close connections with the students and the radical intellectuals of the countries in which they were staying, without this association running into any very precise political action. In the best of cases, we have leaned on the academic prestige of anthropology to consolidate a given political stance. But our initial hope for a kind of fusion between professional practice and political practice has revealed itself, based on experience, to be largely illusory.

What can we learn from this modest or disillusioned appraisal? In the first place, the enterprise has suffered deeply from the general crisis of Marxism from the 1970s on. We were claiming to revitalize anthropology from a Marxist point of departure; however, it would have been necessary for Marxism to preserve its vitality. The shortness of breath of Marxist thought these last years—in itself both sign and effect of the political crisis of Marxism—has in some way carried along with it the asphyxiation of our attempt; if I dare put it this way, our motor was no longer getting any fuel.

In fact, it is with Marxist anthropology as it is with anthropology in general. As I see it, our discipline is incapable—and has always been incapable—of producing its own categories and its own modes of reasoning and demonstration; it is forced to borrow its models from other more or less neighboring sciences. In the nineteenth century, it borrowed it from biology and looked at society as an organism; in the twentieth century, structuralism appealed to linguistics; in our day, some turn to topology, others toward the theory of catastrophes; in short, any anthropology that would be constrained to isolate itself and to close in upon itself very shortly would be condemned to death. That is what happened to Marxist anthropology; from the moment that Marxist research in general declined, Marxist anthropology, which was inspired by the former, had to decline as well.

If one accepts the preceding analysis, one might then, without any extreme risk, put forward a prediction on the future history of the relationship between anthropology and Marxism. In France today, Marxism resembles a palace that has been abandoned by its inhabitants: it is deserted but intact, and one can foresee that it will not remain unoccupied indefinitely; the day will come—sooner perhaps than it may seem—when the analytic power and the critical property of Marxist thought will be rediscovered. The same will happen where anthropology is concerned: if one agrees with me that it is still largely dependent upon the functionalist paradigms inherited from the nineteenth century, if one agrees that these paradigms are beginning to lose their heuristic quality, if, finally, one recognizes that anthropology is obliged to import from the outside the main of its concepts and its approaches, then the layers of its available ideas are not so numerous, and it cannot afford the luxury of letting the Marxist vein remain unexploited for too long. That day, our attempt will be renewed again, and it will be revealed perhaps that, despite all appearances, our own effort has not been absolutely in vain.

Practical Ideology and Ideological Practice: On African Episteme and Marxian Problematic— Ilparakuyo Maasai Transformations

sixteen

Meidip oltung'ani endapana enkiteng' enye
("The hide of his own cow cannot suffice a person")

Peter Rigby

The aim of "African philosophy" or, better still, "African philosophies," is not, as witnessed by *Présence Africaine*, merely to "Africanize" philosophy; it is to create a discursive space in which an epistemology and problematic related to the historical experiences of Africa can be constructed (Mudimbe 1988:164–165, passim). It is not just to make philosophy an *object* of research and study in Africa; it is to provide a reflexive and critical theory for truly revolutionary action.[1]

1. It very well may be objected that the role of intellectuals and their productions, such as this essay and the research and various works to which it refers, are so distant from the "actual *praxis*" of transformation to which it pertains in Africa as to be virtually insignificant. If the reader is of this opinion, I trust he will change his mind as we proceed, since I hope convincingly to demonstrate otherwise. For the moment, and despite its Hegelian overtones, I will concur with Michel Foucault in the following passage (1980:133), in which he says, "The essential political problem for the intellectual is not to criticize the ideological contents supposedly linked to science, or to ensure that his scientific prac-

It is to go *beyond* négritude and "Afro-centricity" in order to create a future free from class, or any other kind of exploitation and oppression. It is both theory and practice.

It might seem ambitious, presumptuous, and even obnoxious for a nonphilosopher to begin an essay in this fashion. I have my reasons which, I hope, will appear as we proceed. And I can perhaps justify such an opening by saying that my position is not at variance with Professor V. Y. Mudimbe's claim for the *"unity* in diversity" of contemporary African philosophy (Mudimbe 1983); in fact, this introductory essay may be taken as an affirmation of African philosophy as a continuing process within which often-heated debate is its most characteristic feature, indicating "the creative power of African self-criticism" (147). I differ somewhat, however, with Mudimbe in respect of the role that Marxism can play in this continuing discourse.

My main concern is that, if a future anthropology (and perhaps any other social science) is to be of any help at all in realizing "development," cultural and social transformation, and "true *freedom"* in Africa, it must be a force in heightening "awareness" of what is involved in "development," and hence in political mobilization toward these ends. Such an accomplishment would engender a process of development in all *four* aspects of a comprehensive political economy: namely, economic disengagement and internally generated transformation, free political praxis toward this end, cultural independence in all its senses, and their accompanying discourses free from the *categories* of thought and dialogue of past and present colonial domination.

It is, therefore, quite obviously not my intention here to summarize or evaluate the extremely diverse views expressed by African philosophers, theologians, and social scientists, even if I were capable of it. This task has been most penetratingly and comprehensively achieved by Professor V. Y. Mudimbe (1983, 1985, 1988). What I attempt in this chapter is to suggest a direction in which a truly radical and subversive African theoretical framework (and, as a result, a basis for political, economic, and cultural praxis) might be derived from a

---

tice is accompanied by a correct ideology, but that of ascertaining the possibility of constituting a new politics of truth . . . It is not a matter of emancipating truth from every system of power (which is a chimera, for truth is already power) but of detaching the power of truth from the forms of hegemony, social economic, and cultural, within which it operates at the present time." This position is consistent with one derived from Gramsci and not at variance with a dialectical Marxist view of praxis.

convergence of African philosophy and a particular *form* of historical materialist theorizing.[2]

During the excursus, I will address the issue of the "Africanization" of Marxist theory as well as the "Marxistization" (if I may coin such a term) of African historical, social, and reflexive studies. This is necessary, I believe, because neither a Marxist theoretical position, nor an African philosophy, on its own, is capable of creating the conditions in which the struggle for freedom in Africa (or elsewhere in the Third World) can proceed and fulfill our expectations. It is immediately clear, of course, that this is no easy task, since the diversity of opinion within Marxist theorizing is as great as the almost intractable controversies that bedevil African philosophical discourse.

II

In an important book on "livestock development" in Kenya Maasailand, Evangelou recently noted (1984:1–2) that

> the underexploited productive potential of range areas, regions mainly utilized by largely self-sufficient, non-market oriented [*sic*] pastoral peoples, is increasingly attracting the attention of national governments.

At the same time, Evangelou continues, "Traditional Maasai social structure and cultural institutions fundamentally constrain development initiatives" (125; see also Doherty 1979).

Both these statements, including the notion of "*livestock* development" itself, and the research upon which they are based, occupy a discursive space totally *displaced* from Maasai society, culture, and politics. The first statement involves the notion that "national governments" represent social categories *distinct* from "largely self-sufficient, nonmarket oriented pastoralists" who, nevertheless, seem to live in areas over which these "national governments" apparently hold sway. It is implied, *ab initio*, that the *interests* of pastoral peoples are essentially different from those of the national government; and, in fact, this is largely true, but for reasons quite at odds with the ones adduced by Evangelou. The only manner in which

---

2. By "Africa" I mean here both the most *general* conditions of African history: the history in which Africa has seen the transformations that occurred before imperialist penetration, the depredations of the period immediately preceding a colonial penetration, and the colonial period itself; and the postcolonial recent past, as well as the more specific and localized historicities, forms of thought and practice related to one or more African peoples. *None* of the latter can be conceived of as "closed systems," since they have never, at any period, been truly isolated from one another.

these diverse interests will coincide is through a relation of inequality between the two parties concerned and, hence, the exercise of power by one over the other. The struggle is predetermined; the outcome is assumed.

The second statement by Evangelou embodies a judgment upon a number of things, the two most important of which are: (1) *Who* defines what "development initiatives" are, and (2) *who* decides that these initiatives are "constrained" by the "traditional" social structure and culture of Maasai pastoralists? The idea of ("good") development occupies an "external" space in relation to the Maasai social formation; the ("bad") traditional social structure and culture are "internal" to Maasai society; we arrive again at a contradiction which can only be resolved by political confrontation and differential power.

It appears as if the investigator is somehow intervening in these two social fields, helping *both* sides resolve an otherwise unresolvable conflict. But, in reality, the researcher has already decided who will (or even should) win and sets about *appropriating* knowledge from the already identified "loser" and supplying it to the "winner." At the very least, this implies hegemonic control by the state over not only the *place* occupied by Maasai but also their entire vision of the future. More than this, Maasai are presumed to adhere to what is called "traditional" culture and institutions, implying another form of *distancing* in both place *and* time, a state of affairs that seems to be accepted without contention by the anthropologist (see Fabian 1983).

"Development" is the "present" and the "future"; Maasai culture and social structure are "traditional" and the "past," soon to be forgotten in the glorious movement of "progress." Does the anthropologist never sit down and think, since Maasai have been involved in peripheral capitalism for at least a hundred years, to them, at least, what is new today is the anthropologist's "tradition" tomorrow? I return to this crucial issue again, since it becomes a central question for what is, or is not, African philosophy. At any rate, "progress" is something decided upon *not* necessarily by "national governments" in many cases but by international capitalism, represented by international development agencies; I would hazard that it does not take much imagination to know *who* will get "developed" in such a case. Yet anthropologists seem content to ally themselves with these organizations, consciously or unconsciously for their own benefit.

The very *language* of development is imposed upon a people who are assumed to occupy a place and a time separate from, and even antagonistic to, those of the planners of progress. Not since the fire-breathing missionaries of the nineteenth century has such misplaced zeal been evident. I have discussed elsewhere (Rigby 1985:92–122) the relationship between the discourse of missionaries and Ilparakuyo Maasai praxis. Contemporary external hegemonic control, in the case of Ilparakuyo and Maasai, is purported to be exercised by the national governments of Kenya and Tanzania. Postcolonial states in contemporary Africa differ a great deal, at least ostensibly, from each other in the forms of the development they pursue. They, in turn, are to a greater or lesser degree dependent upon external sources of power and accumulation for their own precarious reproduction (see Coulson 1979; Kitching 1980; Leys 1975; Shivji 1975; Saul 1979, 1985; Thomas 1984). The reproduction of the state in the Third World, its power, and the status quo depend upon the achievement of certain *class* interests at the national level, even if the specific politico-economic and cultural conditions for the formation of these classes in Africa, and elsewhere in the Third World, are different from those in advanced capitalism.[3]

To the extent that this is true, social formations such as Ilparakuyo and Maasai, other pastoralists (especially in Kenya) and the entire peasantry occupy an exploited and marginal position analogous to, but very different from, the position of the proletariat in advanced capitalist social formations. It is here that an *African* discourse about class struggle and cultural resistance *from within* provides the juxtaposition of a knowledge diametrically opposed to the forms of "knowledge" espoused by commentators such as Evangelou as well as many other theorists of "development interventions." They are committed to a "capitalist" path to a bourgeois revolution in the Third World, whatever comes later (for example, Hyden 1980, 1983; Warren 1980; but see also Hedlund 1979).

In many places, but perhaps most eloquently in his *Decolonizing the Mind* (1986; cf. 1977, 1981a, 1981b, 1982, 1983), Ngugi wa Thiong'o states his position on the relation between class struggle and cultural liberation, a struggle in which the problem of language plays a central part. While I adopt a position on language as a material force in the liberation struggle which is broader than Ngugi's, the elemental point that the theory and practice of class struggle and liberation must occupy the *same* discursive space as that occupied by African history,

---

3. Even among "underdeveloped" countries, the process of class formation, as it is "overdetermined" (Althusser 1977:252–253; Althusser and Balibar 1970: passim), varies a great deal from one country to another, although the *conditions* of class formation remain the same everywhere.

cultures, and languages is brilliantly made by Ngugi (1986:3), and I quote him in extenso:

> Imperialism, led by the USA, presents the struggling peoples of the earth and all those calling for peace, democracy, and socialism with the ultimatum: accept theft or death. The oppressed and exploited of the earth maintain their defiance: liberty from theft. But the biggest weapon wielded and daily actually unleashed by imperialism against that collective defiance is the cultural bomb. The effect of a cultural bomb is to annihilate a people: belief in their names, in their languages, in their country, in their capacities and ultimately in themselves. It makes them see their past as one wasteland of non-achievement . . . Amidst this wasteland which it has created, imperialism presents itself as the cure and demands that the dependent sing hymns of praise with the constant refrain: "Theft is holy!" Indeed, this refrain sums up the new creed of the neo-colonial bourgeoisie in many "independent" African states.

The class struggle, then, is inseparable from a cultural struggle, through which revolutionary praxis unites the past and the present in the *creation* of a future (see Rigby 1985:81–87, passim). The forces and strategies of the ruling class, manifested in cultural hegemony, *become transparent* to the "actors" (the historical subjects) in an alliance of peasants and urban proletariats and lumpenproletariats, *through* recourse to the forms of language and discourse of the people themselves. This constitutes a rejection of cultural imperialism and neocolonialism; awareness, engendered by a reinspired language and discourse, includes an apprehension of the hegemonic control exercised by the postcolonial state. The latter has a power more tenuous than in mature capitalist formations and is more likely to have recourse to physical coercion and cultural censorship. Ngugi (1986:3) concludes:

> The classes fighting against imperialism even in its neo-colonial stage and form, have to confront this threat with the higher and more creative culture of resolute struggle. These classes have to wield even more firmly *the weapons of the struggle contained in their cultures.* They have to speak the united language of the struggle *contained in each of their languages.* (Emphasis added)

In Ngugi's terms, Ilparakuyo and Maasai are not *conservative;* they are positively *revolutionary!*

Before we proceed, I must insert a caveat. As I point out elsewhere, (Rigby, in press, chap.6) by emphasizing the subversive use of African languages and linguistic categories, a *prise de parole* including diverse cultural elements, I am *not* referring to the phenomenon known generally in anthropology as "revitalization movements," or "millenarian cults;" on the contrary, I am referring to the conative power embodied in specific *forms of parole*, not as in Suassure's *parole* but as in Bakhtin's sense of the speech act as "made specifically social, historical, concrete, and dialogized" (Bakhtin 1981:433, passim; see also Clark and Holquist 1984:10–15).

Neither am I proposing an apotheosis of *négritude*, or of the very different ideology of "Afrocentricity," although these ideas have played, and continue to play, an important role in certain places and historical conjunctures. This role is primarily one of a strategy of discourse for political praxis, and it will appear at several places in what follows. Here I must note that "Afrocentricity," or the "Afrocentric Idea," particularly as advanced by Molefi Asante (1980, 1987, passim), is addressed primarily to African-*Americans*, and does not propose a discourse which would mobilize an *African* struggle against current racist and class oppression in Africa. Asante himself notes (1987:124) that "there are *three* ideas [my emphasis] advanced to deal with the questions of blackness as a philosophical issue . . . *negritude, authenticity*, and *Afrocentricity*." But he is incorrect when he concludes that "all are centered in the socio-cultural reality of a geographical region, namely, Africa." He then proceeds to substantiate this claim, in a footnote, as follows (157–158, n.3):

> I maintain that *African-Americans* can never achieve their full psychological potential until they find a congruence between who *they are* and *what their environment says it ought to be.* (Emphasis added)

This statement is true, no doubt, but hardly directed toward promoting the revolutionary struggle much of Africa has to undergo to achieve full freedom and cultural independence, as outlined by Ngugi wa Thiong'o. Asante attempts to separate the "Afrocentric" Ngugi from the "Marxist" Ngugi, an enterprise bound to failure (see also Asante 1987:125, 167); they are dialectically inseparable from each other, and one cannot really have one Ngugi without the other (see Balogun 1987/1988; Kamenju 1985; Nazareth 1985; etc.).

But I must now turn to a brief consideration of the debate about African philosophy, conducted by African philosophers, writers, and social scientists; I then turn to its implications for the social sciences, for Marxist theorizing, and finally, for Ilparakuyo and Maasai studies.

III

There are two questions of fundamental importance in what follows: (1) What constitutes the specificity of *African* philosophy; and (2) what, if any, is the relation between African philosophy and Marxism? As we shall see, these two questions are intimately linked. But another caveat. As I have noted, I am not a philosopher, and therefore my excursion into the territory of African philosophy is fraught with hidden perils. My justification for so doing is twofold: first, the intention and logic of the chapter demands that anthropology, in its broadest sense, *must* cease to define itself on the basis of a reified (and spurious) object; second, this necessary redefinition must involve the production of a knowledge which is both temporally and spatially congruent (or as congruent as possible) with its *subject of discourse* (see Fabian 1983).

The first question involves Paulin Hountondji's work in African philosophy. He has been described as "perhaps the best known of the 'professional philosophers'" (Owomoyela 1987:79; see also Irele 1983: 8). Hountondji's position is highly controversial, since he rejects what has come to be called "ethnophilosophy" in Africa. Because such "ethnophilosophies" are the historical basis for the initial thrust in generating the interest in African philosophy, it is not surprising that his views have been sharply criticized. And, partially because Hountondji was a student of, and influenced by, Louis Althusser, a prominent French philosopher of Marxism, the rejection of Hountondji's position is sometimes taken as a simultaneous repudiation of any possible *rapprochement* between African philosophy and Marxism.

One of the most recent and strongest critiques of Hountondji comes from Kwame Gyekye, of the University of Ghana. He is quite unequivocal in his condemnation of Hountondji's position (Gyekye 1987:36). Hountondji's rejection of a philosophical basis for "traditional" African thought and proposal for a "new concept of African philosophy" is, according to Gyekye, a "tissue of errors ... The so-called new concepts of African philosophy may be 'radically new,' but it is equally radically false and radically unacceptable."

Gyekye is very concerned about Hountondji's criticism of what the latter calls "culturalism." While admitting that Hountondji is not alone is denying the link between culture and philosophy, and hence negating "ethnophilosophy" (Gyekye includes Bodunrin and Wiredu in his critique), he makes a strong case (I think correctly, for reasons that will appear) for deriving African philosophy from its cultural context. Philosophy, however, cannot be *reduced* to culture; if it is, it ceases to exist. This entails another point of contention: that of the *collective* nature of a culturally derived African philosophy versus the *individual* production of philosophies in the Western tradition (Gyekye 1987:24–29). Gyekye also makes a good case for the collective provenance of ancient Greek philosophy from which Western philosophy is said to descend, as interpreted by such eminent scholars as F. M. Cornford. And to Gyekye's argument we can now add that the "collectivity" from which Thales and Aristotle probably derived their philosophical systems was African and Asian rather than "pure Greek," whatever that may be! (Bernal 1987:207, 233, passim).

What Gyekye does *not* deal with is one of the major reasons given by Hountondji for his trenchant critique of "culturalism" in African philosophical discourse. Hountondji's argument is powerful (1983:162):

> Culturalism is an ideological system because it produces an indirect political effect. It eclipses, first, the problem of effective national liberation and, second, the problem of *class struggle*. (Emphasis added)

Not only this, however; for Hountondji (1983), culturalism is a *weapon* of class oppression, as is anthropology and ethnology:

> In independent countries culturalism takes the form of a backward-looking cultural nationalism, flattening out the national culture and denying it its *internal pluralism* and *historical depth,* in order to divert the attention of the exploited classes from the real political and economic conflicts which divide them from the ruling classes under the fallacious protext of their common participation in "the" national culture.

Hountondji then proceeds to ethnology and political anthropology, noting that culturalism is "characteristic of Third World nationalists and Western ethnologists: it is the *locus of their objective complicity*" (emphasis added). He continues (1983:163–164):

> Ethnologists . . . try to isolate the cultural aspects of society and to stress it at the expense of the economic and political aspects. Even when dealing with politics, ethnologists will generally be concerned with the traditional kind, arbitrarily reduced to its precolonial dimension, petrified, ossified and emptied of its internal tensions, discontinuities and confrontations. The political problem of

colonial or neo-colonial domination is never posed . . .
Moreover, when they investigate this precolonial past,
they refuse to see the evolution, revolutions, and discontinuities that may have affected it, and the precarious balance which has made these civilizations temporarily what
they are today. Anthropologists need to play with simple
units, univocal totalities without cracks or dissonances.
They need dead cultures, petrified cultures, always identical to themselves in the homogenous space of an eternal
present.

How true this is will become more evident as we proceed with this
chapter, particularly when I deal with recent work on Kenya Maasai
by anthropologist Paul Spencer. It is quite reasonable to suggest that
Hountondji here (and elsewhere in his book) is being deliberately po-
lemical in suggesting an epistemological and politico-economic origin in common for the ethnophilosophies so carefully constructed by
so many African philosophers on the one hand, and the notoriously
alienated forms of bourgeois social science on the other. For the moment, however, I propose to follow Gyekye's broad suggestion (1987:
9), which is one among many similar statements by other authors, that

the denial of the philosophical component of African
thought cannot really be accepted. The reason is that philosophy, as an intellectual activity, is universal; it cannot
be assumed to be confined to the peoples of the West and
the East. Philosophy of some kind is involved in the
thought and action of every people and constitutes the
sheet anchor of their life in its totality. (Emphasis added)

I have emphasized the words "thought and action" because this
statement, perhaps paradoxically, is not at odds with Hountondji's
position and can easily be conjoined with a historical materialist
problematic. It is precisely Marx's task, in "clearing the philosophical
decks" in order to construct a radical political economy, to do away
with the introspective musings of "*the* philosophers" and thus re-
insert philosophy into history and materialism, and hence into culture. But this must be *theorized;* it cannot be taken for granted, and
this is my longer-term task. For the time being, I note that, in his
Economic and Philosophical Manuscripts of 1844, Marx states
(1975:357):

But since for socialist man the *whole of what is called history* is nothing more than the creation of man through human labor and the development of nature for man, he

therefore has palpable and incontrovertible proof of his self-mediated *birth*, of his *process of emergence*. (Original emphasis)

Colletti, in his gloss upon key terms in these manuscripts (1975: 431), also points out that, for Marx, "Praxis is also the foundation of the 'science of man,' which supersedes both traditional speculative philosophy and political economy, abolishing the opposition between them."

Some of the peculiarities of Hountondji's thinking, which provide the major targets for his critics, are possibly linked to his (mostly silent but continuing) dialogue with Althusser, with whom he had studied at the Ecole Normale Supérieure in Paris, although I would not go so far as to say that he is a "disciple" of Althusser's (Mudimbe 1988 : 160).[4] In his introduction to the English edition of Hountondji's *African Philosophy: Myth and Reality*, Professor Irele notes (1983 : 28):

> The charge of elitism is often linked to what is also perceived as the "theoricism" of Hountondji, ascribed to the influence of his former teacher, Louis Althusser . . . it is possible to consider that Hountondji's emphatic tone betrays him into the occasional simplification or overstatement of his case; to discern a peremptoriness which, while it corresponds to the strength of his conviction, obscures the finer points of his argument and therefore leaves room for its misinterpretation.

It is also important to note that both Irele and Mudimbe feel some of Hountondji's critics go beyond the bounds of intellectual propriety, although I doubt very much if this would worry him. Mudimbe says that Hountondji's critics are "sometimes a bit raucous" (1988 : 160), and Irele suggests that "there is often a tendentious character to the criticisms levelled against Hountondji's ideas" (1983 : 28).

Whatever the case, this discussion is intended to set the scene for the second of my two initial questions: What is the relation between African philosophy and Marxism? For my present purposes, the construction of an epistemology grounded in Ilparakuyo history and experience as well as in historical materialism, this question has two

4. Professor Mudimbe provides a superb account of the context and critique of Hountondji's position in African philosophy; here, I refer only to one or two aspects of the latter's work. It is also important to note that Mudimbe alludes to the influence upon Hountondji of Georges Canguilhem and Gaston Bachelard, through Althusser (see Althusser 1977; Althusser and Balibar 1970).

levels. The first (and most obvious) concerns the way in which various African philosophers read and use (or reject) Marx; the second (and more important) addresses the issue of the Ilparakuyo notions of history and culture and their apprehension of the *transparency* of sociopolitical relations in this social formation, both past and present (Rigby 1985), on the one hand, and what I have called a "specific form of Marxist phenomenology," on the other. Let me deal with these levels in that order.

I have already noted that, in some contexts, the critique of Hountondji's view of African philosophy is taken as a critique of Marxism, translated to Africa. But in many cases, other African philosophers do not necessarily agree. Even Gyekye, for example, while being severely critical of Hountondji and the latter's attack on culturalism, sees the possible, if qualified, relevance of what he calls "nineteenth century European philosophers." This is how he puts it (1987:36):

> The philosophical enterprise is connected ultimately with the search for the wisdom needed to form the basis for a satisfactory way of life . . . African societies in the past half century have certainly been grappling with a variety of problems, most of which are the results of colonialism, imperialism and industrialism. Solving such problems and reconstructing African societies in the postcolonial era will certainly require professional investigation into *fundamental ideas and general principles.* (Emphasis added)

So far, so good; but this is where Gyekye takes evasive action (1987:39):

> It is the task of *modern* African philosophers not only to deal with the consequences of colonialism in African society and culture, but also to face squarely the challenges of *industrialization* and *modernization.* In doing so, they might take their cue from the philosophical activities of nineteenth-century European philosophers like Marx, Hegel, and Saint-Simon, and their responses to the consequences of the French Revolution. I am not referring to the specific doctrines and solutions such philosophers put forward, but to the *way* they responded to the circumstances of their societies. They philosophized with the *contemporary situation in mind;* they gave *conceptual interpretation* to contemporary experience. (Emphasis added)

This passage could easily be interpreted as implying that *(a)* "traditional" African ethnophilosophies cannot handle the problems of contemporary Africa (a position with which Hountondji would probably concur!); and *(b)* the concepts of "modernization" and "industrialization" are *unproblematic* in themselves. I hope these interpretations are not true, for they would seriously undermine the point of Gyekye's book. But nowhere in it are we told what these "fundamental and general principles" *are;* nor is the form and content of "industrialization" and "modernization" in African countries delineated anywhere. Since they are inseparable from *class formation* and growing exploitation, we are left in the air; *this* is what so upsets Hountondji, and myself!

It is also evident, however, that when Gyekye comes to look for these "fundamental ideas and general principles" in *traditional* Akan philosophy (the major subject of his book), he has to abandon any attempt at a "Pan-African philosophy" for an "Akan conceptual scheme," the specific culture of the Akan peoples. So, too, Hallen and Sodipo (1986) focus upon *Yoruba* concepts when they are looking for epistemological ideas, not upon Africa as a whole. It should be noted here that this methodology, used successfully by Gyekye and Hallen and Sodipo for certain limited but rigorous questions, is very different from that of more generalizing studies, such as Tempels's *Bantu Philosophy* or the work of Kagame (what Mudimbe calls the "Tempels and Kagame's school"), and the even larger claims for a "Pan-African" set of philosophical ideas as represented in Mbiti's writings (Mudimbe 1988:154–161, et passim; see also Rigby 1985:74–75).

Mudimbe deals very comprehensively and systematically with the relations between Marxism, African philosophy, and movements for African liberation, both past and present. He carefully explores the historical links of leading African (and other Third World) intellectuals with Marxist intellectuals in Europe and their ideas, particularly in France, devoting a whole section to the question of "J-P Sartre as an African Philosopher?" (Mudimbe 1988:83–87, passim). This is because of the role Sartre played in the promotion of works by African thinkers which expounded the philosophy of négritude. He succinctly sums up this period as follows (Mudimbe 1988:83):

> Up to the 1920's, the entire framework of African social studies was consistent with the rationale of an epistemological field and its sociopolitical expression of conquest. Even then, social realities, such as art, languages, or oral literature, which might have constituted an introduction to otherness, were repressed in support of sameness . . . Within this context, negritude, a student movement that

emerged in the 1930s in Paris, is a literary coterie despite its political implications. Besides, these young men—Aimé Césaire, Léon Damas, Léopold Senghor—mostly used poetry to express and speak about their differences as blacks ... it is Sartre who in 1948 with his essay, *Black Orpheus,* an introduction to Senghor's *Anthology of New Negro and Malagasy Poetry,* transformed negritude into a major political event and a philosophical criticism of colonialism ...

The growing influence of Marxism from the 1930s onwards opened a new era and *made way for the possibility of new types of discourse,* which from the colonial perspective was both absurd and abhorrent. The most original include the négritude movement, the fifth Pan-African Conference and the creation of *Présence Africaine.* Eventually, these signs of an *African will for power* led to political and intellectual confrontations ... In the 1950s, one also witnessed a *radical criticism of anthropology and its inherent preconceptions of non-western cultures.* Since then a stimulating debate about the African significance of social sciences and the humanities has taken place. (Emphasis added)

Despite Sartre's "high-handed" appropriation, then, of négritude for his own theoretical purposes (Mudimbe 1988:84–85), the link with Marxism became crucially important at this time of struggle. Dealing with the period of the end of formal colonialism and the newly found political independence of African nations, Mudimbe continues (1988:85):

First, *Black Orpheus* was in large measure responsible for the blossoming in Francophone Africa of the négritude literature of the 1950s ... A *littérature engagée,* a highly political literature, put forward Sartre's basic positions concerning African spiritual and political autonomy. This new generation of writers born between 1910 and 1920 includes Cheikh Anta Diop, Bernard Dadíe, René Depestre, Frantz Fanon, Keita Fodeba, Camara Laye, Ferdinand Oyono, among others. Second, black intellectuals, particularly Francophone, read Sartre, discussed his anti-colonialist positions and, generally upheld them. Fanon disagrees with Sartre yet offers a good example of his impact. In his *Peau noire, masques blancs,* Fanon accuses Sartre of treason, for Fanon does not believe that "Negritude is dedicated to its own destruction." Some years later, in his *Les Damnés de la terre,* the West Indian theorist firmly applies Sartre's dialectical principle and bluntly states: "there will not be a Black culture: the Black problem is a political one."

The point of this somewhat extended exploration of négritude and Sartre's involvement in the movement will become clearer as we proceed.

I now turn to Léopold Senghor, another major figure whose influence on African politics, culture, and literature remains rightfully enormous: Mudimbe is quite emphatic on this (1988:93):

> Senghor tends to define African socialism as just a stage in a complex process beginning with negritude and oriented towards a *universal civilization.* He emphasizes three major moments: negritude, Marxism, and universal civilization . . . Marxism is, for Senghor, a method. In order to use it adequately, the Senegalese thinker dissociates Marxism as humanism from Marxism as a theory of knowledge. The first offers a convincing explanation of the notion of alienation in its theory of capital and value and exposes the scandal of human beings under capitalism becoming mere means of production and strangers vis-à-vis the product of their work . . . For this reason, Senghor readily accepts Marxism's conclusions insofar as they indicate a recognition of the natural rights of humans, who are and most remain free agents and *creators of culture.* For Senghor, Marxism as a theory of knowledge nevertheless constitutes a problem. (Emphasis added)

Senghor's problem with a Marxist theory of knowledge is really threefold. The first is that Senghor sees Marx as *abandoning* the true nature of a dialectical theory of knowledge and as reverting, instead, "to the old concept of mechanistic materialism" and seeming to "deny the active role of the subject in knowledge" (Senghor 1964:43). While this is a misreading of Marx, it is, nevertheless, unfortunately true of a considerable number of positivist Marxists especially when theory is to be translated into practice. In arriving at this interpretation, Senghor is in agreement with Sartre.

The second part of Senghor's problem is the way in which Marxism-Leninism *in Europe* became distorted by the practices of Stalinism, resulting in often insurmountable problems for European Communist parties and their international ties. We now know, of course, that Senghor was not alone in his feelings at the time; but we cannot pursue this here. In terms of Hountondji's interrogation of "culturalism," with Senghor we again lose sight of class struggle and political mobilization; they become buried once again in ideology, of a different kind from "ethnophilosophy," but much more explicitly this time. As Mudimbe accurately points out (1988:93–94), for Senghor, "it is one thing to use [Marxism's] schemas for analyzing and understanding the complexity of social formations, and another to accept the concept of class struggle and *express the need to deny religion.*" (Emphasis added)

This brings us immediately to the third part of Senghor's problem with Marxism as epistemology: the matter of religion. This is of major concern to any discussion of African philosophy, since so much theorizing about it has been done by African theologians and *in the context of theology* (Mudimbe 1983:133, 1988, passim). Senghor reacts against the reductionist, economistic, and mechanistic strands of a certain period in European communism and laments that "Marxism has lost its soul." It was apparent to him that the Marxist theories current at the time had forgotten Marx's *denial of the need for an ideology of atheism* in a Socialist society, and Engels's attempts to situate early Christianity historically (Engels 1957). In the passage on Socialist man already referred to from the 1844 *Economic and Philosophical Manuscripts,* Marx continues (1975:357):

> Since the *essentiality* [*Wesenhaftigkeit*] of man and of nature, man as the existence of nature for man, has become practically and sensuously perceptible, the question of an *alien* being, a being above nature and man—a question which implies an admission of the universality of nature and of man—has become impossible in practice. *Atheism,* which is a denial of this unreality, no longer has any meaning, for atheism is a *negation of God,* through which negation it asserts the *existence of man.* Its starting point is the *theoretically and practically sensuous consciousness* of man and of nature *as essential beings.* (Original emphasis)

This passage is extremely important for the second level of my initial two questions on African philosophy and Marxism (see above). But before I proceed, I must, in concluding this topic, stress that Senghor does not abandon the Marxist problematic for his project; instead, he adopts an eclectic position by turning to the work of Pierre Teilhard de Chardin, which, Senghor maintains, offers a revitalized dialectical method.[5] This transition by Senghor from Marx and Sartre to Teilhard is perhaps best expressed by Irele (1981:28–29):

> Senghor's *critique* of Marxism does not imply a total negation, for he recognizes that it provides a dynamic vision of man in his relationship to nature, and as a consequence, a *liberating view of social relationships* in which the primary concern is the fulfillment of human virtualities. He believes however that Marxism is a theory that *needs to be completed* in the light of new developments since it was propounded, especially in the sciences, and *modified to fit the African situation.* (Emphasis added)

Having begun this debate on the formal links between African philosophy and Marxism with Hountondji and his critics, we come full circle to end this section with his emphatic plea which, to be fair to him, I must quote in extenso (Hountondji 1983:183):

> We must promote positively a *Marxist theoretical tradition* in our countries—a continuing scientific debate around the work of Marx and his followers. For let us not forget this: Marxism itself is a *tradition*, a plural debate based on the theoretical foundations laid by Marx. There have been plenty of disagreements in this tradition, but the progress of Marxist thought has been possible thanks to public debates between Lenin and Rosa Luxemburg or between Lenin and his fellow countrymen Plekhanov, Bukharin, Bazarov, Trotsky, etc.;[6] and thanks to the theoretical individuality of thinkers like Gramsci or Mao, to cite only the greatest among hundreds.

5. Senghor states (1964:134), "Engels tried to explain . . . [a] . . . unified science in *Dialectics of Nature.* But at that time (about 1890) the great scientific discoveries . . . had not yet been made. Teilhard de Chardin picked up Engels's project in *The Phenomenon of Man*, invoking not only natural sciences, but also physics, chemistry, and even mathematics. Teilhard de Chardin has a twofold advantage: the great scientific discoveries had already been made; as a paleontologist, he was himself a specialist in natural sciences." The epistemology of the natural sciences had not had, at that time, the shake-up they were later to receive. It is also of interest to note that French Marxist Roger Garaudy underwent a "conversion" to the ideas of Teilhard de Chardin (Caute 1964).

6. It should be noted that many of these figures were banished or relegated to the status of "non-persons," certainly deprived of their theoretical standing and importance, during the Stalinist period in the Soviet Union. Many of them, however, have been (or are being) restored to the front ranks of Marxist theoreticians through Gorbachev's *glasnost* and *perestroika* programs.

To which we may add, from these "hundreds," such Third World names as Samir Amin, Amilcar Cabral, Walter Rodney, Archie Mafeje, Ngugi wa Thiong'o, Clive Thomas—and many, many more.

IV

I now turn to the role of historical materialist theory in the specific context of undertanding the political economy and history of particular pastoralist social formations: Ilparakuyo of Tanzania, and other Maasai sections of Kenya and Tanzania. The first stage of this theoretical and practical exercise, the use of the concept of the "Germanic mode of production," was attempted in my book, *Persistent Pastoralists: Nomadic Societies in Transition* (1985), and I cannot rehearse it here.

I have also, in the first part of this chapter, tried to establish some of the more formal links that exist between African philosophical theorizing and Marxism. Focusing now upon the second level of this "problematic of convergence," I wish to explore in somewhat more detail the relationship between Ilparakuyo and Maasai theorizing, both as an abstract scheme of terms and as a "practical ideology," and certain elements of historical materialist theory, particularly those that address the production of social knowledge, language, and discourse, and their expression in political praxis.

But before I come to grips with this rather difficult enterprise, I must deal with some other recent anthropological materials relating to Maasai and other pastoralist and agropastoralist societies, and their epistemological status. It is necessary to relate other discourses on the same social formations; they form a part of the construction (or deconstruction) of the discursive space occupied by the various genres dealing with these social formations, and a brief discussion of some of them (particularly those with which I cannot agree, but also some which *are* epistemologically self-conscious) illuminates the manner at which I arrived at the present one.

The "authenticity" of anthropology has, for some time now, been the center of a theoretical crisis beseting the discipline as a whole (Diamond 1974: Rigby 1985: 1–24). This is not to say that the false epistemological foundations of, say, functionalism (itself derived from theories of marginal utility in economics: see Patterson 1987) or structuralism (whose epistemology leads ultimately to a theory of neurophysiology) are applied by Europeans and Americans exclusively to the study of "the other." On the contrary, as Mafeje has brilliantly pointed out (1976:311, 329, passim), they were, in different ways, paradigmatic of advanced, capitalist (that is, bourgeois) society itself; it applied in mirror-image form both to the Other and to the Self. Both problematics are epistemologically based upon positivist assumptions, as is the vain attempt to achieve an epistemological break through symbolic anthropology (see Geertz 1973, passim).[7]

I use the concept of "epistemological break" in Althusser's sense, without subscribing either to his distinction between "ideology" and "science" or to his differentiation between the "young Marx" and the "mature Marx." In a letter to his translator, Ben Brewster, Althusser (1977:257) compares his use of the concept with those of Bachelard, Canguilhem, and Foucault. As Brewster points out for his translation of Althusser, the kind of break he is thinking of is "Marx's rejection of the Hegelian and Feuerbachian ideology . . . and the construction of the basic concepts of dialectical and historical materialism" (Althusser 1977:249).

What is extremely perplexing in contemporary anthropology, however, is that there is still research being published on various societies around the globe, and on Maasai pastoralists to boot, which is blissfully unaware of any crisis or epistemological problem in the first place. For example, in his study of the Ilmatapato section of Kenya Maasai, Spencer (1988) selects this section on the grounds that in 1975–1977, when he was doing his fieldwork, they were "remote and in the heart of Maasailand, but still accessible," and that they are "more traditional" and "have less administration than any other tribal section," as well as "less contact with recent change and virtually no tourism."

---

7. Fabian, commenting delightfully on anthropological relativism and symbolic anthropology, says (1983:45), "There is now an anthropology which is fascinated with 'symbolic' mirrors (signs, signifiers, symbols) lining the inside walls of 'cultures' and reflecting all interpretive discourse inside the confines of the chosen object. These reflections give to an anthropological observer the illusion of objectivity, coherence, and density (perhaps echoed in Geertz's 'thick description'); in short, they account for much of the pride anthropology takes in its 'classical' ethnographies. One is tempted to continue [Ernst] Bloch's metaphorical reverie [in 1962] and to muse over the fact that such mirrors, if placed at propitious angles, also have the miraculous power to make objects disappear—the analyst of strange cultures as magician or sideshow operator, a role that is not entirely foreign to many a practitioner of anthropology and one that is most easily assumed under the cover of cultural relativism." For another spirited attack upon the more bizarre forms of cultural relativism, see Maurice Bloch (1977).

Spencer does not mention that Namanga, the border town on the main road between Kenya and Tanzania, is in the middle of the Ilmatapato section and where elderly ladies sell Maasai beadwork and jewelry to tourists, even going begging in bad years. But more important, Spencer makes absolutely no mention of the literally voluminous amount of recent writings on "development," history, and change which is now available on both Kenya and Tanzania Maasailand (except for Waller's historical work), and he even ignores the excellent recent studies by Galaty on the semiotics of Maasai rituals, their symbolic structures, and their significance for age-set organization (Galaty 1977, 1982, 1983, passim), topics with which Spencer is ostensibly concerned. A great many of these studies were readily available before Spencer completed his manuscripts in 1987.

This prodigious amount of literature, based upon very diverse methodological and theoretical frameworks, has only one thing in common: that Maasai, particularly in Kenya, have undergone tremendous historical upheavals and transformations, through which they have struggled desperately to maintain and reproduce as much as possible of their unique culture and social organization by adhering to pastoral praxis and its "practical ideology" (Rigby 1985:4, passim). A more blatant example of "bad faith" (in Sartre's sense) and of intellectual distancing through an inexcusable manipulation of history and time than is evident in Spencer's study would be very difficult to imagine.[8]

Furthermore, to the extent that he allows any "theory" to get in the way of his descriptions, Spencer recruits Gluckman's notion of the "rituals of rebellion," dating from the late 1950s and early 1960s, to illuminate Maasai society in the 1970s and (presumably) 1980s. While I have nothing against Gluckman's concept (see Rigby 1968), Spencer does not even refer to what Maurice Bloch calls "Gluckman's many followers" who, despite the fact that they refined this theoretical notion, could not in any case provide a cogent analysis of social change (Bloch 1977:280). As a "conclusion" to his book, Spencer provides us with a discussion of how he thinks the ideas of Freud and

8. "Bad faith" may be defined as follows (Sartre 1957:628): "A lie to oneself within the unity of a single consciousness. Through bad faith a person seeks to escape the *responsible freedom* of Being-in-itself. Bad faith rests on a vacillation between transcendence and facticity which refuses to recognize either one for what it is, or synthesize them."

Plato may help us understand Maasai "rituals and rebellion and the trusteeship of culture."

Quite apart from the fact that Spencer lacks any theoretical sophistication, his ignorance of the work of other scholars, many of them Maasai, demonstrates a serious absence of scholarly integrity.[9] Finally, adding insult to injury, Spencer has the temerity to claim the Ilmatapato Maasai "share a pride in their past, but have *no developed sense of their own history* or of the *changing opportunities of the contemporary scene"* (emphasis added; see Rigby 1985:67–91, passim; and other materials in n. 9, and bibliography). I have dwelt upon this anachronistic work not in order to prosecute an ad hominem attack on Spencer but to emphasize the *positively dangerous* repercussions that such irresponsible studies may have for the future of the peoples and cultures they purport to interpret.

Turning with relief to other literatures, there have been among recent studies of pastoral or semipastoral peoples several "non-Marxist" attempts to overcome the distancing created by what Fabian (1983:21) accurately calls a "schizophrenic use of Time" and its resultant inauthenticity, so aptly exemplified by Spencer's book. These attempts take the form of a certain "reflexivity" in the consciousness of the investigator in approaching his material. An excellent example of this is Paul Riesman's book, *Freedom in Fulani Social Life*. Its subtitle is "An Introspective Ethnography," and Riesman introduces it as follows (1977:1–2):

> The goal which I have set myself in this book . . . is neither an ethnographic description, nor a description of social structure, nor a functional analysis, nor the discovery of social and economic determinations, though I make use of all these approaches in my work. It would be more accurate to say that this book is a *resultant of the encounter of a man belonging to western civilization, and haunted by questions which life there raises for him, with a radically different civilization which he investigates with those questions constantly in mind.* Two principal traits give this essay its shape and focus: first, a theme, the problem of freedom, which takes shape in the presentation as it took shape in the field; second, an attempt to give the

9. On many of these issues, see Rigby 1985, 67–91, passim; Arhem 1985; Sena 1981, 1986; Parkipuny 1975, 1983; Kipury 1983, passim; Galaty 1977, 1982, passim; Sankan 1971, 1979; Mpaayei 1954.

reader an idea of how this encounter took shape. This is
not just for atmosphere; it is an essential aspect of my
methodology, (Emphasis added)

And, certainly, Riesman's is a very illuminating and rewarding study.

This is not the place or the time to determine whether Riesman
achieves entirely what he sets out to do; rather, it is to examine its
epistemological implications. To some extent, Riesman is making explicit what has long been regarded as a standard for good fieldwork
and ethnography, which should be seen, as Bloch reminds us for Mali-
nowski, as a "long conversation taking place among the people with
whom we live during fieldwork and in which we inevitably join"
(Bloch 1977:278). He goes on (1977:290, n. 1):

> This type of view of the subject matter of social study is
> one which runs through the work of many writers in op-
> position to various "structuralist" theories. It is present in
> linguistic philosophy and phenomenology and has through
> this channel influenced recent social scientists including
> Geertz.

This view of the nature of social reality is, not surprisingly, the one
taken by some African social scientists who have written extensively
about their own societies and cultures; although, as we shall see, it
is a methodology that does not guarantee the same quality of results. An excellent example of this is Francis Mading Deng, whose
outstanding work on his own society, the agropastoral Dinka of
Sudan, is widely available (for example, Deng 1971, 1972a, 1972b,
1978, 1986, passim). If one compares closely the results of the "long
conversations" of Geertz and Deng, however, a very major difference,
crucial to what follows, arises.

Through his analysis of Time in Balinese society, American anthropologist Geertz concludes that "Balinese social life lacks climax because it takes place in a motionless present, a vectorless now" (Geertz
1973:404; cf. Bloch 1977:284). Deng, Sudanese jurist and anthropologist, on the other hand, constantly refers to the history of Dinka society and its *historicity*, encompassing precolonial, colonial, and
postcolonial periods. Obviously, "conversations" can be very different in quality. Bloch correctly raises doubts about Geertz's version of
Balinese time concepts and notions of history, noting that, since Bali
has been under two colonialisms (Dutch and Japanese) before Geertz
arrived on the scene, neither of which had been particularly pleasant

for the Balinese, and that they were later involved in the crises of nationalism and the growth of revolutionary parties, somewhere along the line a "linear view of time" and historicity must have been incorporated into Balinese conceptualizations.

Deng shows brilliantly that Dinka not only question explicitly the grounds upon which the authenticity of oral history rests, but also that they *comment* upon the epistemological differences between oral and written sources as well as the *power* that may derive from alternative forms of the appropriation of the latter. Deng begins by noting, for example (1978:29–30):

> A fundamental principle, which paradoxically gives Dinka
> . . . history a dynamic character that makes it adaptable to
> current realities while also rendering it vague, ambiguous,
> and uncertain, is that it is transmitted by word of mouth
> through successive generations. *Authenticity* of informa-
> tion is largely based on the fact that the receiving genera-
> tion not only *listens* to the transmitting generation but
> also has the additional advantage of *proximity and obser-
> vation.* (Emphasis added)

From this it is clear that Dinka do not unquestioningly receive everything they are told by their elders, and the elders frequently express doubts about what they themselves are transmitting. Dinka, therefore, acknowledge that there is often a discrepancy between what is told and what ought to be told; I deal later with the implications of this for Ilparakuyo and Maasai.

There are two consequences that stem from Dinka notions of history: first, that "knowledge of their history is more pervasive and more broadly assimilated than is generally the case in literate societies where the sources of knowledge are available through formal institutions;" and second, that despite this enhanced awareness on the part of the general population, "it does not mean that [a knowledge of history] is equally shared nor does it mean that all are equally knowledgeable" (Deng 1978:30–31).[10] Deng continues (31):

> As a result of these dynamics, it does not always follow
> that the older persons are necessarily better informed than
> the younger . . . Amid all this complexity and uncertainty,

10. These variations in Dinka historical knowledge and consciousness are parallel to Hountondji's insistence that, although a particular African social formation may have a *dominant* ideology, it is not necessarily shared by all the members of that social formation.

the Dinka quite often express a commitment to "the truth" and nothing but the truth.

Dinka also see a commitment to the truth, insofar as history is concerned, to be deeply affected by modern written history. But, significantly, they do not necessarily see history "as written down" as any more reliable. Chief Lino Aguer, for example,

> paradoxically alleges that distinctions and complications have now resulted from the recent recording of tradition in a manner that welds oral literature with other sources and presents the amalgam as an authentic Dinka version. (Deng 1978:33)

Finally, Deng shows:

> While the Dinka now tend to rely on the accuracy of the written word, the traditionals also associate writing and the knowledge derived from it with a degree of secretiveness . . . This rather *suspicious* view of the secret world of the educated appears to stem from the fact that whereas traditional knowledge is open and broadly shared, modern knowledge, acquired from books as it is, *is more exclusive* and therefore seen as "secret." (33, 34; emphasis added)

The writing down of knowledge, Dinka knowledge, whether of the past or the present, Deng goes on to show, is viewed as creating not only "secretiveness" but also a source of *power*, a power that results from a form of *appropriation*. As Deng puts it, "The traditional Dinka do not expect *anyone* to be neutral observer. A researcher may be viewed as a person of *influence* by virtue of status in society or of academic involvement" (34; emphasis added). Foucault in Dinkaland!

What follows from this discussion of what I have called "historical consciousness" for Ilparakuyo and Maasai (Rigby 1985:67–91, passim), or lack of it, is that it applies equally to the specificity of the social formation being discussed, *as well as its interpreter*, the anthropologist, historian, novelist, or whatever. And it appears from these examples, and from numerous others, that reflexivity and a search for a historical consciousness is most likely to be found in the work of people interpreting their own societies, social scientists who adopt a Marxist perspective, anthropologists who are generally more epistemologically sophisticated, especially in linguistics; or, finally, some combination of these three viewpoints. Why is this so? For African societies, can an exploration of African philosophy offer an answer? Or is there something fundamental about the relation between

historical consciousness and an epstemological break from the sti-
fling grip of a Western bourgeois intellectualism?[11]

While I cannot adduce numerical evidence for this assertion, I can
refer briefly to a few examples other than my somewhat detailed
comments on Deng's outstanding contribution and the Ilparakuyo
Maasai material to follow. Going back to Riesman, we find an ac-
knowledgment of the importance for Jelgobe Fulani of certain historical events, particularly concerning religion; although he does state
that "the history of Jelgoji remains to be written" (Riesman 1977:45;
see also 44, 96–101).

Turning to one of the very few studies of African social formations
based upon a historical materialist problematic, Donham (1985:29–
70) emphasizes the privotal importance of historical processes, going
back 2,000 years or more, for an understanding of the Maale social
formation of southwestern Ethiopia. The work of French and other
Marxist anthropologists, such as Coquery-Vidrovitch, Meillassoux,
Bonte, Terray, Bourgeot, etc., amply attest to serious concern with the
need to understand historical processes; indeed it is inseparable from
the Marxist notion of "social formation."

V

There is, however, a difference between the conscious apprehension of history as indispensable to an understanding of *any* social formation, and the use of specific *historicities* as an epistemological
necessity in establishing the relation between theory and praxis in
the social sciences (see Mudimbe 1988: 176–177). If history and the
question of dealing with it on an epistemological level is as important
as I claim it to be, we are faced with a number of problems. These
problems are as common to the construction of an African philosophy (or "philosophies") as they are to the epistemology of African
history; as I noted earlier, one cannot deal with one and not the other.
It behooves us, then, to explore briefly the appearance of an epistemologically sound and critical African history.

The first phase of the postcolonial movement of African history
was to demonstrate the errors of colonialist historiography in which,

11. I do not, of course, claim by this argument that the use of historical materials is
confined to African and Marxist anthropologists. Clearly, the work of such major figures as Bohannan, Goody, Evans-Pritchard, Southall, M. G. Smith, etc., are also closely
concerned with historical processes which are *necessary to their analyses*. An excellent example is Stenning's (1959) work on Wodaabe Fulani. Also, there is the whole
recent literature on "ethnohistories," such as Cassanelli's on Somali society (1982).

notoriously, there was assumed to be *no* history before the imperial-
ists got there. In the immediately postcolonial period, African history
had to refocus its interest upon *Africans* themselves as serious actors
in the process of "making our own history." This movement was exemplified by what came to be called the "Dar es Salaam school." It
constituted a very important movement in the necessary *ideological*
shift required at that time; and Ranger, one of its founding fathers at
the University of Dar es Salaam, aptly called this shift "the need to
recover African *initiative* in Tanzanian history" (Ranger 1969; see
also 1968). History in Africa became "nationalized" precisely at the
time nationalist ideology was politically crucial. The major *methodological* shift was the rise to intellectual respectability of *oral
history.*[12] There is no doubt that this "Afro-centered" period of
historiography produced major studies whose results *and* certain
methodological achievements are still useful for reinterpretation
(Bernstein and Depelchin 1978, 2:31–32), much as many significant
studies in anthropology were produced under the theoretical aegis (or
is it hegemony?) of functionalism.

   Although historical studies in Africa were now focused on Africans, and oral sources became acceptable to most professional
historians, an epistemological break remained elusive. Calling this
movement "professional Africanist history," Temu and Swai (1981:
61) correctly observe:

> Its limits are the inner organizational possibilities of the
> facts under investigation rather than their setting in space
> and history. Postcolonial Africanist historiography de-
> mands that African history should be explained in terms of
> its own *facts.* In this endeavour it is *colonial history* which
> has been regarded as being problematic rather than *profes-
> sional metropolitan history,* which has been viewed as *un-
> problematic* and a model to be emulated consciously. In
> this belief it has been forgotten that colonial historiogra-
> phy and professional metropolitan history share the same
> *empiricist method,* and that imperial history branched off
> from metropolitan history in conformity with the empiri-
> cist parcellization of knowledge. (Emphasis added)

12. The gaining of this *widespread* respectability by oral sources of historical data
could be said to have begun with the publication in 1961 of Professor Jan Vansina's
book, *De la tradition orale: Essai de Méthode historique,* translated as *Oral Tradition*
and published by Routledge and Kegan Paul in 1965.

What is clearly implied here is that *historical research as a whole,*
the entire discipline, requires an epistemological break. Temu and
Swai go beyond the need for a "shake-up" in history, by saying
(1981:160):

> We have been arguing that an objective history of Africa
> must be written within an international problematic which
> takes cognizance of imperialism and the changing charac-
> ter of capital. This, however, should apply [equally] to
> *other disciplines which are concerned with the recovery
> of African social reality.* (Emphasis added)

If my argument on the close analogy or, more strongly, a direct parallel between the epistemological needs and contributions of African
philosophy and African history is accepted, then neither philosophy
nor history can merely be "Africanized"; they must go through an
epistemic transformation. The way in which both may be achieved, I
submit, is through a responsive and constructive historical materialism. This is precisely the argument of Temu and Swai, as well as
Bernstein and Depelchin, for the future of African history; it is my
argument for African philosophy and the construction of a radical and
subversive epistemology for the social sciences in Africa. The difficulties I have already enumerated for the problem of "levels of discourse" for specific African social formations on the one hand, and
Pan-African continuities and uniformities on the other, also apply
equally to both fields. It is significant that two recent attempts to
present a history of Africa as a whole are based upon a historical materialist problematic (Freund 1984; Jaffe 1985).[13]

The central role of a theorized historicity in the revitalization of
all African social sciences has been expressed by Mudimbe. Commenting upon Copan's periodization of African studies (Copans
1976), Mudimbe asserts (1988:177) that

> Marxism achieves a radically new approach. It does not
> westernize a virgin terrain, but confronts inattentiveness,
> the supporting walls which suppose them, and assembles
> under the roof of the analogue, relations, contradictions,
> imaginations. In effect the method results in an original
> type of visibility of differences in terms of theoretical
> traces of *taking the place of* and *representing* [original em-

13. An earlier Marxist attempt to encompass all of Africa (south of the Sahara) on
the basis of a historical materialist problematic in history is E. Sik's *The History of
Black Africa,* 2 vols. (Budapest, 1966).

phasis] . . . The great originality of French Marxists and
their African counterparts in the 1960's resides in this. Beginning with Balandier's proposition on macro perspectives
in the field (1955a, 1955b) a new discourse unites what had
been kept separate and opens the way to a general theory
of *historical and economic derivation* as exemplified in
the work of Osende Afana, Suret-Canale, C. Meillassoux,
C. Coquery-Vidrovitch.
    . . . *The Centrality of history* is thus remarkable in what
Marxism expounds as *African Studies.* (Emphasis added)

Despite the fact that Mudimbe cannot "wholeheartedly" agree
with Copan's analysis of the "succession of methodological paradigms," he nevertheless states (1988:177):

The concept of "African history" marked a radical transformation of anthropological narratives. A new type of
discourse valorizes the diachronic dimension as part of
knowledge about African cultures and encourages new representations of the "native," who previously was a mere
object within European history. Its Marxist version offers
the immediacy of objectivity through systems-signs of socioeconomic relations that permit both good pictures of
local organizations of power and production and intercultural comparisons.

Now, I partially disagree with the position taken here by Mudimbe, since it admits of the synchronic-diachronic dichotomy. In
this, (1) the *epistemological* impact of Marxism is underrated for this
particular discursive space; and (2) the "synchronic" project of Lévi-
Straussian structuralism is overrated. I say this for two reasons: (*a*)
despite the "structuralist" reading of Marx attributed to Althusser,
the latter attempts to *dissolve* the synchronic-diachronic dichotomy
as a false one (Althusser 1977:96–109; Rigby 1985:78–79); (*b*) despite the lengthy critiques of Althusser which abound, his enormous
impact upon anthropology, history, and Marxism has still to be measured (see Callinicos 1982; Elliott 1987), largely because most of the
thinkers (including Hountondji) upon whom he has had this fundamental influence *do not accept his project in its entirety.*
    Finally, the inescapable necessity of beginning at the microlevel for
the construction of an ethnophilosophy (particularly with regard to
its epistemological implications rather than its ethical ones) is not
directly contradictory to broader efforts to establish Pan African continuities; but *neither* level can escape the necessity of taking "cogni-

zance of imperialism and the changing character of capital" if the result is to be relevant to past, present, or future. As Mudimbe tells us, Smet has tried to show the complementarity of the two levels. This is how he puts it (1988:161):

> Smet *dissolves* the methodological and ideological oppositions between ethnophilosophers and their critics in terms of a *diachronic complementarity* of schools. (Emphasis added)

Having realized that one can begin looking for epistemological ideas in African philosophy, the question arises: Can we do so only at the restricted level of relativized ethnophilosophies, or can we move across the spectrum of African *Weltanschauungen* to autocritical reflection?

VI

I have already noted that, while earlier African theological philosophers had attempted to find philosophical continuities within larger groups or categories of African peoples and cultures (Tempels for the "Bantu-speaking" peoples; Mbiti for all of [Black] Arica; see Diop—a nontheologian—for all of Africa), more recent attempts to focus upon epistemological issues with more rigor tend to deal with "single" cultures, even if large populations are involved. In the latter case, the areas chosen for analysis are often defined on the basis of linguistic criteria. Keeping in mind the intellectual trap of "culturalism," which Hountondji has so vigorously attacked, let me refer to a couple of cases.

But to begin with, a reminder of some warnings. First, the *categories* of philosophical discourse in the West are the product of a specific history and its successive modes of production, culminating in capitalist imperialism; they are *not* universal categories, even if some philosophers still maintain that they are. Second, we must avoid a reductionist view of epistemological categories—for example, the reduction of epistemology to worldview (see Mudimbe 1988:144). This is common in a good deal of anthropological theorizing. Third, we must also note, with Hountondji, that however "small" a social formation, and however undifferentiated along class lines, not all the people who make up that social formation at any one point in time have identical ideas. The old myth of "primitive conformity" must be buried, even if, in some anthropological studies, the "total, cosmology" of a people or culture is often derived almost entirely from one "ritual expert." Finally, while philosophical systems differ wildly from one another, there *are* "common problems" with which, for obvious reasons, they must deal.

I return to Gyekye and his essay on Akan philosophical thought. His first concern is to debate with Robin Horton's reduction of philosophy to epistemology (Horton 1976, passim). Horton had suggested that African traditional thought should not be equated with philosophy, since African traditional thought did not, as far as he was concerned, provide any theory of knowledge. After taking issue with the assumptions Horton has made in respect to Western philosophy, Gyekye states that "African traditional thought *did* develop some epistemology, at least of a rudimentary kind" (Gyekye 1987:5). He continues:

> Concepts such as "truth," "mode of reasoning," "skepticism," "explanation," and so on appear in *Akan thought*, and the linguistic expressions, proverbs, and the general metaphysic of African peoples are replete with epistemological ideas and positions . . . Paranormal cognition, for instance, is an important feature of African epistemology. (The fact that this mode of knowing does not occur, or occurs only marginally, in Western epistemology is irrelevant.)

I agree. But what I find most interesting in this debate is Gyekye's quotation, in support of his argument and materials, from Busia (1963:149):

> The African has not offered learned and divergent disputations to the world in writing, but in his expression in *conduct of awe, and reverence for nature, no less than in his use of natural resources, he demonstrates his own epistemology.* (Emphasis added)

Gyekye then proceeds to suggest that, although there is not much evidence that "epistemological ideas or proposals were developed to any high degree in African traditional thought comparable to that achieved in, say post-Socratic Greek thought or post-Renaissance Western thought," that "the position is analogous to that of pre-Socratic Greek philosophical thought, which, of course, is known to have developed great metaphysical systems, but which appears to have paid inadequate attention to the analysis of epistemological concepts as such."

My point here, however, is not to assess whether or not Gyekye wins the argument on the grounds that he has chosen; I am amazed

that he chooses these grounds to begin with, and why he finds it necessary to join battle *here*, in the first place. Gyekye lacks a theory of
ideological forms. Why should Western bourgeois definitions of what
is, or what is not, philosophy constrict the argument? It seems that
in the task I outlined in the beginning, the task of overthrowing Western cultural imperialism, "professional philosophy" in Africa is far
behind history, and even some forms of anthropology. When Gyekye
does get around to specifying what the epistemological foundations
of Akan knowledge are (1987:201–203), he deals mainly with the
"paranormal" aspects of thought, "namely spirit mediumship, divi-
nation, and witchcraft."[14]

In their study of epistemological concepts in Yoruba traditional
thought, Hallen and Sodipo (1986), despite considerable philosophical
hedging over the very real problems of translation, focus upon examining in detail the notions of "to know" (*mo*), and "believe" (*gbagbo*).
After a careful use of oral evidence, and such eminent anthropological
work as Rodney Needham's *Belief, Language and Experience*, Hallen
and Sodipo establish what Dorothy Emmet, in her Foreword, calls "a
Yoruba epistemology more sophisticated than is generally acknowledged in the anthropological literature ... The study of usages of
these particular words show that the Yoruba *onisegun* [sages] are
more sophisticated epistemologically, and more critically, and indeed
empirically, minded than has been generally supposed" (Hallen and
Sodipo 1986:2).

This exercise, while being valuable, reminds me somewhat of
those theologians, one of whose intellectual purposes is predominantly
to demonstrate that African religions are valuable *because* they
approximate in some way, in some set of beliefs, to Christianity.
While I praise the meticulous methodology of Hallen and Sodipo's
achievement, the whole endeavor is based on W.V.O. Quine's "inde-
terminancy of translation" thesis. There is absolutely no social or
historical contextualizing, no reference to the nature of the Yoruba
social formation at *any* time, past, present, or future. They end their
discussion, as did Gyekye, by considering the paranormal theories of
witchcraft, both Yoruba and Western.

But to return, at last, to Professor Busia's claim that "the African ...
in his expression in conduct of awe, and reverence for nature, not less
than his use of natural resources ... demonstrates his own episte-

14. As is common in many such studies, "Akan thought" is frequently generalized
to "African thought" without evidence for this extension being presented. This is particularly a constant feature of Mbiti's *African Religions and Philosophy* (1970).

mology." This, perhaps, could not be a more concise formulation of
the Marxist notion of epistemology! Moving from the most abstract
to the most concrete, as Marx recommended in "The Method of Political Economy" (1973:100–101), I review briefly Marx's concept of
epistemology. In his chapter on the dialects of object and subject, Gollobin (1986:405) notes concisely:

> The history of a very general knowledge is a history of di-
> alectics, logic, and epistemology, three spheres of knowl-
> edge long deemed competitive rather than complementary.
> *Only with Marx's and Engels' discovery of materialist dia-
> lectic*—the revolutionary transformation of idealist dialec-
> tics and of metaphysical materialism—did comprehension
> become possible of the three spheres' *inner connections*, of
> their *ceaseless confluence* in the integral development of
> knowledge.

For Marx, and historical materialism generally, an epistemology
cannot be found *theoretically:* epistemology for Marx *is* the relation
between theory and practice in all human activity which, by definition, is *conscious*. We cannot talk about the theory of knowledge as
distinct from dialectics and logic, since all are conjoined in "the practice of mankind and of human history" (Lenin 1961:280). And "the
bottom line," as it is fashionable to say these days, is that

> if we recall Marx's concept of knowledge—a conception, x,
> is knowledge if, and only if, x is used to alter the world in
> accordance with human needs—we can see that it is a mat-
> ter of extreme epistemological import . . . In non-Marxian
> parlance, but according to Marxian principle, the Good is,
> when realized, the True. (McMurtry 1978:239)

We again return to Hountondji's notion of a "practical ideology" as
the *basis* for an epistemology which is at once *African*, in that it is
identified with African history, experience, and culture, and *Marxist,*
since it would not have been recognized *as* epistemology without
Marx. But let Hountondji speak for himself (1983:178):

> When one observes the daily life of our cities and country-
> side and tries to investigate certain practices, rituals, and
> behaviors, one cannot help feeling that they are really in-
> stitutionalized manifestations of a collective code of con-
> duct, patterns of thought which, viewed as whole, can
> constitute what might be called a *practical ideology*.
> Moreover . . . quite apart from this practical ideology there
> exists a considerable body of oral literature, esoteric or exo-

teric, the importance of which we are only beginning to suspect. We must have the patience to study it, analyze it, investigate its logic, its functions, and its limits . . . my view is that every society in the world possesses practico-theoretical codes or "practical ideologies" on the one hand, and, on the other, written or oral texts, transmitted from generation to generation.

If this is *not* "ethnophilosophy" for Hountondji—and he says it isn't—then so what? He should try going back to Marx rather than going beyond Althusser!

VII

Certainly, the "dogmatic' Marxism of the Second International and Stalinism was (and is) totally inappropriate for any contemporary applications, whether in the third world or in "advanced" capitalism. As Perry Anderson beautifully demonstrates (1984: 15–16), these dogmatisms led, in Europe, to a virtually unbridgeable chasm between the praxis of the Communist parties on the one hand, and the *philosophical* discourse of Marxism, "itself centered on questions of method—that is, more epistemological than substantive in character" (Anderson 1984: 16). The epistemological significance of this philosophical discourse (in the theorizing, for example, of Adorno, Althusser, Gramsci, Korsch, Lukacs, Marcuse, Ernst Bloch, Colletti and, eventually, Sartre) was in creating a historical materialist theory of *cultural processes*, language, and history, a theoretical development of "brilliance and fertility . . . as if in glittering compensation for their neglect of the structures and infrastructures of politics and economics" (Anderson 1984: 17).

The transformation of this philosophical tradition and the rebirth of Marxist political praxis, mainly since the 1960s, has two strands: first, within the capitalist West from the late 1960s (in France, Spain, Portugal, etc.); and second, in the Third World. Despite the influence of such scholars as Althusser and Sartre upon the latter, the European strand of Marxism is at least partially shut out by the continuity of Third World Marxisms of scholars and revolutionaries from the 1920s to the 1940s (for example, C.L.R. James, Mao, Ho Chi Minh, Cabral, and the later Nkrumah) up to the contemporary work of scholars such as Samir Amin, Hountondji, Walter Rodney, Clive Thomas, Archie Mafeje, etc., together with other black intellectuals of the African diaspora such as Oliver Cox and Manning Marable. The strength of Marxist cultural critique in Africa can be seen from the writings of such major figures as Ngugi wa Thiong'o, Sembène Ousmane, Onoge, Nazareth, and numerous others (for example see, Ngara 1985; Gugelberger 1985).

This brings me right back to a consideration of language and the understanding of the "practical ideology" of Ilparakuyo and Maasai and the historical transformations of their social formations. I could, of course, do a study of Maasai concepts similar to those by Gyeke and Hallen and Sodipo, for Akan and Yoruba culture and language, respectively, I do so briefly here. But if I were challenged upon the issue of a *conceptual* epistemology for Maasai, and not on one which is inseparable from pastoral praxis and which I began to elaborate in *Persistent Pastoralists (1985)*, I would first, of course, reiterate that one cannot arrive at an epistemology purely on theoretical or conceptual grounds. Then I would turn to a discussion of linguistic forms, some of which would be following.

In the language of Ilparakuyo and other pastoral Massai, which can be called *enkutuk oo'lMaasai* (lit. "the mouth of the Maasai people"), there is a proliferation of verbs to denote various "shades" of some activity. Simply "to do" is *aas* in its transitive form, of *aasisho,* "to work," intransitive. "To work at" something is *aasishore.* Nouns derived from this verb are *enkiaas* (sing.), *inkiaasin* (pl.): "productive work/s." *Aiko* also means "to do," and to do something in the sense of "prepare" is *aitobir,* and "to do something satisfactorily" is *aitobiraki.* Among the derivative forms of auxiliary verbs are *ang'as,* "to do first," *aitoki,* or *agil* "to do again," or "to repeat something you do"; "to do something soon" is *asioli;* and "to do something early, or early the next day" is *ayooki.* These are auxiliary verbs followed by the simple infinitive or subjunctive: for example, the infinitive of the verb "to milk" is *alep.* Thus, *asioki alep,* "I will milk immediately"; *matasioki aalep,* "Let us / That we may soon, or quickly, milk"; and so on (Tucker and Mpaayei 1955:96–97; Mol 1978:14,56).

These variations upon the verb "to do," "to act," "to practice" would seem to indicate that the Maasai language is focused upon *practices;* and this notion is strengthened by Tucker and Mpaayei's expert opinion (1955:51): they assert, "The verb system in Maasai is very elaborate, and contains the *real spirit of the language*" (emphasis added). This in itself is not, of course, any indication of a "deeper significance." But we may continue a little along these lines.

Ilparalkuyo and Maasai make distinctions among a number of other concepts, some of which have tentatively interesting features. For example, the verb "to believe" is *airuk*, which behaves in the normal fashion for a verb in Class II (those with verb stems beginning with "i"). But it also means "to obey," "to respond," or "to answer when addressed." It could be said that *airuk* refers to "receiving something without question." It is almost a "reflex" response, in which no *thought* is involved. Thinking itself is firmly tied to the notion of *words* or *verbalization*: the same verb *ajo* means "to think" and "to say." There is another verb, *adamu*, which is "to think" and *amus*, which means "to have an idea" or "to guess." [15]

To know is quite another matter. The basic verb is *ayiolo*. Most Maasai verbs remain the same for the present habitual and the future; *ayiolo*, however, more *commonly* takes the suffix *-u* for the future and the subjunctive, which makes it somewhat unusual but not morphologically distinctive. There is a diverbative noun from *ayiolo*, which means "knowledge" in the strict sense: *eyiolounoto*, and which is different from the notion of "wisdom," *eng'eno*, as in *eng'eno oo'lMaasai*, "the wisdom of the Maasai." Both have plural forms: *iyiolounot* and *ing'enoritin*. Then again, there is another verb *ais*, which may on occasion mean to "pretend to knowledge" (Mol 1978:92). Among other verbs which regularly have irregular future forms is *ara*, "to be;" "I will be" is *aaku*. Another diverbative form is *enkitayiolore*, specifically "knowledge." (Mol 1978:92).

"Experience" is represented by a compound form, *oleng'eno*, literally "it of wisdom" or "it of mind," which may also mean "cleverness" but in a very specific sense. Experience is considered *qualitatively* different for the depth of knowledge different people may acquire. Thus there is a metaphorical form denoting someone who knows his surroundings but may not have any depth of knowledge: *enkong'u naipung'o*, literally "the eye which has been out, been places." Finally, the verb "to learn" is *ang'enu*, from the same root as *eng'eno*, and thus means "to gain wisdom," in the future, or conditionally. "To be an expert," on the other hand, can be expressed adjectivally as *-arriya* (sing.), *-arriyiak* (pl.); the noun "expertise" is derived from the same root, *enkarriyiano*.

Despite these elaborations, which demonstrate the richness of Ilparakuyo Maasai conceptual categories dealing with knowledge, belief, and experience, I am, as I have insisted, much more concerned with the *context* of *utterances* than with the linguistic and philo-

15. Other verbs can take these suffixes, but they do not regularly do so. There are also local variations for a number of these verbs.

sophical status of *terms*. Elsewhere (Rigby in press) an analysis of the
dialogical form of discourse, as proposed by Bakhtin/Voloshinov, is
used to illuminate the manner in which Ilparakuyo and other Maasai
deal with the drastic threats to their existence posed by, for example,
government "development" policies. I must be very brief here, in order to define the context.

I elect to use Diamond's discussion of the relation between prose
and poetry, in which he says (1980:320),

> The origin of language—its metaphorical, connotative, as-
> sociative, and yet *concrete* character, are in poetry. Myths
> are imaginative, not abstract, universals, the *poetic per-
> sonification of history*. (Emphasis added).

This represents the very *opposite* of a structuralist approach to
language, such as derived from Saussure by Lévi-Strauss, and which
Voloshinov calls "abstract objectivism: (1973:57–63, passim.) Diamond's conception lies squarely in the *revolutionary* problematic
(prefigured by Saussure but dissolved by modern structuralism and de-
constructionism) for the Marxist understanding developed by Bakhtin/
Volshinov/Medvedev.[16] Holquist (1981:xvii) is quite succinct: "If you
expect a Jacobsonian systematicalness in Baktin, you are bound to be
frustrated." In a characteristic passage in *The Dialogic Imagination*,
Bakhtin says (1981:291):

> At any given moment, languages of various epochs and per-
> iods of sociological life cohabit with one another. Even lan-
> guages of the day exist: one could say that today's and
> yesterday's socio-ideological and political "day" do not, in
> a certain sense, share the same language; every day repre-
> sents another socio-sematic "state of affairs," another ac-
> centual system, with its own slogans, its own ways of
> assigning blame or praise. Poetry depersonalizes "days" in
> language, while prose . . . often deliberately gives them em-
> bodied representation and dialogically opposes them to one
> another in unresolvable dialogue.[17]

16. This of course is not the place to introduce the intractable debate on the "true
identities" of these three pioneering figures in the development of a historical materialist approach to language; but, from my reading of them, certainly, at least Bakhtin
and Voloshinov are the same person!

17. I agree entirely with White (1984:123) that, "since literary structuralism and
deconstruction are ultimately linked to the same debate, I believe Bakhtin's theory
simultaneously encompassed and pushed beyond them too. By 'pushed beyond' I mean
that Bakhtin's work prefigured both structuralist and deconstructionist views of the

But more than this. Voloshinov, referring to Medvedev's work on the "poetic qualities acquired by Language," states that these qualities are also *not inherent* merely in the *form* of the utterance but in the *context* in which the utterance is made. Voloshinov states (1986:183): "Therefore, the proper point of departure for investigation into the specificity of literature is not poetic language (a fiction in any case) but poetic context, poetic construction—literary works of art themselves."

I began this chapter with a reference to a number of "genres" through which Ilparakuyo and Maasai are "represented." One of these is the literature on "development," the other an inauthentic anthropology; in neither case is the discursive space created in any way congruent with the Ilparakuyo social formation and its forms of discourse. The *content* of capitalist development is presented to Ilparakuyo and Maasai, inter alia, in the form of (a) being forced to "settle down" ("sedentarization"), (b) being forced to "cultivate," (c) commoditizing their herds, (d) commoditizing their land (particularly in Kenya), or (e) losing their resource base to non-Ilparakuyo/Maasai cultivators (in Kenya, often large-scale wheat farmers; in Tanzania, peasant farmers or game reserves). But peoples who follow land-use patterns totally different from Ilparakuyo and Maasai have *always* figured in the way in which they create their own identity (Galaty 1978,1982, passim). I therefore end this chapter with a text that comments on this identity-formation process, an analysis that owes a lot to Galaty. But first, a brief note on how a text may be considered a "dialogical utterance," or stream of utterances.

Voloshinov makes it very clear that, although "verbal interaction is the basic reality of language," the nature of the "dialogic" is much broader than this:

> Dialogue in the narrow sense of the word, is, of course, only one of the forms—a very important form to be sure— of verbal interaction. But dialogue can also be understood in a broader sense, meaning not only direct, face-to-face, vocalized verbal communication of *any type whatsoever* [emphasis added]. A book, i.e., a *verbal performance in print*, is also an element of verbal communication [original emphasis] ... Thus the printed verbal performance en-

---

language of literature, but crucially placed them both in a sociolinguistic framework which thereby makes them *responsive to an historical and thoroughly social comprehension of literature*" (emphasis added).

gages, as it were, in ideological colloquy of larger scale: it responds to something, objects to something, anticipates possible responses and objections, seeks support, and so on.

Thus Bakhtin can interpret "Rabelais and His World" not only as a product of the "dialogic imagination" but also as a *struggle* between "folk culture" and the "official middle ages" (Bakhtin 1981:passim).[18]

Here is the Ilparakuyo Maasai text[19] and its interpretation in the social process of its role in the formation of the "practical ideology" of pastoralist praxis:

> *Enkiterunoto oo 'lMaasai o 'lMeek:* "The beginning of Maasai and the Cultivators." When Leeyo (the first Maasai man) became a great elder, he called his children and said, "My children, I am now an elder of many days, and I want to instruct you."
>
> He then asked his eldest son, "What is it that you want from all my treasures?" And the eldest son replied, "I want everything in this country." And the old man said, "Since you want everything, take a few head of cattle, a few small goats and sheep, and some food of the earth [agricultural produce], since there are a large number of things." And the eldest son replied, "very well."
>
> Then Leeyo called his youngest son and said, "And what is it that you want?" And he said, "Father, I wish that I should be given the fly-whisk in your hand." And his father said, "My child, because you have chosen only this fly-whisk, may God give you prosperity [i.e., many wives, children, dependents, and cattle], so that you will have control among your brothers."

And so the one who wanted everything became a cultivator, and he who took the fly whisk became the father of all Maasai.

Although Ilparakuyo and Maasai pastoralists conceive of themselves as "pure pastoralists" as opposed to cultivators (both Maasai-speaking—classified as Ilkurrman, "those of the fields"—and non-Maasai) and "hunters" (Iltorrobo), their continued historical and economic interdependence with these "others" is expressed both mythologically as well as in constantly changing day-to-day exchange of pastoralist products for nonpastoral ones. This reciprocity depends

18. I must emphasize again here that I *do not* subscribe to the Saussurean structuralist notion as developed by, for example, Derrida (1971; see Callinicos 1982), which implies "There is nothing outside the text."

19. This folktale is also recorded by Hollis (1905, 171–173). I have other versions; this translation is my own combination of them.

upon the *maintenance* of distinct identities. But Massai identity also rests upon the interplay between nature and culture, in which cattle (and other livestock) play a mediatory role, both as the *major means of production*, appropriated *directly* at the household as well as the large community, and as symbolic "communicators" between physical and social domains (see Rigby 1971, 1985:48–66).

For Ilparakuyo and Maasai, then, and in keeping with the analysis of verbal forms in the Maasai language, people and "things" are not merely identified by what they *are* (nature, in an ontological sense) but also by what they *do* (culture *as social labor*). Thus Ilparakuyo and Maasai identity relates on the one hand to descent and kinship, as in *enkaji nabo* ("one house," "descendants of one mother"), *osarge obo* ("one blood") and age-set organization, *olaji obo* ("one great house"), and on the other to *esiasi* ("work" as social production) and *olkerreti* ("skin ring" signifying "talent"); in short, in terms of substance as well as praxis

BIBLIOGRAPHY

Althusser, Louis. 1977. *For Marx.* London: New Left Books.

Althusser, Louis, and Etienne Balibar. 1970. *Reading Capital.* London: New Left Books.

Anderson, Perry. 1984. *In the Tracks of Historical Materialism.* Chicago: University of Chicago Press.

Arhem, Kaj. 1985. *Pastoral Man in the Gardeon of Eden: The Maasai of the Ngorongoro Conservation Area.* Tanzania: University of Uppsala, Department of Anthropology; and Scandanavian Institute of African Studies.

Asante, Molefi. 1980. *Afrocentricity: The Theory of Social Change.* Buffalo, N.Y.: Amulefi.

———. 1987. *The Afrocentric Idea.* Philadelphia: Temple University Press.

Bakhtin, Mikhail. 1981. *The Dialogic Imagination.* Trans. Caryl Emerson and Michael Holquist. Austin: University of Texas Press.

———. 1984. *Rabelais and His World.* Trans. Helene Iswolsky. Bloomington: Indiana University Press.

Balandier, Georges. 1955a. *Sociologie des Brazzavilles Noires.* Paris: A. Colin.

———. 1955b. *Sociologie actuelle de l'Afrique noire.* Paris: Presses Universitaires de France.

Balogun, F. Odun. 1987–1988. "Ngugi's *Devil on the Cross:* The Novel as Hagiography of a Marxist." *Ufahamu* 16:76–92.

Bernal, Martin. 1987. *Black Athena: The Afroasiatic Roots of Classical Civilization.* Vol. 1. New Brunswick, N.J.: Rutgers University Press.

Bernstein, Henry, and Jacques Depelchin. 1978. "The Object of African History: A Materialist Perspective." *History in Africa* 5:1–19, 6:17–43.

Bloch, Maurice. 1977. "The Past and the Present in the Present." *Man,* 12:278–292.

Brewster, Ben. 1967. "Glossary" for translation of Louis Althusser, *For Marx.* London: New Left Books.

Busia, K. A. 1963. "The African World-View." In *African Heritage,* ed. Jacob Drachler. New York: Crowell, Collier, and Macmillan.

Callinicos, Alex. 1982. *Is There a Future for Marxism?* London: Macmillan.

Cassanelli, Lee V. 1982. *The Shaping of Somali Society: Reconstructing the History of a Pastoral People.* Philadelphia: University of Pennsylvania Press.

Caute, David. 1964. *Communism and the French Intellectuals.* London: Andre Deutsch.

Clark, Katerina, and Michael Holquist. 1984. *Mikhail Bakhtin.* Cambridge, Mass.: Harvard University Press.

Colletti, Lucio. 1975. "Introduction" to Karl Marx, *Early Writings.* Trans. R. Livingstone and G. Benton. Harmondsworth: Penguin/New Left Books.

Copans, Jean. 1976. "African Studies: A Periodization." In *African Studies: a Radical Reader,* ed. Peter Gutkind and Peter Waterman. New York: Monthly Review.

Coulson, Andrew, ed. 1979. *African Socialism in Practice: The Tanzanian Experience.* London: Spokesman.

Deng, Francis Mading. 1971. *Tradition and Modernization: A Challenge for Law among the Dinka of Sudan.* New Haven: Yale University Press.

———. 1972a. *The Dinka of the Sudan.* New York: Holt, Rhinehart and Winston.

———. 1972b. *The Dinka through Their Songs.* Oxford: Clarendon.

———. 1978. *Africans of Two Worlds.* New Haven: Yale University Press.

———. 1986. *The Man Called Deng Majok.* New Haven: Yale University Press.

Derrida, Jacques. 1972. *Positions.* Paris: Minuit.

Diamond, Stanley. 1974. *In Search of the Primitive.* New Brunswick, N.J.: Transaction Books.

———. 1980. "Theory, Practice, and Poetry in Vico." In *Theory and Practice: Essays Presented to Gene Weltfish.* ed. S. Diamond. The Hague: Mouton.

Diop, Cheikh Anta. 1963. *L'unité culturelle de l'Afrique noire.* Paris: Presence Africaine. Translated as *The Cultural Unity of Black Africa.* Chicago: Third World Press, 1978.

Doherty, Deborah A. 1979. "Factors Inhibiting Economic Development on Rotian Olmakongo Groups Ranch." Institute for Development Studies, Nairobi, Working Paper no. 356. Mimeographed.

Donham, Donald, 1985. *Work and Power in Maale, Ethiopia.* Ann Arbor, Mich.: UMI Research Press.

Elliott, Gregory. 1987. *Althusser: The Detour of Theory.* New York: Verso.

Engels, Frederick. 1957. "On the History of Early Christianity." In *On Religion.* by Karl Marx and Frederick Engels. Moscow: Foreign Languages Press.

Evangelou, Phylo. 1984. *Livestock Development in Kenya Maasailand.* Boulder, Colo.: Westview Press.

Fabian, Johannes. 1983. *Time and the Other: How Anthropology Makes Its Object.* New York: Columbia University Press.

Foucault, Michel. 1980. *Power/Knowledge: Selected Interviews and Other Writings.* Edited by Colin Gordon. New York: Pantheon Books.

Freund, Bill. 1984. *The Making of Contemporary Africa: The Development of African Society since 1900.* Bloomington: Indiana University Press.

Galaty, John G. 1977. *The Pastoral Image: The Dialectic of Maasai Identity.* Unpublished Ph.D. dissertation, University of Chicago

———. 1982. "Being 'Maasai'; Being 'People of Cattle': Ethnic Shifter in East Africa." *American Ethnologist* 9:1–20.

———. 1983. "Ceremony and Society: The Poetics of Maasai Ritual." *Man,* 18:361–382.

Geertz, Clifford. 1973. *The Interpretation of Cultures.* New York: Basic Books.

Gollobin, Ira. 1986. *Dialectical Materialism: Its Laws, Categories, and Practice.* New York: Petra Press.

Gugelberger, Georg M. ed. 1985. *Marxism and African Literature.* Trenton, N.J.: Africa World Press.

Gyekye, Kwame. 1987. *An Essay on African Philosophical Thought: The Akan Conceptual Scheme.* Cambridge: Cambridge University Press.

Hallen, B., and J.O. Sodipo. 1986. *Knowledge, Belief, and Witchcraft: Analytical Experiments in African Philosophy.* London: Ethnographica.

Hedlund, Hans. 1971. "The Impact of Group Ranches on a pastoral Society." Institute of Development Studies, Nairobi, Staff Paper no. 100. Mimeographed.

———. 1979. "Contradictions in the Peripheralization of a Pastoral Society: The Maasai." *Review of African Political Economy* 15–16:15–34.

Hollis, A.C. 1905. *The Masai: Their Language and Folklore.* Oxford: Clarendon. Reprinted by Negro Universities Press, Westport, Conn. 1970.

Holquist, Michael. 1981. "Introduction." In M.M. Bakhtin, *The Dialogic Imagination,* ed. Michael Holquist. Austin, Texas: University of Texas Press.

Horton, Robin. 1976. "Traditional Thought and the Emerging African Philosophy Department: Comment on the Current Debate." *Second Order* 6:54–80.

Hountondji, Paulin. 1970. "African Wisdom and Modern Philosophy." In *African Humanism and Scandinavian Culture,* ed. Torben Lundback. Copenhagen: Danish International Development Agency.

———. 1983. *African Philosophy: Myth and Reality.* Bloomington: Indiana University Press; London: Hutchinson University Library for Africa.

Hyden, Goran. 1980. *Beyond Ujamaa in Tanzania: Underdevelopment and an Uncaptured Peasantry.* London and Nairobi: Heinemann.

———. 1983. *No Shortcuts to Progress: African Development Management in Perspective.* London and Nairobi: Heinemann.

Irele, Abiola. 1981. *The African Experience in Literature and Ideology.* London and Ibadan: Heinemann.

———. 1983. "Introduction." In *African Philosophy: Myth and Reality,* by Paulin Hountondji. Bloomington: Indiana University Press.

Jaffe, Hosea,. 1985. *A History of Africa.* London: Zed Books.

Kamenju, Grant. 1985. "*Petals of Blood* as a Mirror of the African Revolution." In *Marxism and African Literature,* ed. Georg Gugelberger. Trenton, N.J.: Africa World Press.

Kipury, Naomi. 1983. *Oral Literature of the Maasai.* Nairobi and London: Heinemann.

Kitching, Gavin. 1980. *Class and Economic Change in Kenya.* New Haven: Yale University Press.

Lenin, V.I. 1961. *Philosophical Notebooks.* London: Lawrence and Wishart.

Leys, Colin. 1975. *Underdevelopment in Kenya.* London and Nairobi: Heinemann.

McMurtry, John. 1978. *The Structure of Marx's World View.* Princeton: Princeton University Press.

Mafeje, Archie. 1976. "The Problem of Anthropology in Historical Perspective: An Inquiry into the Growth of the Social Sciences." *Canadian Journal of African Studies* 10:307–33.

———. 1977. "Neocolonialism, State Capitalism, or Revolution." In *African Studies: a Radical Reader,* ed. Peter Gutkind and Peter Waterman. New York: Monthly Review.

Marx, Karl. 1973. *Grundrisse,* Harmondsworth: Penguin and New Left Books.

———. 1975. *Early Writings.* Harmondsworth: Penguin and New Left Books.

Mbiti, John. 1970. *African Religions and Philosophy,* Nairobi and London: Heinemann.

Mol, Frans. 1978. *Maa: A Dictionary of the Maasai Language and Folklore.* Nairobi: Marketing and Publishing Limited.

Mpaayei, J. Tompo ole. 1954. *Inkuti Pukunot oo 'lMaasai,* London: Oxford University Press.

Mudimbe, V. Y. 1983. "African Philosophy as Ideological Practice: The Case of French-speaking Africa." *African Studies Review* 26:113–154.

———. 1985. "African Gnosis: Philosophy and the Order of Knowledge: An Introduction." *African Studies Review* 28:149–233.

———. 1988. *The Invention of Africa: Gnosis, Philosophy, and the Order of Knowledge,* Bloomington: Indiana University Press.

Nazareth, Peter. 1985. "The Second Homecoming: Multiple Ngugis in *Petals* of Blood. In Marxism and African Literature, ed. Georg Gugelberger. Trenton, N.J.: Africa World Press.

Ngara, Emmanuel. 1985. Art and Ideology in the African Novel: A Study of the Influence of Marxism on African Writing. Trenton, N.J.: Africa World Press.

Ngugi Wa Thiong'o (James Ngugi). 1977. Petals of Blood. Nairobi and London: Heinemann.

———. 1981a. Writers in Politics. Nairobi and London: Heinemann.

———. 1981b. Detained: A Writer's Prison Diary. Nairobi and London: Heinemann.

———. 1982. Devil on the Cross. Nairobi and London: Heinemann.

———. 1983. Barrel of a Pen: Resistance to Oppression in Neo-Colonial Kenya. Trenton, N.J.: Africa World Press.

———. 1986. Decolonizing the Mind. Nairobi and London: Heinemann.

Owomoyela, Oyekan. 1987. "Africa and the Imperative of Philosophy: A Skeptical Consideration." African Studies Review 30:79–99.

Parkipuny, L.M. ole. 1975. Maasai Predicament and Beyond. Unpublished M.A. thesis, Institute of Development Studies, University of Dar es Salaam.

———. 1979. "Some Crucial Elements of the Maasai Predicament." In African Socialism in Practice: The Tanzanian Experience, ed. Andrew Coulson. London: Spokesman.

———. 1983. "Maasai Struggle for Home Rights in the Land of the Ngorongoro Crater." Paper presented at the International Congres of Anthropological and Ethnological Sciences, Vancouver, August 20–25.

Patterson, Thomas C. 1987. "Development, Ecology, and Marginal Utility." Dialectical Anthropology 12:15–31.

Ranger, Terrence, ed. 1968. Emerging Themes in African History. Nairobi: East African Publishing House.

Ranger, Terrence. 1969. "The Recovery of Local Initiatives in African History." Unpublished paper, University of Dar es Salaam. Mimeographed.

Riesman, Paul 1977. Freedom in Fulani Social Life: An Introspective Ethnography. Chicago: University of Chicago Press.

Rigby, Peter. 1968. "Some Gogo Rituals of Purification: An Essay on Social and Moral Categories." In Dialectic in Practic Religion, ed. Edmund Leach. Cambridge Papers in Social Anthropology no. 5 Cambridge: Cambridge University Press.

———. 1971. "The Symbolic Role of Cattle in Gogo Ritual." In The Translation of Culture: Essays to E. E. Evans-Pritchard. ed. Thomas Beidelman. London: Tavistock.

———. 1985. Persistent Pastoralists: Nomadic Societies in Transition. London: Zed Books.

———. 1987–1988. "Pastoralism, Egalitarianism, and the State: The Eastern African Case." Critique of Anthropology 7:17–32.

Rigby, Peter. In press. *Cattle, Capitalism, and Class.* Philadelphia: Temple
    University Press.
Sankan, S. S. ole. 1971. *The Maasai.* Nairobi: East African Literature Bureau.
————. 1979. *Intepen e Maasai.* Nairobi: East African Literature Bureau.
Sartre, Jean-Paul. 1957. *Being and Nothingness.* London: Methuen.
Saul John. 1979. *The State and Revolution in Eastern Africa.* New York:
    Monthly Review.
————, ed. 1985. *A Difficult Road: The Transition to Socialism in Mozam-
    bique.* New York: Monthly Review.
Sena, Sarone ole. 1981. "Schemes and Schools: Two Agents of Change among
    the Maasai of Kenya." Paper presented at a joint seminar of Temple
    University African Studies Committee and Department of Anthropol-
    ogy, April 15.
————. 1986. *Pastoralists and Education: School Participation and Social
    Change among the Maasai.* Unpublished Ph.D. diss. McGill Univer-
    sity, Montreal.
Senghor, Léopold. 1964. *On African Socialism.* London: Pall Mall.
Shivji, Issa G. 1975. *Class Struggles in Tanzania.* Dar es Salaam: Tanzania
    Publishing House.
Sik, Endre. 1966. *The History of Black Africa.* 2 vols. Budapest.
Spencer, Paul. 1988. *The Maasai of Matapato: A Study of Rituals of Re-
    bellion.* Manchester: Manchester University Press for International Af-
    rican Institute.
Stenning, Derrick. 1959. *Savannah Nomads,* London: Oxford University
    Press for International African Institute.
Temu, Arnold, and Bonaventure Swai. 1981. *Historians and Africanist His-
    tory.* London: Zed Press.
Thomas, Clive. 1984. *The Rise of the Authoritarian State in Peripheral So-
    cieties.* New York: Monthly Review.
Tucker, Archie, and J. Tompo ole Mpaayei. 1955. *A Maasai Grammar.* Lon-
    don: Longman Green.
Vansina, Jan. 1961. *De la tradition orale: Essai de Méthode historique.* An-
    nales du Musee Royal de l'Afrique Centrale, Sciences humaine, no. 36.
    Translated as *Oral Tradition: Historical Methodology.* London: Rout-
    ledge and Kegan Paul, 1965.
Voloshinov, V. N. 1986. *Marxism and the Philosophy of Language,* Cam-
    bridge, Mass.: Harvard University Press.
Warren, Bill. 1980. *Imperialism: Pioneer of Capitalism.* London: Verso.
White, Allon. 1984. "Bakhtin, Sociolinguistics, and Deconstruction." In *The
    Theory of Reading,* ed. Frank Gloversmith. Sussex: Harvester Press;
    and Totowa, N.J.: Barnes and Noble.

seventeen

Formulating Modern Thought in African Languages: Some Theoretical Considerations

Kwasi Wiredu

In his *African Religions in Western Scholarship*,[1] Okot p'Bitek recounts the following story.

In 1911, Italian Catholic priests put before a group of Acholi elders the question "Who created you?"; and because the Luo language does not have an independent concept of *create* or *creation*, the question was rendered to mean "Who moulded you?" But this was still meaningless, because human beings are born of their mothers. The elders told the visitors they did not know. But we are told that this reply was unsatisfactory, and the missionaries insisted that a satisfactory answer must be given. One of the elders remembered that, although a person may be born normally, when he is afflicted with tuberculosis of the spine, then he loses his normal figure, he gets "moulded." So he said, "Rubanga is the one who moulds people." This is the name of the hostile spirit which the Acholi believe causes the hunch or hump on the back. And instead of

1. Okot p'Bitek, *African Religions in Western Scholarship* (Nairobi: East African Literature Bureau, c.1970).

exorcising these hostile spirits and sending them among pigs, the representatives of Jesus Christ began to preach that Rubanga was the Holy Father who created the Acholi. (62)

Let us assume that p'Bitek is right in this account, as he very well might be; then one can expect quite wide-ranging incongruities in the translation of Christian theology into the Luo language; p'Bitek, in fact, went on to illustrate this problem with the translation of the first sentence of St. John's Gospel into Luo. St. John's opening message is, of course: "In the beginning was the Word [Logos] and the *Word* was with God, and the *Word* was God." Now, according to p'Bitek, "[T]he Nilotes, like the early Jews, did not think metaphysically. The concept of *Logos* does not exist in Nilothic thinking; so the word *Word* was translated into *Lok* which means *news* or message . . . And as Nilotes were not very concerned with the beginning or the end of the world, the phrase 'In the beginning' was rendered, 'Nia con ki con,' which is, 'From long long ago.'" In the upshot, the Luo translation read as follows: "Nia con kicon Lok onongo tye, Lok tye bot Lubange, Lod aye ceng Lubanga" which, according to him, retranslates into English as "From long long ago there was News, News was with Hunchback Spirit, News was the Hunchback Spirit" (85). One might not be able to suppress a chuckle, but one must resist any temptation to pass over this as a mere translational curiosity, for serious problems are involved here about communication across cultures.

One obvious question is this: If the concepts of *creation, Logos,* and of *the beginning of the universe* do not exist in the Luo language, why may they not be introduced into it? It may be admitted that the particular attempt to do so which we have just noticed produces quite comical results, but this, it might be suggested, may be blamed on the accidental circumstances of the Italo-Luo conversation recounted (or re-recounted) by Okot p'Bitek. The general idea of introducing new concepts into a language is very extensively relevant to our concerns in this paper, and so we will concentrate on it a while before returning to Luo particularities.

Without presupposing any particular theory about the ontological nature of concepts, it may be said that, roughly speaking, in the more unproblematic cases of translation from one language into another, what happens is an interchange of signs for conceptual materials antecedently existing in both languages. On the other hand, where a concept exists in one language but not in another, there is no longer just an interchange of signs but the creation, so to speak, of a new concept in the latter medium. Two options, at least, are available here. One may devise a new term, which may be a word or phrase, using words that already exist in the language, or one my resort to a new word altogether, which may be a transliteration into the language of a foreign word. In the latter case, there is not only a translation into the language but also an extension of its vocabulary.

It is, however, all too easy to suppose that a given concept does not exist in a particular language on trivial verbal grounds. Observing, for example, that there exists no word for a certain concept in a language, it has sometimes been hastily concluded that the concept does not exist in it. African languages have not infrequently been subjected to such a hasty approach and not only at the hands of aliens. Has not a well-known native writer on African traditional thought suggested that African languages lack a concept of the indefinite future because certain East African languages examined by him did not have any word for expressing the indefinite future?[2] A concept need not be expressed by any one word; it may be expressed by a phrase or even a large set of sentences or, indeed, by a pattern of behavior. Certainly, the absence of a single-word designator does not argue the absence of a periphrasis.

Another side of the error just noted is the attribution of certain concepts (and theories, ways of thought, etc.) to some peoples in a proprietary sense. A concept may be associated with a particular people because it was originated by a person or group of persons belonging thereto, or because it has an important place in their received framework of thought, or simply because it occurs in their popular or even esoteric discourse. In neither sense can it be said that there is anything intrinsically ethnic about the concept itself. Nor can ways of thought also be said to be ethnic in any but an adventitious sense. Accident, ecology, economy, or more mysterious factors may incline a people to ways of thinking strikingly different from those of others, but what we know of the fundamental biological unity of the human species should discourage us from supposing that other peoples might not come, through their own devices or through cultural interaction, to make these ways of thought their "own." Effective appropriation is the only criterion of ownership in this case, and there is obviously no implication of exclusiveness.

2. John S. Mbiti, *African Religions and Philosophy* (London: Heinemann, 1970), chap. 3, esp. 17–18. The suggestion can, of course, be faulted on other grounds. It should be remarked, however, that this chapter of the book is of considerable philosophical interest.

Consider in this connection the unfortunate suggestion, sometimes heard, that logic is not African but Western. If is implied by this that logic as a discipline was not developed in traditional Africa, as it was in the West, it can be largely conceded; though it has to be noted that the discipline was cultivated in other places—for example, in the Orient—centuries in advance of the West. With historical hindsight we can now appreciate how hasty it would have been if in those far-off centuries somebody had said, "Logic is not occidental but oriental." This reflection should also expose the hastiness, not to talk of the absurdity, of a rather more alarming idea which frequently lies behind the remark that logic is non-African. I refer to the idea that logical thinking, not just the construction of systems of logic, is not a characteristic of the African. Again, this notion is entertained not only by some foreigners but also by some apparently patriotic Africans, even by some of those who yield ground to none in execrating Lévy-Bruhl for saying (in his early phase) that Africans have a prelogical mentality. If Africans had no taste for logical thinking, they would have to acquire it or else hold themselves ready for eventual recolonization. But, in fact, that is not the case. Anybody who has observed traditional African elders arguing, for instance, in the adjudication of disputes, must be quite radically obtuse not to have noticed their logical acumen. This comes out not only in their dialectical adroitness but also frequently in their explicit enunciation, in proverbs, as a rule, of formal logical principles. If a person were to fall into contradiction before a gathering of Akan elders, for example, he would invariably be upbraided with some such proverb as that there are no crossroads in the understanding, which, obviously, is an epigrammatic formulation of the principle of Noncontradiction. ("Asu mu nni nkwanta").[3] Or, if one tried to evade both the affirmative and the negative of a proposition, one would invite the contemptuous exclamation: "He will not stand and he will not lie either"—an unmistakable invocation of the principle of Excluded Middle ("Kosi a nkosi, koda a nkoda!").

These exhibits, incidentally, refute the well-intentioned but unwelcome plea, entered on behalf of Africa by some of her friends, that although African thinking does not operate with such principles as Noncontradiction and Excluded Middle, it is none the worse for it,

3. Dr. George P. Hagan of the Institute of African Studies, University of Ghana, has called attention to an alternative Akan traditional formulation of this principle in an unpublished manuscript. He gives it as "Nokware mu nni abra" which means "There is no conflict in truth" (the Akans are an ethnic group in Ghana).

since there are alternative logics.[4] The question of Excluded Middle is somewhat involved,[5] but a quite simple consideration suffices to demonstrate that no coherent logical system or even logical thinking is posssible that dispenses not just with some particular formulation but with the essence of the principle of Noncontradiction. Any system of logic will have to be such as to allow the valid deduction of some propositions from others. But a valid deduction is, by definition, such that the joint assertion of its premises and the negation of its conclusion is self-contradictory, that is, violates the principle of contradiction. If a given system does not have this principle, even at a metalogical level, then the principle is not there to be violated, and the notion of valid deduction must consequently be absent. It follows that dispensing with the principle of Noncontradiction is a logically suicidal abnegation.[6]

The crucial relevance of logic to the concerns of this essay may be seen from the following. Formulating modern thought in African languages will take the form largely, but not wholly, of translating things from other languages. Now, any body of organized knowledge may be viewed in at least two ways: first, as an accumulation of facts; and second, as a method of inquiry. It is only necessary to push the methodology of any subject a little along the path of abstraction to reach the *Logic* of that discipline. A similar exercise on a broader path gives you the *Philosophy* of the discipline. Presupposed by the logic or phi-

4. See, for example, Gordon Hunnings, "Logic, Language and Culture," *Second Order: An African Journal of Philosophy* 4, no.1 (January 1975).

5. See J.E. Wiredu, "Truth as a Logical Constant, with an Application to the Principle of Excluded Middle," *Philosophical Quarterly* (October 1975).

6. In some many-valued systems of logic there is an appearance of the rejection of the principle of Noncontradiction [-(p & -p)]. Thus, in one of Bochvar's systems, -(p & -p) is not a thesis, not being a tautology. The point, however, is that, because the logical constants have different matrices from those of classical logic, the formula -(p & -p) in this context is not identical with the classical principle of Noncontradiction. Moreover, the principle is presupposed at a metalogical level. Note also, in any case, that although -(p & -p) is not a tautology in the system in question, ⊣(p ∧ ⊣p) is. See Nicholas Rescher, *Many Valued Logic*, New York: McGraw-Hill, 1969), chap. 2, esp. 33. There is a grosser trifling with the principle of Noncontradiction in the "paraconsistent logic" or "dialectical logic" recently canvassed by some otherwise solid logicians. See, for example, R. Routley and R.K. Meyer, "Dialectical Logic, Classical Logic and the Consistency of the World," *Studies in Soviet Thought* 16 (1976); or R. Routley, "Dialectical Logic, Semantics and Metamathematics," *Erkentnis* 14 (1979). (For a critique see Joseph Wayne Smith, "Logic and the Consistency of the World," *Erkentnis* 24 [1986]). In my opinion any difference between paraconsistentism and paralogism lies in the possibility of an equivocally consistent interpretation of the proffered symbolisms.

losophy of any discipline is Logic in the fundamental sense of the principles of correct reasoning. This logic or aspects of it can be captured in any number of alternative formalizations; but unless different languages shared basically the same logic, it would be impossible to translate one into another, and any question of translating modern knowledge from, say, French into, say, Luo would lapse. The point is not just that the logic of the disciplines formulated in the medium of a language could not be rendered in another language of a fundamentally disparate logic but also that not even the facts of the subject concerned could be translated.

The point can be pressed further. Language is not just an ad hoc aggregation of sound types and symbols but rather a *system* of these with rules of formation and combination. Unless the principle of Noncontradiction were at least implicitly acknowledged, one could not even begin to talk of the use of rules, for the idea of a rule involves the *intent* of *consistent* application. Logic, then, in the most fundamental sense, is presupposed by language. In this sense logic is appropriately described as the science of consistency, that is, the sustained application of the principle of Noncontradiction.

Let us take stock of the foregoing reflections. They were triggered off by the consideration that some concepts and ways of thinking may exist in one language but not in another. Okot p'Bitek had suggested that the concepts of *Logos* and *creation* did not exist in the Luo language and also that the habit of speculating about the beginning and the end of the world was not found among the speakers of that language. And this, it was suggested, had led to strange results in the translation of Christian theology into Luo. With regard to this, our first priority has been to recommend circumspection regarding such claims in general. Concepts and ways of thought do not belong to particular peoples in any but a historically episodic sense. In the special case of the logical way of thinking, what we have seen is, in effect, that it cannot be absent from any group of articulate beings and that this has a special significance for the possibility of translation.

Nevertheless, with all the circumspection in the world, it still has to be acknowledged that, as a matter of historical fact, there have been, and there are, conceptual and methodological disparities in the thinking of different peoples; and our second priority is to investigate the implications of this for the question of formulating modern thought in our African languages.

Interestingly, the natural and mathematical sciences do not present any intractable difficulties in the present connection. It is true that at present our languages are largely lacking in the vocabulary for expressing modern scientific knowledge. But this is not such a significant disability as might appear at first sight. Language is most fundamentally conceived as a skeleton capable of indefinite fleshing out, or, to change the metaphor a little, as an infinitely flexible framework capable of being bent to any purpose of communication or symbolism in general. If we look at a given language as a set of symbols or types of sound and combination rules together with a definite aggregate of vocabulary, then we may view the adoption of a new word to designate a new perception or attitude or conceptual formation as an accretion. This is legitimate in some contexts. But from the more fundamental point of view, the continual extension of the vocabulary of a language in response to the imperatives of fresh thought and experience is to be seen as just what language is for. We are to think of it not as the enlargement of an instrument but rather as the extended use of it. Thus in Africa we will need to adopt countless new words and symbolic devices in using our languages to domesticate the sciences. But in doing this we would only be exploiting our languages in the natural way.

Three conditions need to be satisfied for the rational and effective pursuit of this aim. The necessity and importance of the enterprise must be clear. Also the ideas and techniques to be thus rendered in our languages must have universal intelligibility and applicability; and finally there must, in any particular case, be an adequate mastery of the given African, or foreign, language and the body of knowledge concerned. That these conditions are either already satisfied or otherwise easily satisfiable is so beyond dispute that one may be tempted to think it superfluous to state them at all in regard to the sciences. But, as we shall see in due course, it is by no means clear that they are all met or can be met in other areas of thought.

How exactly, then, may the requisite vocabulary be devised? By the specialization of old words in our languages and the adoption of new ones from other languages. This is, in fact, no different from the way in which technical terms are introduced into any language. A word may be specialized by the restriction or extension of its meaning or by that analogical transformation of antecedent meaning that is familiar in metaphorical language. A very considerable proportion of African modern scientific vocabulary, however, will have to consist of adopted words from foreign languages; for where, as one can foresee in many cases, the phenomenon to be named has no apparent linkages with previous experience there can be little basis for the specialization of an old word.

As a matter of fact, the vocabulary of science in the languages of the so-called advanced countries is full of adopted and adapted words from the classical languages. Africa can follow suit with good sense. Thus wishing, for example, to express the concept of "electron" in the Akan language of Ghana, there is no reason why we cannot simply say "elɛktrɔn" if an indigenous word does not easily present itself. Our Arab brothers have done this sort of thing quite effectively. The Japanese have thrived on it famously.

It should not be supposed, of course, that articulating scientific knowledge in Africa need always take the passive form of translating things from other languages. Once the program of domesticating the sciences gets under way, Africa, too, can be expected to become a major source of modern scientific knowledge.

When we enter the areas of the humanities and the more intuitive parts of the social sciences, however, we encounter distinctly subtle problems. Concepts and theories in subjects such as art, literature, sociology, theology, and philosophy are apt to reflect the cultural affiliations of their authors or exponents. In such cases not even universal intelligibility, let alone universal validity, can be taken for granted. In such cases, indeed, translation is capable of becoming a form of unwitting transacculturation.

A further look at the problem, commented on by Okot p'Bitek, of translating St. John's opening metaphysics into Luo will help to illumine some aspects of our problem. According to p'Bitek, the concept of *creation* does not exist in Luo. He does not, obviously, mean the concept of creation that is involved when it is said, for example, that a sculptor has created a beautiful piece of sculpture. He is referring to the concept of creation ex nihilo (out of nothing). How plausible is it to suppose that this concept might not exist in a particular language? To be sure, the word "language" in this context refers more directly to vocabulary than to the abstract framework which, as we have seen, constitutes language in the fundamental sense. The vocabulary of a language is, of course, closely connected with the thought habits of its speakers. If, as p'Bitek says, the Luo were not disposed to speculate on such things as the beginning and the end of the world, then it is not inconceivable that they may not have had so transcendental a concept as that of creation out of nothing.

The concept of creation out of nothing is transcendental in the sense that it cannot be defined in terms of anything within human experience. A people can be highly metaphysical without employing transcendental concepts in their thinking, for not all metaphysics is transcendental metaphysics. The Akans of Ghana, for example, are a highly metaphysical people in that they are very curious about such concepts as God, human personality, destiny, free will, causation. But they are preeminently empirical in their intellectual orientation. In particular, their concept of God ("Nyame") is nontranscendental. Nyame (or Nyankopon) is conceived of as being responsible for the world in a sense appropriate to an "Excavator, Hewer, Carver, Creator, Originator, Inventor, Architect."[7] Such a creator is supposed to create, to construct, new things out of something, not out of nothing. The Akan word for this creator is "Ͻbͻͻade." "Bͻ" means to construct, hew, fashion out, etc. To render the notion of creation out of nothing in Akan, one would have to say something that translates back into English in some such phrase as "constructing, hewing, fashioning out something without using anything," which carries its contradictions on its face.

The Akans, then, would seem to be like the Luo in not having a concept of creation out of nothing. Okot p'Bitek seems to suggest that not thinking in terms of concepts of this sort is a sign of a nonmetaphysical outlook. This, as we have pointed out, is not so unless by metaphysics one means transcendental metaphysics, as some people unfortunately do. The urgent question, however, is this: If the idea of creation out of nothing does not exist in Luo and Akan, then how can the Christian belief in that idea be translated into these languages? We have noticed one comic result of the translation of "creator" into Luo as "Rubanga," and one might be tempted, perhaps, to think that no appropriate translation is possible so long as the idea to be translated itself does not exist in the Luo language. Yet a very great number of Akans and Luos are professed Christians and are presumably able to effect some kind of translation.

Let us compare this problem of translation with the problem of translating, say, "electron" into Akan. As of now, the concept of an

7. J.B. Danquah, *The Akan Doctrine of God*, 2d. ed. (London: Frank Cass & Co., 1968), with new introduction by K.A. Dickson. Dr. Danquah, however, does not appear at all times to have abided by the full implications of this wording. George P. Hagan in his "Black Civilization and Philosophy: Akan Tradition of Philosophy" (paper delivered at FESTAC [Festival of African Culture], Lagos, Nigeria, 1977) argues very plausibly from an Akan drum text and a number of sayings that the Akan conception of creation is not creation out of nothing.

electron does not exist in the Akan vocabulary, and the suggestion I
have already made is that we might simply transliterate it as
"elɛktrɔn." To this it might be objected that if the concept does not
exist in Akan, then this collection of letters can register no meaning
on an Akan mind. The objection is well taken. The point is that the
introduction of the word "elɛktrɔn" would have to be part of a peda-
gogic package in which the Akan listener is led to form the concept
of electron through ostensive or periphrastic procedures. We have so
far assumed that the Akan concerned does not speak English or any
other language which has the concept of electron. Where, however,
an Akan speaks some such language as English, matters are simplified
quite considerably. It is then just a matter of his transferring his
thinking in English into Akan.

Notice the following assumptions in these last remarks. It is assumed that it is cognitively useful to try to translate a concept such
as that of electron into Akan, which presupposes that the concept is
transculturally intelligible. We have assumed, furthermore, that the
Akan can assimilate this concept into his received body of thought.
As we have suggested earlier, these assumptions are uncontroversial
as far as concepts (and methods of inquiry) in the natural and mathematical sciences are concerned.

The situation is quite different when we come to a philosophical
concept like creation out of nothing. Being a transcendental concept,
it cannot be introduced into Akan by ostensive methods. Neither can
it be introduced by periphrasis owing to the empirical orientation of
the vocabulary of Akan which produces an apparently contradictory
result when this is attempted. Thus we are left only with the alternative of thinking partially in English while ostensibly speaking (or
writing) in Akan. Not that this is a difficult thing to do. In fact, it
is all too easy; one might simply continue using the Akan word
"Ɔbɔɔade" while annexing to it the signification the word "Creator"
has in Christian metaphysics as articulated in English. This is actually what many Akan Christians educated in English do.

But why should that be done? To exploit one's English-aided grasp
of "electron" in order to transliterate it into Akan—note, by the way,
the classical origin of "electron" itself—is legitimate; we need science in Africa. But it is not obvious why an Akan should think in
English when talking in his mother tongue about cosmic matters. We
are not, let it be noted, considering at this stage the belief in the existence of a transcendental creator; we are only concerned with the

concept itself. Whether or not one uses the Akan word "Ɔbɔɔade" with a transcendental understanding to affirm or deny his existence, the question of the propriety of the practice must press itself on us with equal force.

One danger in this kind of "translation" is liability to fallacies of ambiguity. Take, for example, the oft-repeated claim that we all—the English-speaking Christian as well as the non-English-speaking traditional Akan—worship[8] one and the same God. In the one context "God" refers to a transcendental creator; in the other, it only refers to a hewer writ large, cosmically speaking. Any appearance of truth in the statement is thanks to the ambiguity.

To a large extent, this ambiguity rests on the fact that the transference of the thinking in English into the talking in Akan goes on unconsciously. Any Akan who notices the difference in meaning between the Akan word "Ɔbɔɔade" and the English term "Creator out of nothing" would, most likely, be chary of the sort of claim commented on in the last paragraph. Moreover, observing that trying to translate the notion of creation out of nothing from English into Akan seems to lead to incoherence, he might be constrained to consider whether the fault is in the vocabulary of Akan or in the notion concerned. The resulting meditation may cause him to suggest that Akan vocabulary is inadequate and in need of transcendental enrichment. On the other hand, he may come to think that the concept is, in fact, incoherent. Were he to come to this conclusion, he would not need to restrict his explanations to just pointing out the difficulties besetting any attempt to render the concept in Akan. The reasons underlying these difficulties might be articulated in English as independent considerations.

Such reasoning might, briefly, be as follows. In common discourse, that is, outside the technical language of philosophy, to create is always to fashion something new by manipulating preexisting materials and potentials. Hence to speak of creation out of nothing is to employ a word while failing to abide by all the conditions of its em-

---

8. Though this is not the point immediately at issue here, it might be useful to note that it is not quite correct to say that a people like the traditional Akans *worship* God. It is a questionable assumption that, if a people believe in a Supreme Being, then they must have institutions or procedures describable as worship directed to that Supreme Being. If Christian Europe has such procedures, that is little reason for supposing that all peoples must have them. The Akans conceive of God as a supremely good, powerful, and wise being. It is not clear why such a being has to be worshipped.

ployment. Moreover, *nothing* is, in the standard meaning of the word, just the absence of something, not the presence of any sort of entity or medium *out of* which something might be created.

Valid or invalid, this reasoning is extremely significant, for it shows that, in trying to translate a phrase like "creation out of nothing" into Akan or Luo or any other African language, one is not just trying to translate English but rather a sublanguage within the English language, namely, the technical language of philosophical thought. Technical vocabulary in philosophy is always heavily laden with doctrinal history. Although the vocabulary and grammar of the parent language often does influence the character of the technical language, this influence is never rigidly deterministic. Moreover, its flow is two-way, for the technical language of philosophy has a way of influencing ordinary usage. This makes it all the more necessary that one should be wary in translations in philosophy and cognate fields.

Here again the Luo translation of the opening sentence of the Gospel according to St. John offers a very useful illustration of the problems of translation across cultures. The saint talks of the *Word*. This, of course, is the translation in English of the Greek word "Logos" which has a rather special technical meaning. The philosophical use of "Logos" in Greek philosophy goes as far back at least as to Heraclitus (about 500 B.C.). For him "Logos" meant not just rational thought but the ontological "principle" from which the rational order of the universe emanates. In Plato "Nous" is the principle which is the source of the rational organization of the "intelligible" world of Forms. In due time this "Nous" is more or less identified with Logos. By the time we reach the Stoics we have an all-embracing Logos doctrine according to which Logos is, on the cosmic scale, the creative "principle" which is the source of the rational organization of nature and, on the scale of human individuals, the Reason of the soul. On the cosmic scale Logos was identified with God.

St. John's "the Word was God" reflects the Heraclitean-Platonic-Stoic doctrine surveyed above. The Christian "Word" reflects further the elaborations of this doctrinal tradition by the early Church Fathers. Now, what is a non-English–speaking Luo elder, uninstructed in the semantics of Graeco-Christian metaphysics, to make of the message that "the Word was God" which, by Luo interpretation, re-translates as "News was the Hunchback Spirit"? Perhaps the Luo elders in the Italo-Luo encounter referred to by Okot p'Bitek could have done a better job of translating "God"[9] but it is difficult to see how, without an inkling of the Graeco-Christian philosophy of the "Word" and an ability to think in some language, such as English, already impregnated with that tradition, anyone could possibly make even a preliminary sense of St. John's suggestion.

One perceives in this connection an interesting stratification of the African audience for translations of the sort being considered. From the point of view of intelligibility, the most ill-served stratum is the class of non-Western–educated, traditional Africans for whom we have already by implication expressed our sympathy. There is also the class of those Western-educated Africans who are not initiated into the Western metaphysics of the "Word." To these only a partial apparent understanding is possible. We have, finally, the class of those Western-educated Africans who are at home in the relevant Western traditions of thought. They[10] are capable of as full an understanding of the Western doctrines as the native Westerners themselves, and they have, consequently, no difficulty in understanding the versions of these same doctrines in the pretended translations into the African languages.

But what sort of understanding do they have of the African texts? The answer is that the understanding they have is, in a certain sense, a Western understanding. The mental content engendered by the African text is not integrated into African categories of thought but rather embedded in Western categories. This is what accounts for the symmetry which exists in the relationship between the English text and the Luo rendition in the mind of the African sophisticate and is absent in that of the traditional Luo.

Take the specific case of "The Word was God." In the first case, the symmetry consists in the fact that this English sentence translates into the Luo sentence "Lok aye ceng Lubanga" which, in its Westernized apprehension, translates back into the original English sentence.

9. In the Twi Bible (that is, the Bible as translated into the Akan language), St. John's sentence reads as "Mfiase no na Asem no wo ho, na Asem no ne Nyankopon na ewo ho, na Asem no ye Onyame." The best one can do in rendering Asem into English in this context is to say "a piece of discourse," so, even if we suppress our qualms about translating "Onyame" as "God," a strict retranslation yields: "In the beginning the Piece of Discourse was there, the Piece of Discourse was there with God and the Piece of Discourse was God," which, though not as hilarious as the Luo version, is no more intelligible.

10. They have illustrious historical antecedents in men like St. Cyprian, Tertullian, and St. Augustine.

In the second case, the failure of symmetry consists in the fact that, while the English sentence initially translates into "Lok aye ceng Lubanga," this Luo sentence in its indigenous meaning translates back into English not as the original English sentence but rather as "News was the Hunchback Spirit." Using a downward vertical arrow to stand for translation, we might set the contrast down schematically as follows:

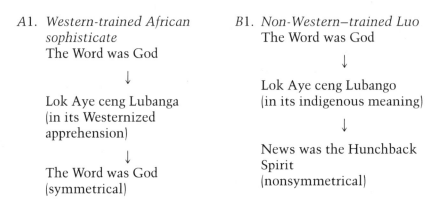

*A*1. *Western-trained African sophisticate*
The Word was God

↓

Lok Aye ceng Lubanga
(in its Westernized apprehension)

↓

The Word was God
(symmetrical)

*B*1. *Non-Western–trained Luo*
The Word was God

↓

Lok Aye ceng Lubango
(in its indigenous meaning)

↓

News was the Hunchback Spirit
(nonsymmetrical)

In an Akan translation the schema would be as follows:

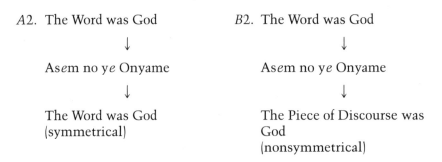

*A*2. The Word was God

↓

Asɛm no yɛ Onyame

↓

The Word was God
(symmetrical)

*B*2. The Word was God

↓

Asɛm no yɛ Onyame

↓

The Piece of Discourse was God
(nonsymmetrical)

In *A* what we might call the Western evangelical point of view is operative in each schema from start to finish: there is a Graeco-Christian message to be communicated. An African sentence is chosen to carry the message without a thorough investigation of the conceptual framework within which it has its meaning. Accordingly, in any reverse translation, what is operative is not the original meaning of the African sentence but the evangelical information or apparent information superimposed upon it. If this translational practice is embraced and perpetuated by a significant enough number of Africans, however, it becomes legitimized. What that means is that in the relevant connection Africans would have become Westernized in what I fear would have to be called an unthinking manner.

It is important to stress that this is not just a verbal question. Nor does it concern an isolated piece of translation. In the domain of religion alone—and we shall see in due course that essentially the same issue is encountered in other spheres as well—the translational practices in question betoken a pervasive eclipsing of unexamined indigenous African modes of thought by equally unexamined imported ones. Modes of thought in so vital an area as religion, of course, have sundry implications for action. Since thought and action in such realms constitute an important facet of a culture, the foregoing considerations show how certain forms of translation can become forms of transacculturation, by the nature of their genesis and not necessarily by the impact of their semantic import.

The schemata under *B* may be viewed as a sort of counter to this sort of acculturation. The first segments represent the tendentious translation of the Christian evangelist; the second represent attempts to give the real meaning of the African sentences involved. The point is not that *B*-type translations are literal and *A*-type translations metaphorical, but rather that the former take African meanings seriously while the latter do not. A metaphor is a certain way of taking a given meaning seriously; it pays tribute to the suggestiveness of that meaning. Far from paying any tribute to African meanings, *A*-type translations, in effect, take them in vain.

What, then, is the lesson of the schemata under *B*? The lesson is that translation in such fields as religion ought to be approached with greater conceptual self-consciousness than has been apparent so far. That there is something wrong with the *B*-schemata is certain; for, surely, translations ought to be symmetrical. In fact, if I am right in my earlier remarks about the Akan language in connection with the concept of creation out of nothing, then the word "God" as signifying the creator of the universe out of nothing is simply not translatable into the Akan language, and not into the Luo either, if Okot p'Bitek is right.

Paradoxically, this does not make rendering the idea of God in Akan impossible; it makes it simpler. It would be quite feasible simply to transliterate and write "Gɔd" in Akan. Similarly, we might say "Lɔgɔs" instead of "Asem." (Here it is obviously better to avoid the

English detour of the "Word") So that "the Word was God" now becomes, in Akan, "Na lɔgɔs no yɛ Gɔd." There is then no longer any pretense that the Akan language already contains concepts equivalent to "Logos" and "God," and the problem of nonsymmetry is effectively and nontendentiously obviated. Moreover, it would now be easily appreciated that if the intended message is to be received by the non-English–speaking, traditional African,[11] then extensive explanations of *"Lɔgɔs"* and *"Gɔd"* will have to be supplied.[12]

How does "Gɔd" as a transliteration into the Akan language compare with "elɛktrɔn?" They both transliterate untranslatable words into the language. But the prospects of their being understood in the recipient language are different. Unlike "electron," which is an empirical concept, a transcendental concept like "Gɔd" can be expected to give rise to difficulties of understanding in an empirically oriented language like Akan, as noted earlier. An English-speaking Akan might have the impression that the idea is easy to understand in Akan, but this is likely to be because, in this matter, he thinks in English and not in Akan. For an African to think in a Western language in this way is a mark of what might be called the colonial mentality. By contrast, he may consciously incorporate his Western-acquired concept of "electron" into Akan without incurring this description for reasons already given. Accordingly, it might be said that while a word like "elɛktrɔn" is to be introduced to encourage the domestication of certain Western concepts and forms of thinking, a work like "Gɔd" is to be introduced to encourage caution in the assimilation of Western ideas.[13]

This caution is, indeed, desirable in connection with a large assortment of Western concepts and categories of thought. In Anthropology, History, and Politics, it is well-known that the use by European students of Africa of words like "family," "tribe," "chief," "brother,"

11. The reference here is to the African who speaks no language in which the relevant concepts are already received.

12. Any dictionary that translates "God" as "Nyame," "Onyankopon," or vice versa glosses over this necessity to the disadvantage of genuine Akan thinking. Christaller, the German author of the first Twi-English Dictionary, did this, but so have Akrofi and Botchey, themselves Ghanaians. See J.G. Christaller, *Dictionary of the Asante and Fante Language Called Tshi (Twi)* (Basel, [1881] 1933); C.A. Akrofi and G.L. Botchey, *English-Twi-Ga Dictionary* (Accra: Waterville Publishing House, 1968; Rev. ed. 1980).

13. The reader might like to be reminded that when concepts and forms of thought are said to be African or Western there is no implication that they are intrinsically ethnic, as explained already.

"cousin," etc., in application to Africa has often betrayed a Eurocentricism.[14] Ironically, this seems to have insinuated itself into the discourse of Africans themselves. Sorting out the intricacies of translation in regard to these and allied concepts is by no means easy, but matters are much worse when we come to relatively more abstract concepts like "Law," "Custom," "Morality," "Religion," "Worship," "Punishment," "Retribution." When we reach the level of abstraction represented by logical, epistemological, and metaphysical concepts, the difficulty is to perceive that there is a problem to start with. It would be a major first step towards the correct formulation of modern thought in African languages if we in Africa were to cultivate the habit of as much as possible *thinking* in our own indigenous languages when *talking* in one metropolitan language or another about issues involving concepts such as "God" (which we have already touched upon), "Mind," "Person," "Soul," "Spirit," "Sentence," "Proposition," "Truth," "Fact," "Substance," "Existence," and about categorical distinctions such as "the Physical and the Spiritual," "the Natural and the Supernatural," "the Religious and the Secular," and "the Mystical and the Nonmystical." Our concern here need not be too narrowly and too directly focused on translation. Our characterizations in foreign languages of African institutions and modes of thought and behavior ought to be critically scrutinized, for they have a crucial bearing on our translations.

To start with a simple example. Consider the relation: mother's sister's son. In Akan a person having this relation to me is called "me nua." Now "me nua" also describes the relationship that my mother's son bears to me. In this case, "me nua" translates unproblematically into English as "my brother." The question is: How are we to translate "me nua" in the first case? The orthodox translation is "my cousin." But this is quite incapable of expressing the strength of kinship bonds connoted by the Akan term for the relationship. To continue to say "cousin" without a sense of uneasiness is to allow ourselves to be controlled by a foreign cultural model in our translations. If we do speak of the extended family, why may we not speak of an extended brother? On the other hand, if we are not careful, an uncritical pursuit of industrialization could so erode our sense of extended kinship solidarity[15] as to make "cousin" the correct transla-

14. See A. Adu Boahen, *Clio and Nation Building,* Inaugural Lecture, Ghana Universities Press, Accra, 1975 : 20 ff.

15. See Kwasi Wiredu, *Philosophy and an African Culture* (Cambridge: Cambridge University Press, 1980), 21–22, 29, 30.

tion, after all. We see, here again, that these issues of translation are not just a matter of words but also of worth.

Even more interesting conceptual issues arise in connection with the translation of a term such as "punishment." The standard temptation is to suppose that there must be an equivalent concept in Akan. In fact, there isn't. There is no comparable blanket concept for reaction to wrongdoing in Akan. If a child or an adolescent misbehaves, what is visited upon him is called "asotwe," literally "ear pulling." This term is never applied to an adult who trifles with the community's rules. The term used depends on the broad category of the offense. If the rule involved is just a custom or a convention, what the misconduct calls for is either an "mpata" which means pacification or compensation, or "nnwanetoa" which means apology through an intercessor. Both may be quite expensive, though frequently a few well-chosen words, reinforced with the right set of proverbs, will settle the matter. On the other hand, one who shows himself heedless to a law of the state brings upon himself "amane" or "adi," that is, trouble or adversity. This might be a fine, a period in banishment, or, in the gravest type of case, death. Any category of offense might have an extrahuman dimension, in which case purificatory rituals might also be incurred.

The following facts are especially worthy of note in regard to the Akan reaction to error. "Asotwe" is explicitly reformative. Of an erring or fractious child it is said that "naso nte asom," that is, his ears do not hear advice; in other words, he is impervious to moral instruction. His ear is figuratively (and at times also literally) pulled to open it to edification. Though primarily reformatory, the exercise is expected, secondarily, to help deter other children. Occasionally, a parent who has temporarily lost his reason through excessive irritation might set upon his erring child in a spirit of retribution. Such loss of perspective is, of course, never held up as a model of parental governance in Akan society. In the case of adult transgression of state laws, on the other hand, retribution is held to be appropriate; it is, indeed, the primary reaction, and this is clear in the language used. When the Akan official announcer proclaims that whoever violates an edict of the "chief" will be overtaken by adversity ("wunii a wobeye [saa], adi aye wo"; " . . . wanya amane"; " . . . amane da wo so"), he is unequivocally warning of retribution. Deterrence does, indeed, enter into the calculation but as a secondary consideration. The reformatory motive is more shadowy. The person concerned may very well "learn sense" ("sua nyansa") from his troubles, but even if he did not the sanction would not be regarded as having proved futile on that account. Actually, the question of reformation does not always arise. A generally continent man whose resistance collapses in the face of the oversexy exhibitionism of a married woman is not particularly in need of reformation, for there is, by hypothesis, no tendency to adultery in his character; nevertheless, he will be dealt with according to law, for he has done wrong. Moreover, even where a misconduct is the manifestation of a settled trait, the principal duty of seeing to the reform of the individual is assigned to his family rather than to any other institution.

Reformatory motives are, again, quite marginal in those cases in which the wrongdoer (frequently together with his family) is expected to pacify ritually his ancestors or some nonhuman forces in order to restore cherished and beneficial relationships. Ideas of deterrence are equally remote, and those of retribution even more so, if operative at all. The same remarks apply a fortiori to the procedures for dealing with offenses that require only an apology or a compensation in an out-of-court setting.

Consider now the question, much debated in Western philosophy, of the justification of punishment. Some philosophers have suggested that punishment is only justified by its deterrent and reformative consequences. Others, the retributivists, have maintained that the commission of a forbidden act is the necessary and sufficient condition of punishment. How are these issues and contentions to be translated into the Akan language? There being no blanket counterpart to "punishment" in Akan, the principal question here has to be raised anew in respect of each of the broad categories of reaction to wrongdoing in Akan society. Suppose, then, that we ask what is the justification of "asotwe." This would amount to asking for the justification of trying to reform bad children and deter other children from wrongdoing. Whatever one may think of this question, one thing that should be absolutely clear is that you cannot answer it by proposing reformation and deterrence, on pain of an obvious circularity. Nor could one suggest retribution, for to seek to justify reformation by retribution would be to chase after a contradiction. Of course, one can ask whether "asotwe" is the right way of trying to reform children; and this, in fact, is the important question. Yet, were we uncritically to translate "asotwe" as "punishment," we would, most likely, be diverted from this question into debating familiar but not quite pertinent Western issues and proposals.

The point applies equally clearly to the retributive way of dealing with (a certain category of) misconduct. If you think of this simply in terms of the Western concept of punishment, you are likely to be encouraged to pursue the topic along the customary Western lines. But from the Akan point of view, the question that might need investigating is whether retribution is the right way, or perhaps one should say the right spirit, for dealing with the class of offenses under consideration. It should be noted that this is quite over and above the issue whether a particular concrete form of retribution is fair to relation to a given offense. Now, to ask for the justification of retribution is immediately to transcend the position of the typical Western retributivist; it is, so to speak, to start the inquiry where he ends it. The interesting thing here is that this approach is fore-shadowed by the preanalytic conceptualizations, in the Akan language, of the phenomena that are studied under what is known in Western philosophy as the Philosophy of Punishment. It is conceivable that a sustained inquiry into the morality of retribution might lead to the conclusion that, say, reformation is a better basis for dealing with wrongdoing of the type under consideration.[16] If this were then to become the received approach, the chances are that there would be quite a thoroughgoing change, possibly in the direction of greater humanity, in the Akan way of speaking about and dealing with large classes of wrong conduct. That would be a remarkable example of the impact philosophy can have on practical affairs. But the Akan philosopher of today who thinks in English or perhaps French is unlikely to be able to maintan those linguistic links of empathy that will enable him to communicate effectively with and influence his traditional kinsmen on issues such as the ones we have been discussing. If with foreign-oriented thinking he translates modern thought in this area, as in various other areas, into his own language, the outcome is likely to do violence (though not premeditatedly) to his indigenous categories of thought. Other Africans, Akans and non-Akans alike, are invited to compare their own notes with mine.

In regard to the procedure of settling offenses through purificatory

16. Note that this would have been arrived at by a different route from that of the Western advocate of reformation. The Western "reformationist" thinks of reformation as the justification of a comprehensive practice called punishment; the Akan "reformationist" would start with a critique of the institution of retribution he encounters in his society, and his reflection would take the form of examining the morality of retribution and, along with it, deterrence, reformation, and any other possible approach to misconduct.

rituals or through compensation or apology, it is even more obvious than in the preceding cases that the (English) concept of punishment and its philosophy are hardly applicable; accordingly, circumspection is doubly necessary in translation.

I come now to a distinctively metaphysical concept, namely, *substance*. Nothing is more tempting in this area of reflection than to suppose that categories of substance and accident or, in more modern language, thing and quality (property) are absolutely essential to all human thought about the world. They have pride of place in Aristotle's list of the categories and are very fundamental in the philosophies of Descartes, Leibniz, and Spinoza. Though the classical British empiricists Locke, Berkeley, and Hume were critical of the notion of substance, they were never completely free of it, since they remained stuck with a notion of quality which was a logical correlate of that substance. Moreover, Locke never succeeded completely in disabusing his mind of it, being to the last committed to the idea of substance as something "he knows not what"; and Berkeley, though contemptuous of the idea of *material* substance, was keen on spiritual *substance*. Hume, the most radical empiricist of all, rejected the notion of substance as an "unintelligible chimera," but in suggesting that things were just collections of qualities, he fell victim indirectly to that notion, for his sugggestion suffered from an incoherence deriving from the fact that his notion of quality was a logical correlate of substance. One way or another, then, the notion of substance has been very influential in Western philosophy.

Aristotle had various ways of characterizing substance, four of which have, in some manner of conflation, become the core of subsequent thought on the topic. Substance was conceived alternatively as a logical subject that is, as a subject of which predicates could be affirmed or denied but never itself a predicate of anything else, as that in which properties or qualities inhered, as that which had independent existence, and as that which remained the same when something underwent changes in quality. There is here an obvious interplay of grammar, logic, and metaphysics. The organization of the materials of discourse into subject and predicate is a circumstance of speech (and of writing, where it exists) which may not be universal among the human species.[17] Nor need it be an invariable aspect of the structure of all human thought. But even granting the contrary, it is

---

17. See Tsu-Lin, Mei, "Chinese Grammar and the Linguistic Movement in Philosophy," *Review of Metaphysics* 14(1961).

not clear why the structure of thought and discourse has to be duplicated in the structure of reality. Yet it is this ontological interpretation of a semantic distinction that has become widely received into philosophical and semiphilosophical discourse (in the West).

In English, for example, one speaks of a thing and its properties or qualities, and it is frequently taken for granted that a thing belongs to an ontological order distinct from that of its properties. A thing is *concrete,* but its properties are *abstract.* Thus, for example, when a table is brown, the brownness is said to be a property of the table but not itself a concrete thing like the table, being only an abstract entity. In this form the substance-accident distinction, not necessarily hinged to its Aristotelian or neo-Aristotelian support, is very current indeed in modern English-speaking philosophy.[18] In contemporary philosophy of logic, an added Platonic complication gives rise to a theory of abstract entities in semantic analysis espoused by some of its most prestigious practitioners.[19] The technical language of philosophy, as noted already, is apt to infiltrate into common discourse, and much ordinary use of the thing-quality distinction bears the marks of an unconscious metaphysic.

When, therefore, we come to consider how the substance-accident, thing-property distinction might be translated into an African language, we have quite a slippery situation with which to reckon. Although the Akan language, for instance, is not inhospitable to the subject-predicate distinction, the hypostatization of subject into a self-subsistent entity and of predicate into a dependent abstract object is unintelligible in that medium as of now. The word for "thing" is "ade" in Akan, and this is the only word that could possibly be used to render "substance." But the referent of "ade" has to be a full-blooded object; the word cannot be used to express the notion of an existent in abstraction from its properties. The notion of the property of an object may be translated as "yɛbea" or "tebea," which literally means "way of being" or better, "the way a thing is" or, better still, "the nature of a thing." Two things must be clear at once: first, it

18. For a critique of this see J.E. Wiredu, "Predication and Abstract Entities," *Legon Journal of the Humanities* 2(1976).

19. See, for instance, Alonzo Church, 'The Need for Abstract Entities in Semantic Analysis," *American Academy of Arts and Sciences Proceedings* 80 (1951). Reprinted in I.M. Copi and J.A. Gould, *Contemporary Readings in Logical Theory* (New York: Macmillan Co., 1967). I have criticized this kind of theory at length in J.E. Wiredu, "Logic and Ontology," *Second Order: An African Journal of Philosophy* (January 1973, July 1973, July 1974, and January 1975).

does not make sense to conceive of the way a thing is as itself a kind of object, and, second, it makes even less sense to envisage the existence of an entity which has no nature. Hence the metaphysical distinction between a thing and its properties cannot be expressed in Akan without unconcealed absurdities.

Of course, the semantic distinction between a thing and its properties can be made in Akan. This just means that one can identify and talk about a thing ("ade") without giving an exhaustive description of the way it is ("ne tebea"). Thus an Akan, mindful of his indigenous categories of thought, is unlikely to take for granted the intelligibility in Akan of the metaphysical distinction between a thing and its properties. In consequence, when translating any piece of discourse involving that distinction into Akan, he will be likely to adopt cautionary devices, including, presumably, transliteration and periphrasis, complete with explanations. Moreover, in contrast to the case of translations in the field of science, it is improbable that the motive of the exercise will be the desire to domesticate culturally either the thought form or its content.

The same critical approach will be called for in translations of concepts such as "Mind," "Person," "Soul," "Spirit," "Sentence," "Proposition," "Truth," "Fact," "Existence," "Free Will," and category contrasts such as "the Physical and the Spiritual," "the Natural and the Supernatural," "the Religious and the Secular," and "the Mystical and the Nonmystical." These were listed earlier. They do not exhaust the range of concepts regarding which an African would need to be specially open-eyed in his translations. But they are wide-ranging enough to discourage any sense of complacency. Hitherto, complacency has reigned in, for example, Akan translations of terms like "Mind," "Soul," "Spirit." It is usual to find "soul" translated as "okra" and "spirit" and "sunsum" (or under Christian influence, "honhom"). "Mind" is rarely directly translated. It may be surmised that this is because in the Akan inventory of the entities that go to constitute a human person nothing that might be called the equivalent of "mind" is mentioned. This is for a very good reason. The fact is that the Akan conception of mind is not of a kind of entity but rather of a capacity and a function.[20] Although

20. Kwasi Wiredu, "Philosophical Research and Teaching in Africa: Some Suggestions [toward Conceptual Decolonisation]" (paper delivered at UNESCO conference on Philosophical Teaching and Research in Africa, Nairobi, Kenya, June 1980). Published in *Teaching and Research in Philosophy* (Paris: UNESCO, 1984). See also Kwasi Wiredu, "The Akan Concept of Mind," *Ibadan Journal of Humanistic Studies*, no. 3 (Oc-

"mind" is not often consciously translated in the literature, it is usually , in effect, identified alternatively with the "okra" and with the "sunsum." The "okra" is supposed to be the entity that accounts for a person being alive. Some authors call it "the principle of life,"[21] others "a life force."[22] Whatever it is called, it is clear beyond peradventure that "mind" cannot mean the "okra." Nor can it mean the "sunsum," which is held to refer to something in a person that gives him the peculiar force of his personality, if for no other reason than that the "sunsum" is thought of as a kind of entity while "mind," "adwane" in Akan, is conceived of simply as the thinking capacity or function. Yet it has become orthodox to equate the "okra" with the soul, which, since the soul is more or less identified with the mind, has the effect of indirectly equating the "okra" with the mind. The scene is, accordingly, set for entangling the Akan concept of mind in Western problems of dualism, idealism, materialism, etc., which, in truth, do not fit into Akan categories of thought.[23]

By a similar circumstance of translation, belief in countless "mystical," "spiritual," and "supernatural" entities has been attributed to the African race. In fact, however, these categories do not exist in Akan thought, for example; they would seem not to exist in the thought of many other African peoples. I would like, however, to see philosophically sophisticated conceptual analyses of the thought of various African peoples by thinkers with an inside understanding of the relevant African languages and cultures before generalizing with any confidence. Still, since one counterexample overthrows a universal generalization, I would like to dwell on the Akan example briefly in considering the universal attributions in question. As I have already observed, the intellectual orientation of the Akan is empirical. To repeat, this does not mean that the metaphysical bent is absent from their thinking. It does not mean, furthermore, that they are unused to thinking with concepts of the highest abstraction. What it means is only that they do not employ in their thinking certain kinds of abstract concepts, namely, those that cannot be defined in terms

tober 1983]; G. Floistad, ed., *Contemporary Philosophy: A New Survey, vol. 5: African Philosophy* (Boston: Kluwer Academic, 1987).

21. Kwame Gyekye: "The Akan Concept of a Person," *International Philosophical Quarterly* (September 1978): 278.

22. K.A. Busia, "The Ashanti," in *African Worlds*, ed. Daryll Ford (Oxford, 1954), 197.

23. I have tried to sort these things out in K. Wiredu, "The Akan Concept of Mind."

deriving from human experience.[24] Now, quite clearly, the concept of the "supernatural" goes beyond the world of human experience. It envisages a world *over and above* this world. By no manner of deduction, extrapolation, or imaginative projection could one arrive at such a concept from empirical beginnings.

The reason why many students of African thought have seen the supernatural, the spiritual, the mystical as being preeminent in the African worldview is because traditional Africans undoubtedly believe in the existence and pervasive influence of a variety of nonhuman beings and powers. But as far at least as the Akans are concerned, these beings and powers are an integral part of this world. They belong as much to the world as the chairs in this room and the trees outside it. Not even Onyame ("God") is supposed to exist outside the world. That would be a veritable contradiction in Akan terms. To exist is to be *there* ("wɔhɔ," and existence is the being there of something ("sɛ bribi wɔ hɔ"). To exist outside the world would mean to be *there* but not at any place, an idea lacking in coherence. Note, incidentally, that the great St. Anselm would have had unmanageable difficulties trying to articulate his ontological argument for the existence of God in vintage Akan, although his definition of the Supreme Being as that than which a greater cannot be conceived is commonplace in that linguistic setting.

There is, then, as Busia puts it, an "apparent absence of any conceptual cleavage between the natural and the supernatural" in Akan traditional thinking.[25] Of a piece with this also in the absence of any conceptual cleavage between the spiritual and the physical. Mbiti observes, speaking of African thought generally, that within it "no line is drawn between the spiritual and the physical."[26] This is assuredly

24. This is not to say that the Akans are empiricists. Of course, not all Akans are philosophers. Nor need an Akan Philosopher be an empiricist. Indeed, if he or she pays due attention to the Akan language, the basic thesis of classical empiricism will be found incoherent. Empiricism is not necessarily truly empirical in orientation. See John Dewey, "An Empirical Survey of Empiricisms," in *Dewey on Experience, Nature and Freedom*. ed. Richard J. Bernstein (New York: Arts Press, 1960). Moreover, we are here directly concerned with Akan traditional categories of thought, not with Akan traditional thought about Akan categories of thought.

25. K.A. Busia, *The Challenge of Africa* (New York: Praeger Paperbacks, 1962), 36. Busia, unfortunately, in this same work as in others (for example, *Africa in Search of Democracy* [London: Routledge and Kegan Paul, 1967]), wrote as if the Akans had a place for the concept of the supernatural in their thought.

26. Mbiti, *African Religions and Philosophy*, 5. This insight, however, as in the case of Busia, is inconstant in Mbiti's pages.

true of Akan thought. No entities are spoken of or even dreamt of in Akan philosophy that are not material to some degree. If we take the maximal limit of materiality to be exemplified by things like chairs and tables, which are subject to all the constraints of space and time and have all the familiar causal susceptibilities, then the difference between such objects, on the one hand, and entities such as "okra" and "sunsum," on the other, is not that the former are material and the latter are immaterial, extensionless, but rather that the former are fully material, and the latter are thought of as only partially so, being only loosely constrained by space and time and commonplace causality.

The foregoing discussion discloses contrasts between Western categories of thought and those of the Akans (and most likely other African peoples) which have enormous implications for translation. Since a good translation should be symmetrical, both translations from foreign into African languages and the converse are affected. The problems in the second aspect of the matter, namely, translations from African, into foreign languages are especially urgent, since at present very much more of that takes place than the reverse. The translations referred to here are not of the simple and straightforward type in which a composed text in an African language is rendered into a corresponding text in a metropolitan language; they take the form rather of accounts of African thought in foreign languages in which, inevitably, African categories of thought are, so to speak, mapped onto Western ones. We have seen that in some important spheres of thought such mappings have sometimes left much to be desired, conceptually , and that this has led in the past to the uncritical assimilation of Western modes of thought. Not only concepts and beliefs have been imported in this way but also philosophical problems. Certain forms of the problem of punishment, as we have seen, need not arise in an Akan philosophy of morals. Similarly, the metaphysical problem of substance and quality has no place in the Akan context. Since, as has just been indicated, mind in Akan thought is not a kind of substance or entity, the time-honored problem in Western philosophy of how mind as a spiritual substance can interact with the body as a physical substance also is nonexistent in that intellectual mileau.

The existence of these problems depends on the character of the languages concerned. Not only are the problems not universally ineluctable for the human mind but also they seem to be pseudoproblems. This has not, of course, been established, though there are hints in the above discussion which foreshadow independent considerations in that direction. What needs to be especially emphasized here is that they are not being said to be pseudoproblems simply because they are based at least in part on interpretations of language. Many important philosophical problems are of this nature. The trouble only comes when they are based on mistaken interpretations. It is to be noted, furthermore, that the fact that these problems do not arise within the Akan language is not taken as a conclusive reason for supposing that they are pseudoproblems. We will return to a certain implication of this remark soon. Meanwhile, it seems prudent to add that it is not being suggested that the philosophical problems mentioned in the last paragraph are pseudoproblems in all their forms.[27] Only the forms of the problems specifically delineated in our discussion are implicated. It is necessary, moreover, to point out that, when the problems in question are called Western, it is not implied that they are entertained by all Western philosophers. On the contrary, there are important Western philosophers who are not taken in by the metaphysical suggestiveness of their language in these matters.[28] The problems have been called Western simply in the sense that they seem to arise quite naturally in the Western context of thought and language. But in such matters, "language can only incline, not necessitate."[29]

27. For example, in the paper on "The Akan Concept of Mind" referred to earlier, I have distinguished four problems of mind, namely, (1) the metaphysical problem of how mind conceived as a nonmaterial entity is related to the body, a material entity; (2) the question of how the concept of mind is related to that of thought; (3) the problem of the basis of the possibility of thought; and (4) the issue of how the category of brain process is related to that of thought. Only the first is declared to be a pseudoproblem not arising within Akan thought.

28. In the case of the metaphysics of substance and quality we have already noted the opposition of David Hume. In contemporary English-speaking philosophy, Bertrand Russell was one of the most unremitting critics of the metaphysical notion of substance: "'Substance' . . . is a metaphysical mistake, due to transference to the world-structure of the structure of sentences composed of a subject and a predicate" (*History of Western Philosophy* [London: George Allen and Unwin, 1946], 225). In an earlier book Russell had called for the expurgation of the metaphysical notion of substance from philosophy and commented, "A great book might be written showing the influence of syntax on philosophy; in such a book, the author could trace in detail the influence of the subject-predicate structure of sentences upon European thought, more particularly in this matter of 'substance'" (*An Outline of Philosophy* New York: Meridian Books, [1927] 1960). Ayer's discussion of *substance* in his *Language, Truth and Logic*, 2d. ed. (London: Victor Gollancz, 1946) was scarcely more accommodating. He actually said that philosophers who advocated the doctrine of substance had been "duped by grammar" (p. 45; see also p. 42).

29. Kwasi Wiredu, *Philosophy and African Culture*, 35.

Let us call concepts, problems, and theses that depend on the contingent characteristics of a given language "tongue dependent." A concept, problem or thesis that is tongue dependent is, of course, necessarily language dependent. On the other hand, language dependency does not necessarily imply tongue dependency. If a problem arises from an absolutely universal feature of language, it is not tongue dependent. There certainly must be such problems. For example, the idea of message-stating must be inherent in any natural language. It must, consequently be pertinent in any natural language to talk of the equivalence of statements. At least any statement will have to be equivalent to itself. In the systematization of the logic of any natural language, therefore, relating equivalence to other logical concepts, by definition or otherwise, must always be a useful enterprise. The particular way in which this is done in a particular language, however, may not have a translational counterpart in some other language.

Consider the following two definitions:

1. "A is equivalent to B" means by definition "A if and only if B."

2. "A is equivalent to B" means by definition "(if A then B) and (if B then A)."

Both (1) and (2) generate obvious logical truths in English.[30] It turns out, however, that while (2) generates a logical truth in Akan, (1) is not even expressible therein simply for the lack of a counterpart of the phrase "if and only if." Of course, Akan has the concept of a conditional. In fact, any language in which the validity of an argument can be discussed must have this concept and hence must be able to express (2) in one way or another. In Akan, (2) might be expressed as follows:

2. "A ne B kosi faako" nkyerease nhyehyεε ne "(sε A a ende B) na (se B a ende A)."

Now, from a logistic point of view, given "(if A then B) and (if B then A)" the phrase "A if and only if B" is superfluous, since the two are definitionally equivalent. And this shows that a logical system in Akan need not be semantically incomplete on account of not having the latter. Actually, in standard presentations of classical logic in English both "A is equivalent to B" and "A if and only if B" are represented by one and the same logical symbol, namely, "↔" or "≡"; which should reinforce our sense of the logistic superfluity of the

---

30. Formulating modern logic in African languages is going to be an important part of the general program of formulating modern knowledge therein. Victor Ocaya made an interesting attempt in this direction in his Master's thesis, *"Logic within the Acholi Language"* (Makerere University, Kampale, Uganda, 1978).

latter. Nevertheless, the fact that a logical truth, such as (1), may exist in one language and not in another is of considerable theoretical significance. It demonstrates, in particular, that some logical truths are tongue-dependent and, therefore, not universal without qualification. Of course, a relative universality might be secured for (1) by taking cognizance of some such qualifications as "provided that both logical concepts are available in the given language." (This is relevant only to a highly informal level of discussion such as the present one, for in any rigorous establishment of a logical system there will be an explicit indication of the basic symbols available and of how to obtain new ones.)

It might be of interest, in view of these last remarks, to determine the minimum set of logical concepts for any natural logic whatever. We will not pursue this question here beyond pointing out the dangers of unconscious tongue-parochialism in an exercise of this sort. A case in point is provided by a British philosopher called David Mitchell in his book *Introduction to Logic*.[31] In the minimum conceptual equipment for logic in any natural language, he cites enthusiastically the distinction between a thing and its qualities or attributes. This distinction, he contends, is not just a linguistic device, "it is rather a *requirement* that the world should present itself to us in this form for it to be thought about" (143; italics in original text). It is clear that by "us" he means at least all human beings, including Africans and Chinese. In the light of our earlier discussion, this claim is debatable.[32]

But Mitchell sallies forth onto even shakier grounds. He goes on to assert that the equivalence of the active and passive voices in grammar corresponds to a categorial principle inescapable for the human mind: "The *necessary* truth that if A acts on B, B is acted on by A, seems to reflect a categorical distinction between active and passive and not a merely linguistic convention; that is to say, it seems that it is linguistically permissible to substitute 'B is acted on by A' for 'A acts on B' only because *we* cannot but think that if A acts on B, B is necessarily acted on by A" (146; my italics). In fact, however, there is, strictly speaking, no passive voice in a language like Akan. The nearest one can come to, "B is acted on by A," is something that retranslates as "What happened to B was due to A," which is not a proper

31. David Mitchell, *Introduction to Logic*, 2d. ed., Hutchinson University Library (London, [1962] 1964).

32. Recall also our reference to the Chinese critic of the subject and predicate distinction in linguistic philosophy; see n. 17 above.

passive. Here then, in Mitchell's "necessary truth," is a tongue-dependent principle, if ever there was one.

An even more interesting example of tongue-dependency in philosophy is the following. In English there is the concept of truth, of fact, and of what is the case, what is so. In Akan, on the other hand, the one notion of what is so ("nea ete saa") is capable, even at the preanalytical level, of doing duty for all the English notions listed. In consequence, though in English it is quite an important philosophical project to try to elucidate the relationship between truth and fact, no corresponding project of comparable importance discloses itself in Akan. There is the word "Nokware" in Akan, which primarily means truthfulness, though by a turn familiar in linguistic usage generally it sometimes means truth in the cognitive sense. But in those contexts in which it has the cognitive sense, the immediate understanding which "εyε nokware" ("it is true") engenders is "εte saa" ("it is so"), and it is exactly in terms of what is so ("nea εte saa") that the notion of fact may be expressed in Akan. "Fact" is to be rendered in Akan by "nea εte saa" or by some variant or synonym of this phrase. Thus, nobody is ever going to be able to pretend to bring enlightenment to an Akan by, for example, informing him in the Akan tongue that truth consists in correspondence with fact. The problem of the relationship between truth and fact, then, is another example of a tongue-dependent issue.[33]

We have now seen that tongue-dependency can issue forth in pseudo-concepts, problems, theses, etc., and also in genuine ones. The second sort of case is, perhaps, the more remarkable, for one is apt to assume that problems arising from the peculiar characteristics of a given language cannot be genuine. But this is to confuse genuineness with uni-

33. I first introduced the notion of tongue-dependency in "The Concept of Truth in the Akan Language" (paper delivered at the International Symposium on Philosophy in Africa held at the University of Ibadan, Nigeria, 15–19 February 1981. See also my paper on "Philosophical Research" cited in n. 19 above). In "Wiredu on Truth as Opinion and Akan Language" (Paper presented at the Annual Conference of the Nigerian Philosophical Association held in Lagos in 1982), Prof. Bedu-Addo of the Universities of Cape Coast, Ghana, and Ife, Nigeria, also an Akan, has disputed the claims advanced above, among other things. This exchange promises an exciting feast of philosophical controversy which should demonstrate at least that, whatever the peculiarities of African philosophy, unanimity is not one of them. ("The Concept of Truth in the Akan Language" together with Prof. Bedu-Addo's critique at the later conference are published in the proceedings of the 1981 conference under the title *Philosophy in Africa: Trends and Perspectives,* edited by Prof. P. O. Budunrin [Ibadan, Nigeria: University of Ibadan Press, 1985]).

versality. Be that as it may, it is important to realize that both sorts of tongue-dependence can bedevil translation. It is as gratuitous to embrace other people's pseudoproblems as to tax oneself unnecessarily with their genuine problems. In formulating modern thought in African languages, African thinkers, for their own part, are going to have not only to translate some foreign ideas into their languages but also to formulate in their languages their own syntheses of any insights gained from such sources and those derived from reflection on their languages and indigenous traditonal thought. In all this, we are going to have to beware lest our translations and formulations be vitiated by tongue-dependent prepossessions from within or from without.

To forestall possible misunderstandings, let me point out that no sort of conceptual relativism is intended or implied by any part of the above discussion. Conceptual disparities among peoples and cultures, even among individuals in limited environs, are a brute fact of the human situation. Doubtless, this is the source of all sorts of complications in translation, particularly across cultures, some of which we have noted. But overriding all such problems is the fact, which is surely one of the most remarkable facts about language, that we can understand even what we cannot translate. This is due to the fact that we can learn languages other than that (or those) in which we were brought up. The fundamental fact here is that, because of the biological unity of mankind, any human being can participate or imaginatively enter into any human life form, however initially strange. The same fact, of course, underlies the possibility of transcultural communication.[34] This, again, is why the well-known insights about the great influence of language on thought obtained by writers like Sapir and Whorf cannot justify relativism of any ultimate sort.[35]

34. On this claim see Kwasi Wiredu, "A Philosophical Perspective on Communication," *International Social Science Journal* 32 no. 2 (1980), esp. 205f. See further Kwasi Wiredu, "Are there Cultural Universals?"—a contribution to the symposium on the same question at the Eighteenth World Congress of Philosophy, Brighton, England, 20–27 August 1988.

35. The equally well-known speculations of Quine on the indeterminacy of translation have no necessary relativistic forebodings for us. To say that "manuals for translating one language into another can be set up in divergent ways, all compatible with the totality of speech dispositions, yet incompatible with one another" (W.V.O. Quine, *Word and Object* [Cambridge, Mass.: MIT Press, 1960], 27), is to say something, which, if true, will affect all translations, not just "radical" translations, for it follows from the point we have just made that all "radical" translations, "that is, translation of the language of an untouched people[!]," can be "de-radicalised" through sustained

Owing to what has just been said, merely pointing out that a concept, problem, or thesis expressed in a given language is not expressible in another language will never be a sufficient reason for dismissing it as in some way defective. If a notion in English, for instance, cannot be expressed in Akan, the Englishman who has mastered Akan or the Akan who has mastered English can investigate in English why that is so. It may turn out, as we have seen in some cases, that the notion in question needs to be introduced into Akan. In the alternative, arguments intelligible in English can and will have to be given for debunking such a notion. I have tried in the body of this paper to give at least brief hints whenever such a job of demolition has seemed just in my eyes. In general, this in the only way in which linguistic discrimination, such as I have been advocating, can be prevented from degenerating into ethnic or racial discrimination.

I have been constrained in this discussion to have recourse again and again to my own mother tongue, namely, Akan. Two reasons account for this. First, the considerations I have been urging require a sort of intimate knowledge of an African language, which I cannot pretend to have of any language except my own. Second, I have found in the relevant literature little in the directions that interested me. There is, I think, an urgent need for highly discriminative conceptual studies of our individual languages in preparation for the domestication of modern knowledge in the African context. Such studies obviously will also prove useful if and when Africa achieves a lingua franca and settles down to perfecting it as a carrier and an instrument of modern knowledge.

Earlier writers on the subject of formulating knowledge in African languages, such as Cheikh Anta Diop, had it as one of their principal aims to prove to detractors of Africa that African languages are capable of becoming the vehicles of advanced knowledge. This is no longer in question in any remotely respectable circles. What the present discussion shows is that we need to develop a greater awareness of the conceptual framework of our own languages. Conceptually speaking, then the maxim of the moment should be "African, know thyself!"

----

cultural intercourse. More radically, the thesis must affect translation inside one and the same language.

The African University: Evaluation and Perspectives

eighteen

Benoît Verhaegen

Preface

By way of introduction to the topic, I would like to confront two works devoted to the African youth and to the role of the student and university elite: *La jeunesse africaine face à l'impérialisme* by Jean-Pierre Ndiaye, published in 1971, and *Les jeunes et l'ordre politique en Afrique noire* by J. A. Mbembe.[1] These two publications are separated by fifteen years. When Ndiaye writes his book, the "African independences" are already a stillborn hope, "their only contribution being, in the author's words, the replacement of the classical colonial structures with more accomplished and less direct structures of oppression."[2] But the student youth still constitutes one hope for combat against "the bureaucratic middle classes at the beck and call of imperialism." Ndiaye dedicates his book to this youth. Fifteen years later, Mbembe draws up an extremely severe appraisal of the role of school-aged youth and particularly of the youth of university level. What Ndiaye feared

1. J.-P. Ndiaye, *La jeunesse africaine face à l'impérialisme* (Paris: F. Maspéro, 1971), J. A. Mbembe, *Les jeunes et l'ordre politique en Afrique noire* (Paris: L'Harmattan, 1985).
2. J.-P. Ndiaye (1971), 11.

has happened. "The African institutions of higher education seem to have led, above all, to an enormous waste of human resources and to a cultural destruction the cost of which remains difficult to gauge." As for the students, "a number of them have become docile technicians and today constitute the relay forces in those bureaucracies that assure the indigenous management of capitalism."[3] Mbembe no longer believes that a combat force can come out of the universities to fight the capitalist bureaucracies. For him "it seems illusory to think that the university might escape being domesticated, as if miraculously, in order to become truly a place of liberty and creativity."[4]

And yet, if one takes a detached look, what a distance has been covered in thirty years! In 1958, the Lovanium University, which had 177 African students, graduated the first seven African students trained in Zaire. In 1986, in Zaire alone, more than 40,000 students were registered in thirty-six establishments of higher learning. The former Lovanium University, having become the University of Kinshasa, teaches more than 7,300 students. Zaire, which had ten graduates with degrees in 1958, has more than 60,000 of them in 1988. Whatever may be the present level of the teaching, the quality of the degrees conferred, and the duties exercised by the academics, it is obvious that this makes a fundamental transformation, the impact of which in the long term undoubtedly will be more important and more durable than the gaining of independence, the forming of the new states, and the present economic crisis.

When it comes to tracing a very somber picture of the situation in Black Africa at the dawn of this last decade of the twentieth century, every observer agrees that the authors who enumerate reasons for hope, outside of the official discourses, are rare indeed. Our plan is not to fantasize about this situation or to substitute ourselves for the social actors who will have to make these hopes concrete, but to conclude that the university is and will be the obligatory passageway toward any hope for change. The city, and in its heart the university, are the center of gravity for any social change. One might regret this (with Frantz Fanon) and decide that this center of gravity is also the favorite place of the bourgeoisie, of a consumer society, and of the foreign influences, that the urban immigration and the weakening of the world of the farmers are synonymous with economic crises, cultural impoverishment, dependency, that the city is an ecological dead

3. Mbembe (1985), 65.
4. Ibid., 68.

end and the university an intellectual mirage. But the facts must be faced: the Africa of the villages, the customs, the peasant culture, the infinite diversity of languages and arts, is beginning to disappear. The present crisis has only precipitated the phenomenon of the stampede toward the city and the academic diploma.

But with what diploma, with which higher learning are we concerned? Let us begin by making a critical appraisal of the present situation.

The Internal Crisis of the University [5]

For twenty-five years (that is, since well before May 1968) the African University has been subjected to shocks that have shaken its foundations. In Zaire, the first shock dates back to March 1964, the year of the revolt of Pierre Mulele and of the Simba, when a general strike completely paralyzed the university for eight days. The movement failed and was harnessed by the academic authorities.[6] From that moment on and up to the important reform of 1971, the demands of the Zairian academics concentrated on the Africanization of the university. At first they put their hopes in an increased intervention by the state. When the latter finally did intervene by nationalizing the universities and by creating the National University of Zaire (UNAZA), it very rapidly became clear that the remedy was worse than the disease and that the movement of protest had missed its mark. Africanization proved to be a deception. The change of personnel and labels in no way modified the university's position of alienation and dependence. Quite the contrary: its increased fragility, its new dependence with regard to the political powers, the closer and closer ties between the leadership class and the academics, all quickly deprived the university of its essential function, that of a critical conscience of a global society. Surely there were, even after 1971, attempts at criticism on different university campuses, but their authors (students or professors) were severely punished. The majority of the protesting professors left the university, some to go into exile, others to go into business. Some accepted the law of the conqueror and were integrated into the circle of the privileged by the powerful. One thing is certain: in 1989, the year of the bicentennial of the

5. Our critical analysis deals with Zaire, about which everyone agrees in saying that it is at one and the same time representative of a general crisis in the African universities and unique by the extent and violence of its contradictions.

6. The strike of 8 March 1964 has been analyzed in *Présence Africaine* 52, (1964): 128–142.

French Revolution, an encephalogram of the critical conscience of the Zairian universities would show up completely flat. If any critical thought survives, one must search for it outside of the university, outside of Zaire.

But the university, so badly treated by the State, has inherited its basic evils: poverty and inadequacy of the necessary means for proper functioning, corruption of people and processes, a complete absence of performance. Higher education represents a not insignificant part of the cost of public service, which is by far the foremost employer of the country. But the professors receive a salary below survival level and have no pedagogical or scientific material available to them with which to exercise their duties. At the end of a costly training that has taken ten to fifteen years, they find themselves deprived laborers in the exercise of their profession. In addition to the total lack of an environment conducive to their teaching, there is the poverty of their personal means that condemns them to rapid disqualification and to intellectual regression.

The corruption that holds sway over every cog of the State machinery has equally contaminated the university. No benefit takes place without payments. From the moment of the student's admission all the way up to his obtaining his final degree, and passing through examinations, tutorials, and practicums, every stage of academic life is an opportunity for making monetary inroads to the advantage of those who, at a given moment, have a piece of the power or the monopoly of a service. This generalized mercantilism of academic performances is more weighty in its consequences in this context than in most other public institutions, because it ends up profoundly distorting the academic rules and procedures. In the extreme case, there will no longer be any teaching activity, nor any dissemination of knowledge, only a financial operation of redistribution. Cheating, fraud, and corruption should not be understood only from a moral angle.[7] They are the gears of a system. For the educator, it is a question of making up for the lack of salary and of surviving; for the student, it is an answer to the inexorable logic of the diploma, without which he is nothing. For lack of a sufficient education, he is condemned to use cheating and corruption.

Another perverse effect of corruption is that it provokes the political docility of the academics who are held hostage by a system in which everyone is delinquent. In Zaire, the compliance of the citizens

7. On this subject, see Mbembe, 56 ff.

with regard to an inefficient and corrupt power astonishes the foreign observer but can be partially explained by the precariousness of the situation. Moreover, one might wonder whether the political system does not favor this very system of corruption among all the groups (especially the academics) that could contest it in order to better control them.

The performance (that is, the ensemble) of the services rendered by the State is often hopelessly inefficient and inadequate. If one considers the three basic functions of the university (dissemination of knowledge, research and production of a new knowledge, and collaboration toward the solution of the practical problems posed to the country), one concludes that the decline is a general one. Far from Africanizing or adapting to the conditions of the country, education has become more and more mimetic, more and more removed from the society. This is the severe judgment of Mbembe:

> In the midst of intellectual structures, numbed by conformity and put to sleep by self-satisfaction and routine, the African universities do not seem to have been able to become true centers of elaboration, of criticism, and of dissemination of new forms of thought. It seems as if the African university has been incapable of integrating into its process of formal training the kinds of non-formal education, the totality of popular knowledge transmitted by the entire collectivity, which tries to answer as much to the different needs of the groups as to the possibilities of apprenticeship offered to all . . . In other words, the African universities have turned their back on the life of the African societies.[8]

The African university is presently no longer in a position to insure the functioning of research and criticism that should be its specific hallmark and domain. The autocratic regimes that have settled themselves in the majority of the African countries cannot tolerate the development of critical thinking and consider research a dangerous luxury.[9]

Finally, the university is not capable of reproducing itself. The level of teaching has fallen too low for it to train its own future educators. Preparation for the doctorate and scientific training are more than

8. Ibid., 61.
9. On the subject of the impasse in research in Zaire see "La crise de la recherche zairoise 1967–1977," in B. Verhaegen, *L'enseignement universitaire au Zaire—de Lovanium à l'UNAZA* (Paris: L'Harmattan, 1978): 171–191.

even entrusted to the foreign universities, and this ends up consolidating the relationship of dependence upon the Western model of education.

The University and Society

For a long time the colonial authorities had slowed down the creation of universities, fearing that these would become centers of dispute. At the time of the African independences, the university could have appeared as a synonym for decolonization and a hope for national development. Reality proved very different. After a few years of nationalist and anticolonial demonstrations, African academicians were integrated into the leadership class, and by implication the university agreed to fulfill the three external functions that characterize it today: a capacity for destroying the values and the culture of the rural and peasant world in the name of technological rationality and economic progress; a tendency toward social stratification by training the leadership classes, and by an academic establishment of the diploma; an ideological role legitimizing the political regime and the economic system. By fulfilling these functions, the university has also played the game of economic dependence and has served as relay for cultural imperialism.

Let us clarify these functions. Every social change implies a process of destructuring, indeed of destruction. The university is not the only institution that uproots the farmer. The school, the city, the merchant economy, salaried labor, and the media all contribute their part. But the university is the key to the vault of the whole system of alienation. It is the university degree that gives its strength and its finality to the entire process of migration and change. It has become the obligatory conclusion to the course of schooling. The intermediary forms of training are no longer really terminal. Since the university degree can be acquired only in the city, it is there that all youth heads in search of hope and a better life.

But social change also supposes a process of restructuring around new values, new rules of life, new social structures. The university was expected to make this reconstruction come true, or at least to define its norms and its stages. What was produced was the opposite. In no way was the unlearning of life and social practices (to which school leads) compensated for by the discovery or the creation of new practices adapted to the social change under way. Everything happens as if unrooting were not leading to any entrenchment, as if cultural impoverishment knew no bounds, as if alienation were a durable state.

The second "external" function of the African university is that of participating in the training of social classes by installing a bourgeoisie of the diploma. In Europe, university education had long been a simple tool for the consolidation of the dominant class that found the real foundations of its power elsewhere—in its birth, fortune, or capital. Today, knowledge or (more simply) having a diploma has become a sufficient condition for claiming to reach the class of those who manage the economy, who govern the others, and who profit by the productive effort of the workers. This is particularly true in the African societies in which instruction and diploma have become the basic tools for social promotion, after the self-taught elites, who emerged at the time of the anticolonial struggles, had left the front of the political stage. Until now, the university degree, by its supposed role of sanction of scientific ability and of rigorous selection, has offered an indisputable and stable base for the training of the leadership classes. It certainly is no longer a sufficient factor, nor the only one that comes into play; ethnic or regional affinities, personal relationships, docility with respect to the political power are other conditions that make access to the leadership class easier.

If the mere possession of a university degree no longer automatically gives one the right to a part of the political power or to a position of economic privilege, it nevertheless remains at the origin of a basic schism in society[10]: those without degrees must benefit from exceptional political support—reserved for the set of those close to the power—in order to step up to the leadership class. Entrepreneurial spirit, personal effort, and concern with saving and investing are only rarely rewarded with durable economic success if they are not accompanied by political support. The one with a degree, however, can always hope to be co-opted by colleagues. Graduates know they are among the reserve of candidates among whom those in power will one day take their pick.

If one were to divide the nation into two categories—the productive classes, farmers, and workers on the one hand, and the nonproductive classes on the other—the academician generally fits in the second category; the services that he renders are most often eco-

10. Concerning the social importance of the degree see R. Dore, *The Diploma Disease: Education, Qualification and Development* (London: George Allen and Unwin, 1976).

nomically sterile. The real function of the degree is to allow the graduate to participate in the sharing of the social profit and not in taking part in the production. Since the largest part of the social profit—at least that which is not exported—is collected or controlled by the State in one way or another, it is the position of the university graduate either in the State apparatus or in relation to the political power that determines the greater or lesser part of the profit he or she can hope to obtain. Whether the advantages obtained are officially linked to the actual practice of a profession or this practice provides only the condition on which one can seize an illicit profit, in either case it is from the State and its power that the graduate must receive the presumed advantages of his degree. This explains, among other things, the astonishing docility that graduates show throughout their studies and afterward, for they know that their position in the State apparatus will not be the fruit of their competence or their professional conscientiousness but of political criteria.

However, it is obvious that the increase in degrees conferred threatens the privileges of the graduates, as much on the level of the real prospects and on behalf of the social profit to be gained as on that of the prestige attached to the degree.

One of the ideological functions of the university is that of legitimizing the political power structure and the economic system through incontestable arguments. It is no longer birth, blood, strength, or ruse that justifies the holding of the power of command but rather scientific knowledge. What can be said of science is that it is a master above all suspicions. He who speaks in its name holds the truth; he who commands in its name must be listened to; and he who organizes the economic life through the inspiration of economic reasoning cannot be wrong, no matter what hardships he imposes on the people. The university is supposed to hold or to produce this scientific knowledge, this ability to rationally organize economic life.

We know that the reality is very different, that science is not neutral, and that reason is a handy tool that can be of multiple use. In the decolonized countries, the recourse to the symbolic legitimacy of scientific knowledge is all the more necessary as inequalities are great and the wealth is of recent date. Similarly, the persistence of extroverted economic structures and of imported models of economic growth must be justified. That was the task of the planners, the international experts, the professors of economics. The important budgets by the State, bilateral cooperation and the international organizations spent on development studies and research found their usefulness at that time.

Limits of a Critical Attitude

The scope of the severe critique of the African university can be reduced or placed in a larger framework by the following three remarks. The first is that we are concerned with a crisis of global dimensions that opened up about twenty years ago. In several countries the university has adapted itself with greater or lesser success. Others are familiar with situations that come close to those of the African countries. At the origin of this worldwide crisis the same factors as in Africa are found: on the one hand, a very marked increase in the demand for higher education resulting from the general democratization of education and social organization; on the other hand, a profound evolution of society, of its professional needs, of its technologies, of its life styles and work, which have had no equivalent in higher education. The reasons for this evolutionary divergence are universal. They fit into the very rigidity of the university system, the conformity of its principal actors and its pedagogy. There is, in fact, a profound contradiction between the efforts made by the faculty toward the acquisition of a stock of knowledge, the normal pedagogical extension of which is transmission, and the permanent putting into question of that acquisition.

The second remark consists of admitting that the university is a microcosm of the global society whose contradictions, conflicts, and impasses it reflects. "The crisis of the university institution is the barometer of a crisis of society," writes Lapassade.[11] The university is a subsystem that depends on the economic and political system. Its degree of autonomy is very slight, particularly in societies in which it is not protected by a long academic tradition and in which an authoritarian power imposes uniformity and monolithism on the institutions. In Zaire, the university has lost all its autonomy with the reform of 1971 and with the creation of one single university that regrouped three campuses and more than thirty establishments of higher learning spread throughout the country.

We have seen that the defects of the university are those of the political society; corruption of the people, the waste and weakness of the means, the formalism of the structures, and the absence of effi-

11. G. Lapassade, *Procès de l'université—institution de classe* (Paris: Belfond, 1969), 154.

ciency are all characteristic of the working of the State, of which the
university is a hostage.

A third remark clarifies the second one. The constraints that weigh
upon the university leave it no margin for maneuvering, no possibility to evolve or to reform itself. These constraints are first of all material ones—the poverty of the means and of the people involved, and
the pressure of the numbers; then there is the everpresent political
order, its propaganda and its police; finally there is, more subtly, the
self-censorship of the individuals who know that their survival depends upon their docility, docility of the students toward the faculty,
docility of the faculty toward all those who hold the political power.
Everyone's conformity is first a political attitude before it becomes a
pedagogical deformation.

To these constraints practiced by the national environment upon
the university one must add the international pressure. The development on a worldwide scale of science and technology, the circulation
of information and the models of consumption, the growing dependence of each country and of each institution with respect to what
happens in the rest of the world, all provoke a permanent erosion of
the intellectual acquisition and an acceleration in the phenomenon
of acculturation. Any isolation becomes utopian. Authenticity is
nothing more than a hollow slogan.

Future Prospects

It would be unreasonable and presumptuous on our part to predict what will become of the African university, and even more so to
define a transformation strategy. The analyst's only possibility is to
attempt to indicate the points of stability and permanence and those
of rupture. It seems to be an established fact that the university (and,
more generally, the institutions of higher learning) will have to face
up to a constantly growing demand, one that will bypass more and
more the possibilities of an adequate reception. Yet it will be impossible for them to resist this pressure, for the political power will force
them into accepting it and adapting themselves to it. Access to higher
education is, indeed, the ultimate source of legitimacy for political
regimes that are deficient in every other domain. Degrees will continue to be devaluated in the same way as money is during a period
of inflation, and unemployment of the graduates will become more
generalized. This will cause tensions between the different generations of students, where the oldest ones will have been completely
integrated into the ruling class, while those who follow will be less

and less so. But the procedures will diminish the contradictions: horizontal solidarities (that is, ethnic and regional ones) will offer an alternative to the generational oppositions, while the power structure will continue to use a strategy of rapidly rotating appointments, thus continuing the illusion that promotions are open to all.

Certain points of rupture in the system seem equally obvious.

Three forces of change are in the process of becoming explosive: the city, youth, and university. Nothing will be able to stop the migrations of the rural population to the cities, which ten years from now will contain more than half of the population in the majority of the African countries. This growth will be most profitable to the capital cities, the managing of which will become the primary problem of the States. The age group between fifteen to twenty-five years old within the total population will continue to increase until the year 2000. In its great majority, it will be located in the urban centers in order to find education, entertainment, and the chance of promotion. The university will remain the principal point of attraction for educated urban youths, but it will only be able to accept a small number of them. The frustrations of the others cannot be compensated for by a politics of employment or by the indefinite extending of "small jobs" and "making do." The limitations of the system are already apparent. One need not be a prophet to predict that the points of rupture for the present African regimes are to be found in the capitals and the largest cities, at the doorsteps of or inside the universities, and that the social actors therein will be the age group between fifteen and twenty-five years old.

Daily Life in Black Africa: nineteen
Elements for a Critique

Paulin J. Hountondji

How is it, in these regions, that we incessantly go in circles, constantly bemoaning the same defects, endlessly returning to square one on a course that is so painfully circular? What is the force that holds us by the ankles and prevents us from moving forward? From where comes this irresistible tendency that makes us waste our most precious time, this repetitive behavior of our very history, this passivity in the face of the events around us?

In the following remarks, I would like to identify some of the encumbrances, some of the occasions that must be removed—in terms of the daily life in our countries—if we want life here to be more agreeable, more productive, and more fruitful.

The first fact: an enormous amount of time is lost and a considerable amount of energy is invested in making the least little thing happen. For example, do you want some information from a public service office? Make a phone call and ask. Nine out of ten times the civil servant who answers will ask you to come in yourself and will be surprised that this has not occurred to you. Your concern about saving time is not readily understood. Of course, if you persist, the information you requested will be offered: however, to obtain it, you will first have to state your identity, to mention your position, to let them know in one way or another that you are a person of importance—an executive, a manager in charge, a businessman, or something of that nature—and on that basis you have special reasons to want to save time, special reasons to be singled out compared to the generally accepted norms. And the civil servants will give you the impression that by sparing you a trip to their office they have done you a tremendous favor, which you should remember well, of course, when the opportunity presents itself.

Is your telephone out of order, as frequently happens after a heavy rain or—and this is more curious—as the celebrations for the New Year approach? Make a phone call from another line to the repair service. They will answer very kindly; they will even make promises. Then you will be obliged to call back one, two, three more times. At last you will end up by understanding. Your "call" does not take care of business: that would be too simple. You must make a trip, devote time to this very important issue. You pay with your person, your time, and occasionally with some small kindness for the privilege of having a phone at home, all the more for having a phone that works. In any case, one pays with a mad waste of energy that, in most cases, one would have preferred to devote to some other issue.

I purposely give these trite examples. They force us to put our finger on this monstrous reality: in this part of our vast world nothing "runs" by itself; we must always push at the wheel. The basic automatic devices that are the strength of modern bureaucracies are nonexistent here. In Paris, forty-eight hours are generally sufficient to have the repair service take care of an out-of-order telephone, and to set the process in motion it is sufficient to submit the necessary information once and only once. The reason is that, over there, they feel the client has rights from the moment he has paid his fees. Here, on the other hand, to pay is not enough. Over and beyond that, one has to invest considerable energy to extract the service to which one has subscribed.

It is not only for lack of equipment and adequate technical means, as they like to say all too often. For, if the means are in fact lacking, what is still more cruelly absent is the will for rational organization, the will to use the few resources available in the best possible manner and to everyone's greatest possible satisfaction. Do they say that the telephone service owns only one small truck? And that one small truck is not enough to insure that the repair teams move among more than a thousand subscribers? That is quite possible. Then why not render service in the order that the complaints have been registered? Why let certain subscribers wait one, two, or more months, while others who are "luckier" (a euphemism that points at otherwise sordid realities) get satisfaction in less than twenty-four hours? The truth is that, beyond the actual technical difficulties it does entail, the shortage of materials here functions as a providential pretext for the justification of all kinds of discrimination among the clients.

Should one incriminate those responsible and the other agents of the services concerned, accuse them of thoughtlessness or incompetence, perhaps even of corruption? No doubt one can do so in certain cases and up to a certain point, but quite frequently things are more complicated. For sometimes everything happens behind the back of the service managers and without their knowledge; as for the agents, often they are themselves the victims as much as they are accomplices. No matter how much the supervisor may rationalize the work, may give orders toward greater efficiency and better productivity, it is the hierarchy itself that will jeopardize this attempt at organization. It is the general leadership itself that will give contradictory orders: a certain minister will have called, a certain member of the Central Committee or of the Political Bureau, a certain counselor or cabinet chairman, the most important of the very important, to notify the services of a breakdown that must be repaired immediately and must take precedence before any other jobs. Naturally, in the face of such commands nobody dares to raise the least objection.

Thus, the inefficiency of the system comes from the top. In truth—in that it allows for all sorts of trading of favors—it suits everyone: everyone but the ordinary client, the man without any influence, the honest citizen who, by necessity or conviction, will not or cannot be intimidating or corrupt.

While other examples could be cited, they are not needed in order to come to this conclusion: daily life here is organized in such a way as to cause everyone to waste the greatest possible amount of time. Apart from any moral or political consideration, and disregarding the enormous handicap that the generalized practice of trading of favors poses for our societies, there can never be enough said about this habitual way of acting according to the position of the client, nor about the absence of the very idea of public service; there can never be enough said about the weight of the burden that this disastrous management of time puts on our future and our desire for progress; there can never be enough said about this habit, so solidly anchored in our mores, of squandering time and causing others to waste it to a maximum degree, about the absence of any economic concern, the absence of any sense of real emergency (whereby everything becomes an emergency at the last minute) so that the agent of a "public" service is able to bargain with the client over the favor of treating him, too, as a case of "emergency."

In this way, corruption appears to be more a result than a cause of the inefficiency of our bureaucracies. Far from being the origin, the trading of favors is perhaps initially only the effect of our relationship to time and of the habit we have adopted to let events happen, before it then becomes, second, the cause or one of the causes of the reinforcement of this habit.

It would, then, be too easy to incriminate individuals. On the contrary, what must be emphasized is the significance of a system that bypasses the individual and whose constraints are imposed on all, a system that, moreover, is set up in such a way that the very people who should be working on its transformation end up finding exactly what they want in that system. The relationship to time is not the whole of this system. However, it is an essential element thereof. For the waste of time has been elevated to the level of an institution in itself: made obligatory for everyone by the very organization of our administrative machine, accepted by everyone as normal and almost inevitable, it is an almost natural fact which must simply be taken into account, without claiming in any way that it might be changed.

This inertia of the system, this acceptance of the fait accompli, sometimes takes on the aspect of a paradox. Thus it often happens—and this will be our second statement—that everyone, even among the decision makers, unanimously recognizes the abnormal character of a situation or (if need be) the very peculiar extent of a given situation, and yet nobody does anything to change it.

For example, everyone complains, not only about the delays in government officialdom but also about the frequency with which files get lost and the obligation that ensues for whoever entered a request into the circuit to follow it up himself on a daily basis under penalty of never seeing it answered or letting it be "forgotten" in the drawer of some functionary. Everyone deplores the presence of these bottlenecks in our administrative machine, but nobody will make any changes, perhaps simply because no one is able to do so. Everyone is helpless in the face of a situation that everyone denounces and of which everyone is or can become the victim at any given moment, directly or indirectly: "there is nothing we can do, that is the way it is!" In all its massive evidence, the system stands facing all the people. The obstacle is imposed on all and forces each person to circumvent it on his own (for better or for worse) in a generalized every-man-for-himself approach that resorts to various dubious devices, instead of all the people coming together to solidify their efforts and to attempt, once and for all, to move the obstacle out of the way.

In a given area of the region, a functionary who wishes to leave the area is required to await the signature of two ministers: the minister under whose guardianship he stands and the minister or home affairs.[1] It is a long procedure, harassing and paper devouring; furthermore, it is perfectly inefficient, since originally it was meant to curtail the exodus abroad of the executives, whereas it has visibly and by everyone's admission failed in its purpose due to the very great permeability of the borders. Today its only effect is to penalize those functionaries who are not candidates for exile, those agents in every category who intend to stay in their jobs but who on occasion would like to go 100–150 kilometers away to a given neighboring capital for a weekend without too much formality. Everyone seems to agree that this administrative weight should be denounced, yet nobody makes any attempts to remedy the situation. Let us be fair: it can happen, and probably has already happened, that a particularly courageous executive in a position of responsibility proposes to eliminate this problem. That attempt is nevertheless vain in a context in which the institution will survive itself by the mere power of inertia, well beyond circumstances that originally could have motivated this attempt, or at the very least given it a beginning of justification.

In such a context, where one finds that the most audacious initiatives are broken by the institutional stagnation, how can it be surprising that these initiatives themselves are becoming more and more rare and that what triumphs everywhere are resignation, the acceptance of the fait accompli, listlessness, cowardice, and collective laziness, up to and including those exceptionally serious circumstances where all people of courage should, as one voice, rise up against the arbitrary in the name of the only values still likely to give some meaning to their collective existence? How can it be surprising that the very meaning of these nonnegotiable values is progressively getting lost?

The African leaders, decidedly, have an easy task: their power is without limits in the face of populations that, all too often, have for-

1. This measure has been extended to pupils and students. A little boy or girl, six or seven years old, pupil at an elementary school, can therefore, in principle, not cross the frontier without the signature of two ministers, whether or not the parents are with the child. Motive: to prevent pupils and students in this country from making the national reform in education fail by escaping toward other educational systems.

gotten what "resistance" means. In the general practice of every-man-for-himself, each one tries to be overlooked or (in the best case possible) tries to survive the victorious barbarism as long as possible—while awaiting the coming of a miracle or, on the contrary, the arrival of the fatal day where one finds oneself, dumbfounded, in the center of the same drama that one had thought could only happen to others.

Whether a supercilious power charges you with some imaginary plot against state security just to "liquidate" you politically or physically, among the pure and hardened ones in charge of holding your trial there will always be those lovely souls who whisper in your ear that they are on your side, that they are convinced of your innocence, that the machine that is crushing you is definitely unfair, etc. Those lovely souls may well be the absolute majority, indeed, the near totality of your judges. Taken one by one, each of the judges will address you as a person. United in the group, they will reproduce in chorus the dominating discourse as they act themselves like the unconscious wheels of that hateful machine they denounce in private.

Only slightly better is the tragic situation of a given hospital where everyone—doctors, nurses, and other nursing staff, administrative executives and clerks—unanimously deplores the bad hygienic conditions, the defective state of the equipment, the accumulation of garbage and other magnets for flies in the immediate proximity of the operating rooms, the permanent presence of a whole army of mosquitos that makes any hospitalized patient into a candidate for the most serious forms of malaria, the invasion of rats that are among the largest and best-fed in the country and that sometimes even go so far as to mutilate bodies kept in the morgue; in short, a mockery of what an academic hospital center should be, which instead (and with everyone's complete knowledge) has become the prime place for microbic infection, unanimously denounced as such by the very people who should be able to improve its functioning: but over the course of the years nothing ever changes. This is more proof that the system dominates us, that the institution, stronger and tougher than its agents, shatters the slightest desire for change and discourages the best ones. So much so that, after a more or less lengthy period of innovative enthusiasm, each newcomer ends up (in spite of himself) by tolerating it, if he is not simply seduced by the vile bait and the possibilities of trading of favors a system of this nature always offers.

The accumulation, the apparent convergence of individual criticisms, thus remains powerless. We are dealing here with a unanimity of the vanquished, the unanimity of people now and henceforth resigned to the evil that they denounce, the evil by which in fact they already profit, only waiting to exploit the collective misery to their personal advantage.

Now let us speak about the quality of the care, or simply the quality of life and death—for one can die badly or well—in our hospitals. It is the custom of certain families to assign to one or more of its members (taking turns if need be) the role of nurse; this custom testifies before everything else to an essential deficiency in the organization of our hospitals, even if the patient has the obvious advantage of feeling less isolated. In this area nothing will change between now and the year 2000: there is no apparent indication that would lead us to hope for a miracle that, in the next dozen years, would shake up this all too familiar landscape of misery and lack of awareness. That relatives should have to search for the nurse to check a defective I.V. or to have the I.V. taken out or replaced; that they should have to remind the nurse that the doctor had prescribed a particular injection to be given at a particular time and that the necessary items—cotton and alcohol—needed to be included (for very often these are not provided and must be purchased by the family); that they should be forced to beg, to corrupt, seduce, or intimidate, just to get the right people to do their jobs; that the sick should die on the operating table following an electrical failure because of a storm and because the person in charge of the emergency generator went "for a walk"; that the dental surgeon should treat an old lady the age of his grandmother with insolence; that a sort of butcher who calls himself a urologist (and is a military doctor from the technical aid sent by a friendly nation) should mix arrogance with incompetence while responding with intimidation to the worried questions of a patient and his family; that a patient should die following the cumulative medical errors of a professor of medicine (probably a great scholar but surely a bad practitioner) who lightheartedly orders a counterprescription: this gives a small inkling of the conditions of the hospitals in our countries and of the predominant relationships between patients and medical staff.

Certainly, it is not necessarily better in the industrialized nations where amidst the most modern technical equipment bad physicians—infinitely more numerous than good ones—also mix arrogance with incompetence, or where, even if competent, many trail their patients behind them without listening to them (like a veterinarian with farm yard animals). (In the hospital Saint-Pierre in Brussels, a woman from Zaire who had just returned from two weeks in her country, who was suffering from a serious malaria epidemic, was sent to the pavilion for serious AIDS patients.)

But the difference is that in those countries structures of organized resistance exist, and the physician can always fear a lawsuit in the case of a major error that may have cost a patient his life or otherwise handicapped him. In the Brussels hospital, the chief of the department concerned had to apologize, fearful at the idea of the tragic results this mistake could have entailed, and at the anger of this confident woman who owed her salvation only to her own firm determination, and who could have been tempted to follow up this affair with a lawsuit.

In these regions, on the other hand, no one dares to institute legal proceedings. In any case, this commotion would not bring the dead person back,.they say to themselves, and after all nothing happens that is not supposed to happen. This is murderous fatalism that leads to accepting anything (no matter what) and to lowering one's resistance, even when it might be possible in the end to improve the quality of life and to remind each other that the patient also has rights and can oppose the limited knowledge of the incompetent doctor with nonnegotiable, minimal demands.

In the restrooms of our airports, you will never find any toilet paper—not even in the largest airports: Dakar, Abidjan, Lagos. Should you wish an explanation, the administrators will explain to you that the rolls very rapidly disappear in the bags of the users and that this is the reason they have stopped providing them. They will forget to tell you that no solution has ever truly been sought—simply because the quality of service holds only a very minor place in the hierarchy of the values of our administrators.

In one four-star hotel in the center of Dakar, the water in the rooms runs rust colored, the pipes are quite old, as in another well-known "grand" hotel on the shore in Lome. But that is not all. In one room, the water leaks through the ceiling, ruining the carpeting and inconveniencing the guest, who asks to change rooms, but the staff turns a deaf ear. It is very simple: the price of the room has been paid in advance by the host company, thus there is no risk that the guest will leave. In another room, there is no leaflet indicating how the telephone works; in yet another, when your key is given to you upon arrival, after registration, toward midnight you discover that your room has not been done. You leave a message for a friend who is supposed to come, but it will not be given to him. You ask that you be awakened at a certain time, but your request is ignored. You have a bottle of mineral water at mealtime, planning to pay for it when you check out, but they will run after you all the way to the elevator, or they will interrupt your afternoon's rest by phoning you in your room: the "extras" must be paid on the spot! Perhaps a soccer team recently came through—and set a bad precedent.

Let us not even speak of the thoughtless delays that have caused our airlines to be given nicknames such as "Air Perhaps," "Air Never," "Air God Willing," etc. Or of the interminable flights that take twice as long as the flights between Africa and Europe for a distance that, as the bird flies, is two or three times shorter: Dakar to Cotonou, eleven hours and twenty-five minutes flying time with four layovers (Bamako, Ouagadougou, Niamey, Abidjan), presence required at the airport two hours before take-off, average expected delay of two hours over and above the official schedule (even if the statistics here are difficult to establish). Upon arrival, for the sake of local color, official searches cause you to stand in a long line for an hour. Then there is health control, police, and customs, as in every other airport in the world, all of which makes for a total of sixteen hours of travel. Compare Dakar to Paris, five hours direct flight without stopovers, presence at the airport two hours before take-off, almost certain punctuality of flights (three large companies, at least, fly this itinerary, while the earlier one is flown only by a single, multinational company). True, upon arrival, there is an interminable line that can also take an hour for passport control—required to fight terrorism, for, of course, there is no paradise anywhere—but on the whole it is a much more relaxed trip, of at most eight hours, from your hotel in Dakar to the exit at Roissy airport.

Therefore, third observation: the quality of service is the last concern of our administrators—especially when they are in a position of holding a monopoly—to the great detriment of the clientele. The examples I mentioned are ordinary, often amusing, never tragic. Yet, it can happen that under certain circumstances this contempt for the client can lead to extremely serious situations. What is needed is something like a powerful league of consumers in order to impose respect for the client on every level and in all sectors of commerce and of public service. This would suppose, it is true, awareness of a collective right, feeling of a common destiny, which (as we have just seen) are so very precarious today. Above all, this would suppose that one dare to confront the unpredictable reactions of a power that is so fragile, so unsure of its own legitimacy, that any appeal to public opinion seems a priori suspicious, even more so any attempt to organize this opinion and make it activist, even in the sectors that at first sight one might have thought apolitical.

In this, the powers are undoubtedly not wrong. By becoming radicalized, the defense of the rights of the consumer and the criticism of daily life can lead to calling the very foundations of the oppression into question; above all, the free expression of one's opinion, the collective pressure that ensues, the custom that some adopt to demand their right each time it is flouted and that causes others to respect this right under penalty of being socially neutralized, progressively establishes the beginnings of democracy, of which many of our regimes, governments, party machines, and union leaderships are still too afraid to risk tolerating.

Of course, things are not that simple, and a league of consumers would not be sufficient—the theoretical possibility of creating one without worrying even less so—to truly improve the quality of life. If that were so, the four star hotel mentioned earlier would never have sunk so low, for, even if our Senegalese friends do not know it, we are numerous in other regions of Africa in our envy of their beautiful freedom of expression (not only political but well-nigh physiological), that spontaneity of speech, that unstoppable volubility, which gives the impression of a power, just like the mustard seed (in the Scriptures)[2] that can raise mountains.[3] On the other hand, even in the industrialized nations, legion are the hotels, restaurants, and other places of this sort, where the service is practically worthless, despite the existence of various organizations that defend the rights of the consumer.

But the difference is that, in the context of a competitive economy and one with relative freedom of expression, the economic sanction of a failing service always comes from within, sooner or later. Hence

2. See The Gospel According to St. Matthew 17:20: "For verily I say unto you, if ye have faith as a grain of mustard seed, ye shall say unto this mountain, Remove hence to yonder place; and it shall remove; and nothing shall be impossible unto you." *Holy Bible*, authorized King James version.

3. We are not claiming, of course, that in Senegal all is for the best in this best of all possible worlds! Alas, the sordid exists everywhere. As does the intolerable. We only want to recognize that where it concerns democratic liberties, and particularly the freedom of expression and of criticism, which entails the acceptance of a multiparty system and of a pluralist press, also where it concerns the independence of the judicial power, Senegal is far ahead of the majority of the countries in the region. What lies hidden behind this democratic facade? To what extent can these practices be considered as irreversible acquisitions, henceforth an integral part of the Senegalese political culture? That, of course, is a whole other question.

this prognosis: the four-star hotel in the heart of Dakar will not do well (despite its sixteen stories and its suspended swimming pool) and it will progressively lose its clientele (within a time period that could be determined almost mathematically) because of the competition of hotels in the same category, even of a lesser category, where the quality of the service is much better. On the other hand, in those countries where the management of the hotels is State run, the monopoly, aggravated by the impossibility of open criticism, makes the temptation of ease irresistible to those in charge and makes it improbable that this respect for the client will be pursued, this effort toward making the customer faithful and instilling the desire to return, which elsewhere urges personnel on to render the most agreeable service possible.

Fourth observation: varying in importance and more or less numerous depending upon the country, some realms of activity are run by laws and other rules that are not only inapplicable but that also give the impression of having been made precisely *in order* not to be applied.

A common example: your water and electricity bill regularly mention the following: "Water and electricity will be cut off without any further notice if the present bill is not paid within two weeks after the date above."[4] However, agents of the company have been telling you for some time that it is no longer two weeks but one; revised bills will soon be circulated. Thus, you rush to pay the bill on the day that it is received. Not a chance: a large sign announces, "Windows closed; return tomorrow or the day after tomorrow." Two days later you return; the same sign is still there. Finally, two weeks have gone by, sometimes more, before the cashier opens up again, but at that point

---

4. Here is the complete text: "This statement is not a receipt. The settlement of the fee on this statement must be made within 5 days after receipt of this statement. Electricity and water will be disconnected without any further notice if settlement of the account has not been made 15 days after presentation of this statement." In its own way, this warning rephrases Article 11 of the "Conditions générales de l'abonnement" (the version presently in effect), set by the Société Béninoise d'Electricité et d'Eau SBEE, a State company: "Payment for electricity furnished is payable within 5 days after presentation of the bill at the subscriber's residence. The subscriber is forbidden to refuse submission of payment under the pretext of error. If rectifications are necessary, this will be taken into account on the bill of the following month. In case of nonpayment within the period allowed, the company can disconnect the service within the 10 days that follow the payment deadline. The charges for disconnection and renewal of the electric current will be the client's." The "Conditions générales," set by the subscription police for the provision of water, restate the same rules in its Article 11.

the waiting in line becomes interminable; every subscriber of this service has received his bill at the same time and, like yourself, is afraid that his water and electricity will be cut off because of nonpayment. They clump together in front of the windows, they push each other for four hours or more. It is like a little Paradise, where, it seems, "from the days of John the Baptist until now the kingdom of heaven suffereth violence, and the violent take it by force."[5] And it is perfectly possible that, after all these hours, you have not been helped and will be obliged to return two or three more times.

This is an institutionalized waste of time and sovereign contempt for the consumer, as we have observed. But there is something worse here: the declaration of an impossible rule, the declaration of an obligation to be adaptable precisely in order to make it (objectively) not noticeable, bad faith on the part of the administration which drives the customer to corruption or intimidation in order to avoid being penalized for imaginary mistakes, the institution of a way of operation that renders everyone a priori at fault and leaves you, at times, at the mercy of the agents in charge of disconnecting the services, said agents being all the more rushed to do since they smell a substantial percentage of the taxes to be remitted before service is reconnected.

Of course, the administration does not always do this on purpose. Thus, in the given example, the "technical" reason for the closing of the windows at the office is explained: the bookkeeping service needs to do its inventory at the end of each two-month period and must stop its books before proceeding with new receipts. But then why not modify the terms of the contract? Why not extend the payment period to thirty days or wait for the actual end of the periodic inventory to present the new bills? Why shorten the already impossible payment to eight days if it is not to frighten the consumer, to terrorize him, to put him in a position of being obliged to the service, as if as a consumer he had no rights but only obligations?

Among the required documents of a driver are, as everywhere else in the world, the driver's license, the registration card (a gray card in France and in Benin, a pink card in Belgium and in Zaire, perhaps a different color elsewhere), the insurance papers (not required in certain countries such as Zaire), and the annual tax label. Beyond this, in certain countries, additional papers may be required: proof of inspection of headlights and proof of inspection of technical items in the logbook, for example. That these different documents, in fact, aim

5. The Gospel According to St. Matthew 11:12.

at providing the State with some extra resources over and beyond maintaining road safety is in and of itself nothing to smile at: who can mention a single country in the world where the State does not keep itself busy exploiting its citizens in every way possible? Only here, in this specific case, it is not just the State that becomes rich off your back but all too often the agents themselves who keep the "order" and who fleece the defenseless customer for their own profit, by cleverly exploiting the numerous institutional obstacles through strict observation of the rules.

At the beginning of the year, you wish to pay your motor vehicle tax, and you discover in all the agencies of the public treasury that the stickers are not yet ready. You return again in January, two or three times in February, then in March, and again in April. They are still not available, and nobody can tell you with any certainty when they will be there. All of a sudden, you are de facto in a situation of committing irregularities. Then you stop going to the treasury for the time being, for after all you could be doing other things, or, quite legitimately, you could decide to wait for December 30 in order to be sure that the stickers will finally be available.

No chance: in September you are stopped on the road. You are breaking the law because the stickers have been on sale since June. The agents are uncompromising. They open the door on the passenger's side, sit down without asking, order you to drive the car to the pound yourself—as if it were the most natural thing in the world! En route, you can negotiate—if you know how, have a "dialogue," as they sometimes call it—and get out of it by paying the equivalent of ten dollars or so, for which, of course, you do not get a receipt. If you are not used to this, if you have just come straight from Mars, or if recent incidents have given the gold-braided officer cause to fear that you are trying to trap him and will then denounce him for corruption, then you will in fact drive your car to the motor vehicle bureau or to the police station, depending on the authoritarian commands of the officer. Once in the pound, your car will spend several nights there, and this will cost you very dearly; the hearing for this infraction will be set as late as possible in order to increase the total sum of the penalty.

This goes on on a daily basis. Who has ever forced a driver to welcome aboard an unknown passenger, hitchhiker, or gold-braided officer? In case of an accident, who would be responsible to the civilian? What law has ever required a citizen to spend money on gasoline and motor oil, and to use his car to transport an agent of the "order" and, on top of everything else, to drive his car to the pound himself? I humbly admit: it has happened to me twice that in such a situation, politely but firmly, I refused to welcome the undesirable guest. I believe that I owe it to the agent's surprise and that of his team, and to the small seed of madness to which they attributed my anomalous behavior, that I was able to return home, safe and sound, both times.

These little trials of the driver are well-known; I shall not emphasize them any more. But let us retain the lesson: if, from the end of February on, you are made to present, at anyone's commands, a sticker that does not go on sale until June; if you must show in your logbook proof of inspection, annually renewable by only the competent official service team, which only keeps its appointments two or three half-days a week—while hundreds of drivers, who sometimes come from more than 800 kilometers away, line up at dawn to wait several hours for them; finally, if you must show proof of headlight inspection, also offered by an official service (the only one capable) during the course of a brief annual campaign in which thousands of drivers jostle each other, and which might well occur when you are not in the area; well, then, it is necessary to recognize that you are always, forcibly, the one who is committing infractions, not through your own fault but through the fault of the State, through the fault of an administrative organization that, by decreeing these rules, at the same time creates the conditions that make them objectively inapplicable and sows the seeds of corruption and of trading of favors.

The contradiction becomes clear and almost caricatural in the sector of commerce. Here again, a few examples will suffice.

In a given country of our region, every importer is required to insure his merchandise from the point of embarkation by the State company that holds the monopoly of insurance and reinsurance, or by his local correspondent. The problem is this: in more than one foreign country, the insurance company in question has no local correspondent. Thus, the importer must have his merchandise insured by another company. Hereby he puts himself de facto in a position of infraction of rules. That is not all. Should this infraction still be tolerated—and with good reason—upon arrival of the goods the importer is still required to submit to the national company his suppliers' and his own freight bills and (calculated on this basis) to pay to this company the insurance charges under the guise of a possible retroactive rule. Meanwhile, the merchandise is already in the harbor waiting to be unloaded.

The same scenario takes place concerning registered packages or mailbags. In our context, registering the mail is frequently one of the best possible insurances—at least, it was so until recently. The importer, however, must once again have his fictitiously retroactive insurance charges calculated upon arrival charges, which are in fact quite useless.

If this is not theft, let another name be found. The rule here can hardly disguise its true purpose: a purely fiscal one, and without any real concern for strengthening the national economy, for making it more dynamic (as the official discourse would wrongly have it) by extending the field of activity of such and such a State company, since not one real accomplishment is made by that company in exchange for the sums of money it extorted from the consumer.

Let us not talk about the rules for authorized profit margins. It is possible to show, with calculator in hand, that in certain cases the strict respect for these rates of margin could force the merchandise to be sold below its manufacturing cost, taking into account the real charges not incorporated in calculating the price of permissible cost. The functionaries who make these rules know this; the department of price control, pitiless by vocation (in spite of the seriousness, the intelligence, and the openmindedness of some of its executives), awaits the merchants in question, to jump on them at the first opportunity, like a voracious eagle. In these conditions, the merchant is forced to beg, to negotiate, to corrupt. Then enfolds the whole gamut of worldly artfulness, the complete panoply of cat-and-mouse games, from the friendly slap on the back to angry scenes (real or mimed), while going through the visits to the house, the stuffed envelopes and other gratuities, the touching allusion to mutual friends, indeed, to some distant relative—through the aunt-in-law of the uncle of the grandmother. This is also called having a "dialogue."

In any event, one thing is certain: only those who can circumvent the existing rules and who can do so with impunity succeed in business. The prerequisite of fraud is inscribed in the very structures under penalty of financial suicide. It is impossible to stick to the letter of the law, which is either nonexistent or has no relationship to the reality it claims to rule.

Under these conditions, there is nothing surprising if at the borders of the different monetary zones the smuggling business occupies such an important place, not only on the private market but all the way up to the connections between the States. It is known that such an area of the region, which to this day has never produced a single ounce of cocoa, regularly exports it every year—several thousand tons of it—and that an impressive part of the State's resources in this country come precisely from the taxes on this product of export. Wanting to obtain a particular article quickly and at a low cost (paper, for example, or a car), a given society or institution of the State will not bother to draw up an order in Europe and await its delivery, when the easy trade of the *naira* and the *cedi*, Nigerian and Ghanaian moneys, can allow it to solve its problem in just a few hours.[6]

We are here in the very heart of the contradiction. The State proscribes and represses smuggling; more precisely, it pretends to proscribe it, knowing full well that it remains necessary, inevitable, and indispensable to its own survival. Nevertheless, smuggling is actually punished, as if by a symbolic ritual, by dealing severely with a few unlucky victims: the small smugglers, those who do not have the means for intimidation or for corrupting on the grand scale—for example, the poor housewives who transport, for household consumption, a can with four liters of kerosene, while the large importers of the same product have it arrive in contraband in the full sight and knowledge of everyone in enormous tanker trucks that make use not of the little paths of the bush but of the great highways, without being in the least worried.

The preceding remarks are intentionally ordinary, in that they are based on experience and make no claim whatsoever to any theoretical profundity. They are, furthermore, partial, incomplete, rhapsodic, dealing with only a few areas taken at random, without any order and even without any systematic classification, among all those that daily life contains in Black Africa. Nevertheless, they will have reached their goal if they have managed to indicate only a possible, needed direction for research: the analysis of the collective experience with a view toward a critique of everyday life.

I will not stress here the justifications for such a project, nor the immense problems of theory and method that are connected with it. First of all, a very rigorous definition would have to be given of what is understood by "everyday life"; also needed would be the specificity of the critical perspective that alone can allow one not only to highlight the contradictions of this daily life and all that therein is pointed out as intolerable but also (in the most elementary fashion) to bring these to light and to make the object, this humdrum existence itself in which we are caught, by supposition.

6. My colleague, John O. Igue, from the Department of Geography at the Université National du Bénin, has brought under scrutiny the smuggling business on the border of Nigerian with its immediate neighbors: Bénin, Niger, and Cameroon. His numerous publications on this subject will be of great interest for the reader (see Bibliography).

This kind of global and all-encompassing approach would have to be situated with respect to the numerous studies and monographs devoted to a given sector, to a given aspect of everyday life: for example, corruption, practices of sorcery and counterwitchcraft, the urban phenomenon, life in the country, economic and political practices, police practices, professional life, and so on. This approach should even be distinguished from similar analyses that aim (apparently) at the same object taken in its globality: for example, in a given sociological survey by Toure on *La civilisation quotidienne en Côte d'Ivoire,*[7] its author seems to be interested only in that which, in urban mores, betrays a "process of Westernization," though he, too, starts from a critical viewpoint. By degrees, the envisioned criticism should, if need be, situate itself with respect to the enormous anthropological and sociological literature devoted to Africa.

This is not the place to proceed with such a delineation of the field. Let us say only this: a radical critique of everyday life can and must retain the lesson of the existing studies and surveys, which restore partial and complementary aspects, fragments, or (better yet) levels of collective experience. But in its role of radical critique, it must go deeper: down to that concrete ground where the different aspects, fragments, and levels originate, all the way down to that unnoticed residue (generally forgotten by the most scholarly analyses) where the possibility of Westernization is knotted to its most comical failures, and still further down to the possibility of repression and terrorism, the possibility of this omnipresent violence, of this accelerated process of becoming savage that contains our daily lot and is the required horizon of every individual existence in so-called modern Africa, much more surely than this "process of Westernization," which is real enough.

Henri Lefebvre has produced a *Critique de la vie quotidienne*[8] centered primarily around the European experience, more precisely around the French one, essentially questioning what he calls the "bureaucratic society of controlled consumption" (*la société bureaucratique de consommation dirigée*), or also "the cyberneticization of the society through the daily slant" (*la cybernétisation de la société par le biais du quotidien*).[9] The analysis of the French philosopher is supported (without being reduced by it) by a critical and nondogmatic

7. Toure (1982).
8. See Lefebvre [1946] 1958, 1962, 1980.
9. Lefebvre, 1968 : 117, 125. See also ibid., all of chap. 2: "La société bureaucratique de consommation dirigée," 133–207.

Marxism, emerging into the plan for a "total revolution" at one and the same time economic, political, and cultural, a revolution that aims at "changing life" in the most ambitious sense of the word.

The plan laid out here is both similar and different. It is similar in that it, too, is borne by a critical intention, by the refusal of accepting things as they are, by the demand for a different life, for the utopia of another society—yet a utopia that does not mean to invent a purely imaginary topos ex nihilo but to free the concrete possibilities for an authentic subversion starting from a real knowledge of the present society and its defects. Yet in other ways it is a different plan, first of all because it is Africa-centered, rooted in the concrete soil of an experience from more than one side only, irreducible to that of a Frenchman of the Liberation, or even of a more recent period; and, second (without forbidding recourse to Marxist illumination—quite the contrary!), because this change in context requires accounting for aspects of daily reality, aspects that are relatively original with respect to the industrialized society or the old Western democracies, aspects that partially determine the very content—the possible contents of the utopia to be furthered.

Other approaches exist, other models of criticism of which one should be aware and that essentially converge at the same point as does Lefebvre's criticism: the plan for a different society. *One Dimensional Man* by Marcuse is a fine example.[10]

As far as Africa is concerned, the reminder of the everyday may produce the salutary effect of demystification, of a return to what is real beyond the pretentious stream of discourses that obscure it. There is still so much to be said, so many crimes to be uncovered, so many myths to be destroyed, so much suffering to be brought to light, that one finds oneself here almost constrained to begin at the beginning: the purely journalistic reconstruction of the facts. One must, then, not be surprised by the purposely anecdotal character of the above remarks. *Journalism-vérité*, if properly practiced, already represents in and of itself an enormous subversion, with respect to the dominant practice which makes journalism, in this part of our wide world, a discourse of justification and the instrument par excellence of the domestication of the masses.[11]

10. Herbert Marcuse, *One Dimensional Man*, translation: *L'homme undimensionnel* (1968).

11. What shows the urgent need for information that is simply precise, a return to unpretentious journalism, is the fact that a testimony such as the one by Jean-Paul Alata could have the effect of a bomb, at the time, when all he did was give an account

Yet the simple narrative can no longer suffice. One must also order, classify, interpret the news item, show therein the real conditions that emerge, detach the structure that makes it possible and that gives it meaning. The critique of the everyday must bring to light this weighty system that clutches at our heels and which we ended up by accepting as normal through sheer habit. The critique must identify this familiar system and make it recognizable, must do the same for the totality of constraints within which our passivity is organized and which delivers us, defenseless, without our even being aware of it, as victims, executioners, or accomplices, to the most abject forms of dehumanization.[12]

---

of facts and practices that, in Guinée, were part of the daily happenings and were known as such by everyone, although accepted passively in the silence of resignation. That *Prison d'Afrique* was not permitted to be sold in France, by a government that claimed to champion the Rights of Man, as do all French governments, tells the tale of contemporary political mores. On this subject, the reader will be interested in the analysis by Patrick Rotman and Hervé Hamon, *L'affaire Alata.*

Idi Amin Dada was not alone, in any case, nor was Jean-Bedel Bokassa, They were— and still are—legion, and we are more comfortable talking about those two or about the Guinean patriarch Sékou Touré, only because they are no more, or are no longer in power. To dare to write, one must be a foreigner, such as Jean Lacouture in his foreword to *Prison d'Afrique* (and I leave it to him, of course): "Henceforth, the danger is every-where, in the very air that one presently breathes, from Kampala to Conakry . . . Or in N'Djamena . . . Or in Brazzaville, in the People's Republic of the Congo . . . In the Cameroon . . . In the Central African Republic . . . [In] Dahomey, today's Republic of Benin, [that] prides itself to be socialist, like Guinea . . . [In] Zaire . . . [In] the Ivory Coast . . . [In] Nigeria." As in the "shame of humanity," South Africa, unanimously decried, it must be said in passing, by the governments of the countries mentioned. One must live in exile, and preferably in a stable democratic country, where one can be assured of solid support, in order to dare to put out a hefty tome such as the recent work of Comi M. Toulabor, *Le Togo sous Eyadema*, which, this time, is not forbidden in France (cohabitation is compelling!), but which in Togo can only be read clandes-tinely, at one's own risk, and which will have no effect on the foreign policy of France, anyway, or of those countries that are similar, nor on the calculations (economic, stra-tegic, geopolitical, etc.) that form this policy's foundation.

What we, on our end, must elucidate are the possible permanent conditions of cari-catures such as Idi Amin Dada and Jean-Bedel Bokassa, the structures, forms, modali-ties of our habitual behavior and, more generally, of our everyday lives, both within and outside of the political field stricto sensu, that make these most outrageous abuses possible, the only ones that we would think of discussing in the best possible circumstances.

12. Should I stress it? My criticism of ethnophilosophy, in its essential inspiration, was already dominated, from one end to the other, by this same refusal of mystifica-tion, this same demand for a return to the real beyond the deceptive idealizations, of which the ethnologic addiction to the past was, all told, but a modality. In this regard,

BIBLIOGRAPHY

Alata, Jean-Paul. 1976. *Prison d'Afrique: 5 ans dans les géôles de Guinée.* Collection Hist. Paris: Editions du Seuil.

Chaliand, Gérard. 1979. *Mythes révolutionnaires du tiers monde: Guérillas et socialismes.* Collection Points. Paris: Editions du Seuil.

Egg, Johnny, and John Igue. 1987. "Echanges invisibles et clandestin." *Inter Tropiques* 22 (May): 4–7.

———. 1987. "Commerçants sans frontières." *Inter Tropiques* 21 (March): 15–17.

Hountondji, Paulin J. 1967. "Charabia et mauvaise conscience: Psychologie du langage chez les intellectuels colonisés." *Présence Africaine* 61: 11–31.

———. 1978. "Recherche théorique africaine et contrat de solidarité." *Travail et Société* 3, nos. 3–4 (July–October): 353–364.

———. 1980. *Sur la "philosophie africaine": Critique de l'ethnophilosophie.* Paris: Editions F. Maspéro, 1977; Yaounde: Editions CLE.

———. 1980. "Distances." *Recherche, Pédagogie et Culture* 49: 27–33.

———. 1982. "Occidentalisme, élitisme: Réponse à deux critiques." *Recherche, Pédagogie et Culture* 56 (January–March): 58–67.

———. 1983. *African Philosophy: Myth and Reality.* Trans. Henri Evans with the collaboration of Jonathan Ree. London: Hutchinson; and Bloomington: Indiana University Press.

———. 1984. "La culture scientifique dans les pays de la périphérie." In *Culture pour tous et pour tous les temps,* 65–78. Paris: Presses de l'UNESCO.

———. 1986. "His Master's Voice—Remarks on the Problem of Human Rights in Africa." In *Philosophical Foundations of Human Rights,* ed. Alwin Diemer, 319–332. Paris: UNESCO Press.

———. Forthcoming. "La dépendance scientifique et le problème de la déconnexion." In *La dimension culturelle du développement,* ed. Samir Amin.

Igue, John O. 1976. "Un aspect des échanges entre le Dahomey et le Nigéria: Le commerce de cacao." *Bulletin de l'IFAN* 38 no. 3, series B: 636–669.

---

one should reread the "Postscript" to Hountondji's *Sur la "philosophie africaine,"* and one will see how the theoretical criticism of unanimism, in the last analysis, refers to the "everyday tragedy of our countries on the road to becoming Fascist"—thus, to something intolerable with respect to which the scholarly assembling of this apologetical discourse seems quite laughable. The articles published since then have recentered the perspective more around this critique of the present.

I am grateful to my colleague Abiola Irele, of the University of Ibadan, for having focused the attention on this point in the beautiful "Introduction" to the English (and American) version of *Sur la "philosophie africaine":* ethnophilosophical criticism has never been, despite the appearances, a purely academic quarrel, but what is really at stake is surely "the improvement of the quality of life on our continent" (Abiola Irele, "Introduction," to Hountondji, *African Philosophy, Myth and Reality,* p. 30).

————. 1976. "Evolution du commerce clandestin entre le Dahomey et le Nigéria depuis la guerre de Biafra." *Revue Canadienne des Etudes Africaines* 10, no. 2:235–257.

————. 1983. "Commerce et intégration en Afrique occidentale." *Politique Africaine* 9:29–51.

————. 1985. "Rente pétrolièree et commerce des produits agricoles à la périphérie du Nigéria: Le cas du Bénin et du Niger." Presented by Johnny Egg, INRA/ESR, Laboratoire d'Economie Internationale, Montpellier, March.

————. Forthcoming. "Le Nigéria et ses périphéries frontalières." In *Le Nigéria: Les limites d'unes puissance*, by D. Bach, J. Egg, et al. Paris: Editions Karthala.

Irele, Abiola. 1983. "Introduction." In *African Philosophy, Myth and Reality*, by Paulin J. Hountondji. Trans. Henri Evans with the collaboration of Jonathan Ree. London: Hutchinson; and Bloomington: Indiana University Press.

Lefebvre, Henri. 1946. *Critique de la vie quotidienne.* Vol. 1, *Introduction.* Paris: Editions Grasset et Fasquelle. Vol. 2, *Fondement d'une sociologie de la quotidienneté.* Paris: L'Arche, 1961. Vol. 3, *Vie quotidienne et modernité.* Paris: L'Arche, 1980.

————. 1968. *La vie quotidienne dans le monde moderne.* Collections Idíes. Paris: Editions Gallimard.

Marcuse, Herbert. 1964. *One Dimensional Man.* Boston: Beacon Press. French trans.: *L'homme unidimensionnel.* Paris: Editions de Minuit, 1968.

Mudimbe, V. Y. 1972. *Réflexions sur la vie quotidienne.* Kinshasa: Objectif 80, Editions du Mont Noir.

Njoh-Mouelle, Ebenezer. 1970. *De la médiocrité à l'excellence: Essai sur la signification humaine du dévoloppement.* Yaounde: Editions CLE.

————. 1970. *Jalons: Essai d'une mentalité neuve.* Yaounde: Editions CLE.

————. 1975. *Jalons II: L'africanisme aujourd'hui.* Yaounde: Editions CLE.

————. 1983. *Considérations actuelles sur l'Afrique.* Yaounde: Editions CLE.

Oruka, H. Odera. [1976] 1985. *Punishment and Terrorism in Africa.* 2d ed. Nairobi: Kenya Literature Bureau.

p'Bitek, Okot. 1966. *Song of Lawino.* Nairobi: East African Publishing House.

————. 1971. *Two Songs (Song of Prisoner; Song of Malaya).* Nairobi: East African Publishing House.

Rotman, Patrick, and Hervé Hamon. 1977. *L'affaire Alata: Pourquoi on interdit un livre en France.* Paris: Editions du Seuil.

Toulabor, Comi M. 1986. *Le Togo sous Eyadema.* Paris: Editions Karthala.

Toure, Abdou. 1982. *La civilisation quotidienne en Côte d'Ivoire: Procès d'occidentalisation.* Paris: Editions Karthala.

part five

A Dialogue on *Présence Africaine*

Historic Witnesses   twenty

Albert H. Berrian (1925–1989)

MUDIMBE: When exactly did you
come into contact with *Présence
Africaine* and how did you react to
its ideology and program?

BERRIAN: I first became aware of the
journal *Présence Africaine* in 1952.
This followed some inquiries I had
made concerning the role of Blacks
in American letters. Professor John
Matheus, some of whose poetry appeared in Alain Locke's *The New
Negro*, informed me of the existence
of Harlem Renaissance literature
and of *Présence Africaine*. My first
visit to the *Présence Africaine* office
took place in 1956, during the time
of my postdoctoral studies at the
Sorbonne. I met Alioune Diop. The
second visit took place in 1959,
while I was en route to Guinea, following an invitation to visit by
President Sékou Touré, who had
been awarded an honorary doctorate
by my institution, North Carolina
Central. The third visit, while I was
en route to Zaire in January 1960.
Subsequent visits were made in
1974, while I was en route to Senegal, and in 1976, while I was visiting
my daughter, Brenda, who was a doctoral student at the Sorbonne.

The ideology espoused by *Présence Africaine* was, I thought,
highly ambitious but valid. My
sense of its validity came from the
fact that I believed that one's vision

367

of the world evolved from within—in this case, from within the Black psyche.

Further, I had maintained for some time that homo sapiens evolved from Africans and that all humankind and their self and worldviews are extensions of those of man's earliest ancestors. This ideal ultimately found expression in a short book, which I entitled *Monophyletic Principle*.

M: As an American, and from the viewpoint of the American situation, how did you evaluate *Présence Africaine*, and what are your feelings now forty years later?

B: During the time of my youth and early adulthood the United States was lacking in humanity socially and politically. For Blacks and Native Americans, America's espoused democratic principles had no meaning. This made the philosophical underpinnings of *Présence Africaine* attractive. As you know, social and political conditions in the United States have improved, but not to the point where what *Présence Africaine* projects becomes subject to question. Nor has my position changed on the validity of a worldview growing out of a Black source.

M: How do you see the contribution of *Présence Africaine* to both the cause of Africans and African Americans?

B: *Présence Africaine* has served to validate the worth of Black civilizations wherever they appear. This publication provides documentation for this worth. The documentation could profit from a more in-depth character—more annotations, for example, but is valuable as it stands. Although I am aware of certain differences, I have always chosen not to separate Blacks on the basis of nationality, ethnicity, or complexion (frequently the result of miscegenation). In this regard I have embraced a White American position.

M: Does *Présence Africaine* have a future?

B: *Présence Africaine* has a future, if for no other reason than its existence as a historical fact. As to whether its future includes having an impact, this depends on Blacks. Whites do not have to be sold on the value of this publication and have probably been more than a little responsible for its continuance. The extent to which Blacks have evolved holistic personalities and a sense of racial pride, ethnic and subtle genetic differences notwithstanding, will determine *Présence Africaine*'s future.

M: What is the lesson you draw from the project, its ideology and its ambition? I mean the lesson you would like to give to the new generation of African-Americans and Africans?

B: The lesson that I personally draw from the project and would like for others to consider is that, as painful and slow as the process might be, persons characterized as Blacks can overcome attempts by humans with less coloration to dehumanize them for reasons that began in economic greed and the thirst for power. I would hope that the new generation of Blacks, wherever they may be found geographically, will not underestimate the time and effort that will be required to root out the myth of race and racial superiority, with all that this entails for maintaining present political and economic advantages. My advice is that Blacks must stay in communication with each other, remain vigilant, and avoid intraethnic conflicts. Finally, they must stand convinced of their responsibility for the regeneration of the human family in all of its shapes and colors.

Simone Howlett

MUDIMBE: Madame Howlett, what is the history that has made you one, that makes you one with Présence Africaine? (And in this "you" I include your late husband, Monsieur Jacques Howlett.) How did all this begin? And when exactly, for each of you?

HOWLETT: After the war years—years of confinement—a wind of freedom and of political initiative took hold of the young intellectuals, and in this—hazardous—encounter (both Alioune Diop and Jacques Howlett were junior teachers at the Lycée Saint-Louis in 1946) there was an opportunity to contribute to another liberation: that of the Black people under colonialism.

For a young philosopher used to Sartrean problematics, what could be more exciting and more worthwhile than a commitment side by side with a man who considered himself the spokesman for the claims of Black culture? As for me, I shared Jacques's ideas. We were a couple who "communicated" well, and thus I helped him with this difficult task throughout his life, without belonging to the staff of Présence Africaine.

M: Jacques Howlett was a philosophy teacher. In that sense he led, in a way, a double life or, more precisely, he had a double face much like Janus: that of a European philosophy teacher—first in the high schools, then at the university—and also that of one of the pillars of Présence. As you know, for many people that seemed akin to a diversion. Philosophers, after all, are allowed their whims. But for you? What explanation do you have for your commitment and your loyalty?

H: The philosophic past of Jacques Howlett was less marked by the academism of the philosophical systems than it was involved with existential interrogation. Philosophy had meaning only in proportion to its ability to listen to the other living being, whether White or Black: existence is less a question of systems than of seeing the other person. This philosophy offered no obstacle whatsoever to the encounter with words of wisdom whose voice had been muffled for too long. For Jacques, meeting Alioune was a political birth, a commitment never denied until 1961 or 1962 (I no longer remember the exact year) with the call of the 121. As I was politicized earlier than Jacques, it is easy to understand my commitment and loyalty. So, their mutual understanding both in choice of themes and in work methods—though never denied—was the target of some ups and downs. Yet, for two years the antagonism was so acute that they had to suspend their collaboration. But—and this was before the Conference of Rome in 1956—this collaboration was renewed on a sounder basis for each of them. From that time on, an abiding and true friendship, deepening with time, continued to bind them until their last days. I later learned through people close to Présence Africaine that Alioune Diop—and this is all to his credit—had always been supportive of Jacques and had shielded him from attacks by certain people, people who were at all times ready to take his place as Présence Africaine's cultural advisor.

M: A very indiscreet question: Alioune, Jacques, Présence . . . how do you see this trinity? What were its problems and what are, today, the consequences of that intimacy?

H: A White European making demands for Black culture, a European listening in on a new eloquence, a European guilty because he is White, and then yet again as many difficulties in the meeting of two, not always identical, discourses where one was more cultural (Alioune Diop) and the other more political (Jacques Howlett). As in all trinities, the separate elements can sometimes remain heterogeneous even though they must unite, but the shared concern for their enterprise compels them not to exacerbate their differences.

M: Many famous people were present at the birth of Présence Africaine: Gide, Sartre, Monod, and quite a few others (was Camus, in fact, not among them?). What did this atmosphere mean to Présence?

H: As a matter of fact, the first issue of the journal Présence Afri-

caine was full of great names of White intellectuals (Camus was not one of them), but this Committee of Patrons was, in my opinion, not very effective in supporting the cause of Présence Africaine. Perhaps I am mistaken.

M: There are also some Europeans who, from the very beginning, sided wholeheartedly with Présence. You are one of them. You work for this publishing house. How many are there? They are not very visible, but they are there. How do you feel? How do the French and the other colleagues who work at Présence Africaine feel?

H: The Europeans who were and still are interested in Présence Africaine are primarily teachers of African literature. As for the readers who are (for the most part) African or Caribbean specialists in economics, politics, literature, law, and so forth, they are friends who speak openly and who do not hesitate to criticize Présence Africaine when the occasion arises during the meetings of our Reading Committee: this is constructive. The staff, all White, is loyal to the house—otherwise, why would it stay? Personally, I feel good at Présence Africaine, though I frequently worry about the future, for we must wage a constant battle, but then I like to fight for causes that mean a great deal to me.

M: Please forgive me for recalling painful memories. Jacques Howlett was very seriously ill when my *Odeur du père* came back from the printer's. He still found time to draft the copy for the cover of my book. I have been told that is was one of the last things he did. I do not know. In any event, true or not, the story makes me feel guilty, I am not sure why. Furthermore, I find such generosity disarming . . .

H: When your *Odeur du père* came back from the printer's, Présence Africaine telephoned me to ask me whether he would be able to write the fourth page of the cover; he signaled "yes" to me with his eyes. He was bedridden, almost entirely paralyzed. Despite great difficulty of speech, he dictated the text to me. When it was finished, he had an intense look of being very much alive, it was the last time. A few days later, he was to die calmly. He respected you, and I don't see why you should feel guilty since you provided him with his last profound intellectual joy.

M: A final question, a crude and direct one: Does Présence Africaine, in the face of the giant publishing houses that work in the American style, have a future?

H: African friendship is spoken of in terms of the family. Just as one does not reject a family member entirely, so there was no question that at the death of Jacques Howlett his presence would disappear from the house. If Présence Africaine was at first a large family rather than well-managed enterprise, it is time to change all that; we are working on it, but it will be very difficult and the attitudes will also have to change. We will not be able to become a giant publishing house in the American style until African literature is recognized and read.

Maurice A. Lubin

MUDIMBE: How did you first come in contact with Alioune and *Présence Africaine*?[1]

LUBIN: I first came in contact with Alioune Diop during the time that I was in Rio de Janeiro, in connection with the First Conference of Black Writers and Artists in 1956. I don't quite remember if it was I who initiated our correspondence. I had a subscription to the journal, *Présence Africaine*, and used to receive my issues regularly in Rio de Janeiro. What I do remember is that Alioune Diop was concerned about having a very strong Black representation at the conference, particularly from the Black diaspora. Now, the Brazilian authorities are extremely sensitive to the issue of race. They will ask you: Why do you want to be in touch with Black people in Brazil? In the eyes of the Brazilian constitution, there are no Blacks, no Whites, no Yellow people, but only Brazilian citizens, without any distinction whatsoever. Because of this racial regulation, any official request from *Présence Africaine* would risk causing a "blanking-out." Furthermore, the economic situation of the Brazilian Black at the time did not permit him to undertake a trip to or to stay in Paris at his own expense. What solution could be found to have Brazilian Blacks represented at this conference, which was of such considerable importance to the Black world? There were, at this time, Black artists of Brazilian nationality living in France. It was at the suggestion of friends of mine that these be invited by *Présence Africaine*.[2] And that is how Wilson Tiberio and other Brazilian Blacks participated in that first conference. I was not present at this international meeting,

1. Alioune Diop, director of the journal *Présence Africaine*.
2. Alioune Diop sent invitations to the First International Conference of Negro Writers and Artists which was held in Sorbonne, Paris, 19–22 September 1956.

but I did send a paper, "The Contribution of Haiti to Black World Poetry."[3]

I did not yet know Paris. When I came to Paris from Italy the following year I was cordially received by Alioune Diop. I believe he had left a meeting to come and welcome me. And from that time on our relationship grew stronger. That is something of which I am proud.

Within the framework of my relationship with Alioune Diop, there is one important detail to be mentioned. I was very well-informed on the subject of Haitian literature at a time when this material did not appear in the academic curriculum in Haiti. I had already published *Panorama de la poésie haitienne*.[4] Anxious to know writers and works from Francophone Africa, I turned to Alioune Diop as the best possible person to help satisfy my earnest desire. He assured me that he was going to publish works by African writers, and was already doing so, and that he would send me some of these for my information. That is how I became familiar with African literature written in French. When Howard University wanted to introduce African literature studies into its curriculum, it sent a contract to me in Port-au-Prince, asking me to come and succeed Dr. Mercer Cook and to teach French and Francophone African literature. I owe it to Alioune Diop that I became a professor of African literature at Howard. This has been very important to me in my life.

During a conference organized by *Présence Africaine* on the integration of the economy in African education,[5] we were able to see each other daily in one of the UNESCO halls where the meeting was held. Once, while speaking, about the political situation in Haiti under Duvalier's dictatorship, he stated how happy he would have been to organize a conference in Haiti, and what a pity it was that he could not do so.

M: What does *Présence Africaine*[6] represent for you?

L: *Présence Africaine* answered my needs. Up to that point, Africa

3. "The Contribution of Haiti to Black World Poetry," *Présence Africaine* 14–15 (June–September 1957): 256–281.

4. Maurice A. Lubin and Carlos Saint Louis, *Panorama de la poésie haitienne*, Collection Haitiana (Port-au-Prince, Haiti: Editions Henri Deschamps, 1950).

5. This was organized in 1962 by Présence Africaine with Martin Ramanoelina and many representatives and students from Africa and the Diaspora.

6. Alioune Diop rarely used his name to sign his articles in *Présence Africaine*. Usually, all editorials, text, introduction of seminars, conferences, roundtables were attributed to *Présence Africaine*. Diop was fully aware we were operating as a team.

and the Black diaspora did not know each other. This was not to the advantage of Blacks. I approved of everything *Présence* had undertaken, since it was in the interest of our project for human promotion.

Haiti has always struggled to safeguard her independence, the liberty of her nationals, and the dignity of Black people. For a long time on the international scale, only Liberia, Ethiopia, and Haiti were considered the representatives of Black people. We were true minorities. Furthermore, every bias, every prejudice against us prevailed. *Présence Africaine*'s ideal responded to the cause of all Haitians. It proposed gathering all Blacks together in clusters and letting the entire world know of their accomplishments and their potential.

Présence Africaine drew up a program that was to command respect for Black people. Various means were mobilized to arrive at the relevant results that we so appreciate today. It is enough to state that *Présence Africaine* worked on what is real. In such matters, we must allow time to do its work, to correct, to modify, which may well be a question of centuries.

M: Forty years later, how do you evaluate the work that is accomplished?

L: At a distance of forty years, the work and successes connected with it are remarkable. What matters now is to continue struggle, while learning from temporary setbacks and taking the experience gained into consideration.

Alioune Diop—the apostle—was a deeply inspired man. He carried out his task well. He understood that isolation has never been an instrument of progress. He worked with the collaboration of all people of goodwill (White, Yellow, or Black) and was open to helping us define African originality and to hastening its integration into the modern world. That is the initial declaration of the father of *Présence Africaine*.

Those who lent their assistance or their moral support are humanists who thought only of the improvement of the human condition. The fact that Blacks have been held back morally affects the most evolved, the most developed nations.

M: Tell me a little about the journal and its projects.

L: We have the best of relationships with the journal and collaborate fully with it. I have not called upon the services of the publishing house because, more than once, Alioune spoke to me of problems he was facing with the publication of manuscripts he received from Africa. I had enough of a sense of discretion not to get in the way of letting an entire continent take advantage of that house's hospitality.

There are plans projected over a long period of time: one has the impression that everything has been meticulously planned and that one is bound to obtain the best results. Yet, there are difficulties that only crop up in the course of the execution, errors that show only after the fact. It makes sense to take these difficulties and these errors into consideration during the analysis of the results.

The results of *Présence Africaine*'s politics are more positive than negative. It is up to the coming generations to continue the work of the pioneers, while taking the new needs and the changing conditions of modern life into account.

M: *Présence Africaine* has been blamed for its politics in Africa, which (so it seems) had a tendency to uphold the new masters.

L: Distinctions should be made. It is not *Présence Africaine* that went to put itself under the yoke of the colonial or the postcolonial powers, nor to strike bargains with them. It is the other way around. The colonial powers or the governments of various countries used the positive results obtained by *Présence Africaine* to consolidate positions, or to grab for their own advantage all that they could exploit.

Fifty years ago, the Black was merely a consumer of other people's culture. He didn't even know his own literature. Today, the Black can draw up a list of writers who do honor to his people, and Wole Soyinka now holds the 1986 Nobel Prize in literature.

Nevertheless, on African soil the dreadful Apartheid continues, the shame of present-day humanity. We remain convinced that this social leprosy is in its final stages.

M: How do you see the future of *Présence Africaine*?

L: *Présence Africaine* is more than a symbol; it is a living reality. It has accomplished a task of enormous importance: to encourage self-awareness in Black people, to develop their sense of human dignity, and to disseminate Black culture. In this way it has assisted in reuniting and consolidating a Black cultural heritage in which literature plays a noteworthy role. There is no need to discuss hard reality.

The generation of Alioune Diop began the task; those who follow will carry it on for the benefit of the Black people and of humankind.

Jacques Rabemananjara

My dear Mudimbe,

I am very touched by your good wishes for the New Year and thank you for those. In return, I, too, send my very best wishes. May 1989 bring you happiness, good health, and the fulfillment of your most cherished plans.

Clearly, your collective project on *Présence Africaine* has enthralled me. I did promise you my contribution. But my predicament is a serious one. It is a question of doing a general checkup of our enterprise.

I wonder if I am qualified to make such a diagnosis. Together with Alioune Diop, I was one of the founders of *Présence Africaine*. Together with him, I have devoted the best of myself and many long years of my life to it, and continue to do so today, together with his widow. Through living there and following all the trials and tribulations, I have ended up identifying myself with the organization itself.

How, then, under those conditions, could I possibly do a clinical examination of the state of the patient? I can say only one thing: I am overjoyed that the child (that the small team surrounding Alioune Diop almost delivered with forceps) has grown, has affirmed itself, has blossomed: I can only take notice and applaud.

For me it is a satisfying subject: the rather splendid celebration of the fortieth anniversary of the birth of *Présence Africaine* attests to our contentment as well as to our pride. This double emotion seems legitimate to us: for a cultural journal, forty years of activity indicates longevity, a feat. Few periodicals of a similar nature reach such an advanced age, such a significant duration; this justifies the ambition of the founders and demonstrates to what extent the creation of an organization of this scope responded to a demand of history: to participate actively in the accession to and in the progress of that history.

In fact, the Black man has been excluded from this history, crossed off, too much held in contempt to be taken seriously and to be worthy of a place on the record of achievements. The Black man existed only to be an object of jeers and gibes; he existed only in humiliation and obliteration. The existence of the Black man had to be reinvented; he had to be thrown resolutely and without complexes into the common path of the human species.

That was and still remains the objective of *Présence Africaine*: to be present in the world in the same way as others.

At that time, racism was accepted as normal; nobody was surprised that the Black was treated differently from the other members of the human race.

That ostracism had to be faced, that secular prejudice had to be denounced, that taboo had to be exorcised: the struggle waged by *Présence Africaine* had no other meaning—to carry out both the rehabilitation of the Black man's values and the general rectification of human attitudes in every domain.

Présence Africaine assigned itself a double mission: to implement the spiritual prophylaxis of both the Black man and the White man, to place them both side by side, on the same level, on the same landing, and to have them look each other straight in the eyes.

The task is far from finished. But many a stage has been cleared and many results are positive and beneficial. There are no longer any serene racists. Those who trail behind and pride themselves on being racist no longer dare to advertise it loudly, tortured by some irrepressible shame. The only country in the world that has instituted apartheid as a principle and as a practice of government has been declared to be beyond the pale of humanity: South Africa has called universal condemnation upon itself—it is the plague that everyone wishes to avoid.

Today's generation is not aware of the progress that has been made. That is the difference between us. We are fully able to measure the distance that separates us from the era out of which we have come; this generation today enjoys a state of grace whose birthing has cost us dearly: it was born in the light, it lives in the light, it does not know that the night has been long, that the dawn did not emerge out of nothingness.

I am not claiming that this victory is due to the single action of *Présence Africaine,* but *Présence Africaine* can insist on the honor of having been in the forefront of the battle, the standard-bearer of those who raised the flag of rebellion to seize their rights and to recuperate their dignity.

However, *Présence Africaine* did not limit itself to playing that role only, the role of raising and breathing life into an insurrectional movement of the Black intelligentsia. It also settled down to the task of showing the creative ability of Black people in every activity of the spirit: poetry, novels, essays, philosophy, theology, sciences, and so on.

Thanks to an atmosphere created by the vitality impelled by *Présence Africaine,* thanks to patient and effective work, great names of the Black world sparkle in the firmament where universal glory shines; the Senghors, the Cheikh Anta Diops, the Aimé Césaires, the

Wole Soyinkas, from now on are part of the heritage of humanity: they have become names as familiar on the lips as Shakespeare, as Hugo or Lamartine.

Présence Africaine's greatest pride lies in its having ventured both to return to Black people the taste for dignity, and to disseminate among other peoples the will to respect the Black people.

Were it only in order to acquire and insure this consideration, it was well worth the trouble to have decided upon this battle and to have led it up to our day.

Jacques

Emile Snyder

Dear V. Y. Mudimbe:

You ask me the question: "What is Présence?" And I answer this with some emotion, as I think of this house with which I have had such close ties for so long, for so many years. What is Présence?

Please note that I simply call it Présence from the start. There's no need to add "Africaine." Among the founding people on the staff, Christiane Diop, Simone Howlett, Aké Loba, Rabemananjara, and Isabelle at the bookstore, they simply say Présence. They say "stop by Présence," "So we'll see each other at Présence," or "Ousmane has just arrived from Dakar; if you want to see him, come by Présence tomorrow around four o'clock, he'll be there."

Présence stands simply and completely for Présence Africaine. And even the young who have just arrived from Africa or who (from Paris) are interested in Africa, quickly learn to abbreviate with full confidence. "So, see you tomorrow at Présence." No need to add Africaine. They know . . . We've known it for forty years! That doesn't make us any younger, does it? But it does warm us when wintertime knocks against our joints, hammers at our arteries: we say "as long as we can still turn up at Présence, then there's still hope."

That is what Présence is. The Présence of a presence, that of friends, with whom one forms a multitude. I come up to the reception desk, just arrived from America, totally unexpected. Madame Diop cries out: "Well, there you are!" And then with a warm, almost maternal voice, such a comfort to my age, she asks: "And how's your health?" She asks the question twice—"So tell me, how's your health?"—as if the second time would bring a more reassuring answer. I tell her that it is all right, that I have come out of my second heart operation fairly well, in the final analysis. She smiles and asks: "For how long will you be in Paris?" And before I can even answer her, she has been called to the phone. She runs as she cries out at me: "Excuse me! Stop by again." I know that I will stop by again. *One always stops by again at Présence!*

That is what Présence is. Personalities always present, who do not leave you, and to whom you always return even when they are no longer there!

Madame Diop has fled. I come into a hall, offices to the right, to the left, hellos to Aké, to Rabe. ("How are you?" "Ah, you're back with us again, for how long?" "And your health?" "How are you feeling now?") For those who don't know: Aké is Aké Loba, the novelist, and Rabe is Rabemananjara, the Malagasy poet. So one moves from Africa to Madagascar, and if Edouard Maunick were to show up suddenly, one would be on the Mauritius Island . . . and Simone Howlett is Parisian and I am an American passing through . . . That, too, is Présence: a presence in the world.

I have a little chat with Aké, with Rabe. Again they inquire after my health. I answer: "It's all right, and yours?" We look at each other, feeling a bit worn out by the years, but seeing each other again is rejuvenating too, isn't it? Then I run into Simone Howlett, who has heard my voice and comes out of her little office. "Ah, there you are!" If Jacques were here—in the time of Jacques and Alioune—Jacques would have taken me in his arms, warmly, and asked: "How are you, my big man?" It should be said that I was minuscule next to him, and that he always used to bend his long, thin body down to embrace me. But Simone, who is my height, embraces me without difficulty. And she, too, says: "How are you? Come into my office." That also is Présence: offices with a presence.

I have visited a number of publishing houses that had large offices, upholstered chairs, sometimes in the style of American big business. In fact, those were absences, well-decorated absences. But at Présence there are presences, little cubbyholes with personality, swarms of personalities, if I can put it that way. In Simone's office (which was formerly Jacques'), there are, as always, books spread out all over, on the chairs, the desk, the cabinets, on the floor. How do you sit down amidst all these presences? You find a space, you get settled, thinking perhaps that it has been a year since you last saw each other, last summer to be exact. You feel wedged in between the books . . . You shuffle these paper presences around a little and, in doing so, you meet old friends, old presences, a *Cahier*, a *Pigments*, an *Epitome*, a reedited *Les écrivains noirs de langue française* by Lilyan Kesteloot, *L'Afrique des africains* by Claude Wauthier, or the studies of Cheikh Anta Diop, all of them fundamental texts that give life to the great, intellectual leap of négritude. And also, squeezed in on the right, on the left, the most recent titles, *Le jeune homme de sable* and *Le zéhéros n'est pas n'importe qui* (to name but two of them), those two novels by the fine Williams Sassine, and the three great novels by Mudimbe: *Entre les eaux, Le bel immonde, L'écart*—and also by him, *L'odeur du père*, that philosophical survey of the African presence. And in this little office I also discover young novelists and poets whom I do not yet know, but whom I expect to take with me—new presences who will be added to my old ones.

That is how it is at Présence. One always meets new presences. I look at these texts while Simone talks to me at that Parisian speed to which I, peasant from the "*Danube*" of "*Lake Monroe*" (Bloomington in the United States) am no longer accustomed. And again: "So, how about your health?" I talk, I explain, I begin to loosen up through this conversation with Simone, only half of whose remarks I hear, I must confess: for I am fascinated by this office where Jacques spent so many years of his life, where he and Alioune must have met so often, must have discussed a presence to be affirmed, to be perpetuated, to be protected, Présence Africaine. Then it is noon. "Come," Simone says to me, "we'll eat at the Chinese place across the street." It is actually a small Vietnamese restaurant, but we understand each other. We arrive. Already seated, a little further down, are Madame Diop and some friends, always other presences around presences. We come back a little later. I need to stop by the bookstore, the *other Présence*, where Isabelle (after all these years I still don't know her last name—she is and always will be, warmly, Isabelle) will greet me warmly: "Ah, you've just come from America, and how's your health?" Everyone is concerned about me: it is wonderful! So many warm presences surrounding my small presence!

I browse through the shelves: literature, humanities, magazines. Since I am traveling by plane, I cannot weigh myself down with all these presences, but I make a list to leave with Isabelle. I know she will take care of it and have everything sent to me. Later on, I will take all these presences out of a large cardboard box and I will add them to my old presences of Présence Africaine in my office at the university. And when winter comes to Bloomington, and when it snows and it is icy, and it is so very much America, I know that I will turn to my Césaire, my Damas, my Sassine, my Mudimbe, and to the newcomers whom I have barely begun to read. Then I will once again feel that human warmth with which Présence Africaine, 25 bis, rue des Ecoles, has overwhelmed me for so many years.

Analysts

twenty-one

Manthia Diawara

MUDIMBE: You are young, belong to the postindependence generation. Is négritude a bad word for you?

DIAWARA: Not necessarily. One must put négritude in a historical context. The concept was useful in the pre-independence era as a modernist movement similar to Surrealism and Existentialism. As such, négritude empowered its founders and enabled them in an undeniable manner to construct African spaces for culture, political independence, and other social organizations. Thus there are some correlations between the word "négritude" and the lived experiences of people in Africa, the West Indies, and Europe. Négritude also participated in the movement to relativize such concepts as realism, civilization, science, and history. One can even go so far as to say that négritude constructed an African identity by inversing the meaning of such words as "nègre," "Black," "femme noire," "Africa," "émotion" at the expense of their counterparts in Europe: White man as superior being , the color white as symbol of truth, Europe as birthplace of history and civilization, science and reason as the most superior qualities in the human being.

As a young scholar of the postindependence generation, I see two contradicting points in négritude's articulation of what Senghor calls "la

382

somme totale des valeurs nègres." In defining the Black identity, the négritude poets found themselves forced to renounce science and materialism which they saw as belonging to Europe. In many ways, Jean-Paul Sartre, Frantz Fanon, Cheikh Anta Diop, and yourself all have in common, in your very different assessments of négritude, a dissatisfaction with a notion of Africa outside of the scientific revolution. In the face of the materialist imperative, Sartre suggests a proletarian phase as the necessary step after négritude; Fanon introduces the concept of a revolutionary national culture; Diop inserts a notion of science moving from place to place, putting Africa at the origin; and you yourself call for an African regime of science which takes into account the sociocultural phenomenon in Africa.

In contradiction to the notion of Africa as the opposite of Europe, Africa as the primitive sister of Europe, the latter being able to teach the former its forgotten values, the négritude poets simultaneously posit a notion of African identity which is no longer defined by binary oppositions between Europe and Africa, civilized and primitive, religious and idolatrous. This contradiction is sustained by the movement of relativism which was practiced at that time by anthropologists, poets, philosophers, and linguists. Through a scientific formulation of the notion of *difference*, it was possible to describe Africans without referring to them as societies outside of history and without culture. It was in this sense that historians such as Joseph Ki-Zerbo, Djibril Tamsir Niane, and Théophile Obenga wrote books on African history; philosophers such as Hountondji and yourself put into play the mode of existence of an African philosophy, and creative writers such as Seydou Badian, Mongo Beti, and Sembène Ousmane challenged the Senghorism (the cultural marriage between African and Europe, the primitive and the civilized) and the view of Africa as a romantic kingdom of the first blacksmith and the first mother (*L'enfant noir*), and began to contextualize the clash between tradition and modernity in the different Francophone regions. Of course, the relativism was most enabling to *Présence Africaine* which could not have survived without it.

As a scholar emerging from the Francophone tradition, I do not see négritude as a bad word in the same manner that it was seen by Wole Soyinka and Ezekiel Mphahlele. I see négritude as a movement from which I came. To me, négritude is the first modernist movement of consciousness in the former French colonies. People of my generation, following the lead of Sembene Ousmane, simply revise or rewrite négritude. We no longer believe, like Senghor for example, that *Francité* is the best mode of expression of African values. In fact, we find it necessary, sometimes, to violate the French grammar in order to express our Africanity. We are also careful to make our definition of African discourse as tight as possible in order to remove from it the French *ratio* that we find so undermining in the Senghorian négritude. The important thing for us is to make our discourse reflect our socioeconomic realities. We criticize négritude, therefore, for marginalizing the majority of our populations, and for not basing its theories on economic, cultural, and social realities in Africa. Négritude was too philosophical and had too little material basis.

M: How do you feel about all this project of promoting African difference? Did it help you to be a more balanced person compared, say, to your grandfather?

D: I have no doubt that the concept of difference, when used self-consciously, is more enabling than universalizing concepts of the world. Michel Foucault says that "there is a certain position of the Western *ratio* that was constituted in its history and provides a foundation for the relation it can have with all other societies, even with the society in which it historically appeared" (*The Order of Things*, 377). From this, it is easy to see the danger of accepting as universal human values the ideas that are specific to European history and culture. We all know, for example, that the Senghorian theory of assimilation rests on a universal view of the world with France in the center. We no longer believe in a theory of universalism that posits the African as the imperfect model of the European.

The concept of difference, on the other hand, seeks to undo hierarchies and create the possibilities for cultures and nations that are diverse in origin, customs, religion, and race to work together. The notion of difference is opposed to imperialist and colonialist structures created by universalist views of the world. The universalist discourse, whether it comes under a marxist, religious, or assimilationist guise, leaves unsaid contradictions between cultures and within societies. We must promote African difference within a condition of relativized desires (sexual, political, and religious) without making repression the norm.

My grandfather was conquered by two opposing but universalizing discourses: Islam and French colonialism. At home he lived by the totalizing worldview of Islam which determined his relation to nonbelievers, women, men, and animals. Outside, in the juridical, political, and economic world, he had to submit to French rules and norms. It was in this sense that one day, when he refused to pay taxes to the colonial administration, the commandant punished him by taking my father away from him and sending him to the colonial school. For the totalizing worldview of the commandant, this was not only to humiliate my grandfather and set an example to other rebels in the village but also to "civilize" my father. For my grandfather, the beginning of the colonial school meant the loss of my father to the devil. My father went on to become a grafter in mango fields before changing professions after Independence. He remained a Moslem all his life.

My values are more complex. I started school after the independence of Guinea when most schoolteachers have been exposed to the influence of Fanon, Sékou Touré, Richard Wright, and other "rebels." We were also seduced by the eloquence of Sartre and Mao, popular music, and American "B" movies. We grew up listening to James Brown singing "Say it Loud, I'm Black and Proud." Our role models were not only from French films and popular music, we also admired Malcolm X, the Black Panthers, Mohamed Ali, Otis Redding, Sékou Touré, Patrice Lumumba, Kwame Nkrumah, and Sembène Ousmane. Unlike my grandfather, I am able to see beauty and sense in the contradictory formative forces in my life such as Islam, the Fanonian notion of national culture, Western "high" culture, popular culture, and the Black diaspora.

M: Theoretically, how do you evaluate Présence Africaine?

D: For a long time Présence Africaine has been the African discursive space in the Francophone world. Other Paris-based publication houses such as Le Seuil published African authors, but Présence was until recently the dominant space for African voices. The Présence books were defined largely by their commitment to African values, national culture, and the diaspora. Présence's attempt to define its space by adhering to these principles led it to exclude counterhegemonic texts; texts that either attacked a specific African government or exposed a repressive organ of African tradition.

Since 1969, with the creation of the Agence de Coopération Culturelle et Technique (ACCT), several smaller presses have emerged, competing with Présence for funds. One has only to look at the success of such books as *Le devoir de violence* by Yambo Ouologuem and *Les soleils des indépendances* by Ahmadou Kourouma to see that good African texts do not have to be celebratory. The present African conditions require that certain practices be put into question and their agents named. Well-established publication houses like Plon and Le Seuil, and new ones like Karthala, L'Harmattan, Silex, and Jeune Afrique have understood this, and have quickly published books that attack Ahidjo's Cameroon, Mobutu's Zaire, Boigny's Ivory Coast, and Touré's Guinea. Présence is also losing some market to Africa-based publication houses like Les Nouvelles Editions Africaines (NEA), CEDA (an affiliate of Hatier), and Les Editions Clé.

The biggest contradiction facing Présence—in this sense it is not unlike many serious publication houses in France—is its attempt to be both a commercial and a nonprofit organization. As a nonprofit branch of the Maison de Société Africaine which caters to the funds of the ACCT and other Francophone organizations, Présence can ill afford to publish books that attack African governments and traditions. As a commercial organ, it needs to be bold and take risks.

M: Personally, do you not think that such concepts as "otherness," "identity," "race" are conceptual traps? I mean, in the way they have been used by the négritude ideology and Présence Africaine?

D: Given that the négritude movement was created in France with French people as its primary audience, the poets had to use French discursive spaces (ethnology, literary canons, Marxism, and Christianity) to speak about Blackness. Now, since Michèle Duchet's *Anthropologie aux siècles des lumières*, and Foucault's *Les mots et les choses*, it has become well-known that the Western ethnologist only sees Europe even as his gaze is turned toward Africa. Thus, from the anthropology of Buffon to that of Leo Frobenius, the Africa that Western discourse knows is the opposite of Europe: either monstrous or primitive. The fact that relativists such as Frobenius, Marcel Griaule, and Lévi-Strauss spent much time discovering other cultures and civilizations had more to do with the contestation of the theories of Enlightenment than with the "real" contours of Africa. The speech of the "Other" was only retained if it could be used in the war of opposing paradigms in Europe. The identity that was imposed on Africans was either one of people outside of history, or of people with exotic cultures.

Both négritude and Présence Africaine were trapped in these essentialist notions of "otherness," "identity," and "race." To refute the Manichean construction of Africa by the theories of En-

lightenment, Présence was used by relativists (White and Black) as
a space to insist on an inalienable African identity, a Black way of
being. Ironically, such négritude categories that sees the Black
as warm, rhythmic, musical, and emotional come from a well-
established source in literature existent since the Enlightenment,
and rethematized in the nineteenth century by the archracist
Gobineau. As I have tried to show in my response to your second
question, it is clear that relativizing values and desires were necessary to move beyond a Eurocentric view of the world. But the
way in which négritude used the concepts of identity and race was
equally totalizing and ethnocentrist. For example, categories such
as African culture and African identity leave unsaid the diversity
of cultures, the relativity of desires and identities in the different
African countries.

M: How do you see the future of Présence Africaine vis-à-vis the
economy of African studies?

D: African studies, today, is a terrain of contestation of such disciplines as anthropology and history. Researchers are more interested in exposing the way in which nondiscursive institution such
as imperialism, and (neo)colonialism determine the discourse of
social scientists and humanists. The totalitarian African regimes
have also become the target of much criticism. Furthermore, we
are at the end of innocence and exoticism in Africa. Many revolutions have failed, and the concept of the hero has died. We are left
with ambivalent readings of Nkrumah, Sékou Touré, Nyerere, Nas-
ser, Sankara, Amin Dada, and others. The urgent issues are no
longer political independence for the African nations. We must
deal with the repression of Africans by Africans in the same way
that we fight Western racism, imperialism, and (neo)colonialism.
The most important debates in African studies today concern
feminism and the need for an economic base which reflects the
social and cultural conditions in Africa. Governments should be
held accountable for such disasters as famine and epidemic disease.

Présence Africaine should accommodate these new areas of research. There should be more space for radical feminism that puts
into question the subjugation of women. There should also be
space to criticize the failure of African governments. In addition to
the books and the journal that Présence publishes, maybe it should
create journals specializing in these issues. Présence is already doing a good work celebrating Black voices in Africa, Latin America,
the United States, and the West Indies. It has also assumed a lead-

ership role in disseminating ideas of such new philosophers as Houtondji, Towa, and yourself. The time has now come to publish works that dare to attack African governments and traditions.

Lilyan Kesteloot

MUDIMBE: *Présence Africaine* began forty years ago. It has been about twenty-five years since your doctoral dissertation made né- gritude and *Présence* famous. What do you presently think of the two events?

KESTELOOT: What you say is true enough, and I am grateful to you for so simply recognizing the merits of my doctoral dissertation. Its passages and even its structures have been cited too frequently since, without any indication of their source, even to the point where today it is deemed necessary to mention it only when dis- puting it (for example, Mateso). But when they describe the famous itinerary—Negro Renaissance, *Légitime Défense, L'Etudiant Noir, Présence Africaine,* and the advent of négritude throughout these stages—rare are the intellectuals who mention that this history was established in 1961, by Lilyan Kesteloot, which nevertheless is based on a strict, scientific reading. Fortunately, this thesis has been translated in America, and on the matter of bibliographical references the Anglo-Saxons believe more in fairplay than does the French-speaking world.

M: If you had to do the work again, would you do it differently?

K: Having said all this, I am also perfectly aware that this work had gaps and that I could have avoided those, had I had more time and greater financial means available to me. If I were to do it again today? The tone is what would change the most, that enthusias- tic and youthful tone, linked to the period (the eve of the Inde- pendences, the conferences of Paris and Rome!), at times marked by naivete, especially in the sociological section, where I have a tendency to take all declarations of intention for acts already in force, where I never evaluate the role of illusion, of bluff—in other words, of manipulation. If I had to redo this thesis, I would also, of course, fill in the many details of which I had no knowledge until after its publication. Actually, many people have provided me with information that would have been very useful earlier. It was, there- fore, in the real sense, as much a breaking of new ground as it was a decoding, since I had to discover this itinerary as much as interpret it. Now if I had to do this investigation today, I would no longer have the help and the availability with which the Black writers provided me at that time. They were not like the ones today, famous and overwhelmed with interviews. It was the first scientific work devoted to them. People like Damas, Césaire, Fanon, Mongo Beti, and Senghor really *wanted* to help me: they gave me documentation, they gave me hours and hours of conversation, they tried to answer myriads of questions (many more than there are in the questionnaires in the book). Unfortunately, I could not afford to buy a tape recorder and could only take notes. Similarly, professors like Georges Balandier in Paris, Mr. Wauthier and Luc de Heusch in Brussels, and Marc Lagneau and Paul Vercauteren in Louvain advised me with such insight or corrected me with such patience. I don't know whether I would find this kindness and this devotion, free of charge, again today.

M: How do you evaluate the field of African literature today?

K: The field of African literature is in constant expansion, so much so that we are today witnessing multiple tendencies to a fragmentation of the literature, notably (and oddly) with the professors practicing in France. You are aware of the debate on national literatures. We could no longer speak of African literature, much less of a Black African one, for there are the American Blacks and the French-speaking and English-speaking Africans, who apparently no longer have anything in common. Better yet: supposedly, we cannot even speak of Francophone African literature any longer, because the Cameroonians, the Ivorians, the Congolese, the Senegalese would speak such different (French) languages that they can only be understood and linked to the exact roots within the interior of the borders created by colonialization.

Jean Derive has elucidated all these ambiguities and the fallacies remarkably well in a article that appeared in Abidjan in a collection, a work in which professors Kotchy, Dailly, and others participated, *Littérature et méthodologie*. It must be recognized that in Dakar the teaching staff is also not yet ready to abandon the ecumenism of African literature in favor of emphasizing Senegalese literature, even if the latter is among the most profuse. What to say about poor Central-Africa, or Burkina Faso, or Niger? Parceling, cultural Balkanization—is Africa not too divided on the political level already?—and, above all, breaking up the movement of the wholeness of the Black consciousness, which was precisely what founded this literature, which made it coherent and effective.

Recuperation, the most lucid one will say. Here, then, is one of the threats to the future of African literature (and to the U.S. African Literature Association as well), for its present expansion would be annulled by the fragmentation into national literatures (which, moreover, exclude oral literatures in national African languages!). Each literary corpus would be seen, from here on, in the narrowness of its state of origin and solely in its French or English context. Alas, several of our colleagues outside of Africa have allowed themselves to be seduced by the novelty of this formula, without realizing what it contained in terms of imprecision and perniciousness for the sense of history of the Africans and for the consciousness of cultural and ideological growth of their continent.

Well, as far as the direction this African literature is presently taking, there are essentially two directions:

a) There is the realistic and critical approach (critical of present mores, of the corruption of the executives, of the diversion of the administrative and political moneys to the advantage of private interests, of the various and negative consequences on all levels of African society). This gives us the type of novel written by Ngugi or Soyinka, Sassine or Fantouré, B. Nanga or Aminata Sow Fall, Sembène Ousmane, Alpha Diarra. *Le bel immonde* belongs in this group, Mudimbe, with Kanyinda and *La Pourriture* at the other extreme in popular style! But the most exemplary narrative of this kind, it seems to me, is the very tough *The Beautiful Ones are Not Yet Born*, by the Ghanaian Ayi Kwei Armah.

b) The other direction would be the one of the more or less surrealist narrative (which is, by the way, another way of speaking about the same thing). It is the last Monenembo, *Ecailles du ciel;* it is the Fantouré of *Récit du cirque;* it is *Wirriamu* by Sassine or *Le prix de l'âme* by Moussa Konaté, or Yodi Karone with *Nègre de paille* . . . At any given moment, the sordid or agonizing situations surge toward the dream, the hallucination. You do something of this sort in your novel *L'écart,* and Ibrahima Ly takes off similarly in *Toiles d'araignée,* and of course Sony Labou Tansi in *l'anté-peuple,* his last novel having sunk down in chaos. For, naturally, it is a more intellectual, more sophisticated direction in which style plays a more active role and becomes an instrument of liberation as much as an incantation, for which more important linguistic means are needed.

Beyond these two directions of critical realism and visionary hallucination, there remain the earlier currents already set in motion during the first years of the Independences: revolutionary militantism (in the style of Dongala, Sepamla, or Gnaoule), devastating satire (in the style of Lopez or Ch. Ndao). Love or philosophical lyricism finds refuge in poetry (Tati-Loutard, Bélinga, P. Ngandu, M. Aliou, L. Sall), although there, too, the militant current is always active (Dakeyo, Makouta, Nohan, J. M. Adiaffi, Zadi, Pacéré Titinga), as well as the longing for the African soil and the African past (M. T. Tshibinda, P. Kayo, Th. Obenga, Kadima). This is nothing but a quick sketch, too hastily presented, and I will confess to you that what I have read this year with greatest enthusiasm is Soyinka's (auto)biography, *Ako, les années d'enfance*, by far the most beautiful of its kind in Africa, in my opinion.

M: And the future?

K: I am thinking of my friend Bernard Fonlon, who used to love to repeat this line of Nkrumah's: "Only the best is good for Africa." That is my deepest hope. In addition, I wish that *the writers would not lose the sense of their unity, of their solidarity, for that is what makes their strength;* beyond the languages and ethnicities (the 200 African languages), beyond the French, the English, the Portuguese, may they remain conscious of the fact that their hearts beat in the same rhythm, that of Black African civilization, that which today causes all of Africa to rise up against apartheid. For they will need to be stronger and more united still for the battles of tomorrow . . . under penalty of disappearance. Witness this article by the Cameroonian writer Kum'a Ndumbe on the death of Sankara. I ask you to publish it, for it shows to what extent the concerns of our writers remain Pan-African.

Jeune Afrique, 18 November 1987: Dr. Kum'a Ndumbe III, President of the Association Nationale des Poètes et Écrivains Camerounais (APEC), vice-president of the Association des Écrivains de l'Afrique Centrale (AEAC), Brazzaville, Congo.

African writers question themselves . . .

It is with great emotion that we have learned of the death of Thomas Sankara and his close collaborators. Our sorrow has been great for, with this death, Africa once again loses one of her most worthy, most devoted sons. Why must we, in Africa, always begin from the beginning, at the zero point? A multitude of questions preoccupy us, African writers . . .

1. Is it necessary, in Africa, always to assassinate in order to settle a basic political conflict? Must the errors, the deviations of
   the "revolutionary comrades" or the "companions in struggle"
   always be accounted for through their physical disappearance?
2. Are those who eliminated Sankara and his closest allies sure
   that they hold the key to the problems that face their country
   and our continent? Will they not, in turn, be mistaken?
3. And should it happen that they are wrong, that they are not able
   to solve the immense problems that attack their country and our
   continent, would they agree that the best solution would be
   their own physical elimination?
4. When do the African leaders think that the Africans will be mature enough to discuss, openly and publicly, the problems of
   their nations, their continent, their century, to boost the divergent tendencies of the regimes now in place or of the ruling
   class, to defend different courses bearing upon the future of the
   nation without risking the need to go into exile, to find themselves in the corner of a prison cell, to swim inertly in a river of
   blood, to be furtively buried or made to disappear without leaving a trace?

These are the questions that torment us, African writers, when
hope is assassinated under our eyes, under our skies. We are weary of
polemics and it is not our intention to contribute to them. But we are
calling for answers to these questions, so urgent for the future of Africa, of each country, of our continent. You, Burkinabe leaders, you
who have seized the reins of power, what are your answers? We will
not weep for Sankara; he has been sacrificed on the altar of a true,
African liberation. We will not weep for the writers who fell by his
side, such as Bamouni and others. We, African writers, we must not
weep any more. Africa has wept too much for her sons, her daughters,
ever since slavery and colonization. Today, we Africans, we ourselves
will orchestrate the parade of the dance of death. And though we trail
at the tail-end of the development, of the well-being of all peoples,
with adequacy, intolerance, confusion. But the African writers say
this: it is enough! Africa does not need these exterminations; Africa
needs liberty, tolerance, a spirit of initiative, allowing for the possibility of making mistakes. Africa needs generosity. The other roads have
led only to material and human misery . . . We ask of you, men of
politics, that you create the structures and the climate in which hope
may be reborn in Africa.

Fernando Lambert

MUDIMBE: You are a Canadian, you have spent many years in Africa, and you are active in research in the field of literature. Can you place your interests in relation to Présence Africaine and to ideologies of independence?

LAMBERT: My first contact with Africa goes back to 1955. Without anything being obvious, my first contract for three years was renewed until it became a period of fifteen years (that is, until 1970). Since then, several stays—some longer, some shorter—have allowed me to continue the contact and to take stock of Africa regularly with my African friends and colleagues.

From 1959 on, I knew of the existence of the journal *Présence Africaine.* I must confess that my reading of the first issues that came into my hands aroused many questions in me. I was teaching in Cameroon, where the colonial environment was shaken by major events from 1955 on. Ruben Um Nyobe was leading the resistance in the underground. *Le pauvre Christ de Bomba* by Mongo Béti (1956) had aroused reactions that I was following closely. At the time, *Présence Africaine* was speaking of African culture, of Black culture in the whole of the diaspora, of a committed literature, of African philosophy, history, geography. This was a very different discourse from the one I was hearing in the teaching environment. I was profoundly challenged, and I began to feel a bit uncomfortable with my classical French authors and my favorite Latin authors. (I was teaching French literature and Latin language and literature.)

It was in 1964 that I crossed the threshold of the 25 bis, rue des Ecoles for the first time. But I felt too ignorant of African culture to dare ask for the person in charge of the publishing house, Alioune Diop. My foray was a brief one, in fact, but I came out of it with a copy of *Nations nègres et cultures* by Cheikh Anta Diop, the 1954 edition. This trenchant work was to open the ways of thinking, of history, and of the culture of Africa for me.

From 1968 on, my relationship with Présence Africaine become a good deal more stable. I met the much lamented Alioune Diop, Madame Diop, Rabemananjara, Kala Lobe, everyone else in the house. I never missed a single issue of the journal. I closely followed the list of publications. I was interested in the activities of the Société Africaine de Culture. Présence Africaine was for me a privileged place where various discourses on Africa were organized and articulated.

Even if information was rather badly circulated in the country where I was (Cameroon), I used to follow all the political movements that came across Africa with close attention and interest. On the one hand, I was present at the attempt to make African nationalisms emerge and organize them. On the other hand, plans for regrouping the States according to the larger region of Africa were being born. Then came the Pan-Africanism of Kwame Nkrumah. All these vast political plans seemed far removed from the preoccupations of the ordinary people for whom the tomorrows of independence still made no music. Before anything else, I was a witness to the numerous disappointments that independence provoked; I was not paying much attention to the different ideologies that circulated, insofar as several of those who supported these were fairly rapidly retrieved by the system in place, as soon as it offered them an administrative position.

When I look at the past of Présence Africaine, it seems to me that it never neglected the great political debates. It had recognized as its role that of letting all the voices that came forth from Africa and the diaspora be heard, and clearly not that of deciding about the political options. Still, Présence Africaine devoted its largest space to African culture. I am indebted to it for having aroused and maintained in me an ever renewable interest in the philosophy, the religions, the arts, the literature, and the history of Africa, and for constantly having put the whole of the Black culture across the diaspora in perspective with African culture. Présence Africaine has had a basic function of animating through its journal, through the activities of the Société Africaine de Culture (SAC), through the orientations of its publishing house, all the while providing a meeting place without equal for all Black people and for all those who were looking for a different view of Africa.

M: You seem to be a happy academician. Are you really? And where is your place in the face of what seems to be, in Africa, the failure of the ideologies of difference?

L: Happiness is eminently fluctuating and fragile. The next best thing to a perpetually cloudless sky is that I can say that academic life is made up of activities that fulfill me: teaching, research, sharing of knowledge—on the one hand scientific activities, and on the other a preoccupation with an integration in the society. This double window offers everything for a full personal blooming.

The object of my study, for many years now, has been African literature. My point of departure has been African literature written in French. What held me back, in an earlier stage, were the specific conditions of that literary production. The Africans, a few political men essentially (Senghor, Dadié), especially young intellectuals (Mongo Beti, Ferdinand Oyono, Cheikh Hamidou Kane) all in the European sphere of influence, were all speaking out (and in French at that) to denounce the colonial system either through poetic writing or (on more of a massive scale) through the writing of fiction. Those were the first texts with which I came in contact. These works from the fifties sent me back to the earlier works of Hazoumé and Socé (also in French), one of whose aims it was to cast an inside look on Africa and to put certain African customs that were different from those of the Whites in context.

From the first moments of this African literary production written in French, a discourse on difference began to take place that seems to me, to this day, to be the obligatory side of the discourse on identity. Besides, I was also seeing the same phenomenon, though to a different degree, in the Québécois literature of the 1950s and 1960s. Is it because of domination, of being held in the "minority" position, that one must first place oneself in relation to the Other when one wants to define one's own identity? Both Québécois literature and African literature seemed to be going in the direction of that hypothesis. The corroboration was stronger still for the African literature, since the African writers were borrowing the language of the Other.

Given the very conditions of the surfacing of this African literature, can one speak of the failure of the ideologies of difference? It seems to me, rather, that the discourse on difference is one phase of a much vaster process. The model proposed by Edouard Glissant in his *Discours antillais* is enlightening in this regard. This model includes three motions: the going, the detour, the return. The discourse on difference, in my opinion, is located in the stage of the detour, of the passage through space, through the gaze of the Other. The failure, then, would be to stop at the apparently obligatory moment in an altogether specific process within which the production of African literature takes place.

What is perhaps more of a question is the fact that a literature that is relatively strong continues to be written in French in Africa.

M: Your field is oral literature. Since when has it really been "literature" and to what end, in your eyes?

L: The African novels that I read, those by Beti and Oyono, were the ones that referred me to oral literature. I wanted to find out what narrative experience the African writer owed to the oral tradition. I was making the hypothesis that, for the first African novelists, the model of the oral narrative was more deeply anchored, more visceral in them than was the model of the European novel they had learned at school, therefore purely acquired from books.

As I wanted to do serious work in the school of orality, I first learned one of the languages of Cameroon, Ewondo. In this way, I was giving myself access to a specific corpus that would serve me later as a terrain for verification and as a point of reference. My initial plan was aimed at gathering, transcribing, and translating oral texts. My first analytical work was of a thematic order. Little by little I came around to questions that dealt with narrative. I then became interested in the characterization of long and short narratives in Black Africa.

The literary establishment was very late in assigning a literary status to oral narratives. For several decades, following Delafosse and even Equilbecq (that is, from 1913 on), they spoke of folklore with the contemptuous connotation of "naive and popular literature." Even if Equilbecq introduced his *Contes indigènes de l'ouest-africain français* with an "Essai sur la littérature merveilleuse des noirs," what interests him in the first place is not the literary value of the tales and fables, but rather "their usefulness for the study of indigenous psychology." Nevertheless, one must credit him with having been the first to qualify the African tales as "littérature merveilleuse."

Senghor is, without a doubt, one of the first to have included the tales as being uniquely representative of Black African literature. It is enough to read his preface to the *Contes de l'ouest africain* by Roland Colin to see the African tale emerge from its place fixed in folklore and to see it make its way to recognition as true literature. Moreover, Roland Colin also spoke of "traditional Black African literature."

As far as the intervention of criticism is concerned—criticism applied first to the tales, then to the other types of oral texts—one had to wait for the 70s. It is not until then that the tale was studied for its own merits, as narrative text, as literary narrative. One may recall the works of Denise Paulme on the morphology of the African tales, the works of Amadou Hampaté Ba on the epic and on oral poetry. This change in status from folklore to oral literature is not only the case for Africa. The same phenomenon has occurred in Québec, in Acadia (on a smaller scale, undoubtedly), but there, as in Africa, there was a deeply felt need to give back their dynamism and their function as role model to the past and to the values of that past, notably the cultural values. The literary establishment came to affirm this enterprise, and we know that any intervention on its part is never innocent.

Thus, at the moment that much is being said about the renewal of literary forms, the African oral literature can inspire African authors and creators (which it has done anyway since the beginnings of the literature written in French), and it can suggest still other formal models. African theater is coming back to these models, with the Koteba, for example, and why not the novel, too?

M: How do you see the future of your field?

L: If I stick to a personal perspective, I can say that already African literature offers me the possibility of remaining very busy until my retirement and even beyond that. In a more serious vein, I remember very well all those prophets, Black and White, who were predicting the death of African literature in European languages for the 60s. Thirty years later, I manage, but with difficulty, to stay abreast of all that is published in French alone and by Africans. Despite the problems of publication, the problems of distribution, the African writers do produce.

If the production in African languages were to develop, if the writers were to create in their own language, I would find the time to pick up my Ewondo again and to learn Wolof and Bambara in order not to lose track of my favorite authors. In a more pragmatic way, I imagine that the organization of a worldwide Francophone territory (as is presently under way with the Summits held in Paris, in Québec, and in Dakar) will promote the development of cultural creation, thus including the production of African literature written in French. Still, the impact of an international French-speaking body has yet to be demonstrated. Despite everything, the future of my field of research and teaching does not yet seem to be threatened in the short or even medium term.

Since we do not lack "primary material," we can continue the work. But criticism should also be renewed. There is much left to be done in the realm of methodology. For a few years now, the studies devoted to African literature are calling upon more rigorous analytical methods. Even if they were conceived in a framework foreign to Africa, the formal methods have allowed a new reading of the African work. The effort certainly needs to be continued. Also, work should be done on developing "reading tools," methods that are more appropriate to this literature and that allow for a realization of its entire specificity.

M: Does Présence Africaine have a future and, if so, what kind?

L: Spontaneously, I would be tempted to answer: I hope so. Only because it will not happen without problems; it does not happen by itself. Présence Africaine is now forty years old. One man, Alioune Diop, has been the soul of that house, surrounded by his wife and a few faithful friends. Alioune Diop is no more. Those who remain are now of retirement age, and still they continue. It is admirable, and that must be recognized. But the publishing world is not a quiet one. The rules of competition and rivalry are pitiless. That Présence Africaine should have lived for forty years, that its journal should have maintained itself all that time while upholding a high standard of quality, that its cultural activities of international breadth—such as the festivals and the colloquia—should have taken place, is quite simply a feat in itself.

Présence Africaine still continues today, but under conditions that have not become any easier, conditions that have become even more complicated these last few years. Présence Africaine's present challenge is to reconcile its first and essential role as cultural agent, as promoter of African creativeness, of criticism, of scientific thought on Africa, and its status as a publishing house facing the demands of the business world. Can this be done without change (certainly important enough) in the style of Présence and in the manner of business management? It is an extremely delicate question, because it involves people whom I deeply love and value. But it seems to me that it should be asked, despite everything.

Présence Africaine has accumulated, over the years, a unique store that should be available at all times according to needs and that should call upon modern technical support. Moreover, Présence Africaine should keep its role as leader in its field, a field that it created and then developed in a remarkable and irreplaceable way. In the face of such extraordinary work, I can only be quite modest in my intervention and my vision of the future of Présence Africaine.

Thus, without any affectation, it seems to me that the future of Présence Africaine depends on the possibility of its finding new breath, of its adjusting to and even being ahead of the present demands and constraints of the publishing world. One of the conditions for changing the direction of this future, for mastering it, is perhaps at first the regrouping around those in charge at Présence Africaine, of all those who still believe in the essential role of the house. The enterprise needs much strength. In addition, I believe that this future is going through the very specific implication of a few African personalities, widely recognized in the cultural field and the field of African studies. In another connection, should Présence Africaine continue on its own? Should it take the leadership in a consortium of African books? The questions come easily, but it is up to those in charge at Présence Africaine to evaluate the situation, to make the decisions that they will consider the best ones for the future of the house.

What is certain for me is that on the one hand Présence Africaine must continue, and that on the other hand those who have built Présence Africaine deserve all our respect and our profound admiration.

BIBLIOGRAPHY

Beti, Mongo. *Le pauvre Christ de Bomba.* Paris: Buchet/Chastel, 1956.
Colin, Roland. *Contes de l'ouest africain.* Paris: Présence Africaine, 1955.
Diop, Cheikh Anta. *Nations nègres et cultures.* Paris: Présence Africaine, 1954.
Equilbecq, F.-V. *Contes indigènes de l'ouest-africain français.* Paris: E. Lerouge, 1913.
Glissant, Edouard. *Le discours antillais.* Paris: Editions du Seuil, 1981.

Henri Moniot

MUDIMBE: What significance does a French academic like yourself bestow upon Présence Africaine? My question refers specifically to your own field, that of African history.

MONIOT: Présence Africaine has been—intellectually and editorially—an active, open, magnetic place that spread knowledge and encouraged discussion of many aspects of the African civilizations and of the present-day situation in Africa, while offering a variety of viewpoints represented by the African writers themselves. It has vigorously upheld the notion that history and progress were not the business of the West alone. It was a kind of permanent proclamation for decentralization, and a permanent proposal for thinking of history and of humanity as coming from one of several centers:

Africa. It very simply asserted Black dignity, and, in a more problematic or magical way, the key idea of *one* Black genius, of *one*
African civilization.

In a more anecdotal manner, Présence Africaine was for me, in
the early 1960s, a group I frequently visited, quietly but happily, in
a way that was refreshing as an alternative to the academic strict-
ness and the militant rigidity of the Paris of that period.

MU: At what point exactly did Présence Africaine take the form of a
question mark for you? And is it really that?

MO: Présence Africaine has not been a question mark for me. I discovered it at the end of the 50s, already well settled in the landscape, and I accepted it as it was, without thinking of having
to question it. On the other hand, it is true that my regular contact with it had its delicate side for me and a kind of constant
ambivalence.

In one way, Présence Africaine gave me the feeling that it responded fully to one of the good causes I had chosen: to bring
history off-center, to read human history in every society and especially in the African societies, to hunt down the incredible denial of the dignity of other peoples and the incredible sense of
superiority the Westerners had assigned themselves by the invocation of History. The complicity in this was profound.

On the other hand, in many of its publications, Présence Africaine propounded a history that shocked another of my wishes,
namely for a rigorous, always lucid, scholarly history, constructed
against ideological discourse and its complacencies. Too often, I
saw the Eurocentric diagrams reappearing there, sometimes the
most outdated ones, numbed once again by history without looking at it too closely. Thus, at one and the same time I had the feeling that I was working on the same side as Présence Africaine (and
even accepting its tutelary guidance at times), and yet, that I was
working against it in the name of the historian's history. On the
immediate, practical level I did not let it bother me, since I was
obviously well aware that what, in *my* position, seemed merely an
opportunity for cultural argumentation took on a whole other
meaning and another thrust in the position of the colonized. But I
broke away from it.

Over time, I am sure, this experience has contributed to sharp-
ening my "epistemological" appreciations: to being more and more
truly interested in the way in which historical knowledge really
functions, to having a better sense of how and to what point the

historian's discipline—which does not live in the academic regions—is bound not only to a small battery of methodological or problematic requirements but to figures of historical discourse within which the conditions of production and reception of historical studies form an integral part of that which must be appreciated. This Présence Africaine had not expected to teach to such an extent nor in such a format—and it was far from being the only one to teach me this. But it did do so.

MU: Your research as well as your teaching would have taken shape with or without Présence Africaine, would they not?

MO: Yes, undoubtedly. The question is a bit unrealistic: there were many earlier incentives for my choices, and toward 1958–1959, with Présence Africaine already well established, how could I imagine what the context I did find would have been without it? Once I had finished my classical studies of history, the most important and the most decisive of my learnings came from Georges Balandier and Paul Mercier, who were friends of Présence Africaine from its very beginnings and who, at the same time, obviously had an outstanding intellectual influence of their own (I must add the name of André Leroi-Gourhan, who was not an "Africanist").

Speaking more globally, my interest in constructing an African history came from being trained as a historian, where (to put it briefly) the *Annales* and the sixth section of the Ecole des Hautes Etudes led me to make the judgment that the vacuum that characterized the history of the other continents was at once peculiar and intellectually scandalous, and it was not only possible but exciting to attempt to fill that emptiness. Présence Africaine had nothing to do with it at this particular point. But—still speaking intellectually—it would have been quite wrong to fill this vacuum, to give Africa's past a voice, without listening to the Africans of today, for it is not by pure intuition that problematics are constructed. In this regard, Présence Africaine arrived in the nick of time, by mobilizing this past through activism in an accessible way, not too incompatible for the French public.

MU: My plan is not to celebrate Présence Africaine unconditionally but to think of its weaknesses, its limitations, and, if I could, to restate its strengths. What is your feeling on this subject? Is there only strength?

MO: I don't feel that I am in a position to evaluate the weaknesses, the strengths, or the limitations of Présence Africaine. An African would be better equipped to do so, or an author of an in-depth analysis of the political and intellectual evolution of the years 1950–1990. Otherwise, one can comment endlessly upon the advantages, the disadvantages, and the implications of a choice that is more cultural than political, more humanist and open (thus varied) than rigorous and dogmatic. If I might bring up one point, gingerly, I would raise this one: Is there really *one* Black culture, *one* Black genius, *one* Black African situation, or is there diversity and expansion? In that case, the distinguishing train constructed from this ideology must have paid dearly, off and on, in contradictions, in certain forms of powerlessness when in contact with the realities. But this ideology is not constructed in isolation. And it is so long ago that it was constructed—an inheritance of the thinking of the "great discoveries," of the trade, of the polemics against the trade, of the relationship with nineteenth century Black America, of the generalized colonization of the continent, of the common reaction against servitude—that inevitably it has been distanced from reality since then.

MU: In your honest opinion, has the ideological undertaking of Présence Africaine in the realm of history failed or succeeded? And, in any case, how do you explain its credibility at the onset and its later significance?

MO: How can one judge? Présence Africaine has occupied a place that it was very useful to hold—in the moral transition between colonial times and those of the independences, between Western paternalism and a more worldwide fraternalism—for the launching of African history before its becoming academically standardized and managed. Présence Africaine did this in French, yet the colonial discourse and the universalist French discourse gave it a helping hand and required answers, primarily with a humanist Christian emphasis, yet it also provided a wide-open shore that remained free from the theoretical rigidity of political militantism.

MU: And what impact do you see on Africa's destiny? Toward what future, in your opinion?

MO: I feel incapable of forecasting the future. I don't know whether what I am going to say answers this question, or whether it adds to the answers of the preceding questions. From my very limited and very personal viewpoint as a European and a historian, Présence Africaine, as I knew it around 1960, seems to me to be able to anticipate something that we need in the near future, and to have made it (mutatis mutandis) into a kind of (partial and approximate) dress rehearsal. Well then, two more remarks that are connected:

the former academic simplicities, the dogmatic freedoms of what preceded yesterday, yesterday's argumentative nonsense of the dominant ideology, have all been very much weakened by the present intellectual situation. This situation deprives the social sciences of the optimism, the sense of triumph, and the acquired respect that for a long time supported their rapid progress; and it provokes them not into withdrawing but rather very simply into relying better upon what they truly are. This situation suggests a great reevaluation, at a new cost, of our scholarship and its risks (risks of knowledge, of legitimacies, of identities). To write and to present history calls for a conscious and renewed judgment of what is ventured and what is accomplished. Présence Africaine did not have this truly scholarly and epistemological ambition. But it offered, in an ideologically more difficult time, one more certain of itself, a place for diversification, for decentralization—a style more generally accepted today.

History—I mean the discipline of history—has since responded to the challenge of making space for the history of "others": history today touches everyone and is not reserved for the West alone (if we now have a *Cambridge History of Africa* in six volumes, that is a clear sign in the corporate body of history.) But it will now have to rise to another challenge: to maintain and to cultivate its critical exigencies and its rigorous processes, to break with the uniformity of one kind of Western historical "modern" discourse, one which has been very deeply associated with its development but is not inevitably and eternally linked to it. There will come a time for a plurality of historical discourses, nourished by other cultural inspirations—even if the implications of that diversification are still so foreign to us that we have trouble imagining them. It is the very vitality of multiple cultural formulations in the world that will allow the ripening of these new historical writings. From this point of view, therefore, the need for an African cultural voice on a larger scale still exists.

part six
Conclusions

The Politics of "Othering": A Discussion

THE WORD DELIVERED: Essay for a Critical Testimony

Marc Rombaut

In Limine

How does one become a writer? What is that incites a person to shed light on the word which is and makes our mystery? With what legitimacy does our place in the abyss claim kinship with the letter? From what place and why do we write? And, first of all, does writing not issue forth from the desire to sublimate reality? In another connection, does this desire not arise as much from the artistic posture as from the inner necessity to live the totality of the test of surpassing what the demand implies? If we allow ourselves to be directed by writing, we do so in order to complete an offering and a deliverance.

As the Black African writers have taught us, we must dance our word, for in human speech, as in dance, lies an offering. To speak and to write is also to offer oneself to the other; it is to be reborn together. "Every true word is resurrectional," writes Valère Novrina.

Our plan here is to remove a few misunderstandings and to call for a listening to the other as other, to the other who is in each of us. Herein poetry shows us the truth and the mystery.

twenty-two

Human beings are alone and direct their daily destiny through an effort that is amply justified by the grandeur of the adventure of our species, the wonder of the universe and of life, the satisfaction of the untarnished heart and the respect for natural imperatives.

Jacques Stephen Alexis

"What endures is the work of poets," Hölderlin said. Thus we have infinity, eternity, mystery, transcendence on the one hand, and the world of things—that is to say, death—on the other hand. As Bossuet said: "All that is measurable perishes." Poetry is the antithesis of metaphysics, and is carried out much like a crossing from writing, confronted, to the infinite and to duration—Homer, Virgil, Dante, Rimbaud, Proust—whose works, at once fundamental and fracturing, recreate time and space in opposition to a finite world.

In other words, and in a different political-historical context, in his own poetic way, Franz Kafka will say from and within his unique solitude, "that to write is to make a leap beyond the rank of the assassins."[1] This means, then, to leave death and the society of the friends in crime behind. It is precisely modern poetry that introjects, through biographical bias, the dismissal and the refusal of the "human, all too human" trade.[2] What bears witness to this violence of the world are the biographical calamities suffered by a number of modern poets such as Hölderlin, Baudelaire, Rimbaud, Nerval, Poe, Lautréamont, Artaud, and Mayakovsky.

The world hardly seems to care for living poets. For the world is on the side of death and not of love, which is a co-birthing. And very quickly we come to see and hear in all great poetry a meditation on the misery of truth.

The Encounter with the Other

At the edge of this "disenchantment with the world,"[3] the dense murmur from Africa and the African diaspora stood outlined against the horizon of the 1960s, on the march toward the reconquest of the self, which poets, stripping everything clean, highlighted with thrusts of extraordinary lyricism and salvos prophesying revolt. Thus, two telluric powers of absolute beauty and truth telescoped and spread through us a shock wave from which we were never to recover. We were on the verge of our adolescence when this simultaneous discovery both of the biographical tragedy of Western poets and of the tragedy of the cultural genocide of Africa took place. Because of this shock we began to awaken to ourselves, and at first we tried to pro-

---

1. Franz Kafka, *Journal*, in *Oeuvres Complètes*, vol. 3, *Collection de la Pléiade* (Paris: Editions Gallimard, 1984).

2. Friedrich Nietzsche, *Humain trop humain et fragments posthumes*, vol. 3, *Oeuvres philosophiques complètes* (Paris: Editions Gallimard, 1988).

3. Marcel Gauchet, *Le désenchantement du monde* (Paris: Editions Gallimard, 1985).

claim all (or almost all) its effects: the reality and its truths, the dreams and our fantasies, the misery (in every meaning of the word) of the Black people, and our own deficiencies in being.

From the beginning, we were swallowed up inside innumerable misunderstandings. Out of a settling of the account with ourselves and our own culture we created a dance of close support against the colonial order of the world. We will need long years of true-false struggles in order to grasp the total grandeur that can be gained each day against oneself, and to garner (despite the world's malevolence) the quivering impatiences of life, to hear the quaking of time. Black African writer-poets—Senghor, Césaire, Damas, David Diop, Brière—each one in his own poetic language gave back to us, under harmonies, modes, and rhythms that were other, the out-of-tune-with-the-world voices of Hölderlin or Artaud, the revolutionary resurgencies of Rimbaud, the splendid and dreadful incantations of Baudelaire, to be heard once again. Thus, the négritude poets restored to us the taste of our language as trodden by the poets. A vocation born from a provocation to the French (or the English) language, we became involved by way of the négritude poets in the art of writing, whose pitiless law meant to us that to write is to name the world and humankind from within the language. But this emergence of the Other in our imaginary settled itself upon our biographical history, where the data took pleasure in signaling each other to the point of overflow and of very rapidly causing a confusion of the values and the symbols involved.

Présence Africaine, Third World-ism and Black Orpheuses

The year 1960 consecrates African independences. The Algerian War was bringing our revolt and the passion for life of our twenties into focus. The crisis of Western thought expressed itself in terms of ideological debates. The so-called consumer society had not yet been declared nor sociologically coded, and Mao Tse-tung, not yet deified, was turning up on the red horizon.

Marxists, Existentialists, Christians on the left were seeking to channel the revolutionary dreams and the lost opportunities for living of a youth short of an ideal. But the progressive slogans were breaking up like leakages of gas, and the "alarm signals," so dear to Mayakovsky, resounded in other latitudes. The "Black continent" illuminated us with new words uttered by Black men who were "upright and free."[4] From the former colonies that had become un-

4. Aimé Césaire, *Cahier d'un retour au pays natal* (Paris: Présence Africaine, 1956).

derdeveloped nations, then nations under development before defining themselves as "young nations," a new outcry arose that suddenly lit up the grayness of our armchair polemics. "The wretched of the earth"[5] (whom Frantz Fanon threw in our face) became for a certain number among us voices of identification, of projection, and of transference from our directionless rebellion. Our ideology was to be prematurely "Third-World-ist." In the beginning there was Jean-Paul Sartre, who, in a preface to Fanon's work, provided his moral and intellectual guarantee for this discourse on the "other," for this "other speech," and this was so extraordinary that we were obliged to go by way of this already established mediation. For again it was Sartre, Sartre the bastard, assuming and insisting on his bastardy, who initiated us into the new songs of the Black Orpheuses. Négritude pounced upon us just as Existentialism seized us in our very being. Thus, "the-individual-in-the-Black-world" seemed to us from the onset to be the subject of our "Passion," transcending our own sense of inadequacy. When we read the remarks by Sartre on the Negro in "Black Orpheus"[6]—"Thus he is held to authenticity. Insulted, enslaved, he redresses himself; he accepts the word "Negro" which is hurled at him as stone, and he asserts himself, in pride, as a black in the face of the white"—we understood them well beyond their significance, by reinterpreting them as closely as possible to our own problematics. Denied, rejected, acculturated, we were able to experience ourselves in all subjectivity by the touchstone of Sartrean négritude as other and different and fully proud thereof. When, in 1963, the exegetic and historic work of Lilyan Kesteloot[7] appeared, the event (and it was as such that the work was received and honored) revealed to us not only the négritude writers—Senghor, Césaire, Damas—in their essence and their condition as writers first of all but also the history of Africa, of the Black diaspora as well as the sources of a culture about whose foundation we knew nothing at all. In a single book we were given the revelation of "the Black world," whose artistic and literary expressions, political manifestations, and cultural

5. Frantz Fanon, *Les damnés de la terre* (Paris: Editions Maspéro, 1961).

6. Jean-Paul Sartre, "Orphée noir," preface in *Anthologie de la nouvelle poésie nègre et malgache de langue française,* by L. S. Senghor (Paris: Presses Universitaires de France, 1948; reissued 1969).

7. Lilyan Kesteloot, *Les écrivains noirs de langue française: Naissance d'une littérature* (Brussels: Editions de l'Institut de Sociologie de l'Université Libre de Bruxelles, 1963).

witnesses were brought by the journal *Présence Africaine*. When we would read these words of Damas—"Arising out of the culture, my hatred grows heavier"[8]—we were obsessed by their full savor and the strength of the denial of a society and its values.

Black voices spoke within us, we spoke within them, as if the "miraculous weaponry"[9] extolled by the Black poets committed us to undreamt-of excesses. Via the journal *Présence Africaine*, the echoes of the Conferences of Rome (1956) and of Paris (1959) reached us belatedly. Conferences where the Poet, the Politician and the Man of Culture had expressed themselves on behalf of their race and their peoples, and had all enjoyed the same status of legitimacy. There we, the children banished by Plato, finally found the sounds of our own liberation and of our legitimacy. With our sensitivity revitalized at the sources of négritude, and after the enchantment of the exotic and with our biographical peculiarities accounted for, we were able at last to be in harmony with works born from Black African cultural values, works that revealed themselves to be by writers (in the first and universal sense of the word) for whom every language is foreign and who are, essentially, devoted to creating and inventing forms of language derived from reality. We found ourselves again, as if within ourselves, in certain distressing verselines of Aimé Césaire's, where "cowardice rediscovered" under "the wide smile of complicity" made us question ourselves beyond communal and racial relationships.

With the sounds of *kora* and *balafon* (new to our ears), Senghor initiated us into the realities (magical, symbolic, sensitive) of the Black word. "The Negro, in particular," he said, "comes from a world where word spontaneously becomes rhythm as soon as man is moved, brought back to himself, to his authenticity. Yes, word becomes poem."[10] When Damas advised the Negroes to "invade Senegal,"[11] we heard how urgent it was that our ridiculed values be reappropriated, values that had been distorted by those whose duty and responsibility it was to see to their full blooming. But there was more: we became conscious of our own identities as writers and we published these

8. Léon Gontran Damas, *Pigments* (Paris: Editions G. L. M., 1937; reissued Paris: Présence Africaine, 1962).

9. Aimé Césaire, *Les armes miraculeuses* (Paris: Editions Gallimard, 1946; reissued Paris: Poésie-Gallimard, 1970).

10. Lépold Sédar Senghor, postscript to *Ethiopiques* (Paris: Editions du Seuil, 1956).

11. Damas, poem "Et caetera," in Damas, *Pigments* (Paris: Guy Levis Mano, 1937; reprinted in 1962).

writings immediately, from our very first moments of the contact with the works of the négritude poets, with the echo and the expansion given them by *Présence Africaine,* with the universal dimension their writings carried, and of their battle for the dignity of man. Our words born somewhere out of those of the négritude writers.

Postnégritude

Sartre brought us to the discovery of the négritude writers through "Black Orpheus," his preface to L. S. Senghor's *Anthologie,* [12] the founding work of négritude as far as the expression of the combined cultural values of the Black world was concerned. Today, the names and the works of Senghor, Césaire, Damas, David Diop, Birago Diop, Brière, and the actions of Alioune Diop are points of reference; for us, at the age of twenty, they were fascinating, as strange, and as literally revolutionary as were those of Artaud, Breton, or Michaux. As we were living the breakdown of the values of civilization of the Western world—according to the formula so dear to Malraux—from the inside, we tasted of the other and "spiritual nourishment," asserting négritude values that the poets, the writers, and politicians brought us; and we did so with the eagerness of our youth, breaking with family and society (in those days we were still enamored of Gide's famous "families, I hate you"). We had placed ourselves under the aegis of *Présence Africaine.* Long before the condemnation of the Gulag reminded the materialistic West that "man does not live by bread alone," [13] African and her diaspora guided us into the channels of renewing ethical openness and of investing the poetic values of transcendence (doing so under the sign of négritude) by way of its poets and *Présence Africaine,* its mouthpiece. To stretch a point, we dared to say that the négritude poets authorized us to sow anew the words of Dante, Hölderlin, Rimbaud—and to hear in the language of those like Claudel, Jouve, and Char the quakings of time to infinity from the finite world. Here came the sons who killed the fathers. That is the—human—law. Thus the followers of négritude instituted the procession of négritude. They were not able to accept certain historical limitations, nor could they be satisfied with certain aesthetic and ethical contingencies, such as the "emotion is Negro" kind, or above all the "moment of negativity" so dear to Jean-Paul Sartre. It continued to the point where the very concept of négritude burst

12. Sartre, in Senghor, [1948] 1969.
13. Vladimir Doudintsev, *L'homme ne vit pas seulement de pain* (Paris: Editions Julliard, 1957).

apart—into melanism,[14] authenticity, Africanism, etc.—*Les soleils des indépendances*[15] shed their rays at a slant. The testing of the liberation of peoples—and thus of languages—stood up against the blows of misunderstandings, disillusions, and dreams destroyed. An entire, watchful generation of African writers saw itself led astray in its mythical (indeed, mystical) passion for Africa and experienced itself in the disenchantments of the world in general, in the breakdown of the social consensus in particular, in the conflicts between the modern and the traditional—and suddenly found itself to be a subject of history. Somewhere, the postnégritude generation carried problematics in its heart of hearts that on certain levels were related to those we Western writers and intellectuals were experiencing ourselves. And then we would encounter writers who, before placing themselves conceptually in relation to négritude and other melanisms, would often question themselves in anguish and despair precisely about the legitimacy of their status as writers. Therein, too, they joined somewhere with the fragility of the being-a-writer-in-the-world, and they experienced themselves as creators within loneliness and doubt. The books that, from then on, accompanied our real or imaginary travels had titles such as *L'aventure ambiguë, Entre les eaux, Epitomé, Mascareignes, Dramouss, Le devoir de violence, Le pauvre Christ de Bomba, Racines Congolaises, Les bouts de bois de Dieu, Soundjata, Réveil dans un nid de flammes, Béatrice du Congo, La mort de Chaka, L'exil d'Albouri*, and so forth. As for their authors, their names became familiar to us; they became accessories in fact or in imagination in the crossover of signals. We are talking about Cheikh Hamidou Kane, V. Y. Mudimbe, Tchicaya U'Tamsi, Edouard Maunick, Camara Laye, Yambo Ouologuem, Mongo Beti, J. B. Tati-Loutard, Sembène Ousmane, Djibril Tamsir Niane, Matala Mukadi, Bernard Dadié, Seydou Badian, Cheikh Ndao, Davertige (and today also Sony Labou Tamsi, Williams Sassine, Thierno Monenembo, and Aminata Sow Fall). Thus, before we knew her in reality, Africa appeared to us in the form of a fabulous and unlimited library. To these names and these titles, in recognition of an immeasurable debt, we want to add those of the historians (Cheikh Anta Diop, Ki-Zerbo), of the sociologists and political economists (S. Anozie, J. Nyerere, J. Kenyatta, N'Krumah, Thomas Kanza), of the translators and inter-

14. Stanislas Adotevi, *Négritude et négrologues* (Paris: Union Générale d'Editions, 1972).

15. Ahmadou Kourouma, *Les soleils des indépendances* (Paris: Editions du Seuil, 1970).

preters of the traditional oral literature (Amadou Hampaté Ba, Alfa
Ibrahima Sow), of the musicologists (Francis Bebey), as well as of the
great writers of English-speaking Africa (Chinua Achebe, J. P. Clark,
and Wole Soyinka)—a list of authors and works that is by no means
exhaustive and indicates our journey through African literature and
thought.

As for the action that would be brought against Négritude—and to
which we will attest as an official witness—it came forth out of historical necessity, to put it succinctly. Passion often engenders murder,
even symbolically. The new generations had to break with the myth
of négritude in order to invent themselves and to endow themselves
with a specific identity and legitimacy. In doing so, they came up
against the new, often violent realities of an Africa that was not at all
mythical but epic in her very real tragedy. The Independences were
not the single voice of a unanimous choir of new men but the confrontation of contradictory interests, of the antagonisms of peoples
and powers that poured out of "immediate history"[16] full of disillusionment. And to find oneself a writer, involved in the uproar of
events, solitary, and responsible for one's people, subjects of History's
nightmare! Therein, too, they broke away from the Negro myth—a
bit unanimous in how we had perceived their elders—by first assuming a writer's identity. In their turn, they could now make theirs the
words of James Joyce (I quote from memory): "History is a nightmare
from which I try to extract myself." Subject to a new and pitiless
individuality, they endowed themselves with a different conscience
whose requirements were expressed in terms of personal responsibilities, often in the trials and tribulations of exile or confinement.

The double cultural belonging, the deviation from one's native
tongue to the foreign tongue, the exile (interior or exterior), the negation of one's person by the members of one's race, the break with
the sociocultural, traditional structures: all of these seize the Black
African author in all his truth and his identity as writer. The author's
biography becomes the material of the work, and a people's tragedy is
condensed into the tension of the writing as it collides with the im-
passable wall of the real. Thus, the postnégritude writer goes beyond
the plan of his "fathers" and stands out against the Other and against
himself in his unique strangeness of "being-in-the-world." "I is an
Other," said Rimbaud, and where it concerns the postnégritude

16. Benoît Verhaegen, *Introduction à l'histoire immédiate* (Gembloux: Duculot,
1974).

writer, his "I" is written outside of the parental community, in the positively stated difference and the singularity of his name. From now on, he is a subject of History and of the letter of his name.

Thus, all actions brought against négritude in the name of Negrism, Melanism, and other Africanisms seem to us displaced or at least secondary, in the face of the demands of the work that is written and still inscribed to fit on the edge of sociability. The oeuvre is offered to be seen, heard, and read to the extent of the desire that engenders it. And to desire is a destiny for humankind.

In Fine

All great work, all great literature questions Evil, Evil ensconced in man, Evil at work in the world since time began. "Darkness reigns over the abyss," wrote the African bishop of Hippo, Saint Augustine, at the time of the barbarian invasions that destroyed the Roman Empire.

Barbarism, in our technocratic and scientist century, is expressed in terms of genocides (Armenians, Jews, Khmers), of population massacres (particularly in the Third World), of the violation of the Human Rights, of famines caused by man, and of the reification of man.

If "writing is an act of love" as Jean Cocteau said it was, how can one not name the Evil that murders love, without lying to oneself and others? Our contemporary literature taps all the ingredients of an immeasurable tragedy, which is that of man losing his human qualities. Only in the truth of the human is there love. But if the human has absented himself or herself, where and to whom does one address an act of love? The Black African writers of today bring forth, from within the language, metamorphoses of the verb (and the verb is action, movement, life) in their quest for the human and the desire to love. This movement toward the Other established them in a literary outpouring from which a language of desire is written and invented. All language is foreign to writers; and they stand out at first as pioneers in unknown territory. For where would be the hope of the world if the Black African writers did not first of all bear witness (as they now do) to this tireless quest for the truth of humankind and the world, to this demand for love that "moves the sun and the other stars" (in Dante's words) without which nothing in this finite world would make sense? And if our voice took shape from the breath of the Black word, it was in this action of the being seeking itself and wanting to be within the desire of the world that goes beyond the world.

A QUESTION OF TASTE

Roberta Ann Dunbar

The foundation of African studies in the United States was in some respects analagous to the emergence of cubism in Europe. Just as African sculpture in the *salles* of Paris provided the springboard for the cubists' liberation from the conventions of Realism, so did the decolonization of Africa enable historians coming of age between 1945 and 1965 in the United States—perhaps more than other social scientists—to break free of the hegemony of the written word and of a conception of history limited to the activities and ideas of the (White) elite and the State. Of course, Black American scholars, for reasons too obvious and painful to reiterate, were well in advance of this trend. The conceptions and writing of W. E. B. Du Bois, Carter Woodson, and Leo Hansberry—to name a few from the longer list identified by Professor Hill-Lubin—were more in tune with the evolution of historical and anthropological thought of Europeans and Africans in Europe than the rest of American academe.

Beyond extending the legitimacy of new kinds of evidence and subject matter, a fundamental appeal of African studies, at least as it became more widely institutionalized, was the invitation to slough off ethnocentric preoccupations and to value the contributions of peoples outside the dominant culture both in America and abroad.

For many young American scholars at the time, the ideological and methodological transformations offered by African studies could find no better symbol than *Présence Africaine*. Founded and sustained by Africans, it embraced within its pages those in the diaspora. It welcomed articles from the range of academic disciplines, and it gave voice to the creative artist. Its multilingual format created a forum for exchange among African, Latin American, West Indian, European, and North American intellectuals that highlighted the commonalities as well as the differences of their experiences. Its congresses and colloquies identified and stimulated research on topics held to be important for Africa. That it has survived through the disillusionment and turmoil of the last four decades is cause for this reflection: both tribute and critique of its program are possible. As questions are raised about the fundamental nature of knowledge, as we face the consequences of the realization that "history is both a discourse of knowledge and a discourse of power" (Mudimbe 1988: 188), we may strive toward concept and strategy that encompass both this near if flawed past and the critiques of it. *Présence Africaine* provides a fitting forum for this exercise because of the plurality of its voices and their intentions.

As a project it reflects the tension between the search for understanding the processes at work in Africa and how we articulate them on the one hand, and the moral imperative to do so in the name of envisioning the future on the other. The articles presented in this book reflect the trajectory of our course in this effort. They comment on this tension and on the difficulty of escaping, even when acknowledged, the framework of Hegelian opposites that has dominated historical and social scientific thought since the nineteenth century. They also call attention both explicitly and implicitly to the importance of language.

In "Conjugating Cultural Realities" (Chap. 2, this vol.), Jules-Rosette addresses the necessity of delineating the relationship between cultural and political forms. Her paper contains an interesting analysis of themes explored by the group associated with *Présence Africaine* and includes some valuable interview data with individuals who were principal actors in the publishing venture. In creating a cultural reality that was both source and symbol for a unique discourse, *Présence Africaine* embraced themes that were not always unified but contained the potential for meaning at different levels and to diverse audiences. Idyllic, "natural" Africa is evoked as a source of unity and strength. This task was important, in Rabemananjara's words, to achieve the goals of revitalization, illustration, or explanation that would assist in the creation of new values. The symbol had to be powerful enough to overcome the repression of colonialism and the fragmentation of knowledge that Africans had of themselves. The writers (in particular, Alioune Diop and Frantz Fanon) were at the same time wary of those like Sartre who would make of this cultural renaissance a mere analytical proposition. The image of "scientific Africa" reflected the awareness of the model of ideology and research that was both comprehensive and interdisciplinary. The author suggests that the multiplicity of these images was necessary to their symbolic power, but that carried to their logical extension they deprived Africa and the Black man of a uniqueness critical to the revalorization desired by the *Présence* group. By the time of the First International Congress of Black Writers and Artists in 1956, Africa was shifting from cultural sign to the domain of social action. The ambiguities remained: a "holistic formulation of black culture" articulated by Senghor diverged from Césaire's vision of the diversity of

Black cultures in Africa and the diaspora that were nevertheless united by colonial repression. Fanon voiced his wariness of placing too great a faith in purely literary and artistic endeavors at the expense of ignoring the social and political realities. The interviews with participants of the present day reflect a continuing importance of cultural affirmation and provision of a forum for African and Black voices, along with some malaise about *Présence Africaine*'s capacity to meet the needs of the next generation.

Among the points identified for a research agenda, I wish to comment on the first and the last. Referring to Margoulis's division of the journal's work into three periods: 1947–1949, 1950–1954, 1955 onward, Jules-Rosette notes the importance of a more extensive study of the third which by now encompasses nearly three-quarters of the journal's existence. She herself begins such a project with an analysis of the themes and conflicts of the 1956 conference. This conference looms large as a symbol of the *Présence* undertaking and plays a prominent role in any discussion of the movement (see for example, July 1987). However, what is needed is a more precise historical study of the evolution of thought that appears in *Présence Africaine;* how has it changed, in what direction, etc.[1] A superficial examination of the journal's issues since 1980 reveals the persistence of its commitment to provide a forum for African poets and writers—over half the content consists of texts and literary criticism. Culture and politics is the second largest category of articles followed by about equal attention to history and social science. Articles on the arts, religion, philosophy, economy, science, and technology comprise roughly 9 percent of the content, while law—perhaps the most obvious of colonial impositions—merits infinitesimal space.[2] At the same time, the contents of those articles (for instance, on philosophy) reflect at least the range if not the volume of the lively and contentious debate about the origins of knowledge about Africa.

Jules-Rosette's proposal to examine *Présence Africaine* in its own right and in its social context as a point of departure for the analysis of the diffusion of this intellectual movement I applaud. The comment by Professor Obenga during the discussion following the presen-

1. Aliko Songolo makes a similar suggestion in "Early P.A.: Muffled Discourse" that appeared in a series of essays in commemoration of *Présence Africaine*'s fortieth anniversary in the *ALA Bulletin* 14, no. 3 (Summer 1988).

2. The basis of this rough estimate is an extension of the categories used by Jacques Howlett in pp. 213–216 of his *Index alphabétique des auteurs et matières 1947–1976*.

tations that one should distinguish the commercial venture *Présence Africaine* from the activities of the Society of African Culture spoke to the same point, noting that there are materials (in the archives of SAC) representing voices of the Black community from all corners of the globe. In particular, biographies of some of the principals of either the society or the journal remain illusive. I was struck, for instance, by how little we learn of Alioune Diop as a man in the pages of the journal he founded. Beyond the testimony his writings supply of him as an articulate creator and guardian of the revitalization movement, there is precious little about his life. Even his passage from the scene, unless overlooked in my rapid survey, is unremarked.

In *"Présence Africaine* as Historiography: Historicity of Societies and Specificity of Black African Culture" (Chap. 5, this vol.), Bogumil Jewsiewicki confronts the "anguish [of] the link between historiography and politics in contemporary Africa" and "the place narrative reason has in culture and the practice of politics." There is anguish because the conception of history in *Présence* belies the radical posture, the will to end colonial domination, and the promise of a profound transformation of society. He observes that the project did not promise a revolution in epistemology. But the brunt of his analysis is that it could not, imprisoned as it was by a nineteenth-century epistemology that characterized history as both the manifestation of objective laws to be decoded by historiography and as the collective conscience but belittled the latter. In the painful metaphor of torture, the historians of the 1960s were drawn and quartered between proving their professionalism and bringing their ideology to fruition. Their intentions of political and cultural engagement were undermined by a conception of science that led them not only to step outside their present but to be preoccupied with origins in an effort to provide the antithesis to the Hegelian (Western) thesis. The result was a philosophy of history or what Jewsiewicki calls a *chronosophie* (which I propose to translate as science of time) that enabled them to pick up the thread of a great past—broken by the parenthetical experience of the slave trade and colonialism—and tie it firmly to the realization of a magnificent, essentially African future. But in the process the present is lost sight of: semantically, to pick up a metaphor from the preceding discussion but with different results, the present is conjugated out. A corollary of its historiography focused on the legitimacy of the sovereignty of this or that political authority in the precolonial world and reinforced the notion of the communal character of African society. Such a view has resulted in the expulsion of the concept of social and class conflict from the interior of African society to the exterior: Africa's relations with the rest of the world; but it is a view, Jewsiewicki argues, that ill serves the needs of contemporary nationalist historiographies.

Why a nationalist historiography should be important is not explained here and is made clearer with reference to Jewsiewicki's 1987 paper on Africanist and African historiography. There he argues that, after three decades of independence, both ideology and political practice should be moving away from Pan-African unity. A nationalist focus also derives from the "practical" matter that historians employed in African universities are expected by governments and the public to create a historical past that is relevant to contemporary problems. The voices of African historians militating for the abandonment of "borrowed paradigms" propose movement in the direction of a *particularity* that takes into account not only the legacies of those paradigms but also the issues of "social differentiation, shifting sex roles and the materiality of social artifacts as consciousness and identity." By implication here, *Présence Africaine* did not fully seize this initiative however understandable the reasons. The documentation for this characterization of the journal's historiography is careful. To suggest that hints of the critiques that were to emerge outside its pages may have existed here and there in the first two decades of *Présence Africaine* (for instance, Fanon's warning at the first congress), or that a study of the historical writing since 1970 (the latest quotation cited) might be fruitful is not to detract from the elegance and convincing quality of his analysis. This is another instance in which a historical study that looks more closely at the evolution of *Présence Africaine* within the past four decades is warranted.

In Chapter 13 (this vol.), Professor K. A. Appiah's "Inventing an African Practice in Philosophy," situated on the edge of *Présence Africaine*'s future with little reference to its past views, nevertheless addresses philosophical issues that have been fundamental to its pages. The narrative sets forth both epistemological and moral positions. In identifying the grounds for possibilities of an African system of thought, he makes two assumptions. The first is that it is necessary to analyze *modern identities* that include the concepts and beliefs of people in a variety of social, educational, class settings: "African intellectuals are no less African than peasants." In recognizing that there will be diversity, we should also celebrate it: the multiple discourses of human kind are not a babel but a chorus. He notes that there are a number of intellectual barriers that prevent action on these principles, including the way systems and concepts address one another, the difficulty of translation, and the effect of demanding that different discourses are often required to "compete for the truth."

Working through formulations by Donald Davidson, Appiah stresses that each kind of knowledge is situated in a kind of interest. The interests that drive theory will change, and the way in which they change may be driven by theory. He suggests that it is foolish to ask which theory is true; rather one should ask if they care for one another. Society can handle differences, even conflicts, so long as it doesn't impose the notion that the truth is at stake. Appiah notes that natural scientists hold that Africa is a biological treasure house of diversity; he argues that the continent is a cultural treasure house of diversity as well. He pleads that philosophers celebrate that richness and cultivate it.

Although focusing upon different aspects of human thought, each of these articles raises questions having to do with levels of analysis, oppositions, potential and real conflicts. There are some final observations I would like to make by way of linking their discussions to the general debate about sources and knowledge.

In *The Invention of Africa: Gnosis, Philosophy, and the Order of Knowledge* (1988), Mudimbe notes that Africa of the 1980s is reliving the crisis of the 1950s:

> To create myths which would give a meaning to its hopes for improvement, Africa seems to hesitate between two principal sources, Marxist and traditionalist, and to worry endlessly about the evidence about the superiority of the Same over the Other and the possible virtues of the inverse relationships. (96)

Contained within these sources and the debates about them is the tension between whether one can conceive of human universals in Africa and at the same time escape the hegemonic formulations of the past, or whether Africa must focus on its particularity to control its ideology.

To the extent that they are related, the concepts of particularity and nationalist historiography pose a dilemma not in their logic but in their translation from abstract concepts to implementation.[3] Perhaps

---

3. In addition to the works specifically cited, others that were useful in consideration of the themes of this essay were *The Afrocentric Idea*, by Molefi Kete Asante; *African Historiographies: What History for Which Africa?* Bogumil Jewsiewicki and David Newbury; and *The Messages of Tourist Art: An African Semiotic System in Comparative Perspective*, by Bennetta Jules-Rosette.

it's a matter of terminology, perhaps a figment of the gender and generation of my own discourse and historical memory, but nationalist historiography suggests the kind of ethnocentrism that is problematical: in the West it led to arrogance, and in the reality of historical relations among peoples enclosed by the arbitrary boundaries of African states it has led to civil strife more than to fulfillment. If what is needed is better knowledge of people, their perceptions and experience at the local levels of civil society, fine. The emphasis on distinctiveness, however, may lead to a static view of culture. In *The Predicament of Culture* (1988), James Clifford calls into question the usefulness of essentialist views of culture and argues that personal and cultural identities are negotiated (275). Looking at them as open-ended processes helps to reinforce the selective capacities of cultures to choose from the past and avoid the *huis clos* of a we-they cycle: "Interpreting the direction of meaning of the historical record always depends on present possibilities. When the future is open, so is the meaning of the past" (343). Although the agenda would differ in significant respects, this notion of negotiated identity seems consonant with at least one of the implications of *gnosis* as set forth in Mudimbe's work: the redefinition of human freedom (198). He and these articles have served *Présence Africaine* well by exhorting its attention to a redefinition of ideology that lies inherent if neglected in its history.

BIBLIOGRAPHY

Asante, Molefi Kete. 1987. *The Afrocentric Idea.* Philadelphia: Temple University Press.

Clifford, James. 1988. *The Predicament of Culture: Twentieth Century Ethnography, Literature, and Art.* Cambridge, Mass.: Harvard University Press.

Howlett, Jacques. 1977. *Index alphabétique des auteurs et des matières 1947–1976.* Paris: Présence Africaine.

Jewsiewicki, Bogumil. 1987. *African Historical Studies as Academic Knowledge: Radical Scholarship and Usable Past, 1956–1986.* Paper commissioned by the ACLS/SSRC Joint Committee on African Studies for presentation at the thirtieth annual meeting of the African Studies Association, November 20–22, 1987, Denver.

Jewsiewicki, Bogumil, and David Newbury, eds. 1986. *African Historiographies: What History for Which Africa?* Beverly Hills, Calif.: Sage.

Jules-Rosette, Bennetta. 1984. *The Messages of Tourist Art: An African Semiotic System in Comparative Perspective.* New York: Plenum Press.

July, Robert W. 1987. *An African Voice: The Role of the Humanities in African Independence.* Durham, N.C.: Duke University Press.

Mudimbe, V. Y. 1988. *The Invention of Africa: Gnosis, Philosophy, and the Order of Knowledge.* Bloomington: Indiana University Press.

Songolo, Aliko. 1988. "Early P. A.: Muffled Discourse." *ALA Bulletin* 14, no. 3 (Summer).

ON SPEAKING AND HEARING:
Toward a Free and
Liberating Discourse

Eileen Julien

It is known widely as the land of Khaddafy, Amin, coups d'état, famine, and South African music. Yet, how might it best articulate itself? How might it best be apprehended?

Forty years ago, these questions were at the heart of the *Présence Africaine* project. Just as important now as then, they are a common thread in the many diverse papers that make up this volume. We continuously confront the question of the parameters of a healthy discourse, whether we follow Mouralis, Jules-Rosette, and Bjornson in this volume as they focus more specifically on the history and practices of the publishing house and journal or whether we follow Martin and Cailler in their more general discussions of fruitful and sterile methodologies. The first three writers address primarily issues affecting the production of "speech" or, more precisely, the language act which was *Présence Africaine* and the African voices who spoke through it, while the latter two examine especially the possibilities for hearing those voices and the limits placed on the ability to hear them.

Their arguments, read side by side, have much to say about the conditions of a free and liberating discourse and the constraints that render such a discourse impossible, and it is to this set of issues that I shall confine my remarks. Mouralis signals the necessity of a free space, "un lieu utopique qui permet à la pensée de conserver indépendance et efficacité critique." He sees *Présence Africaine* as fulfilling precisely that role. For Mouralis, the journal and publishing house have maintained, throughout the years of political debate and struggle, its position as a forum, an institution above the foray, dedicated to the *process of thought* because it did not espouse any particular form of government (apart from its denunciation of colonialism and imperialism) and was not the disciple of any particular African personality or head of state. Whether or not one agrees with this particular judgment, the principle of a free space seems fundamental. If there is any lesson—thematic or material—in African literatures today, it is surely the necessity, for both physical and intellectual well-being, of an ideology-free zone.

Bjornson's analysis of Hazoumé's assimilationist stance and Oyono's revision of it buttresses this argument as well. Referring to Irele's "In Praise of Alienation," he describes the impetus to distance oneself from one's present state of consciousness in a movement toward knowledge. If, indeed, such "alienation" is vital, the necessity of dogma-free and reprisal-free inquiry becomes clear. Ultimately, a "free space" allows for growth and for the expression of diversity.

But such a space and the will to reject obsolete and distorted images or values may not be enough, as we are reminded by Jules-Rosette, when she describes the several images of Africa and the periodicization of African history projected in the pages of *Présence Africaine* itself or in the works of writers associated with the publishing house. Jules-Rosette concludes, "Writers have engaged in a . . . complex process of devising counterimagery to identify and reaffirm themselves while simultaneously regenerating idyllic images." Furthermore, she notes with regard to the collaboration of Black writers and French anthropologists, that the perceptions of the African subject were not used to revise anthropological theory or modify methods of scientific analysis: "Although the new anthropology introduced African societies and cultures to France with an unprecedented degree of methodological care and detail, the voice of the African subjects remained strangely silent."

Indeed, we all—listeners and speakers, readers and writers alike—are affected, if not entrapped, by given paradigms. It is not, of course, a mere neat intellectual problem but is quite material. Soyinka expresses this another way in the preface to *Death and the King's Horseman* when he refuses the notion of a "clash of cultures." One cannot speak of a random and free encounter or debate between contenders of unequal strength. Writers and readers, then, even when we are most self-aware, are precisely such contenders in the face of persuasive, seemingly immemorial paradigms. Bjornson's discussion of *Doguicimi*, a novel meant in some sense to "redeem" Africa, is a case in point. In the reconciliation of "traditional African" values and "Western" ones, for example, is it always true that Christianity introduces the principle of "universal love" or "respect for individual rights?" Could neither of those principles, in whatever guise, have preceded Christianity in some societies? Or why do we assume, for example, that the reconciliation of African and Western values requires an evolution in traditional customs while newly assimilated values will stand intact in such a marriage? These assumptions seem to me to betray the view that Africa is still a point of departure. Clearly, to rethink methodology and categories, to challenge stereotypes without reinforcing them or creating others is an awesome responsibility for us all.

All three essays, then, bring us to the heart of Martin's astute critique: the rampant tendency in academic, political, and cultural spheres to project a singular and uniform image of diverse and porous civilizations. Witness the everpresent tags—Francophone, Anglophone, Maghrebian, sub-Saharan, Black, Islamic, *and* Madagascar, *and* Ethiopia—which belie this myth of cultural homogeneity.

Martin's analysis of the myth's workings is perhaps answer enough to the question of its origins. In the academic realm, Africa is, for Martin, as for Jules-Rosette, the object, never the subject, of methodologies ("on applique des recettes mises au point ailleurs"). Not only does research produced in this mold fail to advance knowledge about Africa, but it is, more precisely and disturbingly, "une vaste entreprise de travestissement des réalités." In the public realm, attitudes toward Africa around the world, he argues, are of two types: at worst, condemnation; at best, sympathy; and in neither case, understanding.

Martin's warning obviously is directed toward each and every one of us who studies and, for better or worse, represents that array of peoples and practices which go by the name Africa. The problem is, of course, dual: both to correct the image of an undifferentiated and yet utterly different continent *and* to refuse the powerlessness of balkanization and fragmentation fueled by petty pride. One is reminded of Césaire's insight that we lose our identity either by walling ourselves into our specificity or diluting ourselves in the universal. Thus, to assert that there are common cultural practices across regions, to assess common histories of the slave trade, colonialism, and their aftermath obviously should not necessarily lead to the denial of particularity. Nor should it lead to the conclusion of an extraneous and singular destiny, where singularity—if we refer to Jameson's discussion of alterity and identity, the impulse to define another as what I am not—means of necessity inferiority, both technologically and politically, vis-à-vis the rest of the world. Once again, we face the trap of redefining self in reaction to given, often essentialist, definitions, which in turn leads to new ones. Thus a further challenge is to get beyond defining self, for the preoccupation with differential definitions *(what to be)* is ultimately distracting from the more crucial problem of *what to do.*

Martin's suggestion for the future of African humanities is that we study Africa as other continents are studied: focusing on precise periods and regions, well-defined problems, internal and external factors; exchanging researchers and comparing Africa to other civilizations—not normatively nor as the mere variables for others' formulas, of course, but on equal terms. We have already come a long way from "Femme noire" to *Ségou.* These practices in academe, in the press, and in government will go still farther in taking out of the ghetto.

Cailler's text is therefore, in some sense, a perfect response to the issues raised by Martin, for her analyses of three poems by Fodéba, Hughes, and Niger highlight both what is common and what is individual about these three sons of Africa from different continents. Furthermore, her problematizing of her own position as a teacher of "Francophone" African literature(s) in a large state university of the United States is a telling testimony to the relationship between political climate and the study of literature and humanities, between the status of Africa in public opinion and the possibilities for the study of Africa and the diaspora in higher education in the United States. Her incorporation of these two issues in a single essay, like Martin's inclusion of both public and scholarly attitudes toward Africa, is precisely the kind of textual analysis I think is required: it is an admirable demonstration of her thesis that form is meaning, that poetry is not frivolous and, what is more, that any truly rigorous textual analysis must also be contextual.

It becomes clear, then, that the journey begun by Présence Africaine must be carried on by all of us.

African humanities in America, at least, are the Black women of the academy; they suffer what all humanities suffer, and that condition is compounded by issues of race and the myth of singularity. Of necessity, then, they call us to see the limits to thought (of methodologies and paradigms) to which we have been blind.

Thus, in the realm of literature, we must cease to think of culture, from the narrowest academic perspective, as a sedentary and textual activity but rather as of a whole with other arts.

In the teaching of literature, it is not simply digestion (passive understanding) for which we must strive but reinvigoration, a height-

ening of the reader's own sense of creativity, power, and responsibility. There lies the durable, transferable legacy of reading and
responding—the conviction of one's own *présence.*

Finally, African voices reveal more emphatically than any I know
the interrelationship of peoples and nations on this planet. Theirs is
an undeniable testimony to particularity and yet to the artificiality of
so many boundaries and borders.

ALIOUNE DIOP AND THE UNFINISHED TEMPLE OF KNOWLEDGE

Christopher L. Miller

Looking back to the origin of Présence Africaine through the
optic of the recollections in this volume, the belated observer is
struck by the understatement with which its powerful discursive machine was launched. Created at the apogee of French colonial power,
Présence Africaine the publishing house and *Présence Africaine* the
journal were conceived within the terms and conditions of hegemony,
but as a first step toward the dismantling of colonial power from
within. Thus Présence Africaine was founded and remains in Paris,
the center of the colonial empire, absent from the Africa whose presence it began to pursue, describe, and advocate. Nothing could be
done about France without France: the most necessary condition for
any anticolonial struggle that would transcend ethnic boundaries was
the French language and its literacy. Without Paris, then, without the
absence of Africa, there would be no Présence Africaine.

Should we deduce from this that the role of Présence Africaine has
been to "mainstream," to preserve a geography of marginality and
centrality by its very attempts to promote writers and ideas? Should
we agree with Louise Fiber Luce's assertion that Présence Africaine is
"tied directly to the notion of legitimation on the one hand, and, indirectly, to elitism on the other," perpetuating "a system of *dominé-
dominant* relationships" that add up to a form of colonialism?[1] If any
form of control, selection, and manipulation of power constitutes
"colonialism," then all publishing houses and journals would be
guilty. Luce finds Présence Africaine's position to be "ambiguous," as

1. Louise Fibert Luce, "Neo-Colonialism and *Présence Africaine." African Studies
Review* 29, no. 1 (March 1986): 10.

if there were any other kind of position conceivable within the given context of its emergence and development. If an analysis of Présence Africaine in the late 1980s must come to terms with the dangers of institutionalization and with the possibility that institutions can "become destructive of the very changes they had hoped to bring about,"[2] a look back to the late 1940s reveals both the original hopes and the structural conditions that governed their realization.

Knowing what Présence Africaine would become in the 1950s and 1960s—"the crucible of a certain critical consciousness," the locus of an "esthetic of struggle," the "yeast" that would produce important cultural congresses[3]—one is surprised by the modesty of Alioune Diop's tone in "Niam n'goura ou les raisons d'être de *Présence Africaine*" ("Niam n'goura or *Présence Africaine*'s raison d'être"), the manifesto that appeared in the first issue of the journal. In sharp contrast to its precursor *Légitime Défense*, which had streaked across the Paris horizon in a blaze of revolutionary rhetoric and burned out almost immediately, *Présence Africaine* begins by renouncing ideological allegiances: "Cette revue ne se place sous l'obédience d'aucune idéologie philosophique ou politique" ("This review is not under the bidding of any philosophical or political ideology").[4] The explicit method will be the "collaboration of all men of good will," the goal will be to "define the African's creativity and to hasten his integration in the modern world." The journal, Diop states, "is pleased with being French, with living in the air of French thought [se félicite . . . d'être française, de vivre dans un cadre français]" (12, 190). But both France and Africa will apparently remain contingent within a larger conceptualization of the colonizing and colonized globe:

> Dépassant le strict plan de la colonisation française, [*Présence Africaine*] veut poser et étudier le problème général des rapports de l'Europe avec le reste du monde, mais en prenant pour exemple l'Afrique. D'autant plus que son humanité noire se trouve être la plus déshéritée.
>
> Reaching beyond the confines of French colonization, it intends to raise and study the general problem of Eu-

2. Ibid.

3. Locha Mateso, *La littérature africaine et sa critique* (Paris: Editions Karthala, 1986), 116, 118, 121.

4. Alioune Diop, "Niam n'goura ou les raisons d'être de *Présence Africaine*," *Présence Africaine* 1 (1947): 7; the translation, by Richard Wright and Thomas Diop, was published in the same issue, 185–192.

rope's relations with the rest of the world, taking Africa as
an example, especially since her black mankind finds itself
to be the most disinherited.

Diop's phrasing is a masterpiece of understatement. It is clear that
Africa was meant to be much more than one example among others;
by relativizing the role of France, Diop passes the essential binary
opposition off as part of a "general problem." In light of the militancy
that would follow, it therefore appears charmingly modest on Diop's
part to inquire meekly, "Serait-il téméraire d'ajouter que [*Présence
Africaine*] pourrait même enrichir la civilisation européenne?"
("Would it be rash to suggest that it can even enrich European
civilization?").

The terms that Diop lays down are those of a universal humanism
familiar to students of négritude ideology; négritude envisioned humanity as a single orchestra composed of different sections. The fact
that European powers control the universe—conduct the orchestra—is taken for granted. Modernity is European modernity, from
which Africa has been excluded; Présence Africaine will work to
change this absence into a presence:

> Le noir qui brille par son absence dans l'élaboration de la
> cité moderne, pourra, peu à peu, signifier sa présence en
> contribuant à la recréation d'un humanisme à la vraie me-
> sure de l'homme. (13)

> The black man, conspicuous by his absence in the build-
> ing up of the modern city, will be able to signify his pres-
> ence little by little by contributing to the recreating of a
> humanism reflecting the true measure of man. (191)

The space evoked here is reminiscent of the space implicit in Léopold
Sédar Senghor's early essay "Ce que l'homme noir apporte" ("What
the Black man brings"): the level of universal collaboration commands the most prestige; modernity is a condition to which Africans
will contribute even if Europeans discovered it first. Thus, for Senghor, the Black will "bring" contributions to, for example, a universal
"contemporary music" ("la musique contemporaine") that is controlled and produced in the West.[5] For Diop, authentic universalism
can only be attained if Africans accept and appropriate the necessary European tools: "Il importe seulement que certains déshérités

5. Senghor, "Ce que l'homme noir apporte" (1939), in *Liberté I: Négritude et humanisme* (Paris: Editions du Seuil, 1964), 38.

reçoivent de l'Europe, de la France en particulier, les instruments né-
cessaires à cet édifice à venir" (13) ("It is essential that certain disinherited peoples receive from Europe, from France in particular, the
instruments necessary for the future building," 191). The shopping
list of these necessary instruments begins with Francophone literacy,
from which it follows that, as Diop says, "La littérature devient elle-
même une institution aussi utile que le Parlement" (12) ("literature
itself becomes an institution as useful as Parliament," 190).

At the origin of Présence Africaine, the premises defined by Diop's
declaration thus resemble the premises of négritude: the assumption
that liberation will come only through the appropriation of European
means of discursive production (such as writing in French), through
participation in the global economy on terms that remain for the
most part unchanged (such as producing books in Paris and distrib-
uting them out toward the margins), and through faith in the utility
and reversibility of discourse itself. Liberation is elaborated as access
to universalism, as free and equal exchange among counterparts.

But Diop's manifesto seems to offer a metaphorical critique of the
very universalism within which he appears to be trapped:

> Pour l'instant l'universalisme prend la figure d'un tem-
> ple où la perfection se lit sur la façade, mais où l'arrière-
> plan, jamais exposé au regard, à l'admiration ni à la cri-
> tique, se trouve inachevé et absurde. Pourtant, l'Européen
> non plus, ne saurait se voir sous tous les angles. L'homme
> d'outre-mer pourrait précisément servir de miroir à sa
> beauté, qui ne sera parfaite qu'en devenant *aussi* notre
> beauté. Sans quoi, l'Europe risque de s'étioler dans une
> sorte de narcissisme stérile pour tous. (13)

> For the moment, universalism assumes the aspect of a
> temple on the facade of which perfection is read, but to the
> rear of which, never exposed to sight, to admiration and
> criticism, one finds that which is unfinished and absurd.
> The European, however, cannot see himself from all angles
> either. The overseas man could well serve as a mirror to his
> beauty, which will be perfect only by becoming also our
> beauty. Else Europe runs the risk of wilting in a kind of
> fruitless narcissism. (191)

Apparently investing in universalism, Diop has nonetheless managed
to suggest its demise. On the one hand, he shows faith in the emergence of a single universal beauty, a fully constructed temple. The
allegory then switches from the figure of the temple to that of the

mirror, in order to seduce the European reader with the prospect of achieving perfect beauty. But on the other hand, this paragraph which obstensibly calls for universalism simultaneously calls it into question, revealing its ugly and absurd, rotten foundations. For the retrospective reader, Diop's metaphors take on a prophetic valency. The corruption he described as a "risk" of failed universalism is now more likely to be seen as intrinsic to any project in which the Black serves as a mirror to the beauty of the White. Diop's use of the phrase "sterile narcissism" stands as an implied reproach to those Europeans who can only conceive of the "overseas man" as a mirror for their own beauty; his rhetoric suggests that the universalist project is based on vanity. The same phrase seems to reflect on the future reputation of those premises that Diop and Présence Africaine shared with négritude. Thus for Stanislas Adotevi, the harshest of critics, "Négritude in its entirety is castrated desire, mobile *sterility*."[6] Diop's rhetoric, while laboring to construct the temple of universalism, analyzed its weakness and anticipated its collapse.

The dualism in Diop's writing may be considered as an effect of implied censorship. Jacques Rabemananjara reminds us that under the colonial régime, "the 'natives' had no right to anything because they were not citizens . . . The wish to create, in these conditions, a review in which one could express oneself freely smacked of provocation, and certain *milieux* . . . viewed this enterprise malevolently. They swore its destruction."[7] How easy it is to forget such factors now. Under these conditions, Diop's appeal to universalism can only be a form of surreptitious speech.

Diop's self-destructing temple remains a valid metaphor for certain trends of the present time. The Francophone movement that Senghor refers to in this volume shares a certain number of assumptions with the universalism of négritude; Senghor's ethical faith in the possibility of reciprocal dialogue allows him to foresee *Francophonie* as the "political reality" of tomorrow.[8] At the heart of this structure for Senghor is *Francité*, the spirit of French culture. The appeal to French interests parallels the use of beauty in Diop's article: according to one

6. Stanislas Adotevi, *Négritude et négrologues* (Paris: Union Générale d'Editions, 1972), 82 (my emphasis).

7. Jacques Rabemananjara, "Fortieth Anniversary of the Review *Présence Africaine*," *Présence Africiane* 144 (1987): 12.

8. See Senghor, "La francophonie comme culture," in *Liberté III: Négritude et civilisation de l'universel* (Paris: Editions du Seuil, 1977), 80–89

analysis, French governments were originally indifferent to the Francophone movement; France had to be seduced into participation, made to see—narcissistically—its own self-interest.[9] For Manthia Diawara, things need no longer be conceived in this fashion: "We no longer believe, like Senghor for example, that *Francité* is the best mode of expression of African values."[10] For the generation represented by Diawara, the centrality of France is open to question; values are more complex and overdetermined, and no single temple of culture is envisioned. Fernando Lambert wonders what pragmatic gains will come from the Francophone movement: everything remains to be seen.[11]

If the reason and the ideal behind the construction of Présence Africaine, of négritude and of Francophone African literature in general appear to have been repudiated, if there is no longer any faith in universalizing ideologies of difference (see Mudimbe's reference to the apparent "failure of the ideologies of difference" in Africa),[12] what remains of the temple? For those who believe in a mystical Francophonie, nothing has changed, the dream of completing the temple continues to seduce. For Senghor, the reality of Francophonie is just around the corner. For a critic like Lilyan Kesteloot, the old pieties about unity and consciousness remain compelling: to focus on the inevitable entropy in the emergence of national and regional literatures is to be guilty of "balkanization."[13]

9. See Philip A. Allen, "Francophonie Considered," *Africa Report* 13, no 6 (June 1968): "President de Gaulle is not the only prospective protagonist to treat OCAM's [Organisation Commune Africaine et Malgache, which set forth a plan for organizing francophonie in 1966] project with less than francophone fervor . . . Some unorthodox Africans . . . have not hesitated to define Francophonie as insurance for continued French aid. They understand French policy as insisting on cultural allegiance in return for economic benefits" (9).

10. Diawara (this vol., Chap. 21).

11. Lambert (this vol., Chap. 21).

12. Ibid.

13. Kesteloot (this vol., Chap. 21) states that the literature faculty at the Université Cheikh Anta Diop "is also not ready to abandon the ecumenism of African literature in favor of emphasizing Senegalese literature," but the dean of literary studies at Dakar, Mohamadou Kane, while indeed reticent about national literatures, is the leading exponent of "fragmentation" on another level: the study of literature according to "aires culturelles," concentrating on ethnic and regional values. See Kane's *Roman africain et traditions* (Dakar: Nouvelles Editions Africaines, 1982): "Un [des] volet[s] d'une action tendant à faire ressortir les différences culturelles—en vue d'une grande fidélité à la personnalité des uns et des autres—est constitué par l'étude des traditions dans le roman qui permettent de retrouver de véritables aires culturelles" (22).

More objectively speaking, the centrality of France remains stable: Présence Africaine remains there, and especially its fellow publishers of Africana—L'Harmattan, Karthala—are flourishing in the old colonial capital, while Les Nouvelles Editions Africaines struggles to survive on the African continent. Francophonie in its strictest sense, as the mere use of the French language, remains the prime condition of written expression. But Francophonie and *Francité* seem to be going their separate ways: French is used as a means toward other ends. The long and proud process of construction has produced a literature whose content differs considerably from the original plan. The temple has been built, but deconsecrated. The easy, symmetrical formulations of culture have been profaned. People now mill about in the space of Francophonie as if it were an apartment building instead of a temple.

In this atmosphere, Présence Africaine becomes a fragment of the real more than the embodiment of an idea; Maurice Lubin comments, startingly: "On ne discute pas ce qui est réel."[14] The forty-year history of Présence Africaine is undeniably real, and, as they say in French, *indiscutable*. What has been published has become a matter of fact. But what can and must be discussed is where this history leave us, the readers of *Présence Africaine*. Paulin Hountondji's trenchant analysis of the international knowledge industry ("Recapturing") comes as close to a true discussion of the real as one could imagine. The unequal division of discourse, between Western theory at the center and African raw information in the periphery, sets up an enormous centripetal force, sweeping "toutes les compétences intellectuelles et scientifiques . . . vers le centre du système."[15] According to Hountondji's analysis, no cog like Présence Africaine could help but be part of the neocolonial machine, and until his own work and work by others like him succeeds in reversing the movement, we will all continue to labor within the existing system. For an American scholar, positioned at an extreme margin in relation to Africa, yet living at what Hountondji calls the very "center of the center" of the knowledge industry, the contradiction could not be greater.

Within this system, the spector of legitimation, elitism, and dominance is naturally omnipresent, and all positions are ambiguous. If this rapid glimpse at the origin of Présence Africaine offers any les-

14. Lubin (this vol., Chap. 20).
15. Hountondji (this vol., Chap. 14).

son, it is that ambiguity is an enabling condition. Diop's tactical appeal to European narcissism, after all, *worked:* Présence Africaine was built and has survived within Europe. The challenge posed by Hountondji sets the agenda for the next forty years: to overcome that narcissism and profoundly to alter the balance of trade in knowledge.

Finale

twenty-three

V. Y. Mudimbe

What the preceding pages demonstrate is that in the span of forty years *Présence Africaine* succeeded in organizing a new literary and intellectual space for "a surreptitious speech." This space is not the other side of what we may call the Western space. In fact, it belongs to it, though it is true that from the beginning *Présence* defines itself on the margin of this center it challenges. There is a political reason to this. André Gide made it explicit in the first issue of the journal. Why should *Présence* speak according to the expectations of a culture that was violating what *Présence* wanted to promote?

A space is always a construct. It is a theoretical articulation that claims to render and represent operations or, put simply, the reality of a place, that is, a primary experience. A space is, to say the least, a second-order plane reflecting upon a first-order practice of life and human experience. This second-degree organization, by its very being, considerably alters and transforms the primary logic in which it claims to root itself. To that extent, its narratives as well as its postulations invent "what is really out there" in the field of everyday place. Methods of faithfully expressing the place, at least in social and human sciences, undergo regular transformations in order to reflect better the reality of an experience and its complexity.

Indeed, after reading the contribu-

435

tions to this volume, one could deduce that, until the founding of *Présence Africaine*, African cultures and their designations were submitted to the European space which actualized them as figures of its own past, precisely as anterior to the rupture that radically separated prehistory from history. The memory of the European space would appear thus, diachronically and synchronically, as the paradigm of human experience and, at the same time, as that which historically has muted all other human differences by reducing them to the project of an evolutionary becoming. In this perspective, *Présence Africaine* could appear to signify the unthinkable: an otherness spatializing itself from a nowhere which cannot be but a utopian project. In effect, its surreptitious voice faces Western culture in the name of an absolute alterity; yet this very alterity seems to spring from the Western space.

I might emphasize another aspect. First, an epistemological shift in social and human sciences has taken place since the beginning of the century and its consequences, apropos the traditional division between the civilized and the primitive, are visible in the years that follow the end of the First World War. Michel Foucault has hypothesized that this shift can be understood as a radical transformation of intellectual grids. Traditional perspectives used to articulate the concepts of function, conflict, and signification, antagonizing a normative center to its margins, the normal to the abnormal, signification to its negation, and thus elaborated discourses on pathological modes of being, beliefs, or societies (for example, Blondel, Durkheim, Lévy-Bruhl). On the other hand, since the 1920s, one sees more analyses conducted "from the point of view of the norm, the rule, and the system, each area provided its own coherence and its own validity; it was no longer possible to speak of 'morbid consciousness' (even referring to the sick), of 'primitive mentalities' (even with reference to societies left behind by history), or of insignificant discourse (even when referring to absurd stories, or the apparently incoherent legends). Everything may be thought within the order of the system, the rule, and the norm" (Foucault 1973:360–361).

Thus *Présence Africaine* and its objective become analytically comprehensible. It is not an accident that Marcel Griaule, the French ethnologist who in the 1940s was expounding the logic of Western African mythologies, believed in *Présence Africaine*'s aims. Nor is it an accident that one of the first books Alioune Diop, the founder of *Présence Africaine*, invested in and promoted was Placide Tempels's *Bantu Philosophy*, a text in which the future of Bantu peoples is, at least in principle, postulated from a narrative which theoretically accounts for and exceeds a defined locale. With the intervention of Georges Balandier's, Claude Lévi-Strauss's, and Louis Althusser's disciples in anthropology, this transformation of grids led ultimately in the 1950s and 1960s to a questioning of the very concept of the primitive and to a reinterpretation of the opposition between the civilized and the primitive.

Second, we may note that if *Présence Africaine* has brought about a visibly new space of representation, this is due, at least partially, to the fact that it has inherited a discreet but well-established tradition of spatializing African experiences and cultures. There is, on the one hand, a recent mode of *diegesis* (narrative), which was promoted by Christian missionaries and Western anthropologists. This brought to light what I call the "new African text," that is, a written text in conformity with, or later in opposition to, both the Christian and colonial paradigms.

Always to be kept in mind is the fact that Africans have been articulating antithetical voices and assuming oppositional stances in the margins of Western discourses for quite a long time. Through its safe negations or, more generally, reproductions as was the case before 1700, this marginal genre witnesses to mimesis: in effect, it "imitates" what it integrates as well as what it exceeds and questions.

Let me be more demonstrative. I shall address first the question of the "new African text"; second, that of a marginal tradition of African discourses within Western history since the eighteenth century; and finally, I shall reflect upon the meaning of *Présence Africaine* as an event in the mid-twentieth century.

My hypothesis is that the African text has been postulated by three main systems of spatialization that made it possible and largely still account for its predicament: anthropology, Christianity (or Islam), and the concept of literature. These systems are not, at least at the end of the nineteenth century, only models (in the wide sense of the word) which gave rise to new African texts claiming to speak about and represent in a credible way the "native" experience of being and existing. They carry with them three interrelated projects. As a matter of fact, anthropology is a science defining rules and methods on how to describe human cultures and situate them in the whole picture of humankind's history. Christianity, as well as Islam, brings with it a belief in the only true Revelation, and its theology is presented as a scientific discourse on God and the human condition. Finally, literature, even as a simple art of ordering stories and fictions steadily delivers a message, categorizing beauty and ugliness, thus witnessing a dialogue with aesthetics which is defined then as a scientific discipline.

I am using the concept of science in a very specific sense. The literature of the fin de siècle, in the humanities as well as in the social sciences, shared one unanimous assumption. It was accepted that science evolves: successive discoveries produce a better, more accurate understanding of physical phenomena and of human beings, and that a definitive knowledge will emerge with time. Anthropology, theology, and aesthetics are moved by this same dream: the constitution of methodological grids that could translate as precisely as possible the tension between observed and experienced facts on the one hand, and deduced and theoretical hypotheses on the other. It is from this background that we should understand, in anthropology, the effort of Lévy-Bruhl to found in reason and in science the deviation between prelogical and logical mentalities. In theology, at least, in Catholicism, the condemnation of Modernism by Pius X reaffirmed the absolute primacy of Revelation over the "lyrical vagaries of scientism." Finally, in Africa, through Western education, the aesthetics of literature are actualized and simultaneously illustrated through the canonical works of the Western past.

These are the systems that the African faced as signs and justifications for submitting to, or resisting colonization as well as its orders for human domestication; namely, those justified by anthropological knowledge; the order for spiritual salvation as accounted for by Christianity or Islam and the new aesthetic order, as a condition for a cultural transformation.

I am not concerned here with colonization. I am not even preoccupied by the intellectual and spiritual violence effectively actualized by the formation and installation of these systems of conversion. What interest me are the formal knowledge and discourse that they brought about. In their African practice, these systems, perhaps more openly than elsewhere, demonstrate their common characteristics. First, they evaluate the meaning of conversion to their rationality from a method, an enumerative technique. For example, if an x belongs to a statistical population of y's, on the basis of the real frequency of x's in a concrete and observed sample of y's, x should then be necessarily a member of y. To illustrate this, one could think of propositions such as a Nigerian who belongs to a statistical population of Christians, on the basis of an actual frequency of Christians, cannot but be a Christian. Other things considered and being equal, the probability that a Nigerian—let us say an x—is a Christian or a member of y is postulated on the basis of a larger sample of y's, the supposition being that there should be a greater probability of x's in the sample espousing the frequency of y's in the whole population. Strictly speaking, this is an enumerative induction which, as a method, claims to be able to establish general propositions. Yet, as technique, this type of induction cannot imply that it is the only one, the best method for leading to an accurate and general knowledge of experience. A similar method accounted for misleading statistics which valorized a popular 1950s notion of a "Westernization" of Black Africa on the basis of a supposedly increasing number of "évolués" (that is, of Africans moving from the domain studied by anthropology to that analyzed by sociology, in other words, from "primitiveness" to "modernity"). More specifically, one could focus, for example, on colonial statistics of cultural and thus aesthetic conversion: those outlining the estimates of the progress of literacy, expansion of libraries, investments in the promotion of good quality reading and writing among "natives."

Besides this manipulation of an enumerative induction, one notes that anthropology, Christian practice, and European literature favor retrodiction as a way of establishing themselves as systems of truth. In the African context, these systems justify their discourses by moving from the effect of their power upon the native to hypothetical reasons or causes that testify to their effectiveness. The move is an efficient one and is simultaneously an epistemological orientation. The humblest missionary knows that his speech goes back to the Old Testament and duplicates the Revelation of the only true God. The anthropologist can refer his methods and results to the capacity of science in general. And the teacher of French or English literature possesses the certainty of what the beauty of a text is about: it is European, and its history goes as far back as to the time of Homer.

The first African modern texts reproduce the paradigms of these three models. The literature written in African languages, which was available, for example, in South Africa at the beginning of this century as well as the African literature promoted in the Congo or in Nigeria in the 1920s, are really anthropological literature. One could even define them as the nonscientific discourse which is the other side of anthropology. It is a functional text that spatialized the ground from the constructs of anthropology. Second, this literature concerned itself with the tension between oral tradition and written text and, often explicitly or implicitly, implied that it had the power of modernizing, transforming, and redeeming an oral tradition. The most striking illustration might be, on the one hand, the monumental work in the 1940s of Alexis Kagame retracing in Kinyarwanda the history of the creation of the universe and of the world from a Christian viewpoint and, on the other hand, the popular plays and stories that missionaries write to implement the basics of Christianity in African mentalities.

Thus, one could think that the very condition of possibility of these new genres links them to policies apropos the new organization of power which establish a modern economic and political structure of inequalities. Second, these texts, insofar as they are linked to a symbolic power, comment upon procedures for an innovative appropriation of ancient symbols and subsequently on the meanings of the new social regulations represented in the colonial order.

Even in their potential heresies, these new texts seem to double an order that is organizing African social formations. Indeed, they claim to witness an epistemological break represented in the passage from orality to writing and carry with them a new will to truth whose clearest manifestation resides in what I may call the aestheticization of traditional genres such as epics, proverbs, fables, riddles, etc. These, in effect, enter the "colonial library," and depending on their context and style, are classified as pre-or paramodern on the basis of the new interpretative criteria.

In brief, a new conception of history literally colonized the African text at the very moment that it made it possible and meaningful. The African literature in English, French, Spanish, or Portuguese exemplifies this. Aesthetically, it submits to the canonical models that reflect what literature has been in the European or Islamic experience and what its practice should mean. In its singularity, it places itself as an application of these models and an illustration of their procedures. For example, the efforts of the négritude narratives since the 1930s did, paradoxically, constitute the best degree of conformity to both the aim of literature as art and as a political commitment despite the fact that they seem, as noted by Sartre, to blur the distinction between poetry and prose. Their spirit is encompassed in the same awareness that makes Sartre insist on the hiatus between the language of the poet and the engagement of the militant writer of prose. As he put it himself, "Doubtless, emotion, even passion—and why not anger, social indignation, and political hatred?—are at the origin of the poem. But they are not *expressly* there, as in a pamphlet or in a confession. Insofar as the writer of prose exhibits feelings, he illustrates them; whereas, if the poet injects his feelings into his poem, he ceases to recognize them; the words take hold of them, penetrate them, and metamorphose them; they do not signify them, even in his eyes." In sum, the négritude poet is, in the very tradition of the genre, a man of meditation who withdraws from the disorder of the world into the music of words and its apocalyptic powers. On the other hand, prose writers, whether novelists (Mongo Beti, Ferdinand Oyono) or essayists (Fanon, Nkrumah, or Lumumba), to use Sartre's words, "choose a method of secondary action which we may call action by disclosure." Directly dependent upon a political objective, this "disclosure" is a critique of social relations of production as well as a critique of the organization of both production and political power.

One can recognize a thesis in this analysis. I am implying that even the most radical contemporary African discourses, which invoke a complete reorganization of African economic spaces and thus challenge the present-day neocolonial regimes, emerge from the very systems of representation that made possible the reality of a modern African text. I would tend to believe that all the orientations we can observe today in African anthropology on the continent, in Christian discourses as well as in literature, are still enclosed within the framework of their potential as texts for knowledge and power that is, as pretexts.

If this is the situation, then one might ask, Is there a way out? I do not really know what it would mean to wish to speak absolutely outside of these three systems, or independently from the new will to truth they have thematized and actualized in a number of African minds. Having said that, I see three questions which require a response and are directly linked to the role and signification of these three systems. Their systematized meaning has been internalized to the point that some Africans today recite their tradition as a reflection of anthropological or missionary texts. The hiatus between the listener or the reader and, on the other hand, the speaker or the writer seems bridged. But does this mean that we have gone beyond the separation implied by anthropology's traditional vocation, namely, the distinction between reason and unreason, or metaphorically, between civilization and savagery? The Christian missionary paradigms have imposed themselves as signs of the universality of Christianity, to the point of imposing themselves as conditions of a fellowship of truth. But does not this very project, which emphasizes the sacrifice of the intellect, validate the negation of the freedom of God's children? Finally, and here is my last question: What literature has brought about, at least in the African context of the last years, is a discourse about political power which has silenced aesthetic issues. In itself this elision constitutes a question mark.

As for the second point concerning an African discourse in the Western tradition, one may refer to and use Donald E. Herdeck's *African Authors* from 1300 to 1973 (1973), and particularly his appendix E on African authors by chronological period (1973:511–530) that I have occasionally checked against Janheinz Jahn's *Die Neoafrikanische Literatur* (1965) and *Who's Who In African Literature* (1972). Herdeck's book should be considered here for what it is: an encyclopedic project. The general picture it gives is well executed. Any specialist in the field of African studies would also notice that the book is not exhaustive in its presentation of African authors and texts. But one can hardly deny its relative completeness. Thus I am using it for what it is: a symbolic framework; nothing more, nothing less. What is striking in the progressive constitution of this marginal library? Statistically, the library is dominated in the eighteenth century by Arabic texts. In the nineteenth century, texts in European languages are in competition with those in African languages, and by the 1920s, and especially after 1940, the African text is essentially conveyed in a European language. It is at this very moment that the European presence in Africa and its interaction with local cultures is being questioned by the very texts that, interestingly witness its success. In effect, the African predicament is then discussed in English, French, Spanish, or Portuguese.

In brief, a remarkable rupture took place between 1910 and 1940. The intensification of European colonization of the continent progressively transformed all the local social formations. The process of production as well as their consequent social relations of production are now dependent upon a conquering capitalist model. Thus it is not an accident that it is during this period that the first African Communist party organized itself in the most marked country, South Africa. There as well as elsewhere, the paradigms for the organization of power and the political discourse that accounts for them expound the absolute pertinence of a European historical experience. At the ideological level, the general framework as well as its speculative and concrete practices—for example, in Christian missionizing, applied anthropology, and programs of education—reinforce the pertinence of a radical conversion from "primitiveness" to "civilization." In any case, the policies of this general movement signify and explicitly want to exemplify the possibility of a new African history. Thus the

African who writes at that time faces not only the exigencies and representations of what this rupture means but also witnesses it. He has been schooled in a new mode of thinking and perceiving both history and the world. What he writes has, in actuality, been made possible and provoked by this very rupture. Even when he opposes the implications of the conversion and its procedures, the polemics or the dialogue he can bring about constitutes a symbol. He is already part of the new cultural economy. This fact is illustrated well by the expansion of European languages, and their geographical expansion over the continent between 1940 and 1959.

To be sure, the picture presented by Herdeck's book is not a faithful reproduction of African writing from 1300 to 1973. Names and titles are missing here and there. For example, the achievements of Protestant-trained journalists writing in African languages in the 1920s seem played down; Alexis Kagame's philosophical works are not mentioned; such an influential thinker as Mabika Kalanda of Zaire is not presented, etc. Yet, the general image of the book conveys, I believe, a dependable framework. In its organization, it accounts for the progressive growing of a marginal text and its disconcerting richness.

Seen from this background, *Présence Africaine* constituted the revolution that it claimed to be and which has been analyzed at length in this volume. It made highly visible a marginal discourse and its dreams. *Présence Africaine* is surely distinct from this past, that one could call its marginality, that is, the rhetorics of "Black authors" who preceded it. Yet, its possibility as well as its objective explain this past. Its main originality was to situate itself forcefully on a level of political and ideological struggle in Paris. On the other hand, as shown by a number of articles in this volume, the establishment of *Présence Africaine* coincides with a new will to truth in the European consciousness. At a deep level, it combines with currents that have been questioning the myths of rationality, scientism, and progress since the beginning of this century, and that led in the 1930s and 1940s to the promotion of philosophies and ideologies of subjectivity and otherness, as represented, for example, in France by Emmanuel Mounier's Personalism and Jean-Paul Sartre's and Simone de Beauvoir's Existentialism. Moreover, ideologically, *Présence Africaine* found traveling companions among all those who, dissatisfied with primitivist and functionalist anthropology, dogmatic Christianity, and traditional aesthetics were looking for ways of pluralizing discourses and interpretations about the diversity of human experience.

Because of this extraordinary convergence, one could have expected that, after the achievement of African political independences, *Présence Africaine* would transcend its capitalization on cultural demands in the name of a racial duty and become an exacting locus for rigorously rethinking power relations and their contradictions in the newly independent countries.

Throughout the volume, what also very clearly imposes itself are the values of humanity and friendship that have characterized Présence Africaine since its inception. I still remember my own accidental first contact with the house. During an afternoon in November 1969 we were an international group of young "enseignants" discussing in a café on la rue des Ecoles what was going on at Nanterre where I was then teaching. I incidently brought into the conversation my frustration apropos a manuscript I had sent to a well-established French publishing house the year before and noting something like "they did not even condescend to let me know that they had received it." What I did not know then is that not only had they written to me but the manuscript was accepted for publication. But the news sent to my African address was lost in the mail between Paris and Kinshasa. There and then a friend advised me to try *Présence Africaine*: "They are just around the corner." And that cold afternoon of November, without appointment, I walked into Présence Africaine. It was the beginning of a faithful friendship with the most humane and generous people I have met in my life. They were, very seriously, working hard for the promotion of a new African text and a new speech (*dire*) about the continent.

Présence Africaine participated, and magnificently, in both the questioning of canonical paradigms and the expansion to Africa of a normative commodity: a new text and speech. Paradoxically, this principle specified itself de facto as a means of stabilizing the oral into the written and subsequently appeared as a way of creatively transforming the tables of marginal memories and identities into the taxonomies of a modern discourse. Let me note two facts. First, Présence Africaine publishes "African" texts that claim to respond to the authority of an African context or experience. But these texts should and at the same time do fit into French circuits. That the best of such texts cannot help being controversial seems obvious, since they have to cover themselves with the credentials of a marginal representation and at the same time attest to the sequences of the French imagination, literature, and demands. Second, just as other publishers, Présence Africaine had to follow some specific rules for the promotion of a text, particularly the exigencies about the language and the content and the message of the text that should correspond more or less to the wish of potential consumers. It is clear that the tensions implied by the first fact can allow remarkable contradictions in the second. On the other hand, the exigencies represented by the second fact may lead through to the other side. Indeed, one might imagine that even excellent texts by Africans could have been rejected by *Présence Africaine* because they were stimulating values which apparently or in reality were negating its basic philosophy.

Présence Africaine is, as the chapters of this book show, a monument in the very ordinary sense of the concept, that is, an achievement. Its signs of representation have articulated themselves in the contradictory networks that signify the difficult dialogue of cultures in this century. That *Présence Africaine* has been able to maintain itself for forty years as a symbol of the right to alterity and subjectivity witnesses to the intelligence of its founders and the dedication of its members. What made it possible as well as what has sustained it so far seems to be the most generous, yet the simplest of dreams: to rethink the roles that history as ideology plays in human interactions.

BIBLIOGRAPHY

Foucault, M. 1973. *The Order of Things.* New York: Pantheon.
Herdeck, E. D., ed. 1973. *African Authors: A Companion to Black African Writing 1300–1973.* Washington, D.C.: Black Orpheus Press.
Jahn, J. 1965. *Die neoafrikanische Literatur: Gesamtbibliographie von den Anfängen bis zur Gegenwart.* Düsseldorf-Köln: Eugen Diederichs.
———1972. *Who's Who in African Literature.* Tübingen: Horst Erdmann.
Sartre, J. P. 1947. *Qu'est-ce que la littérature?* Paris: Editions Gallimard.

Contributors

K. ANTHONY APPIAH teaches philosophy and African-American studies at Harvard University. He previously taught philosophy at the universities of Ghana, Cornell, Yale, and Duke. Among his publications are *Assertion and Conditionals, for Truth in Semantics,* and contributions to *"Race," Writing and Difference* (ed. Henry Louis Gates, Jr.). He is currently preparing *In My Father's House: Africa in the Philosophy of Culture* and *Bu me Bé: The Proverbs of the Akan* (with Peggy Appiah).

ALBERT H. BERRIAN, Ph.D. (1925–1989), served as chairman of the Foreign Languages Department at Clark College, Atlanta (1942–1952); professor of French at Central State College (1956–1958); North Carolina College, Durham (1958–1960); and Plattsburg State College (1962–1963); professor and dean of the faculty at Hampton University; and associate commissioner of higher education, New York State Education Department. In 1960–1962 he was director of the English Language Teaching Program, AID, in Léopoldville, Congo. His many publications include *Négritude: Essays and Studies* (1967), *Education for Life in a Multi-Cultural Society* (1968), *Educational Policy and Program Alternatives: A Black Perspective* (1976), *Monophyletic Perspectives: The Roots of Humankind* (1978), *Africa: Roots and Branches* (1978).

RICHARD BJORNSON received his B.A. from Lawrence University, his M.A. from Northwestern University, and his Ph.D. from the University of Paris (Sorbonne). He is currently professor of French and comparative literature at the Ohio State University, having taught previously at the University of Wisconsin and the University of Yaoundé in the Cameroon Republic. He has written extensively on European, American, and African literature. His most recent book is *The African Quest for Freedom and Identity: Cameroonian Writing and the National Experience* (1991). His *Mongo Beti* will be published in the near future. He is also the author of *The Picaresque Hero in European Fiction* (1977). A former president of the American Literary Translators Association, he has translated works by René Philombe, Mongo Beti, Ferdinand Oyono, Paul Hazoumé, and Léopold Sédar Senghor.

BERNADETTE CAILLER received a Licence and a Diplôme d'Etudes Supérieures (English) from the University of Poitiers, the CAPES from the University of Paris, an M.A. (English) and a Ph.D. (Comparative Literature) from Cornell University. She has been teaching at the University of Florida, Gainesville, since 1974. She is the author of two books: *Proposition poétique: Une lecture de l'oeuvre d'Aimé Césaire* (1976), and *Conquérants de la nuit nue: Edouard Glissant et l'histoire antillaise* (1988). She was co-organizer of the 1980 Meeting of the *African Literature Association* (Gainesville),and coeditor of the 1980 *ALA Selected Papers: Toward Defining the African Aesthetic* (1982).

CATHERINE COQUERY-VIDROVITCH is a professor of history at the University of Paris and director of the Institute "Tiers-Monde, Afrique" affiliated with the CNRS. Her main research interests are social and political changes in twentieth century Africa and in urbanization. Her publications include *Le Congo au temps des grandes compagnies concessionnaires* (1972), *L'Afrique noire de 1800 à nos jours* with Henri Moniot (1974; rev. 1984), *Africa: Endurance and Change South of the Sahara* (1988). She edited, alone or in collaboration, several Third World studies, such as *Tiers-monde: Approche pluridisciplinaire* (1982), *Sociétés paysannes du tiers-monde* (1984), *Décolonisations et nouvelles dépendances* (1986), *Pour une Histoire du développement* (1988).

MANTHIA DIAWARA received his Ph.D. in comparative literature from Indiana University. He is professor of English at the University of Pennsylvania, Philadelphia.

CHRISTIANE YANDE DIOP is the widow of Alioune Diop. She has participated in all his accomplishments and has shared his joys, his struggles, his disappointments, and his hopes. She is presently general secretary of the Société Africaine de Culture and executive president of the publishing house Présence Africaine.

MAMADOU DIOUF is maître-assistant in contemporary history at the Faculté des Lettres et Sciences Humaines, Université Cheikh Anta Diop, Dakar, Sénégal. He specializes in the social history of Sénégal in the nineteenth and twentieth centuries. He is presently editing a political history of Sénégal after Independence.

ROBERTA ANN DUNBAR is associate professor in The Curriculum in African and Afro-American studies at the University of North Carolina at Chapel Hill. A historian, she teaches courses on African civilization, women in Africa, African literature, and African art for undergraduates, and a graduate course on social change in twentieth-century West Africa. Her recent research in West African social and intellectual history concerns the interaction of Muslim and civil law and its effect on the status of women.

MILDRED A. HILL-LUBIN is an associate professor, Department of English, with a joint appointment in the Center for African Studies, University of Florida, Gainesville. One of the editors of *Toward Defining the African Aesthetic* (1982), she has published articles on parallels in African and African-American literature, folklore, the Ghanaian author Ama Ata Aidoo, and the image of the Black grandmother.

PAULIN J. HOUNTONDJI is professor of philosophy at the National University of Benin, Cotonou, and, since March 1990, minister of education in the transitional government of Benin. His many publications include *African Philosophy: Myth and Reality* (1983).

SIMONE HOWLETT, the widow of the late Jacques Howlett, is an editor at *Présence Africaine* in Paris.

ABIOLA IRELE received his B.A. in 1960 from the University College of Ibadan (in special relationship with the University of London) and his Ph.D. from the University of Paris. He was formerly professor of French and Head of the Department of Modern Languages, University of Ibadan, Nigeria; he is now professor of African, French, and comparative literature at the Ohio State University, Columbus. He is the author of numerous articles on African literature in English and French and on ideological movements in Africa. A collection of his articles has been published under the title *The African Experience in Literature and Ideology* (1981, reprinted 1990). He has also edited a selection of the poetry of Léopold Sédar Senghor, and is general editor of the series Cambridge Studies in African and Caribbean Literature. His annotated edition of Aimé Césaire's *Cahier d'un retour au pays natal* is in press.

BOGUMIL JEWSIEWICKI is professor of history at Laval University, Québec, Canada. His research has focused primarily on the economic and social history of modern Zaire. He taught history in Zaire from 1968 to 1976.

BENNETTA JULES-ROSETTE is a professor of sociology at the University of California, San Diego. Her research interests include semiotic studies of religious discourse, tourist art, and new technologies in Africa. Since 1969 she has conducted a series of field studies in Zaire, Zambia, the Côte d'Ivoire and Kenya. Dr. Jules-Rosette's major publications include *African Apostles* (1975), *A Paradigm for Looking* (1977), *The New Religions of Africa* (1979), *Symbols of Change* (1981), and *The Messages of Tourist Art* (1984). Her most recent book, *Terminal Signs: Computers and Social Change in Africa* (1991), deals with the effects of computers and new technologies in Kenya and Côte d'Ivoire.

EILEEN JULIEN is associate professor of French and African literatures at Boston University. She writes primarily on sub-Saharan literature of French expression and is the author of *African Novels and the Question of Orality.*

LILYAN KESTELOOT, a docteur ès lettres d'état in general and comparative literature from the Sorbonne III, is professor at the University Cheikh Anta Diop and a fellow of the IFAN in Dakar, Sénégal. Her publications include *Les écrivains noirs de langue française* (*Black Writers in French*) (1962), *Négritude et situation coloniale* (1966), *La poésie traditionelle* (1971), *Aimé Césaire: l'homme et l'oeuvre* with B. Kotchy (1973), *Contes et mythes wolof* (1983), *Binton Koulibaly: Fondateur de l'empire de Ségou* (1983).

FERNANDO LAMBERT is a professor of literature at Laval University in Québec, Canada. He has written widely on African literature.

MAURICE A. LUBIN is a former associate professor of French and African literature of French expression at Howard University. He is now retired in Gainesville, Florida. He is the author of *De l'enseignement en Haiti*

(1947), *Panorama de la poésie haitienne* (1950), *Poésies haitiennes* (1954), *L'Afrique dans la poésie haitienne* (1965), *Jacmel et la poésie haitienne* (1967), *Florilège Jacmélien* (1969), *Afrique et politique* (1973), *Haiti and Culture* (1974), *Caribbean Writers* (1979) (editor of the Francophone section). His research interests are on Haitian culture and history.

DENIS-CONSTANT MARTIN does research at the Centre d'Etudes et de Recherches Internationales of la Fondation Nationale des Sciences Politiques in Paris. He has devoted numerous publications to the analysis of political systems in Africa, especially East-Africa (including *Tanzanie: L'invention d'une culture politique* [1988]), as well as to the sociology of music (including *L'Amérique de Mingus, Musique et politique: les "Fables of Faubus" de Charles Mingus* [1990]). He is a co-director with Christian Coulon of *Les Afriques politiques* (1991).

MOMAMAD MBODJ, maître-assistant in contemporary history at the Faculté des Lettres et Sciences Humaines, Université Cheikh Anta Diop, Dakar Sénégal. He specializes in the economic history of Sénégal in the nineteenth and twentieth centuries. He is presently at work on an economic and social history of the Gambia and its relations with Senegal.

CHRISTOPHER L. MILLER is professor of French and of African and African-American studies at Yale University. He is the author of *Blank Darkness: Africanist Discourse in French* (University of Chicago Press, 1985) and of *Theories of Africans: Francophone Literature and Anthropology in Africa* (University of Chicago Press, 1990).

HENRI MONIOT is maître de conférences at the University of Paris VII, where he teaches didactics of history and African history. With Catherine Coquery-Vidrovitch he has written *L'Afrique noire de 1800 à nos jours* (1974). He has also edited *Le mal de voir: Ethnologie et orientalismes* (1976) and *Enseigner l'histoire: Des manuels à la mémoire* (1984).

BERNARD MOURALIS is a professor at the Université of Lille III (France). His teaching and his research deal with Black-African literature written in French. He is the author of *Individu et collectivité dans le roman négro-africain d'expression française* (1969), *Les contre-littératures* (1975), *L'oeuvre de Mongo Beti* (1981), *Littérature et développement* (1984), *V. Y. Mudimbe ou le discours, l'écart et l'écriture* (1988), *Montaigne et le mythe du bon sauvage, de l'antiquité à Rousseau* (1989), and *Birago Diop* (1991).

V. Y. MUDIMBE is the Ruth F. DeVarney Professor of Romance Studies and Comparative Literature at Duke University. His publications include *The Invention of Africa* (1988) and *Parables and Fables* (1991).

M. ELISABETH MUDIMBE-BOYI is an associate professor in the Romance Studies Department at Duke University. She also has taught at Haverford College, the University of Pittsburgh, in Zaire, and in Burundi. Her publications include *L'oeuvre romanesque de Jacques-Stephen Alexis, écrivain haïtien* (1975). She is particularly interested in the representation of the Other in literary works.

JACQUES RABEMANANJARA, a former vice-president of the government and a State minister of foreign affairs of the Republic of Madagascar, is presently a senior editor at Présence Africaine in Paris, France. He is a poet and the author of *Antidote, Les ordalies, Rien qu'encens et filigrane,* and *Thrènes d'avant l'Aurore.* His theoretical publications include *Nationalisme et problèmes malgaches* published by Présence Africaine.

PETER RIGBY is professor of anthropology at Temple University in Philadelphia. His research has been primarily in the political economy, history, and structure of pastoralism in Eastern Africa, with particular reference to the Gogo and Maasai social formations of Tanzania and Kenya. He is the author of *Cattle and Kinship among the Gogo: A Semi-Pastoral Society of Central Tanzania* (1969) and *Persistent Pastoralists: Nomadic Societies in Transition* (1985), as well as numerous papers in Eastern African studies.

MARC ROMBAUT is a writer and a producer of cultural broadcasts with the Francophone Belgian Radio-Television. He has taught African literature in Brussels (Belgium) and in Conakry (Guinée) and participated in the First Festival of Black Arts of Dakar (Sénégal) and in the First Pan-African Festival of Culture of Algiers (Algeria). He is the author of several collections of poetry, the most recent *La lettre du nom* (1990); of a novel, *Suite en jouï-dire* (1978); of an essay on the transcription of poetry-music, *Matière d'oubli* (1983); and he was the codirector of two collective works, *Le récit et sa représentation* (1978) and *Minorités dans la pensée* (1979). Among his works devoted to African literature should be noted *La poésie négro-africaine d'expression française* (1976) and *La parole noire* (1976). He is also the author of *The Painting of Paul Delvaux* (1989; English trans. 1990), and *Pier Paolo Pasolini* (1991).

LÉOPOLD SÉDAR SENGHOR was educated at the Lycée-Louis-Le-Grand and at the Ecole Normale Supérieure in Paris where he received the *agrégation* in 1934. In 1935 he joined the faculty of the Lycée at Tours. He was a member of the French Constituent Assemblies as a deputy for Sénégal in 1945 and 1946, and in 1946 he was elected to both the French National Assembly and the General Council of Sénégal. In 1948 Mr. Senghor was appointed to a professorship at the Ecole Nationale de la France d'Outre Mer in Paris. In 1955–1956 he served in the French government and over the next few years worked with others for the independence of Sénégal. In 1960 he became the first president of an independent Sénégal, a position he held until his retirement in January 1981. He is the author of several books and essays as well as volumes of poetry. Mr. Senghor is one of the founders of the négritude movement and a member of the French Academy.

EMILE SNYDER, a former president of the U.S. African Literature Association, is professor emeritus at the University of Indiana, Bloomington. He has authored collections of poetry, among them *Faux-papiers 1950–1972* (1973), *La troisième voix: Poèmes en marge d'une autobiographie* (1976), *Un matin le temps m'est venu* (1985). He is also the translator of Aimé Césaire's *Cahier d'un retour au pay natal* and Michel Leiris's *Abanico para los toros.*

EMMANUEL TERRAY, a graduate of the *Ecole Normale Supérieure,* is a philosopher and an anthropologist who worked for years with Louis Althusser. He is professor of ethnology and directeur d'études at L'Ecole des Hautes Etudes en Sciences Sociales in Paris. His many publications include *Le marxisme devant les sociétés "primitives"* (1969).

BENOÎT VERHAEGEN taught political science for twenty-nine years in Zaire. He is presently the director of the Centre d'Etudes de Documentation sur l'Afrique Centrale in Brussels, Belgium. He is the author of *Rébellions au Congo* and *Introduction à l'histoire immédiate* (1974) and was coauthor of the series on *Congo* from 1959 to 1967.

KWASI WIREDU is professor of philosophy at the University of South Florida in Tampa. He previously taught philosophy at the University of Ghana. His publications include *Philosophy and an African Culture* (1980).

Index

453